D1553478

Trees

A field guide to the trees of Britain and Northern Europe

John White, Jill White, and
S. Max Walters

OXFORD
UNIVERSITY PRESS

Great Clarendon Street, Oxford OX2 6DP

Oxford University Press is a department of the University of Oxford.
It furthers the University's objective of excellence in research, scholarship, and education by publishing worldwide in

Oxford New York
Auckland Cape Town Dar es Salaam Hong Kong Karachi Kuala Lumpur
Madrid Melbourne Mexico City Nairobi New Delhi Shanghai Taipei Toronto

With offices in
Argentina Austria Brazil Chile Czech Republic France Greece Guatemala
Hungary Italy Japan Poland Portugal Singapore South Korea Switzerland
Thailand Turkey Ukraine Vietnam

Oxford is a registered trade mark of Oxford University Press
in the UK and in certain other countries

Published in the United States
by Oxford University Press Inc., New York

First published by Oxford University Press 2005

British Library Cataloguing in Publication Data
Data available

Library of Congress Cataloging in Publication Data
Data available

ISBN 0-19-851574-X

1 3 5 7 9 10 8 6 4 2

Typeset by Pantek Arts Ltd,
Maidstone, Kent
and bound in China by
Phoenix Offset Ltd

Contents

Pictorial key to icons

Chapter 1

Palm-like trees

Chapter 2

Scale-leaved conifers

Chapter 3

Single-needle conifers

Chapter 4

Pines

Chapter 5

Simple untoothed leaves: alternate

Chapter 6

Simple untoothed leaves: opposite

Chapter 7

Simple toothed leaves: alternate saw toothed

Chapter 8

Simple toothed leaves: opposite

Chapter 9

Lobed leaves: alternate

Chapter 10

Lobed leaves: opposite

Chapter 11

Lobed leaves, clearly toothed: alternate

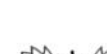

Chapter 12

Lobed leaves, clearly toothed: opposite

Chapter 13

Digitate leaves

Chapter 14

Trifoliate leaves: alternate

Chapter 15

Trifoliate leaves: opposite

Chapter 16

Pinnate leaves: alternate

Chapter 17

Pinnate leaves: opposite

Introduction

About this book

If when trying to identify an unfamiliar tree in the field you consult a tree book written from a botanical perspective, with species arranged according to scientific classification, you will inevitably waste a lot of time. Such books only work properly if you already know the name of your tree. If the book you are using is sufficiently well illustrated you will probably end up thumbing laboriously through the pictures hoping to recognize something familiar.

This book works differently, by a process of elimination. Depending on the quality of field information it should be possible to narrow down the options to a small group of plants, a genus, or the exact species very quickly.

The approach taken here is concerned only with features that can be seen straight away in the field. Using a series of simple, easily recognizable icons the options that dictate identity are progressively reduced. Even 'thumbing through' now becomes a more realistic option. Each group of plants with obvious similarities is relatively small. The text always accompanies the photographs so confirmation or elimination can be determined at a glance. The sole objective of this book is identification. Having found a name or group of names the observer is encouraged to consult more specialist works for additional detailed botanic or cultural information. There is a bibliography and further reading list towards the end of this book.

The icon system chosen here to facilitate broad identification is based primarily on leaf shape and configuration (except for palm like trees). This cuts across the more traditional, systematic botanical arrangement of plants based on taxonomic principles but is far more useful when standing under an unidentified tree. Morphologically diverse genera such as the Maples (*Acer*), for example, appear in different places in completely different iconic groups because the foliage is so variable. Leaves may be entire, lobed, trifolate (i.e. having three leaflets) or pinnate (i.e. having five or more leaflets arranged along a central axis). Margins may be toothed or entire. Maple leaves however are all arranged in opposite pairs on the shoot so a relatively small number of starting points soon become obvious.

How to identify trees

Each tree group can be identified by comparing the shape of a tree's leaves to the leaf icons opposite. The key to these icons is explained in more detail below. Once you have identified the group of your tree, turn to the corresponding section in the book. You'll find the icons printed in the margin of every left-hand page.

Scale, needle or strap-like leaves

1 Distinctive, palm-like structure (*Dicksonia, Trachycarpus, Cordyline*)

2 Scale-like leaves (*Sequoiadendron, Tamarix, Cryptomeria, Araucaria, Juniperus*)

3 Evergreen or deciduous, needle-like leaves borne singly (alternate or opposite) or tufted (*Cedrus, Larix, Picea, Taxus, Sequoia*, etc.)

4 Fascicled (bunched) needles (*Pinus*), in twos threes or fives

Simple leaves

Untoothed or with minute teeth, barely visible to the naked eye, including ciliate, sinuate, recurved, undulate or crenate margins

5 Alternate or in tufts

6 Opposite or whorled

Simple leaves

Clearly toothed, including dentate, bristle toothed and spiny margins

7 Alternate or in tufts

7A Saw toothed

7B Coarse or irregular teeth

7C Finely toothed

8 Opposite or whorled

Lobed leaves

Untoothed or with minute teeth

9 Alternate or in tufts (*Ginkgo, Populus alba*, some *Quercus*)

10 Opposite or whorled (*Acer campestre, Paulownia*)

Lobed leaves

Clearly toothed, including pointed lobes

11 Alternate or in tufts (*Crataegus, Quercus rubra*, etc.)

12 Opposite or whorled (most *Acer*)

Distinctive leaf shapes

Toothed or untoothed

13 Digitate (*Aesculus*)

14 Trifoliate alternate (*Laburnum*)

15 Trifoliate opposite (some *Acer*)

16 Pinnate alternate, including bipinnate (*Ailanthus*, some *Sorbus*)

17 Pinnate opposite (*Fraxinus*)

Plants with other intermediate characteristics (e.g. *Betula* which may be deeply toothed or shallowly lobed) should be searched for under more than one icon.

Advice for the identification of trees in winter is given on page x.

Rogue leaves (e.g. occasional lobed leaves in *Morus*) should be ignored.

Arrangement of the text within each iconic group

Family

The Family is a major taxonomic category often consisting of a large number of broadly related individuals. For example, the Beech family (*Fagaceae*) contains seven genera of trees including, in this book, Sweet chestnut, Beech, Southern beech and Oak. The category superior to Family is the Order (not included in this text because most Orders cover such a wide range of plants that Order inclusion would not assist field identification): for example, the Beech tree Order (*Fagales*) also includes Alder, Birch, Hornbeam, Hop hornbeam and Hazel.

Scientific name

This consists of two or more parts. The first, **Genus**, refers to a closely related group of species. *Genus* is written in a Latinized form so it can be understood internationally by everyone whatever their native language. Names mostly follow the rules of gender, number and case in Latin. The origin of many though may be classical Greek. The name of a genus is substantive in the singular number, or a word treated as such, and is always written with a capital initial letter (International Code of Botanical Nomenclature 1987).

The second part of the scientific name refers to the **species**: a designation that cannot stand alone and is always combined with an appropriate genus. Species is usually an adjective and is written with a lower case initial letter. It is regarded as the basic unit in botanical classification – a stable breeding group of plants normally distinct from all other related groups within the genus. It has unique attributes or combinations of attributes. If species cross with one another the resulting progeny are often sterile so the integrity of the original species is not compromised, but there are exceptions to this and consequently some species designations can become blurred. Hybridization between Sallow willow species, for example, has made material that exactly matches the type specimen of *Salix caprea* difficult to find in many areas. The binomial arrangement of genus and species to create a scientific name was devised by Carl von Linne (*Linnaeus*) and published by him in 1753. Before that scientific names were more wordy descriptions. Common juniper (*Juniperus communis* of Linnaeus) was described in Threlkeld's 1726 Irish Flora as *Juniperus Vulgaris Baccis Parvis Purpureis* (the Juniper which is common with small bright purple (red, black) berries).

Names become valid only when they are published with a precise description in a reputable botanical journal. In order that a name can be verified, or disputed, the author's name or names are also cited, usually in an abbreviated form after the species name (*Juniperus communis L.* meaning Linnaeus or Carl von Linne, 1753). Short names may be written in full, for example, Spach = Edouard Spach, 1801–79. When an author publishes a name already ascribed in part to another person that name appears first followed by 'ex' then the original author's name, for example, *Cupressus macrocarpa Hartw.* ex Gordon. Authors within the same family are recognized by their initials or f. (*filius* = son of). Plants of garden origin can also be ascribed to hort. meaning hortulanorum. When a plant is successfully reassessed for rank or identity the original author's name(s) are written in parentheses followed by the author who effected the alteration. Further updated information on authorities can be obtained from the International Code of Botanical Nomenclature that is revised at intervals by the International Botanical Congress.

Subordinate to Species there are several **infraspecific** categories in the classification hierarchy that are relevant to this work. **Subspecies** (subsp.) are biotypes with more or less regional distribution altered morphologically or ecologically in some way by geographical isolation over a long period. They usually remain genetically similar to the species from which they diverged and if reunited are mostly capable of successfully hybridizing with it. **Varieties** (var.) are morphological variants of a species not necessarily with a particular geographical distribution. Varieties, such as those with an abnormal flower size or colour, are often perpetuated in horticulture. A **cultivar** (cv.), written with an initial capital letter and always in single inverted commas (e.g. *Alnus incana* 'Lacinata'), has been selected using artificial horticultural techniques, for example, plant breeding. Most cultivars are propagated vegetatively to ensure continuous uniformity and integrity. A form (**forma**) is a wild segregate population genetically diverse enough to make it physiologically distinct.

Name changes

Ever-changing scientific names can be a great source of annoyance particularly in the horticultural world. During a long interim period when some nursery catalogues list invalid names and others print new names there is always confusion and argument. Because information is poorly disseminated, particularly in herbaceous garden plants, it has been known for the same plant to occur under different names, old and new, for many years. It is not really surprising therefore that names have been misapplied in the past.

The binomial system was formulated in 1753 but this was 200 years before any strict rules of nomenclature were produced. Type specimens, on which original descriptions were based and names invented, have not always turned out to be typical. Sometimes early designation was incorrect, often because the entire population had yet to be discovered. There is also a principle of 'priority of publication' to be upheld. This means the earliest known, accurate description and associated name is always accepted as valid, and authentic early manuscripts are still being discovered by modern researchers that may predate the name in common use. Synonyms have also occurred due to communication breakdowns between taxonomists in the past.

Common name

Common names are of limited value because they vary regionally, but they may reassure observers who are not particularly comfortable with scientific names. Originally, common names were simple and often reflected the use of the tree, its wood or its place in society. The Spindle tree, still a valid English name, for example, referred to a small tree with hard wood from which spindles were made for the textile industry. Beech has a less obvious meaning in English – it is related to the Early German and Scandinavian buche and boc. Norse writing was often on thin, cleft sheets of beech, hence the related word book.

Descriptions

The text here follows a consistent format often with a headline at the beginning if there is a specific feature of prime importance to look for that will immediately assist identification. If the tree is particularly difficult (or easy) to identify this is stated. Sizes are in metric units. Tree heights and stem diameters are realistic average mature sizes appropriate to an area where the tree is ecologically well suited.

Photographs are indicated in the relevant part of the text by a white number in a black box: for example, **1**. The description may be reduced or modified accordingly if the photograph is sufficiently explicit. The description appears first immediately followed by the boxed number that links it to the relevant photograph.

Habitat and Ecology

This is a brief reference to the wild habitat of the tree if this is known. Many natural habitats no longer exist but surviving trees have adapted to artificial conditions that have become familiar. For example, the *Sorbus torminalis* illustrated **1** has been planted in a picnic area, a woodland tree now thriving in a managed open space.

Similar species

As much information as possible is given, where space permits, about taxa that may be confused with the species described. Some are cross-referenced by page number, others, which are beyond the remit of this work, can be found described in some of the books listed in the bibliography and further reading. Sometimes similar, 'look-alike' species are illustrated where this is thought likely to be helpful.

Range maps

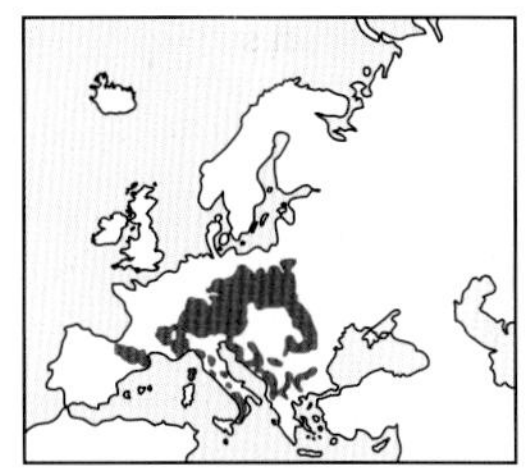

The natural distribution of each native North European species is indicated on a small, inset map. The location of populations that extend beyond the limits of the map or those from other parts of the world are described under the heading **Natural range**.

Cultivated distribution

Cultivated distribution is usually difficult to define precisely so terms such as 'widely distributed in gardens' are used for commonplace trees, or 'rare in cultivation' for infrequently seen species. As a rule of thumb in the field, an unidentified tree is more likely to be common than rare if all other identification features prove inconclusive, not so in a Botanic Garden or comprehensive Arboretum. Climatic change is important here too because formerly tender species, such as *Eucalyptus gunnii* for example, have an extended northerly tolerance range. This is rapidly being exploited by the establishment of plantations and amenity planting. In some cases the uses of the tree are described in the text if this helps with the identification, for example, orchard trees for the production of cider and fruit.

Photography

Trees are naturally photogenic but the aim of this work is to be instructional and not especially picturesque. We have tried to photograph salient identification features wherever possible and resorted to line drawings where a photograph could not do the subject justice. Except for a few irresistible exceptions ordinary run of the mill specimens have been photographed in places where most readers are likely to see them. Many of the trees illustrated are growing in East Anglia, not the most obvious choice of venue for a dendrological purist, but nevertheless an area of remarkable diversity and in many respects similar to adjacent parts of mainland Europe (Turkish hazel in the City of Norwich **2**).

The equipment and materials used were as follows. For the majority of the field work a Minolta Dynax 404 si Camera was used always with a tripod or monopod. A 28–80 mm AF Zoom lens fitted with a Hoya 62 mm Skylight proved very satisfactory. Manual focus was usually required to unscramble twigs and leaves. Studio work was achieved using an old, specially modified Pentax Spotmatic camera with a Super-Macro Takumar 1.4/50 mm lens focusing down to 8 cm. Most of the photographs were taken using Fujichrome Provia 100F and Sensia 200 slide film in daylight. Kodachrome 64 film was used where extra-fine grain was required and long exposures and small apertures were possible to achieve an adequate depth of field. It is a myth that trees stand perfectly still and are easy to photograph. Something somewhere on a tree is constantly on the move in the slightest breeze.

Identification

The identification of a deciduous species is easiest in summer when the foliage is intact. However the arrangement of buds on the shoot in winter will still give an indication of the configuration. Providing that all the dead leaves have not been swept up or blown away it is often possible to piece together enough clues from the ground to arrive at a short list of possibilities. Enough to relate the plant to an **Icon**. Young plants or heavily pruned (coppiced or pollarded) trees sometimes produce foliage which is not typical, so care is needed when dealing with these. The size and vigour of foliage is often exaggerated.

The outline of a tree is sometimes a valuable guide to identification but beware, individual specimens seldom conform to a stereotype. Environmental conditions play a vital role in determining tree shape (Wind and salt sculptured Hawthorn **3**). It is always worth spending plenty of time observing small details about a tree and its location and making as many on-site notes as possible. Vital information can often be discovered after a second look or perhaps a return visit; a vestige of a dead flower, squirrel chewed nuts or cones, a distinctive smell or a better specimen of the same thing nearby. Identifying a tree is pure detective work, linking together random bits of information to form an overall picture. Extra time on site is time well spent.

We aim to provide enough information here for the reader, when confronted by an unknown tree, to identify it accurately or to within a small, similar looking group. Over 400 trees are described and additional reference notes are included about more obscure taxa for which they might be mistaken. At this stage some readers may be content, they may at least know what the tree is not, or they will have a starting point for further botanical study.

In our opinion the trees most likely to be found in the countryside or confronted in urban parks and gardens are included. In an Arboretum or Botanic Garden however identification at this level becomes more risky. It would be unwise to assume anything positive without due reference to the collection catalogue or the plant label. In this situation even the most familiar tree may turn out to be something quite special or not at all what it seems.

Unlike birds and animals, which exhibit fairly constant colouration and size, there is no easy descriptive formula for identifying trees. Whatever the species a tree is a dynamic living structure that changes its size, colour and form continually throughout the year. It would be possible to write a completely different description for the same tree during each of the four seasons. Natural morphological diversity exists between individuals of the same species, or

even between different parts of the same tree. Very confusingly provenances of the American Lodgepole pine in European plantations, for example, depending on their origin, produce a range of needle lengths equal to almost all of the other twin-needled pine species.

The size of the problem

In Britain and Europe there are two fundamentally different but parallel tree populations, native or introduced. The former are relatively stable or in some instances in decline (Black poplar **4**). The latter are rapidly increasing both in diversity and extent (Arboretum planting **5**). If we confined ourselves here to European native species identification, in theory it would be relatively straightforward. Probably less than 100 descriptions would suffice. Less still in the British Isles where there are only around 35 authentic native trees. But as an aid to identification in the field this would be useless. The non-specialist observer may not be certain if the tree in question is native or not. The term native, where it applies, is defined here as post-glacial arrivals in a particular place without human encouragement or interference. The incredibly low figure of 35 in Britain is disputed by some. Botanists continue to argue about the status of Beech (*Fagus sylvatica*), Box (*Buxus sempervirens*) and some Elms (*Ulmus* spp.). Others challenge the generally accepted basic definition of a tree (a woody plant able to exceed 6 metres in height). Trees in the 6 metre + category introduced from outside Europe push the total number growing in Britain to well over 2000 species. If you add to this the increasing number of artificially cultivated plants positive identification, by morphological means without access to historical notes or DNA analysis, becomes impractical and unsafe. By the end of the twentieth century 550 named forms of Lawson cypress (a single species *Chamaecyparis lawsoniana*) existed. Similar numbers of cherries and maples were also listed and it is reckoned that in Italy over one million different cultivars of poplar had been developed for the production of paper pulp and timber products.

Environmental diversity

Trees survive through their great diversity and ability to change especially from one seed generation to the next. Some are in a constant state of evolution. Human interference,

4

5

particularly by moving trees from one place to another in the world, has hastened the process. Generally trees love it, they are infinitely adaptable, but taxonomists are driven to despair. Eucalyptus, for example, is a genus with many named species that have evolved only through geographic isolation in the vastness of Australia. However when these species were artificially moved into the close proximity of collections they immediately began to hybridize. New seedling intermediates are rapidly developing, in some instances the integrity of the old regional species is being lost – a kind of 'speeded-up' example of what evolution is about (Eucalyptus of uncertain origin growing in Scotland **6**).

The direct effect of environmental conditions is usually obvious. A few trees tend only to occur in the natural environment in which they evolved so their size and shape is more or less predictable. Many others however can thrive in various natural or artificial environments such as woodland, agricultural landscapes, rural estates, parks, urban open spaces, gardens or streets. For these little can now be described as constant. For some reaching statutory tree height (6 m) may take a lifetime, perhaps hundreds of years, while others in another place achieve it in a few years. Some trees can genetically override environmental influences, Holly, Thorn and Mulberry, for example, are never gigantic even in sheltered places. Conversely Noble Fir can be excessively large even in extreme exposure or isolation. Size then is a poor indicator of identity. A Mountain ash growing on the side of a mountain will never measure up to another growing in a city park. Size and shape can also be influenced by past management. If this has been neglected for a long time it may not be immediately obvious. Pollards can be especially problematical. Many remain smaller and slower growing than uncut specimens (Ancient boundary Ash pollard **7**); others regrow with great vigour but their outline remains different to an open grown tree (Sweet chestnut **8**). Orchard trees also fail to conform to expected size limits. As well as frequent pruning, which is fairly

obvious, trees are often grafted on to widely differing rootstocks that may produce vigorous or dwarf trees.

Site management is a factor that is increasingly affecting the appearance of trees. Sophisticated earth moving equipment, intentional or unintentional nutrition imbalance, drainage and pesticide use can all cause abnormalities. Stunted or exaggerated growth or foliage deformity caused by artificial conditions may confuse the identity of a species. Features such as these cannot possibly be anticipated when writing a general description for a healthy specimen.

Seasonal variation

Seasonal variation has a profound effect on what trees look like on a particular day or in a particular light. Foliage differences can be observed almost on a daily basis. The problem for authors is how best to put all this information into a reasonably sized book. It is easy to describe a tree from a single specimen on a particular day, but this will not be the tree or the day the reader is experiencing. Not surprisingly, describing every aspect of seasonal variation properly even for a single species would fill volumes and become very tedious for the reader only looking for the name of the tree. Such a volume would inevitably contain information that the ordinary observer would seldom see. For example, consider the prominent upright cones of Silver fir (*Abies*) which begin to appear in late spring when they are brilliant but transient pale glaucous green. As they mature they become bloomed purple, blue, deep brown or almost black. On ripening they fade to pale brown before totally disintegrating. To describe this remarkable succession, which usually occurs amongst the inaccessible brittle top branches of a very tall tree, would require pages of text and numerous coloured illustrations. If this were not bad enough actually describing colour is subjective. One person's idea of greenish-blue will be another person's bluish-green and quite different (Young Silver fir cone **9**).

Young growth often presents additional difficulties for the observer struggling with identification. New leaves begin to emerge in spring which are quite unlike those on older foliage. Most conifers take around two months before the young growth is fully extended. Some broadleaved trees continue to produce new non-typical growth all summer. Oak, if seriously predated, can produce a whole new flush of leaves in summer (Lammas growth) which are not only a different size and shape but a different bronze colour. Young trees of many species produce juvenile foliage that is quite unlike adult growth. Pines do this for one to five years and some Junipers never grow out of their spiny juvenile foliage stage.

For enthusiastic observers of trees there can be no substitute for frequent visits to an Arboretum or comprehensive tree collection. These have aptly been described as 'living textbooks' reflecting seasonal changes on a daily, even hourly basis, something that a real book cannot do. Continuous access to a live tree will surpass any written or pictorial description in any medium yet devised (Kilmun Arboretum in West Scotland **10**).

Age and longevity

There are basically two categories of tree, pioneer opportunists and stoic potential 'climax' species. The former never make veteran status, for them (e.g. Alder, Birch, Elder and Poplar) 100 years is a long life. They usually pack disturbed ground with numerous fertile seeds that grow rapidly, tightly crammed together until suppression and limited light kills out the weaklings (Willow and Alder colonization of a wetland bog **11**). Their objective achieved, bare ground having been converted to tree cover, pioneer trees gradually die out, having seeded on to marginal land elsewhere. The resulting gaps are filled in due course by more permanent climax species such as Oak and Beech (**12** Climax Oak wood), which are generally distributed by forgetful birds or animals whose stores of buried winter nuts are overlooked. Climax trees may dominate a particular site for 1000 years (Kett's Oak near Downham Market in East Anglia **13**). Pioneer trees tend to be easier to identify because longevity does not change their appearance very much. Birch bark, for example, remains

fairly recognizable whatever age the tree may be. Conifers, many of which are pioneers, have recognizable bark from a fairly early age until post-maturity. Oak bark, on the other hand, changes from the smoothness of youth to an excessively rough, craggy, fissured weather-beaten appearance.

Age, or rather the onset of decline, has a profound effect on the shape, outline and vigour of a tree so special care is needed when trying to identify a particular ancient specimen. Unexpected help in this matter comes from the relatively short list of species to choose from that achieve great age as standard extant trees (not coppice or sucker regeneration). In Northern Europe these are, in order of recorded age:

Yew	3000+	years, could be layered or broken and regenerated.
Oak	1000+	years, Common and Sessile oaks.
Sweet chestnut	800	years, could be layered, considerable dead wood.
Hornbeam	800+	years, often pollarded in the past.
Ash	500	years, pollards may last up to 800 years.
Field maple	4–500	years, often cut back as a hedge in the past.
Hawthorn		as Field maple.
Holly	400	years.
Scots pine	400	years, if given space to develop a broad top.
Elm	400	years, often from existing suckering roots up to 5000 years old.
Juniper	400+	years, in harsh upland conditions.
Mulberry	400	years, seldom stands up but grows in a reclining position.
Sycamore	400	years.
European larch	300	years.
Plane	300	years, Oriental plane may layer and live longer.
Beech	300	years, most break up before 200 years.

An ancient churchyard Yew in Hampshire dated by adjacent burials **14**.

Small leaved lime, Wild cherry, Aspen, Wild service and Box can all grow from ancient root systems but visible stems only last 50–200 years before being replaced. Tree willows and some poplars grow to great size and may appear to be ancient but generally they are not. Another valuable age related list to aid identification in some circumstances, this time of exotic trees, is their date of introduction. With the exception of American Redwoods and some Firs few comparatively recent introductions will be excessively large. The largest

specimens of all trees growing in the British Isles are kept on a Tree Register data base (see the Bibliography and further reading). Introduction dates are comprehensively listed in *The Hillier Manual of Trees and Shrubs* (again, see the bibliography).

Where to find trees

There has been a great increase in amenity planting in recent years so some of the greatest diversity of trees can now be found in urban open spaces, large gardens and suburban streets. Cities such as Cardiff and London have magnificent collections almost as complete as any Arboretum. For the serious student of tree identification there are Botanic Gardens and reference Arboreta where the majority of specimens are catalogued and labelled. A valuable confidence boost for the beginner, if time permits, is to identify the tree before checking the label. In this way it soon becomes possible to recognize salient features on other specimens of the same species in other places without labels. Outside formal collections very few trees are actually labelled and some may even have the wrong names attached to them. Surprisingly quickly names are likely to be forgotten, even by collection holders. Garden owners usually remember the names of trees they have planted themselves but often they have problems with trees inherited from previous occupants. Trees generally live much longer than people so most specimens fall into the inherited category.

To aid identification or verify a doubtful specimen it is tempting to pick a leaf, flower, seed or foliage sample. In many European countries it is now illegal to pick material from wild plants. Better perhaps to take close-up photographs or make notes and sketches. Picking up leaves, etc. from the ground is not illegal but proving where specimens came from would be difficult if you are challenged. Picking foliage from private or local authority trees is also against the law as is trespass or any other damage to property. Always seek permission before entering private property or collecting specimens. The proliferation of alarm systems, guard dogs and security cameras have put many opportunities for casually observing trees completely out-of-bounds. When appropriate permission has been obtained avoid damage of any sort, do not disturb wildlife or game and be aware of the danger of fire. Remember to report back any findings, especially any rare plants.

Finally the importance of safety where trees are concerned must never be underestimated. Needless to say trees should never be climbed, especially those tempting veterans with great limbs reaching down to the ground. Beware too of roots that extend above ground. They can trip you up or turn an ankle, and when wet or denuded of bark they become incredibly slippery. Also beware of poisonous plants, irritant foliage and pollen which may cause an allergic reaction.

Many seemingly harmless species can adversely affect some people. For example, Cypress oil from the foliage of Lawson and Leyland cypress can cause a nasty rash on bare arms and hands. If in any doubt wear gloves or avoid touching foliage. Even some smells can cause discomfort: the foliage of the Tree of Heaven, for example, can induce a violent headache on a hot, still summer day.

If you encounter tree maintenance work in progress keep well clear. Contractors are obliged to fence and sign unsafe areas in places where there is public access. Never creep up from behind when someone is operating a chainsaw and never approach forest machinery on the blind side. Beware of potentially dangerous log piles and vehicles being loaded with logs. The wind is also something to watch out for, especially in forests where selective felling or thinning has recently been done. Falling branches from retained trees can kill. It is best to avoid the woods and proximity of large or old trees on windy days. Last of all, and most dramatic, remember that trees conduct lightning, sometimes spectacularly. Something that is not usually seen by the unfortunate people actually sheltering under the wrong tree.

About the authors

John White took up forestry in 1957, becoming curator and botanist at Westonbirt Arboretum in 1975. He was appointed Forestry Commission Research Dendrologist in 1987, and now works as a freelance illustrator, author, and consultant.

Jill White is closely involved with dendrological consultancy work, site surveys, photographic assignments, and writing. She specializes in the interactions between people and trees and the pragmatic education of young children in natural sciences. Together, John and Jill took every photograph featured in this field guide themselves.

Dr S. Max Walters was Curator of the Herbarium and Lecturer in Botany at the Department of Plant Sciences (formerly the Botany School) in the University of Cambridge, and was then Director of the University Botanic Garden there for ten years up to his retirement in 1983. He is the author of numerous botanical books, most notably the *Atlas of the British Flora* (with F. H. Perring), and *Flora Europaea* on which he was a member of the Editorial and Organizing Committee, with a special interest in Russia and Eastern Europe.

Acknowledgements

We would like to thank all those people who have provided encouragement, location details, and herbarium specimens that have helped us to compile this work, particularly Eric Rogers, Gilbert Addison, Neville Danby, David Alderman, Peter Gregory, Andrew White, and Lady Anne Wake-Walker. We would also like to thank the many owners and custodians who have generously allowed us to photograph trees on their property, primarily the Director and staff of the University of Cambridge Botanic Garden without whom our task would have been difficult, and for some taxa impossible. We would particularly like to thank Piers Pratt who has generously allowed us the freedom of his Ryston estate and Arboretum, and also the Allhousen family who have, time after time, given us unrestricted access to their magnificent Arboretum at Bradenham in Norfolk. The Forestry Commission must be credited with providing the inspiration for this work; their Arboreta at Kilmun, Lynford, Speech House in the Royal forest of Dean, Brechfa, Westonbirt, and Bedgebury are among the finest tree collections in the world. Other notable establishments and organizations that have helped us are The National Trust, The Irish National Botanic Garden Glasnevin, The Church Commissioners – especially the diocese of Norwich and of Winchester – St. Edmundsbury Borough Council, Springfield Garden in Spalding, The University of East Anglia, Kings Lynn Borough Council, Bath Botanic Gardens, Stannage Park near Knighton, Kimberly Park Estate, Crarae Forest Garden, Bath City Council, Barnwell Country Park at Oundle, Long Ashton Research Station at Bristol, and many other town, city, and parish councils, as well as individual gardeners throughout the British Isles. We would also like to express our thanks to the hard working production team, and to Mike Wood for assisting with the production of the Natural range maps.

John White, Jill White, and S. Max Walters, 2005

FAMILY Agavaceae

Cordyline australis (Forst.f.) Hook.f.

Cabbage palm or Cabbage tree

Description • Of the two or three palm-like trees that will grow in Northern Europe this is the most familiar. There are no branches as such, only occasional major forks on some specimens. The trunk always terminates in a dense rosette of tough, slender, grey-green leaves between 45 and 90 cm long by 3–8 cm wide, each tapering to a fine point. Dead leaves hang on to the stem below the actively growing top for a time **1** then fall away leaving a clean trunk with shallowly furrowed, hard, grey-brown bark **2**. Often several trunks grow together in a suckering cluster. Eventually trees over 10 m tall develop with palm like foliage confined to the very top pointing upwards initially then outwards and finally drooping down, a process that takes a green leaf around five years to complete **3**. The 1 cm six-petalled flowers, in huge terminal panicles, are creamy white and scented. They appear in early summer and last most of the season transforming the outline of the tree **4**. Globose, 6 mm, pale grey-blue berries are seldom produced in Northern Europe. With continuing climatic change to warmer conditions in most places this may soon change. **Habitat and Ecology** • In Northern Europe only found in mild areas especially close to the sea. Salt spray is tolerated but strong wind frequently causes damage, especially to the inflorescences. **Similar species** • The Spanish bayonet, *Yucca aloifolia* L., and Adam's needle, *Yucca gloriosa* L., which only has a short stem and quite different flowers.

Natural range
New Zealand.

Cultivated distribution
Mostly close to the Atlantic and North Sea coasts but increasingly in sheltered gardens further inland. Often planted close to walls and against houses, quite unsuitable places for a suckering tree of this potential size.

FAMILY Dicksoniaceae

Dicksonia antarctica Labill.

Soft tree fern

Description • Not a tree at all but a fern which having become established in the soil continues to grow on top of a trunk-like structure composed only of dead frond bases and roots. This fibrous, reddish 'stem' can expand to 60 cm in diameter and grow upwards indefinitely until the whole plant becomes unstable and topples over. Once clear of the ground the living fronds are sustained only by the nutrients and moisture they recycle for themselves. Plants are sold in nurseries and garden centres without basal roots **5**. The tri-pinnate fronds extend 2 m in all directions from the crown **6**. **Habitat and Ecology** • Sub-tropical genus from Central America, South East Asia, Polynesia and (this species) Australasia. **Similar species** • Other tree ferns will grow in Europe, but they are rare or only found in conservatories.

Natural range
Australia and Tasmania.

Cultivated distribution
Frequently used in fashionable landscape gardening but unlikely to survive in windy, hot, dry, sunny conditions.

1
2
3
4
5
6

FAMILY Palmae

Trachycarpus fortunei (Hook.) H. Wendl.

Chusan palm

Description • This palm extends further into Northern Europe than any others, noticeably assisted in recent decades by favourable climate change. It is a single-stemmed tree up to 14 m tall **1**. The bark is distinctive being composed of soft, reddish-brown, fibrous, discarded leaf bases **2**. This is reminiscent of the Tree fern (p2) but unlike Tree ferns the Palm stems have a core of wood. The live foliage is confined to the top of the tree; there are no branches in the strict sense. The leaves are held on a 60–80 cm stiff-spined petiole, 2–3 cm thick with a fibrous sheath at the base. They are roundish, about 1 m across, and divided almost to the base into narrow, pleated strips. They face upwards towards the light for several years then droop down round the top of the stem as they are replaced. Most become dysfunctional because they are shredded by the wind. The flowers appear in mild or protected places such as against a wall or inside a building, on a stout, light-coloured stalk **3** protected at first with a yellowish sheath. A branched inflorescence supports fragrant yellow flowers, male and female sometimes on separate trees, followed in hot countries by 2 cm purple-bloomed fruits like small three-lobed dates. **Habitat and Ecology** • The natural environment in China has been obscured by centuries of cultivation. In Northern Europe this tree has traditionally been used as an amenity species in seaside towns. **Similar species** • *Chamaerops humilis* L. The European fan palm **4** is broadly similar except that in Northern Europe it seldom exceeds 1.5 m in height. It too is benefiting from warmer conditions. In its natural state it tends to sucker and produce a picturesque group of Palm trees. Another Palm grown out of doors in the extreme south of the region (e.g. the Channel Islands) is *Phoenix canariensis* Chab. Canary Island palm. It is a 15–20 m tree with a terminal rosette of huge 6 m pinnate feathery leaves each with numerous opposite pairs of lanceolate leaflets reminiscent of the closely related Date palm.

Natural range
China, North Vietnam and Northern Burma. Obscured by extensive cultivation.

Cultivated distribution
Grown in its natural range for the fibrous leaf sheath that is like coarse cloth. Traditionally this was sewn together to make a strong waterproof fabric. In Europe, Chusan palm is a fashionable seaside amenity and garden tree, which was brought to Germany in 1830 and from there to Britain in 1837. New material was introduced from China in 1849.

European fan palm

1

2

3

4

FAMILY Araucariaceae

Araucaria araucana (Molina) K. Koch

Monkey puzzle or Chile pine

Description • To the majority of people this must be one of the easiest trees to recognise from its symmetrical outline at a distance and its scaly foliage at close range. Although from remote Chile it has been planted on a vast scale throughout the temperate world since its discovery around 1795. It is a stiff, straight, monopodial tree up to 30 m tall, but often a lot less, with a maximum stem diameter of about 1 m. The bark is very distinctive somehow reminiscent of the skin of an elephant **1**. Branches occur in distinct horizontal whorls **2** bending downwards as they extend. The actively growing dense foliage at the top of the tree shades out lower branches which die, or are cut off, leaving a long bare stem and a domed 'umbrella' top. The shoot is completely disguised by decurrent leaf bases. Leaves are hard, succulent, triangular scales with a viciously sharp, forward-pointing tip. Each one is 3–5 cm long and about 2 cm wide at the base. They are arranged radially, each one partially overlapping the base of the next **3**. A formidable arrangement which resists browsing or harmful interference of any sort. The colour is deep green with a waxy film produced by minute lines of grey stomata. Dead foliage turns rusty-brown. There is no seasonal leaf fall. After many years whole, lower dead branches often fall off intact. The flowers, male and female on separate trees, are cone-like on previous season's growth. Males up to 15 cm long persist all summer. Green female flowers develop into huge coconut-sized deciduous cones **4**. Edible, 4 cm, brown seeds are shed in the autumn. **Habitat and Ecology** • This species is a relic of a primitive vegetation type that was widespread when dinosaurs roamed the earth. Only a small vestige of the original Araucaria forests in South America have survived exploitation in the nineteenth and twentieth centuries. Although conservation and reafforestation programmes have been put in place the genetic diversity of the wild population is seriously limited. The high-quality softwood timber has always been sought after. Early pruned stems eventually yield long, blemish-free runs of honey-coloured wood. As a forest tree it is moderately shade tolerant, very hardy and grows well in Northern Europe **5**. **Similar species** • None.

Natural range
Chile and Argentina on mountain slopes (often volcanic) to 1500 m elevation, rapidly recolonising volcanic ash following eruptions.

Cultivated distribution
Introduced to Europe soon after 1795 by Archibold Menzies who was given the seed to eat by South American Indians. It was re-introduced by William Lobb in 1844 then became popular as a garden tree particularly in Britain.

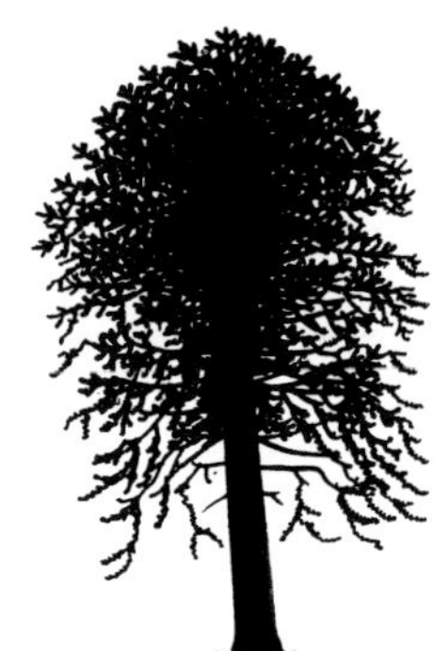

Monkey puzzle

Araucaria heterophylla (Salsb.) Franco

Norfolk Island pine

Description • A tender symmetrical tree that can grow 40 m tall in its native Norfolk Island in the Pacific. Increasingly seen in Europe as an indoor feature in shopping malls and luxury offices. It has a straight persistent stem and tiered branches. On young specimens the juvenile foliage **6** has 1.5 cm blunt-tipped, decurrent leaf scales radially arranged. Pot-grown specimens retain juvenile foliage, sometimes indefinitely.

Araucaria heterophylla

1
2
3
4
5
6

FAMILY Cupressaceae

Thuja plicata D. Don
Western red cedar

Description • A large, straight forest tree frequently over 30 m tall with pendulous, glossy evergreen foliage **1**. The stem is often fluted towards the base and old, open grown trees develop heavy bottom branches that appear to be layering. The bark is fibrous, orange or red-brown **2** with shallow vertical ridges. Shoots are purplish-brown. The foliage is in flat sprays **3** bright green and sweetly aromatic, a little like orange peel. Individual scale leaves, 4–6 mm long, in opposite pairs, are light-green on the underside **4**. Flowers are abundant, males shed huge clouds of pollen in spring. Females on weak side shoot tips develop into small, light-green, erect, leathery cones with 8–10 scales. They turn brown and open in the autumn but usually remain on the tree for a second year **4**. **Habitat and Ecology** • Peaty or mineral wet ground in mountainous country with high rainfall. **Similar species** • Chinese arbor-vitae (below), Lawson cypress (p14) and *Thuja occidentalis* L. American arbor-vitae.

Natural range
Western North America from Alaska through Canada and along the west coast to Northern California. Also east of the Rocky Mountains from British Columbia to Idaho.

Cultivated distribution
Occasionally grown as a forest tree in Europe. The durable timber (Red cedar) is in great demand. A plant once used for hedging but prone to disease in this situation.

Thuja orientalis L.f.
Chinese arbor-vitae

Description • A conical or rounded tree with spreading branches and upright shoots **5**. The bark is reddish-brown developing thin papery scales. The dense evergreen foliage is bright green on both sides **6**. Individual scale leaves have free tips on vigorous shoots but are pressed against weaker branches. The silvery-blue cones, up to 2.5 cm long, each have six pointed scales **7** that ripen to red-brown before shedding seeds. **Habitat and Ecology** • A tree of wet ground in high rainfall areas. **Similar species** • *Thuja occidentalis* L. the American counterpart is a larger 20 m wetland species.

Natural range
North and West China and Korea. Cultivated elsewhere, including Japan, since ancient times.

Cultivated distribution
This and the American arbor-vitae are mostly represented in cultivation by named cultivars many of which are dwarf garden plants.

Thujopsis dolabrata (L.f.) Sieb. and Zuccarini
Hiba

Description • This pyramidal 20 m tree has leathery, bright green foliage. In cultivation open grown trees often appear to layer forming a circular thicket **8**. The underside of each scale leaf is intricately marked with white stomatal patches **9**. After several years old foliage turns orange-brown. The bark is purplish-brown then grey-brown and vertically shredded. Cones are globose, blue-green, ripening to brown. **Habitat and Ecology** • Moist valleys in mountainous country. **Similar species** • Many cultivars including 'Variegata' **10**.

Natural range
Japan, where the species is divided obscurely into northern and southern subspecies.

Cultivated distribution
Grown in Japan as a forest tree for its high-quality timber. Seen in Europe only as an ornamental curiosity.

1
2
3
4
5
6
7
8
9
10

FAMILY Taxodiaceae

Sequoiadendron giganteum (Lindl.) Buchh.

Wellingtonia or Giant redwood

Description • An unmistakable tree growing to massive proportions, 50 m tall so far in Europe and over 90 m in its native America. Stems in Europe exceed 3 m in diameter but in America trees 9 m across are known. In much of Europe growth is rapid for the first 100 years then slows down **1** and often lightning strikes take out the top section. As a plantation this species looks very promising **2** but the timber lacks quality. The bark is reddish-brown, distinctly fibrous and very soft. On the largest trees it may be 30 cm thick on the strongly buttressed base **3**. The function of such a thick bark is insulation against forest fire. It burns poorly even when the fire is very intense. Stems taper rapidly into a conical crown. They are hardly ever forked and branches are relatively light. In the open, bottom branches sometimes sweep downwards to the ground from where they subsequently form a ring of subordinate trees. Although appearing to be layered most of these boughs are simply resting on the surface of the ground. The leaves are short, overlapping, 5 mm evergreen scales **4**. They are deep green but bloomed with blue-grey and have twin white lines of stomata on the underside. The foliage is slender and bunched, often pendulous on the branch extremities and towards the bottom of the tree. Current growth on the shoot tips generally points upwards in the first year. The flowers appear in late winter. For this reason hardly any fertile seed is set because in cold weather the pollen dies. Woody cones, with or without seed in them, appear in clusters **4**. These are green for one year, mature the second year then turn brown but remain on the tree for several more seasons. Each light brown, flat seed has two short wings that enable it to flutter away from the parent tree in the wind. **Habitat and Ecology** • A primitive forest species adapted to lightning strikes and fire, the heat breaks the wax seal on the cones which start to open after the danger of burning has passed. **Similar species** • The cultivar 'Pendulum' has similar foliage but it develops into weird upright or pendulous shapes **5**. Coast redwood (p46) has similar spongy bark.

Natural range
Western slopes of the Sierra Nevada in Central California now confined to protected reserves like Yosemite, Kings Canyon and Sequoia National Park.

Cultivated distribution
When first discovered by loggers in 1841 trees were felled for museums and as 3000-year-old curiosities (e.g. to see how many people could stand on a stump). Many were left to rot once a slice had been removed from the base. The survivors have been protected since 1900. In Europe, widely grown on old private estates and in large parks since 1853. Still planted as an ornamental landscape and avenue feature now, but on a much reduced scale. The excessive size, lightning risk, falling debris, etc. make this an unsuitable tree for most urban situations.

1
2
3
5
4

FAMILY Cupressaceae

Chamaecyparis nootkatensis (D.Don) Spach

Nootka cypress

Description • The best distinguishing feature of this tree, which superficially resembles Lawson cypress (p14) is its pointed outline **1**. Almost every open grown specimen over ten years old will develop this distinctive cone shape adapted to shed snow. The lax, drooping shoot tips enhance this further and, unless trimmed, the foliage extends down to the ground. Fully-grown specimens reach 20–30 m in height with stems up to 1 m in diameter. The durable timber is harvested in America as Alaska cedar. The 3 mm scale-like, pointed, spreading leaves in four ranks cling tightly to the shoot and obscure it **2**. The flowers are small – males being yellow, females green – becoming blue-green and bloomed as they expand into distinctive cones **2**. These ripen to reddish-brown and open to release the seeds after two years. **Habitat and Ecology** • Adapted to harsh mountain top and Arctic winter conditions, an aerodynamic shape, flexible snow-shedding foliage and minimal transpiration. Grows on poor, wet, acid, mineral soil sometimes in pure forests. **Similar species** • Other Cypress and False cypress species and Incense cedar (p22).

Natural range
The Pacific coast of Alaska then south along the Rocky Mountains to Oregon and just into Northern California.

Cultivated distribution
A valuable, durable timber tree. Introduced to Germany before 1854 and planted as an ornamental on large estates in Northern Europe, particularly in high rainfall areas. Not common in the British Isles and often replaced by, or mistaken for, Lawson cypress.

Chamaecyparis pisifera (Sieb. and Zucc.) Endl.

Sawara cypress

Description • A forest tree in Japan superficially similar to Lawson cypress (p14) and very like Hinoki cypress (below). It thrives best in fairly mild regions with acid sandy soil such as South East England. Trees there exceed 29 m in height with stems 70–90 cm diameter. This species has scale-like leaves with in-curved points that are white at the base. The foliage is in flat sprays with evenly spaced shoots like the barbs on a feather **3**. Although flat the sprays point in various directions giving a billowing effect but retaining a conical outline **4**. The bark is red-brown becoming grey with age **5**. Cones are globular, 5–7 mm across, similar to Lawson cypress. Turning from waxy pale green to red-brown and shedding seed in one season. **Habitat and Ecology** • A wet mountainous forest species. Occasionally cultivated as an ornamental but of little merit. **Similar species** • *Chamaecyparis obtusa (Sieb. and Zucc.) Endl.* Hinoki cypress also from Japan. Foliage closer to Lawson cypress and cones larger, 1.2 cm across, yellowish-green then orange-brown.

Natural range
Japan, from Kyushu to Honshu.

Cultivated distribution
Seldom used as a species for ornament but there are many popular cultivated varieties some of which retain fine-needled juvenile foliage (e.g. 'Squarrosa'), or semi-juvenile foliage indefinitely (e.g. 'Plumosa').

1
2
3
4
5

FAMILY Cupressaceae

Chamaecyparis lawsoniana (Murr.) Parl.
Lawson cypress

Description • A large, conical, dark evergreen tree with drooping, flat sprays of foliage **1**. In the wild it grows to 40 m tall but is generally much smaller in Europe. Branches are mostly small and flexible but obscured by persistently green foliage. The stem is straight and if forked at all divides into vertical trunks like organ pipes. The bark is smooth at first and grey-green sometimes exfoliating to reveal red or purplish-brown patches. As it matures it becomes fissured and fibrous red-brown eventually bleaching to grey in full light **2**. The leaves are 2 mm scales pressed firmly against the shoot in opposite pairs. The acute tips may be free and point inwards or outward usually depending on the vigour of the particular shoot. This tree is very shade tolerant so lax fronds of foliage with diminutive leaf scales can be found in deep shade that are quite different to others in full light. One constant feature is the rather unpleasant resinous smell of crushed foliage. Male flowers on the previous season's growth are black in winter opening red and black on the first warm days of spring. They are 4 mm long and appear in large clusters, exceptionally large clusters on the cultivar 'Wisselli' **7**. Female flowers on the tip of side shoots are green, quickly developing into globular, 10 mm bloomed cones **3**, which turn brown, open and shed numerous fertile seeds in the autumn. **Habitat and Ecology** • A forest tree able to grow in pure, close-spaced plantations **4** excluding all other trees, shrubs or ground vegetation in the gloom below. This is one of the least demanding of all trees. It will grow on poor soils unable to sustain other conifers. **Similar species** • In Europe, most often confused with Western red cedar (p8) simply because both species have been frequently planted. The crushed foliage of Western red cedar however has a sweet sickly smell. Also similar to several other Cypress species and Incense cedar (p22).

Natural range
Two separate populations in a narrow coastal belt through South West Oregon to North West California (Port Orford cedar) and further inland around Mount Shasta up to 1500 m elevation.

Cultivated distribution
Strangely when this species was introduced to Europe, originally from the upper Sacramento valley in 1854, it began to produce numerous sports and aberrations that were subsequently raised by nurserymen as cultivars. 'Intertexta' is a large, open, ascending tree with wayward branches and strongly pendulous shoots **5**. There are also many golden forms including the original 1872 cultivar 'Lutea' **6**. 'Wisselii' is a hideously deformed foliage type **7**. This species was a popular garden hedge plant until eclipsed by Leyland cypress (p20) in the late twentieth century.

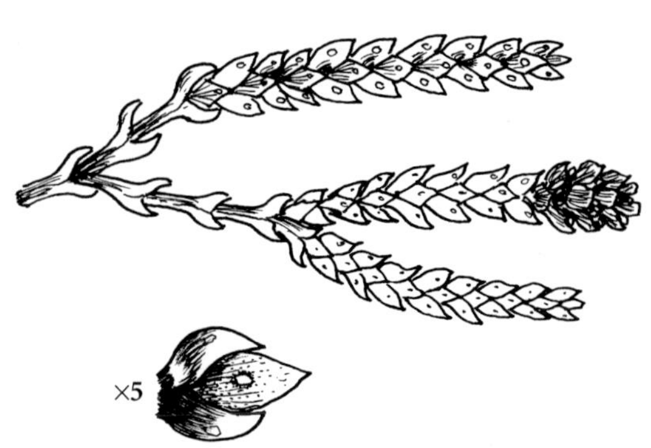

Lawson cypress foliage and flower

1
2
3
4
5
6
7

FAMILY Cupressaceae

Cupressus macrocarpa Hartw. ex Gord.

Monterey cypress

Description • In the milder parts of North-west Europe, where rainfall is sufficient, this is a stately 20–30 m tree **1**. Stems may exceed 1 m in diameter but by this time heavy upright branches start to break off in gales exposing the gaunt, grey stem **2**. Sometimes picturesque, sometimes ugly, but always unpredictable. The bark is brown when shaded then grey-brown and fibrous, finely ridged vertically or on a gentle spiral round the stem **3**. On very old trees the surface may break up into shallow scales and the whole trunk bleaches to almost white. This contrasts dramatically with the dark, ragged evergreen foliage. The 2 mm blunt leaf scales in four ranks are pressed against the shoots which are arranged haphazardly and not in flat sprays. The 6 mm male flowers are yellow in dense clusters. Females are less conspicuous and develop into conelets in one year and full sized 3–4 cm woody cones the second year. Sometimes these occur in large clusters **4**, sometimes singly. Seeds are shed in the autumn, winter or spring when the sun is hot enough but the cones remain on the tree for years with some viable seed in them. It is likely that in nature the heat from fast-moving forest fires would open dormant cones sufficiently for seed to be shed later into the cooled ashes as for *Sequoiadendron* (p10). **Habitat and Ecology** • Geological evidence suggests a much wider range for this species than it now occupies. Climate and geography have confined it to granite cliffs and headlands in extreme heat and close proximity to the Pacific Ocean. In cool conditions in Europe and elsewhere it changes dramatically from a stunted, sun-scorched, gnarled scrub to a tall forest tree. **Similar species** • Other *Cupressus* species and some Leyland cypress cultivars (p20). This is a parent of many Leyland cultivars. In the stunted form it resembles some species of Juniper in their adult foliage state. The smell of crushed foliage, like lemons, is said to be distinctive.

Natural range
Confined to two groves in California, Point Lobos Reserve and Del Monte Forest near Monterey and Carmel. It has been unable to spread further since the last ice age.

Cultivated distribution
Extensively used in Europe for shelter and hedging. Thrives best near the Atlantic coast. Trials for forestry show that heavy, acute-angled branches are a problem and susceptibility to incurable Coryneum canker (*Seiridium cardinale* Wag.) is an unacceptable risk. There are extensive plantations in South Africa, New Zealand and Australia. As an ornamental specimen tree the golden forms are good, notably 'Donard Gold' **5** from Ireland.

Cupressus macrocarpa foliage

1
2
4
3
5

FAMILY Cupressaceae

Cupressus sempervirens L.
Italian cypress

Description • From a foliage sample alone it is difficult to separate this species from several other Cypress species but as a tree it is quite distinctive, especially the narrow fastigiate forms which can be up to 30 m tall benefiting now from a warmer climate in Northern Europe. The form *horizontalis* is probably most hardy. Horizontalis is a reference to the fine branches not the shape of the whole tree **1**. The fastigiate type, forma *sempervirens*, has the distinctive slender 'Italian' upright outline **2**. There are extremely narrow selections cultivated from it (e.g. 'Totem') **3**. Italian cypress foliage is thread-like and the 3 cm cones are ovoid **4**. **Habitat and Ecology** • Obscured by centuries of cultivation but grows best on hot stony ground. **Similar species** • Other *Cupressus*, *Thuja* and *Chamaecyparis*.

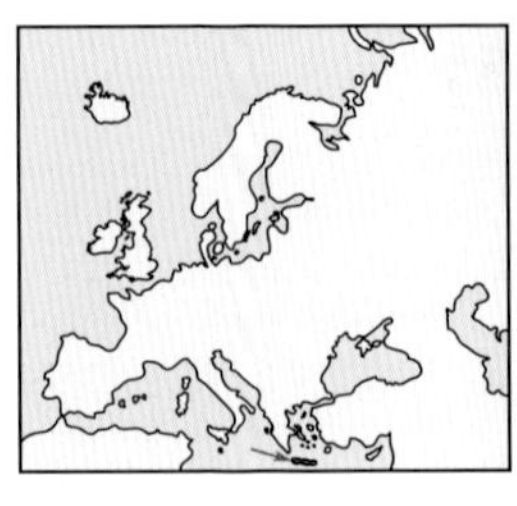

Natural range

Cultivated distribution
Traditionally Southern Europe close to the Mediterranean but extending northwards as an ornamental landscape feature.

Cupressus glabra Sudw.
Smooth Arizona cypress

Description • Potentially an 18 m tree with a straight, smooth, purplish-brown, grey and buff, scaly barked, resinous stem **7**. The stiff foliage is grey-green with numerous yellow male flowers in early spring **5**. Small, green female flowers develop into globular, grey-brown, 2 cm cones similar to those of Italian cypress. The whole tree is distinctive because of its sage green colour **6**. **Habitat and Ecology** • A desert species growing slowly in hot very dry conditions. **Similar species** • *Cupressus arizonica* Greene, which is a smaller tree with stringy bark and greener foliage. Probably intergrades with *Cupressus glabra* which is considered by some authorities to be a variety of it.

Natural range
Central Arizona as a segregate population of *Cupressus arizonica* that extends to North Mexico and Trans-Pecos Texas.

Cultivated distribution
In cool, North European conditions this tree grows vigorously enough in many places to be a potential forest tree where water is a limiting factor. It is already common as an ornamental with several cultivated forms.

Cupressus lusitanica Mill.
Mexican cypress or Cedar of Goa

Description • A large 20 m tree with reddish-brown, scaly bark **8** and grey-green, thread-like lax foliage. The young, globular cones are bloomed grey-green **9**, turning brown at maturity. Originally from Central Mexico this tree has a confusing history. In Europe it is planted as a forest tree. The species name suggests Portugal as its origin, but it was introduced to Portugal around 1640. The alternative common name Goa is a reference to a former Portuguese colony in Western India. **Habitat and Ecology** • Dry semi-desert. **Similar species** • Monterey cypress (p16).

Natural range
Central America from Mexico to Guatemala in desert conditions.

Cultivated distribution
Grown as a timber tree in South-east Europe and occasionally as an ornamental curiosity in Northern Europe.

1
2
3
4
5
6
7
8
9

FAMILY Cupressaceae

X Cupressocyparis leylandii Dallim.

Leyland cypress

Description • An artificial, intergeneric, hybrid evergreen tree up to 40 m tall with a stem diameter in excess of 1 m in 70 years **1**. New coloured forms in yellow, blue-grey and with degrees of variegated foliage have been planted in parks and gardens recently. The original green clones were produced spontaneously in Northern Ireland in 1870 and Wales in 1888, where the parent trees, *Cupressus macrocarpa* (p16) × *Chamaecyparis nootkatensis* (p12), were growing adjacent to one another in ornamental conifer collections. Morphological identification of Leyland cypress is difficult; identification of individual green clones is virtually impossible and certainly unwise. Historical planting notes are essential if diagnosis is to be well-grounded. Mature stems are purplish-brown, usually straight and persistent **2**, vertically fissured and buttressed in old age. Branches are up-swept but lax towards the tip of the flattened foliage giving a feathery effect. Scale leaves obscure new shoots but in the second year red-brown coloration begins to show through. Individual overlapping, in-curved, keeled scales are 5–10 mm long with acute points. Flowers are rare, male and female on the same tree in late winter. Sterile cones **3** are about 2 cm in diameter, globose, with a blunt point on each scale. They take two years to mature. Seed is rarely fertile, vegetative propagation is advised. **Habitat and Ecology** • Clonal forests of Leyland cypress, although highly productive, have a negative environmental impact. Ground vegetation is totally eradicated, trees are identical **4**, so consequently liable to the rapid spread of disease or forest fire. Fast growth often leads to instability or stem snap. **Similar species** • Other cypress species although most grow more slowly. Also clones, for example, 'Harlequin' which has foliage 'peppered' with creamy-white **5** and even variegated cones **6**.

Note: Some authorities in Britain question the genus designation of the parent *Chamaecyparis nootkatensis*, suggesting *Cupressus* instead, while in America *Cupressus macrocarpa* is thought by some to be *Chamaecyparis macrocarpa*. The resulting taxonomy is confused.

Natural range

This intergeneric hybrid does not occur in the natural state in America. The parents' ranges do not overlap.

Cultivated distribution

Widespread particularly in urban Britain where the promise of instant evergreen hedging has caused problems for many householders when their hedges become excessively large and will not stop growing. There are several yellow forms in cultivation.

The earliest commercial cultivar of Leyland cypress 'Rostrevor' was produced in Ireland in 1870. The most commonly planted clones 'Haggerston Grey' 1888 and 'Leighton Green' 1911 originated at Leighton Hall in Wales.

1
2
3
4
5
6

FAMILY Cupressaceae

Calocedrus decurrens (Torr.) Florin

Incense cedar

Description • Initially at first sight this tree resembles many other kinds of Thuja, Cypress and False cypress. Identification in Europe is however made easier because most early introductions intended for amenity planting were the narrow-crowned fastigiate form, sometimes called 'Columnaris'. Old trees are unmistakably narrow in outline. Subsequent seedlings from these have produced a second generation of fairly narrow distinctly 'upswept' trees **1**. The stem, which is usually obscured by foliage down to the ground, is straight and vertical, sometimes forking in the crown but still heading straight upwards. The bark is red-brown and stringy **2**, but not soft like a Redwood (p10). The foliage develops into flat but lax fronds **3**. The leaves, 2 mm pointed scales, are bright green on both sides, very resinous and aromatic when crushed. Flowers on second-year wood occur in spring, they are separate, tiny, yellow male and green female cones. The females develop in one season into 2 cm six-scaled, light-green, leathery cones **4**, which turn light brown and open to shed the winged seed in early winter. Most cones only produce two viable seeds. **Habitat and Ecology** • Mixed forest in Western North America on warm, dry hillsides with *Pinus ponderosa* Laws. and *Quercus kelloggii* Newb. Specimens 55 m tall have been recorded. **Similar species** • Closely related to *Thuja* and has similar foliage to Cypress species and cultivars.

Natural range
West North America from the Santian River in Oregon along the Cascade Mountains to the Sierra Nevada in California, also along the Pacific coastal mountain ranges from Mendocino to central Baja California.

Cultivated distribution
Introduced to Europe in 1853 by John Jeffrey mainly as an ornamental tree although in America the lumber is widely used and high-quality wood is reserved for joinery and pencils. Its aromatic properties repel clothes moths. The former genus name *Libocedrus* refers to the same tree.

FAMILY Taxodiaceae

Cryptomeria japonica (L.f.) D. Don

Japanese cedar

Description • The hard, evergreen, spiky foliage of this forest conifer is distinctive. It is reminiscent of Redwood (p10) but the curved pointed 1–1.5 cm scales are longer **5** and **6**. Plantation trees in Europe are infrequent but reach over 32 m in height in Ireland. Unless wind blown in their youth, stems are straight and clean **7**. The bark is red to orange-brown, fibrous and scaly **8**. Shoots are green with spaced out radially arranged slender pointed scales **5**. The flowers develop in late winter on weak side shoots developing into green and then brown 2 cm cones each with around 25 spiky scales **6**. Each fully formed scale protects several seeds but these are seldom viable. **Habitat and Ecology** • In Japan and China this is highly valued as a quality timber tree. It tolerates infertile ground but requires good water supplies. It is shade tolerant but susceptible to wind damage. **Similar species** • Many cultivated forms.

Natural range
Southern Japan and a small area in Southern China. (var. sinensis Sieb. and Zucc.)

Cultivated distribution
The species, which is not particularly ornamental, is seldom grown in Europe now but numerous ornamental cultivars of it are. Some of these are fixed in the juvenile foliage state with long, very fine, soft needles quite unlike the species. Several turn bronze or brown in winter.

1
2
3
4
5
6
7
8

FAMILY Cupressaceae

Juniperus communis L.
Common juniper

Description • This large shrub or small tree comes in various sizes and shapes depending upon where it is growing. It has no preference for particular soil and can be found on anything from chalk downland to acid, rocky mountain sides. There is no typical shape or form – growth is either strongly vertical or almost prostrate. The largest trees can be around 8 m tall by which time they are usually starting to break up, lean or fall over. Fallen individuals, if they are not 'tidied up' will usually continue to grow perfectly well and soon adapt to their new status. Trees are usually recognized by their dense evergreen foliage and compact up-swept branches **1**. Stems are usually obscured by persistent foliage often down to ground level. The bark is reddish-brown soon developing vertical fissures and hard scaly ridges **2**. Shoots are pale yellowish-green becoming brown the second year then purplish-brown on the main branches. Lower side shoots are often semi-pendulous **3**, particularly on more prostrate forms from alpine or sub-tundra locations. The needles are stiff, around 1 cm long and arranged in threes. Each one is tapered to a fine point and has a glaucous line of stomata on the outer surface. The flowers are very small, yellowish and appearing in spring on the previous season's shoot. There are separate male and female trees. Fruits persist on the plants in various stages of development during a three-year ripening process **4**. First they are sea-green with white bloom, then blue, still with waxy white bloom, and finally purplish-black. **Habitat and Ecology** • A tough, very hardy species that can grow in complete isolation from other woody plants or on forest edges. Particularly associated with pine woods extending their margins into hostile bare ground often at high elevation along the tree line. **Similar species** • Other junipers, which like this species only produce the juvenile type of spiny foliage. There are also many cultivated forms and regional subspecies. The Swedish juniper, forma *suecica* (Mill.) Beissn. is an upright plant **5** with thick deep green foliage **6**. Irish juniper 'Hibernica' is similar but forms a 3–4 m slender column until it is broken open by snow or the sheer weight of foliage.

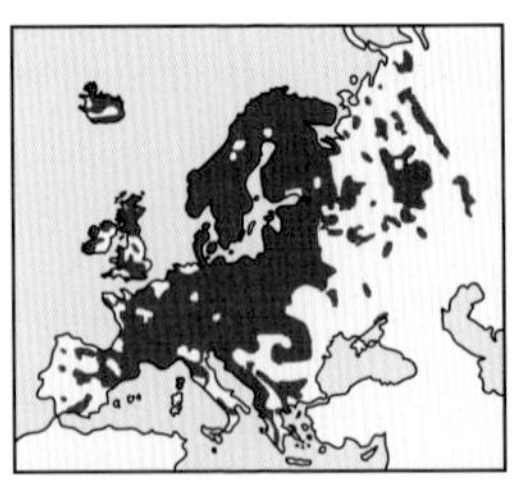

Natural range

Cultivated distribution
The wild tree is encouraged for environmental reasons and the fruit is occasionally used to flavour drinks but it is not generally cultivated. There are however several ornamental selections that are popular in horticulture. Subspecies *alpina* (Suter) Celak is a good rockery or alpine garden plant. 'Compressa' is a miniature upright form. Except for one or two mediocre golden-leaved forms cultivated plants have been selected for extremes of columnar or prostrate growth. The columnar 'Hibernica' has often been used as a substitute for the upright form of Italian cypress (p18) in cold northern landscaped gardens in the Italian style.

1
2
3
4
5
6

FAMILY Cupressaceae

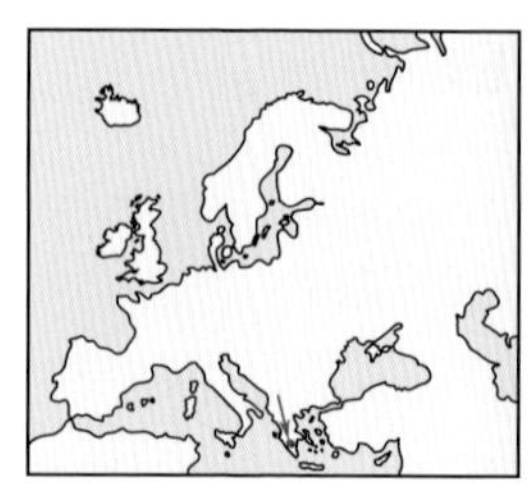

Juniperus drupacea Labill.
Syrian juniper

Description • Second only to the Tiger-tail spruce, *Picea polita* Carr., for viciously sharp needles this species will draw blood if the tree is simply touched. It is usually a statuesque, narrow columnar specimen, 10–12 m tall **1**. The bark is orange-brown but hardly ever seen because foliage persists down to the ground. Needles are in threes arranged spirally round the shoot in alternate sets so that when viewed from above they appear to project in six ways **2**. Each one is 2 cm long, drawn out to a very sharp point. Flowers are on separate male and female trees. Males are globular and yellow, females are like miniature cones. They develop into ovoid, 25 mm woody cones with around eight flat-ended scales. In summer these are glaucous blue-green **2** ripening to bloomed black. **Habitat and Ecology** • Very dry, hot, rocky ground. **Similar species** • Like other Juniper species that retain juvenile foliage but individual needles are longer and fairly distinctive.

Natural range
Southern Greece, Turkey and parts of Syria.

Cultivated distribution
Planted in gardens and specialist tree collections. Antisocial in public parks. Female trees are said to be particularly rare.

Juniperus virginiana L.
Pencil cedar

Description • Potentially 18 m tall with a stem of 1 m diameter. Conical when young but spreading out of shape in old age **3**. The foliage is pale coloured when young then characteristically dark green consisting almost entirely of adult scale leaves (reminiscent of Cypress p16) **4**. Fruits are 5 mm long, ovoid and so thickly bloomed that individual scales can hardly be seen **5**. They ripen in one season to dark violet-brown still with considerable pale grey, translucent, waxy bloom. **Habitat and Ecology** • Tolerant of dry, rocky places or wet, swampy ground. Thrives in limestone areas. **Similar species** • Without the fruit this tree resembles Cypress and *Chamaecyparis* (p14). The fruit resembles that of Chinese juniper *Juniperus chinensis* L. **6**, but Chinese juniper has a greater mixture of scaly adult and spiny juvenile foliage.

Natural range
Eastern North America from Canada to Florida and west to Texas.

Cultivated distribution
Occasionally grown as an ornamental in Northern Europe but usually represented by one of the many named cultivars. Often replaced in cultivation by the spectacular *Juniperus scopulorum* 'Skyrocket' one of the narrowest of all Junipers **7**. Pencils made from the wood, rarely these days, sharpen easily and have a distinctive smell of resin.

1
2
3
4
5
6
7

FAMILY Tamaricaceae

Tamarix parviflora DC.
Tamarisk

Description • A more or less deciduous, small tree or spreading shrub 6–8 m tall often a thicket of suckers and layered reclining tangled branches. Superficially it is similar to most other *Tamarix* species except that it flowers early on lateral shoots on the previous year's branches. The foliage is glaucous-green on dark purplish-brown or almost black shoots. These are upright but slender and flex in the wind. Flowers are light pink, bisexual in stiff catkin-like 2–4 cm racemes often frequent and appearing to cover the whole plant in early summer **1**. Each minute individual flower has four to five petals and stamens and three styles. The fruit consists of a dry capsule with many seeds in three compartments. Each seed has a tuft of hairs that aids windblown distribution. Long-established plants may develop one or more substantial trunks **2**. Stem diameters over 50 cm are known. The bark is pale grey roughly broken into vertical plates divided by deep, dark grey fissures. **Habitat and Ecology** • Maritime cliffs and shingle banks, also hedgerows close to the sea. One of the nearest woody plants to the high tide line. **Similar species** • *Tamarix tetrandra* Pall. Ex Bieb., is virtually identical. Stems are possibly a little darker.

Natural range

Coastal fringes of the Balkan Peninsula and the Aegean Sea.

Cultivated distribution

Tamarisk is planted to aid coastal protection and as a seaside amenity plant. Local authorities seldom take into account which species is being used. This tree is probably slightly less hardy than *Tamarix gallica* (below) and flowering is over before the summer holiday season begins.

Tamarix gallica L.
French tamarisk

Description • This species is different to *Tamarix parviflora* (above) mainly because the flowers are in terminal panicles. Infloescences consist of a showy mass of 3–5 cm racemes. Because the flowers have to wait until the current shoots are fully extended the flowering season is later in the summer. This is a tree up to 8 m tall or a thicket of storm-tossed, arching stems and suckers **3**. The leaves are dull, bluish-green ovate to lanceolate scales under 1 mm long packed tightly round the stem. In all but the severest winters they are evergreen. Young shoots are purplish-brown with alternate green shootlets each subtended by a 2 mm pointed bract. Towards the tip only the bracts occur. Flowers are pink and minute, with four to five petals appearing in great profusion **4**. Numerous seeds are produced in dry capsules. **Habitat and Ecology** • Originally from Southern Europe this species has now become naturalized along much of the Atlantic and North Sea coasts of Northern Europe. It survives well on former marsh and shingle banks. **Similar species** • *Tamarix anglica* Webb, English tamarisk, is almost identical but usually a much smaller bush.

Natural range

The Atlantic coasts of France, Spain and Portugal also Gibraltar and parts of Morocco. Naturalized, but probably not native in Britain.

Cultivated distribution

Frequently planted on coasts for protection and amenity. One of the most hardy species which also keeps some green foliage in the winter even when there is frost **5**. Later summer flowering is also an attraction in seaside resorts.

1

2

3

4

5

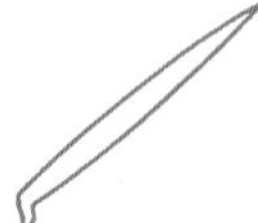

FAMILY Pinaceae

Abies alba Mill.

European silver fir

Description • Still a common forest tree in mainland Europe but virtually replaced in the British Isles by more productive American species and because of its susceptibility to insect predation. Usually found in Britain now as a relic of older plantations or tree collections towering over the surrounding exotic specimens or subsequent invading neglected woodland **1**. The largest trees on record are 50 m tall with stems up to 2 m in diameter. In the nineteenth century it was noted by Loudon (1838) how *Abies alba* was used to distinguish the residences of the landed gentry by its imposing stature. The bark is silvery-grey and smooth for many years becoming slightly roughened and less silvery in old age **2**. Stems are usually very straight and vertical until the top-most shoots are blasted out by adverse weather. Even trees that fork, usually because the single leading shoot has been broken out by birds or the wind, produce twin or multiple stems that resume their strictly vertical progress reminiscent of organ pipes. Side branches are mostly light and horizontal producing a columnar outline. The foliage is variable depending on the provenance. In the Balkans, intermediate forms occur between this species and *Abies cephalonica* (p32). One such form has been named as a species *Abies borisii-regis* Mattf., which has dark, glossy, green needles up to 3 cm long with two glaucous bands on the underside **3**. North European trees have fawn-brown shoots with horizontally spreading ranks of green 2–3 cm needles with grey-green bands of stomata on the underside **4**. Male flowers are pale yellow, 2 cm, cone-like structures. Females, confined to the top of the tree, are upright miniature cones. Mature cones, produced singly or in clusters, are cylindrical with tapered rounded ends and down-turned bracts. They are up to 15 cm long, ripen from green to rusty-brown and disintegrate at the end of one season. **Habitat and Ecology** • Cool northern or mountain forests. Natural pure stands, once extensive, have been managed and re-planted for centuries. At low elevation *Abies alba* often grows in the company of Beech (p86). **Similar species** • Several other species of *Abies.*

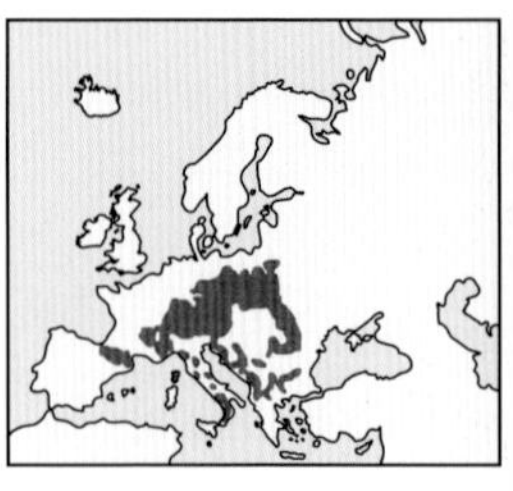

Natural range

Cultivated distribution
Formerly grown as an amenity and plantation tree beyond its Natural range, but blighted by the Aphid *Adelges nordmannianae* which sucks the sap from the needles and weakens the tree's defence against other diseases or environmental stress. Severe attacks can cause complete defoliation and death. In Britain, poorly chosen provenance of cankered and moribund European larch (p64) forest plantations were frequently enriched with this shade tolerant species; sadly this strategy did not work.

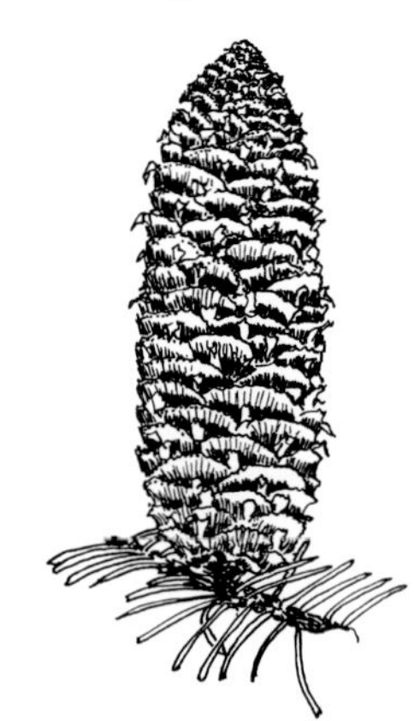

1

2

3

4

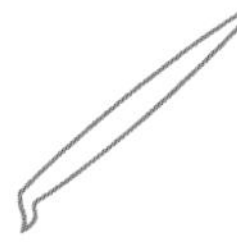

FAMILY Pinaceae

Abies cephalonica Loud.
Grecian fir

Description • A potentially large tree up to 30 m tall with a mature stem diameter around 1 m. Young trees are conical **1**, becoming wide-spreading with an untidy top and very long side branches **3**. The bark is pinkish-brown **2**, bleaching to grey-brown when exposed to the sun and wind; it remains smooth for many years eventually becoming scaly and slightly fissured. Shoots are red-brown, shiny and stiff for one or two years **4**. The waxy orange-brown winter buds have prominent resinous scales. The 2–3 cm needles spread all round the shoot but are distinctly parted on the underside, glossy green above and almost white below **4**, having two distinct, broad, stomatal bands. The tip is pointed but not particularly sharp. Male flowers are yellowish and globular, distributed all over the tree beneath the young shoots. The upright female cones, usually confined to the tree top, are 15 cm long, cylindrical, tapered at each end and mostly pointed at the tip. Each cone scale has a projecting down-curved bract. Cones start off green and ripen to brown, then disintegrate in the autumn to shed the winged seed. **Habitat and Ecology** • A high-elevation mountain species on dry, calcareous, rocky soils. **Similar species** • *Abies cilicica* (Antoine & Kotschy) Carr. and *Abies x vilmorinii* (p36).

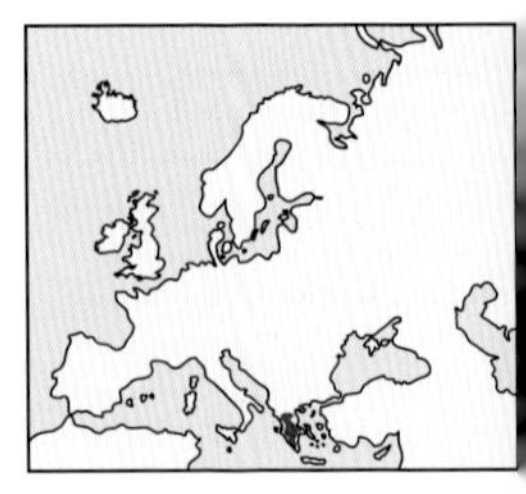

Natural range

Cultivated distribution
A good specimen tree with potential for timber production, but it comes into leaf early and is frequently cu back by spring frost. Cultivated in Northern Europe since 1824 but seldon seen outside specialist collections.

Abies numidica De Lannoy ex Carr.
Algerian fir

Description • A large tree up to 25 m with a very graceful conical outline **5**; then the top tends to flatten out in old trees producing a more ragged appearance. The bark is grey with a hint of pinkish-brown when young **6**. Very old trees develop curling scales, shallow fissures and a network of cracks. Shoots are orange-brown with densely packed, upward curving, 1–2 cm, blunt, notched needles. They are distinctly parted on the pale greenish-white underside, and the upper side is dark green **7**. The non-resinous buds are small, light red to dark brown, with free-tipped basal scales. Flowers emerge from side buds on the previous year's shoots. The males are yellow, numerous and short-lived. Small cone-shaped females develop in one season into upright cylindrical 15 cm cones which start off pale green then become purplish-brown. Bracts do not project from between the cone scales. **Habitat and Ecology** • Restricted to a small, high-elevation, cold, dry area in the Atlas Mountains in Algeria. **Similar species** • Spanish fir (p36).

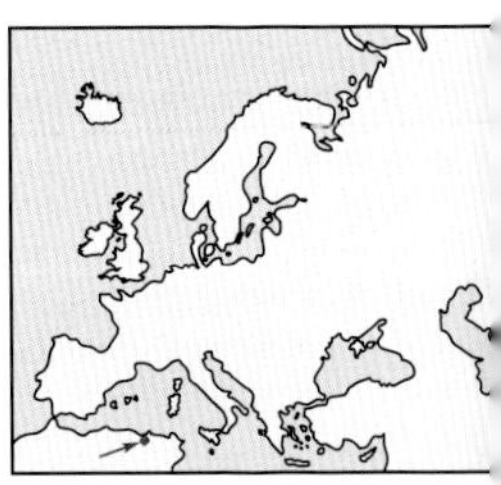

Natural range

Cultivated distribution
Introduced in 1861 but never grown on a large scale in Northern Europe and only found in specialist collection

1
2
3
4
5
6
7

FAMILY Pinaceae

Abies nordmanniana (Steven) Spach

Caucasian fir

Description • Of all the evergreen conifers Caucasian fir retains its needles for longest. A few remain on the branches of most specimens for around 25 years. This is a large columnar tree with a persistent straight stem and dark green foliage. The outline is regular with a conical top until post-maturity when the whole tree becomes ragged with spreading uneven horizontal branches **1**, a stark contrast to symmetrical youngsters **2**. Although rare as a forest tree outside its natural range this is also an impressive species in that role **3**. Growth is even and stems are clean with only light branches. Relative shade tolerance means that a large number of trees per hectare can be sustained. The foliage is always dense and rarely unhealthy **4**. Needles are 2–3 cm long, the longest arranged laterally and shorter ones curving upwards and forward along the upper side of the shoot **5**. They have rolled back margins and an abrupt squarish tip mostly with a small central notch. There are twin grey bands of stomata on the underside. The shoot, although mostly hidden, is olive-green then brown with pale hairs at first. Buds are brown and not resinous. Flowers are infrequent and seldom seen at all on the lower branches of the tree. Males are prominent, cone-like structures that turn bright yellow when shedding pollen. Female flowers, confined to side shoot tips close to the top of the tree, are deep pink and upright. Cones are 15 cm long by about 5 cm wide, pale green then brown with white blobs of hardened resin. Bracts between the scales are exserted and reflexed. When ripe the whole cone disintegrates and falls from the tree as a shower of winged seeds and debris. Intact cones are rarely seen. **Habitat and Ecology** • A forest tree which survives in a remarkably wide range of climatic and soil conditions. It is extremely hardy and moderately drought tolerant. **Similar species** • *Abies borisii-regis* (p30) and *Abies bornmuelleriana* Mattf. **6** are considered to be subspecies. This species itself is probably an extension of *Abies alba*, European silver fir (p30). It will hybridize with Grecian fir (p32).

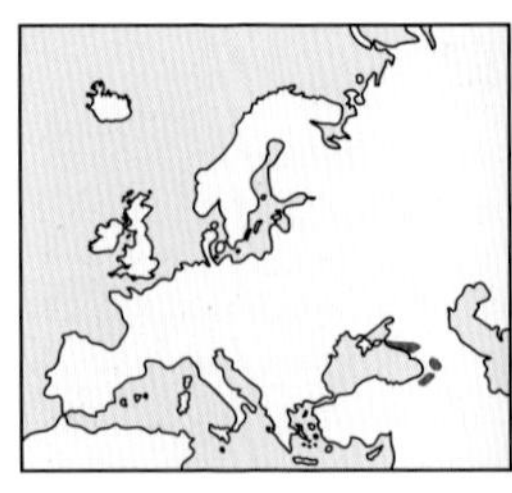

Natural range

Cultivated distribution
Discovered in 1836 Caucasian fir was introduced (to Berlin) in 1848, but has been overlooked by foresters in many countries probably because of disease problems associated with *Abies alba*, a worry now known to be largely unfounded. In Britain, it is less productive than modern Silver firs from America. Recently it has become fashionable as a Christmas tree.

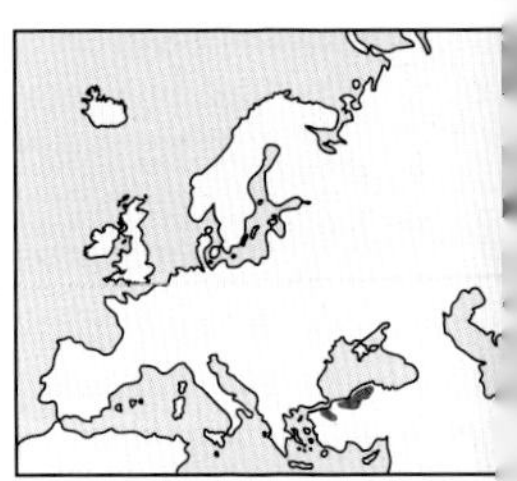

Natural range
Abies bornmuellerana

Cultivated distribution
Very rare, only found in specialist collections. Seldom taxonomically separated from its close relatives with certainty.

1
2
3
4
5
6

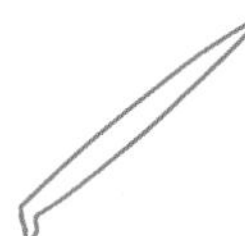

FAMILY Pinaceae

Abies pinsapo Boiss.
Spanish fir

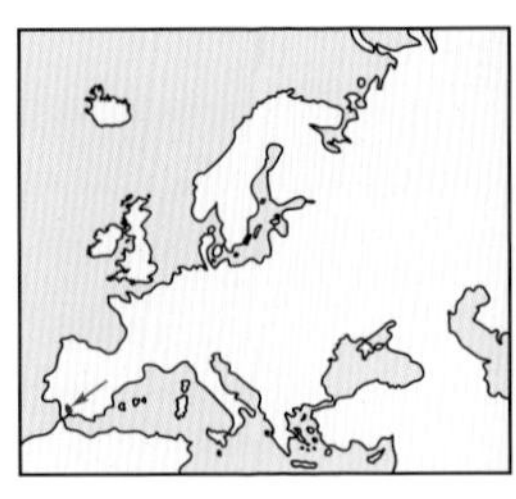

Description • A fine, shapely tree at first **1** until it reaches optimum height, around 20 m, after which the shape becomes irregular. The bark is dark grey and smooth for many years **2**, but in old age it becomes rough with shallow fissures and small, scaly plates. The shoots are greenish-brown at first, becoming warm brown but remaining smooth and glabrous. The distinctive needles are around 1–5 cm long and stick out from the stem in all directions (even downwards on the shaded side) **3** and **4**. Individual needles are stiff and pointed, but not very sharp, and deep, waxy, blue-green with wide bands of stomata on the lower surface. Flowers develop from side buds on previous season's growth. Males are crimson, then yellow when the pollen is shed. Females, only at the top of the tree, are miniature cones which develop in an upright position to about 12 cm in length. They are pale green ripening to light purplish-brown without exposed bract scales. **Habitat and Ecology** • A high-elevation mountain species in Southern Spain in mixed or pure thickets or small areas of forest. **Similar species** • The blue needled form 'Glauca' **4**, the hybrid *Abies x vilmorinii* (below) and *Abies numidica* (p32).

Natural range

Cultivated distribution
Frequently grown in Northern Europe as an ornamental curiosity. Tends to grow slowly in most collections. First described in 1837 and cultivated in Britain since 1839.

Abies x vilmorinii Mast.

Description • A spontaneous and cultivated hybrid between *Abies pinsapo* (above) and *Abies cephalonica* (p32). Like Spanish fir, a fine, straight, shapely tree with a conical outline **5**. Specimens around 20 m tall are known. The bark is pinkish-grey and lightly fissured in old age. Needles spread in all directions but are less dense than Spanish fir and have much sharper points **6**. They are glossy green above with two grey-green bands of stomata on the underside. Shoots are green at first then bright orange-brown. Buds are brown covered with hard, waxy, grey resin. Cones are around 16 cm long with exserted and reflexed bracts between each scale. **Habitat and Ecology** • As the parent species. **Similar species** • *Abies cephalonica.*

Natural range
Forms an intermediate race between the ranges of the parent species, but this is not well defined or researched.

Cultivated distribution
Raised by Maurice L. de Vilmorin at his Des Barres Arboretum in 1867. Infrequent in collections, probably because it has never been widely available in the nursery trade. Certainly a tree worthy of greater prominence.

1
2
3
4
5
6

FAMILY Pinaceae

Abies grandis (Dougl. Ex D. Don) Lindl.

Grand fir or Giant fir

Description • In wet, western forests in the British Isles no other conifer grows as fast as this tree. Good specimens can reach 40 m in about 50 years with straight stems over 50 cm in diameter **1**. In Scotland a number of specimens have exceeded 65 m in height with stems over 2 m in diameter. Unfortunately such rapid growth of soft wood is often accompanied by radial cracking. Cracks sometimes spiral several metres up a tree trunk and the resulting wound, apparent on the bark, may be a helpful diagnostic characteristic. Branches are slender, more or less horizontal, and persistently green well down the tree even in shade. Its shade tolerance ensures that a Grand fir forest is extremely dense, typically with stems of various diameters all standing together. Young trees are beautifully conical with regularly spaced flat tiers of foliage **2**. The bark is grey and smooth with prominent resin blisters at first **3**, bleaching to silver-grey with age and often developing long vertical fissures **4**. Young growth in early summer is fresh green **2**. Individual needles are 3–5 cm long held in two horizontal ranks on each side of the finely pubescent, greenish-brown shoot. They each have two, bright white bands of stomata on the underside and a rounded notched tip. The upper surface is glossy green **5**. Male flowers are small but numerous on the underside of the shoot. They change from pale green to purplish-red then yellow when the pollen is shed. Female flowers, erect, ovoid miniature cones, are less frequent, often confined, singly or in clusters of two or three, to the top-most five years of growth **6**. When fully formed by midsummer, cones are around 10 cm long, bright pale green with rounded scales but no visible projecting bracts. They ripen to dull brown with white spots of hardened resin and by early winter break up to shed the winged seed. **Habitat and Ecology** • A hardy forest species that thrives only in wet conditions, rainfall in excess of 1000 mm pcr annum. **Similar species** • *Abies concolor* (Gord.) Lindl. which has even longer grey-green needles and *Abies concolor* var. *lowiana* (Gord.) Lemm., a geographical variety intermediate between *Abies concolor* and Grand fir.

Natural range
Southern British Columbia along the Pacific coast of North America to California. Also in the Rocky mountains eastwards to Central Idaho.

Cultivated distribution
Introduced to Europe in 1830, and then again on a much larger scale in 1852. Most of the hardy Scottish trees that have grown so large came from the Fraser River Valley in British Columbia. Plantations are mostly on lower and middle slopes in upland districts. Extensively planted to replace ailing European silver fir (p30) in Britain in the nineteenth and twentieth centuries.

1
2
3
4
5
6

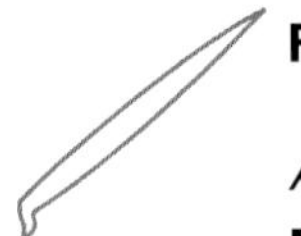

FAMILY Pinaceae

Abies procera Rehd.
Noble fir

Description • Few conifers growing in Europe are as tough as this species, or as impervious to detrimental climatic conditions. Even when planted high up on a snow-covered mountainside in a ferocious prevailing wind stems will usually grow vertically upwards without bending out of shape. In less severe conditions trees will easily exceed 40 m in height with a stem over 1 m in diameter. Young specimens are columnar with a conical top and evenly tiered foliage **1**. Branches leave the trunk almost horizontally and mostly in distinct rings of annual growth. Between these 'nodes' the timber is knot free and the stem is clean. Branch tips tend to droop a little under the weight of the thick foliage **2**. The bark is smooth and silver-grey until minor fissures develop from the base **3**. By this time trees will have taken on monumental dimensions and become distinctively awe-inspiring. Semi-mature plantations have a cathedral like ambience. Being shade-tolerant, trees thrive at close spacing **4**. The 2–4 cm needles occur all round the shoot on small 'pads' but they bend into an 'S' shape in order to form two horizontal ranks facing upwards **5**: few *Abies* species are as distinctly curved. They are stiff and very crowded on the upper side like a hair brush. Each one is 2 mm wide and four-sided with a rounded tip. The upper surface is dark, lustrous green and there are bands of dull grey stomata on the underside. The twigs are orange-brown with rusty hairs, mostly obscured for three to four years, then totally smooth when the needles are shed. The flowers are spectacular but seldom seen. Males are very much like ripe raspberries in colour and shape, held below and sometimes all round weak side shoots. Females, confined to the tree top, are erect miniature cones. The mature cones are like fat candles, 18 cm tall with many round-ended scales arranged in a complex double helix design. Each scale is obscured by a greenish, recurved, papery bract bending down from above it. Each bract is rounded but has a central 6–8 mm projection also directed downwards. Like all *Abies* cones this whole elaborate structure falls into pieces in the autumn leaving only the vertical, woody, central spike. **Habitat and Ecology** • A mixed coniferous forest tree on moist mountain sites. **Similar species** • California red fir, *Abies magnifica* A. Murr., has similar twisted needles.

Natural range
North America west of the Rocky Mountains, from Oregon and Washington to Northern California along the Cascade and Coastal Ranges, up to 2600 m elevation.

Cultivated distribution
Discovered by a European in 1825 and introduced from 1831. Planted extensively in severe climatic conditions particularly where there was prolonged snow cover. The 'blue' needled form 'Glauca' is a large decorative foliage plant **6**.

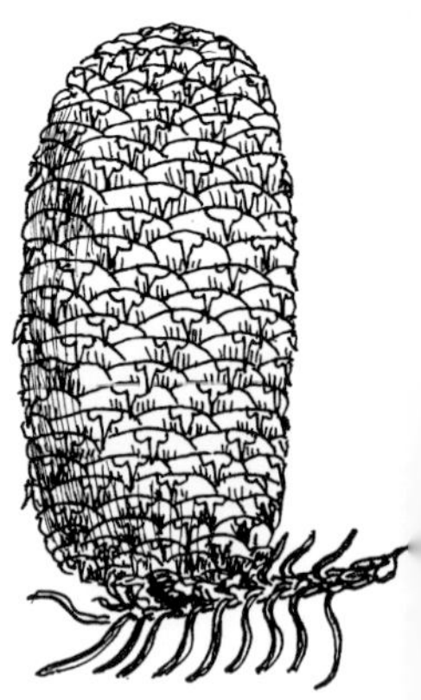

1
2
3
4
5
6

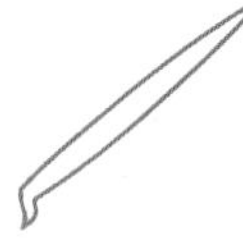

FAMILY Pinaceae

Pseudotsuga menziesii (Mirb.) Franco

Douglas fir

Description • A common, twentieth century forest tree in the British Isles on the lower slopes of mountains and fertile moist hillsides. It is straight stemmed with a conical top until it reaches maturity **1**. Individuals 65 m tall are known in Scotland and stem diameters over 1 m are frequent **2**. A crop of durable structural timber may be expected 40–60 years after planting **3**. Eventually tops blow out, limbs fail, and on clays particularly, trees blow down. The bark is smooth, dark purplish-brown and resinous at first. As the tree matures it becomes corky and ridged, exhibiting an array of colours, red and yellow in the fissures and browns, reds and grey on the ridges. On old trees the bark becomes excessively craggy and thick, but not particularly hard, and reddish-brown in colour **2**. The very soft, flexible, evergreen needles occur singly all round the shoot on new growth and facing more or less upwards on weaker side shoots **4**. They are bright green and around 3 cm long. The foliage has a distinctive resinous smell especially on hot, sunny days in summer. On lower branches it hangs down in pendulous swags. The buds are characteristic, reddish-brown, glabrous and sharply pointed, reminiscent of Common beech (p86). Flowers appear in spring, males are pale yellowish-pink, downward pointing, 2–3 cm cones occurring all over the tree. Females are usually higher up. They are upright, 3 cm, light pink structures consisting of a tuft of free, embryonic cone scales and pointed bracts. Mature cones are diagnostic of this genus **5**, being 5–9 cm long, with tapered ends and papery, rounded scales. Each of these has a trident bract below it with protruding pointed tips. Seeds, two per scale, each have a membraneous wing. They are shed in the autumn and blow away in the wind. **Habitat and Ecology** • A mountain side and valley species often in pure stands. There is a coastal form thriving on river flood plains and alluvium, and a distinctive inland form (Blue Douglas fir) which extends into mountainous country up to 1800 m elevation. **Similar species** • This is a small unique genus. The other species are very rare in Europe. There are many features, soft foliage, bark colours and cones that set Douglas fir apart from other commercial forest conifers.

Natural range

British Columbia down the Pacific coast of North America to central California. Also in the Rocky Mountains from South East Arizona to Central Mexico (only at high elevation).

Cultivated distribution

Introduced to Europe in 1827 some 35 years after its discovery by David Douglas in America. Early plantations were enormously successful and the species is still unsurpassed for productivity and timber quality on rocky hill sides with mineral soils. It requires non-calcareous conditions but does not thrive on acid peat. Wind blast and gale damage are serious problems and air pollution can also be damaging.

1

2

3

4

5

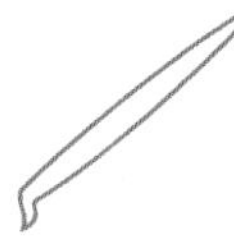

FAMILY Pinaceae

Tsuga heterophylla (Raf.) Sarg.

Western hemlock

Description • A straight, dense, evergreen forest species **1**, so shade tolerant that virtually nothing grows beneath it in plantations. Specimens 35 m tall are common with stems 90 cm in diameter **2**. The graceful outline is conical when young with pendulous side and leading shoot tips. New growth is flexible and soft **3**. The linear leaves are in flat sprays. Each one is about 2.5 mm wide and 1–2 cm long with a blunt point and almost non-existent petiole. Dull green with two broad, greyish lines of stomata on the underside. Flowers on second year shoots are numerous, rose pink, 3 mm male, and pale coloured females developing rapidly into pea green, 2.5 cm cones. Each has 10–15 scales fringed with pale brown. Cones ripen to uniform pale brown and open wide to shed seed in the autumn **4**. Fertility is usually exceptional and tightly packed seedlings grow in sun flecks and on forest road sides. **Habitat and Ecology** • Moist mountain slopes and boggy acid ground, seldom in isolation. **Similar species** • A unique, soft needled genus but individual species are difficult to separate. Part of the population was split in pre-history by the formation of the Pacific Ocean. Trees in western America closely resemble those in eastern Asia (e.g. *Tsuga sieboldii* Carr. Southern Japanese hemlock **5**). Eastern hemlock *Tsuga canadensis* (L.) Carr. from Eastern North America has similar foliage but is usually an ugly coarse tree in Europe.

Natural range
Southern Alaska to Northern California on either side of the Rocky Mountains. Discovered in 1826 and sent to Europe in 1852 and 1861.

Cultivated distribution
Although picturesque in isolation usually grown as a commercial forest species particularly on the Atlantic fringe of Europe with high rainfall and low light intensity.

FAMILY Taxaceae

Torreya californica Torr.

Californian nutmeg

Description • A dark evergreen at first sight reminiscent of Yew (p50). Usually conical 10–15 m tall with greyish-brown stringy bark **6**. Distinctive, sharply spined, hard, 4–5 cm needles occur in two horizontal ranks **7**. Brilliant glossy green above and paler below **8**. The shoot is finely marked with green and red-brown. Male and female flowers occur on separate trees. Males are pale yellow in leaf axils and females terminate some lesser side shoots. The fleshy fruit is plum-like, 3–4 cm long, green with diffuse purplish-brown stripes. Each contains a single seed developing fully in the second year. **Habitat and Ecology** • Valley bottoms and moist sites in California. **Similar species** • There are several species in the genus, also closely related *Podocarpus* and *Cephalotaxus* species.

Natural range
Coastal mountains of California including the western slope of the Sierra Nevada: rare.

Cultivated distribution
Uncommon but planted on a range of sites in Europe as a curiosity. Best where ground water is plentiful. The buff coloured, soft timber is of high quality but seldom seen This is not the spice nutmeg *Myristica fragrans* Houtt.

1
2
3
4
5
6
7
8

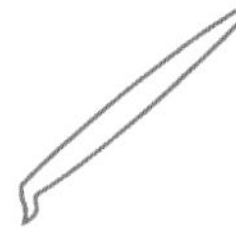

FAMILY Taxodiaceae

Sequoia sempervirens (D.Don) Endl.
Coast redwood

Description • Immediately recognizable by its soft, spongy, red bark **1** and flat, evergreen, needle-like foliage. There is no other tree which combines these two distinctive features. In America this is the world's tallest tree (over 112 m). In Europe it is also a large tree, 47 m tall in Wales and in excess of 247 cm stem diameter in Ireland. On the Atlantic fringe of Europe it can be relied upon to increase its height by 1.3 m each year for about 30 years after becoming established **2**. This is a good forest species, moderately shade tolerant, with fine straight stems **3** that will grow close together. Open grown specimens have a conical top and retain green foliage down to ground level **4**. The stems become massive in less than 100 years, with thick, spongy, fire resistant bark. The leaves are flat needles up to 2 cm long and 3 mm wide. On old or low-growing shoots they form two ranks facing up to the light. On leading shoots they are shorter and spread all round in a spiral arrangement. All the foliage is dark green, with pale stomatal bands on the underside of the leaf which do not show up clearly **5**. Shoots are light reddish-brown and rough from the second year onwards. Needles begin to fall after four years. Flowers occur on the ends of side shoots in late winter. In cold weather they fail to develop properly, turn brown and wither away. When fruit does form it is a 3 cm round or barrel-shaped green cone with about 20 flat-ended scales **6**. They ripen in one season but remain closed on the tree for several years. In the natural state it takes the heat of a forest fire to break the waxy seal and initiate opening. Seed does not emerge for a day or so, after the fire has moved on or extinguished. **Habitat and Ecology** • A relic of once extensive forests that covered large areas of the world. Now confined to a relatively small strip of mixed conifer forest close to the Pacific coast of North America, sustained by cool, moist fog from the sea. It was much depleted by logging in the eighteenth and nineteenth centuries. Now that forest fires are less frequent natural regeneration is also hampered. **Similar species** • The bark is exactly like Wellingtonia (p10), the foliage is like the Hemlocks (p44).

Natural range
Discontinuous along a 500 mile (804 km) strip down the Pacific coast from South West Oregon to Central California. Growing on coastal flats and extending in places to 900 m elevation mountain sides but never more than 35 miles (56 km) inland.

Cultivated distribution
Introduced to Europe, by way of Russia, in 1843 and immediately planted on country estates and in town parks. In most places it was less popular than Wellingtonia so is now less frequently seen as a big mature tree. The foliage tends to go brown in dry areas with exposure and the outline is sometimes ragged and less formal.

1
2
3
4
5
6

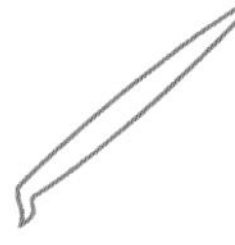

FAMILY Taxodiaceae

Cunninghamia lanceolata (Lamb.) Hook. f.

Chinese fir

Description • A 15 m tall conifer with distinctly garish colours. Luxuriant, bright, glossy green foliage **1**, orange brown bark and bright red-brown dead leaves. It is shade tolerant and keeps green foliage on low branches for many years **2**. The bark is vertically fissured and stringy but hard, on stems up to 70 cm diameter in Northern Europe **3**. Shoots are green with 6–8 cm, down-curved, sharply pointed needles in two ranks facing up to the light **4** with bands of white stomata on the underside. Cones are 4 cm long and oval. **Habitat and Ecology** • A forest tree where ground water is plentiful. **Similar species** • Reminiscent of Monkey puzzle (p6) but clearly different on close inspection. The foliage resembles *Torreya* (p44).

Natural range
Central and Southern China possibly into Vietnam.

Cultivated distribution
Rare in cultivation. Accumulations of brown dysfunctional foliage in dry areas makes it unpopular as an amenity tree.

FAMILY Podocarpaceae

Podocarpus andinus Endl.

Plum-fruited yew

Description • One of several *Podocarpus* species cultivated in Europe. The common name is apt, a yew-like tree with dark green 1–3 cm needles in compact sprays but the fruits are like bloomed, black, fleshy, 2 cm plums. Most specimens have foliage to the ground **5**. The stem is smooth and purplish-grey **6**. Horizontal branches have up-turned ends **7**. **Habitat and Ecology** • Most of the 100 or so species in this genus are tropical. A few occur in mixed temperate forests. **Similar species** • The foliage resembles Yew (p50).

Natural range
The Andes in Southern Chile

Cultivated distribution
Introduced to Europe in 186[illegible] but of little amenity value an[illegible] only grown as a curiosity by plant collectors or botanic gardens.

FAMILY Sciadopitaceae

Sciadopitys verticillata (Thunb.) Sieb. and Zucc.

Umbrella pine

Description • Superficially like a one-needled pine tree having a conical outline and ultimate height around 15 m. The foliage is dark green and stiff **8**. Needles are 8–12 cm long arranged in whorls like the spokes of an umbrella **9**. Flowers are yellow, 2.5 cm, cone-like structures followed by 5 cm, green cones that ripen over two years. **Habitat and Ecology** • Wet woodlands. **Similar species** • A unique primitive conifer better known in fossils.

Natural range
Central Japan.

Cultivated distribution
Rare in Europe as an ornamental and facing extinction in a much reduce[illegible] range.

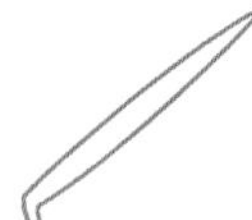

FAMILY Taxaceae

Taxus baccata L.

Common yew

Description • The dark form of the Yew tree is familiar to most people. Its dense foliage shades out everything beneath, producing a sombre, dank environment that attracts dust and dirt and usually smells unpleasant. It is often an indicator of a religious place, usually a churchyard but perhaps relating to pre-Christian use of the site. This is an evergreen tree with soft, 2–3 cm, flat needles arranged in two horizontal ranks on side branches and all round the shoot on actively growing branch tips. Although individuals over 20 m are known it is not usually a tall tree, generally at around 8 m the crown splits into two or more parts which grow in different directions **1**. Sound stems may be 1 m in diameter. Ancient broken trunks 3 m or more across are known. The bark is rich red or purplish-brown scaling off in thin plates. Even on trees hundreds of years old the bark is never thick **2**. Male flowers in great numbers on separate trees are 2–3 mm cones under the needles **3**. They are pale cream when ripe and shed clouds of pollen on the first suitably warm day in late winter. Female flowers occur singly or in groups of two or three near the shoot tips. They develop into remarkable fruits. At first a small, exposed, 3 mm, blue-grey seed set in a shallow, silvery green, fleshy cup, which rapidly swells into a juicy, pink, translucent casing that covers all but the tip of the seed **4**. **Habitat and Ecology** • Ancient yew woods, a kind of open scrub, can be found particularly on lime rich and chalk soils. Ancient trees are rich habitats in themselves sheltering invertebrates and small animals, and also providing a place for epiphytes to grow in the trees' decomposing mould. **Similar species** • The genus is fairly distinct but there are several different species world-wide. Common yew has produced many cultivated forms. The best known is probably Irish yew 'Fastigiata' **6**, a female clone discovered in Ireland in 1780. There are also more recent male clones of much the same form. 'Elegantissima' is a dense bushy tree with light coloured foliage **7**, a female tree which produces abundant fruit **8**. There are several yellow-leaved yews, none have especially bright colouring.

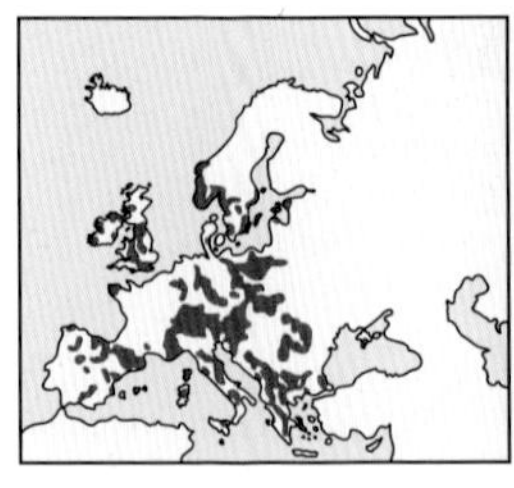

Natural range

Cultivated distribution
In their long history yew trees have been cultivated for many different purposes; famously for long bows used by English archers. The wood is still sought after for veneers, turnery and fine furniture but strangely plantations have never been established to service this requirement. As an ornamental plant Yew is good for hedging, screening and topiary **5**, but its poisonous properties tend to make it unpopular.

1

2

3

4

5

7

8

FAMILY Pinaceae

Picea abies (L.) Karst.

Norway spruce

Description • To most people their best recollection of this fine tree is as a traditional, old-fashioned Christmas tree, the universal Christmas tree until 'non-needle-shedding' species and plastic alternatives appeared. This is a native North European species. A fine, straight conifer with dense, rich, green foliage **1**. Individuals over 50 m tall are known and stems almost 150 cm diameter have been measured. However trees up to 30 m tall are more likely and once stems exceed 80 cm there is a fair chance of rot in them. It is not unusual for such stems to fail just above ground level and send the whole tree crashing down **2**. The bark is distinctive, smooth, orange-brown and slightly peeling in small papery scales **3**. The solitary 2–3 cm, stiff, sharply pointed needles are rhombic in cross-section. They are densely arranged above the shoot and parted below it on side branches, but occur evenly all round the leading shoots. Each needle is held on a buff coloured woody peg that persists on the branch when the needles have been shed, after about five years on a healthy specimen **4**. Separate male and female flowers occur on the same tree. Females at the top where they are more likely to be pollinated by other trees further up the hill. They are erect and brilliantly coloured purplish-red. They rapidly expand into miniature leathery cones **5**, finally turning light brown and then pointing downwards. A good cone will be around 15 cm long and may contain over 100 winged seeds **6**. These are gradually liberated in the autumn and flutter away on the wind. **Habitat and Ecology** • A moderately shade tolerant forest tree that will stand closely spaced for a long time. It performs best as a timber producer in high rainfall areas or where available soil moisture is not limited, although cold, hardy, spring frosts can damage the soft emerging foliage. Young plants will not tolerate the close company of Heather, *Calluna vulgaris* (L.) Hull, on moorland sites. **Similar species** • Several Spruces, but the nearest is *Picea obovata* Ledeb. (p54) the Siberian spruce and hybrids between the two where their natural ranges overlap. There are also numerous cultivated forms. Probably the most curious are the 'snake-bark' spruces such as the French clone 'Virgata' 1853 and the English counterpart 'Cranstonii' 1855. These seldom produce any side shoots so long sinuous branches prevail in a distinctive way.

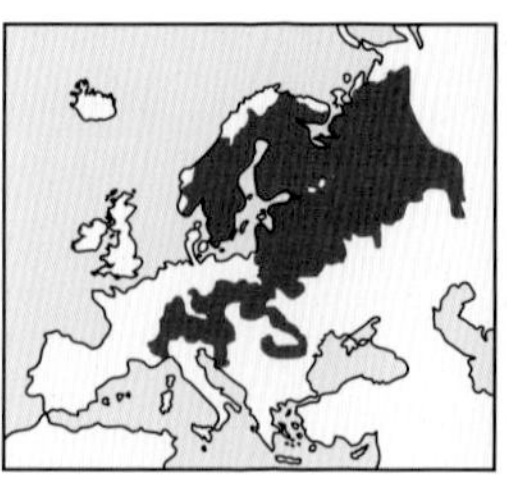

Natural range
Extends from Europe into South-east Russia.

Cultivated distribution
Natural forests have been managed on Mainland Europe for hundreds of years and this species has been widely planted beyond its native range. In Britain, where it was introduced around 1500, it was the third most planted forest conifer in the twentieth century. Disease, beetle damage and instability on shallow soils have reduced its popularity now. There is also a public dislike of conifer monocultures. The low resin content and long wood fibre length make this an ideal species for manufacturing paper pulp. The soft timber 'White deal' has numerous structural uses.

'Cranstonii'

1
2
3
4
5
6

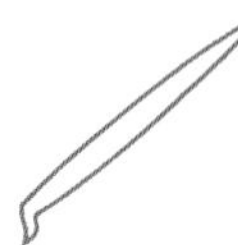

FAMILY Pinaceae

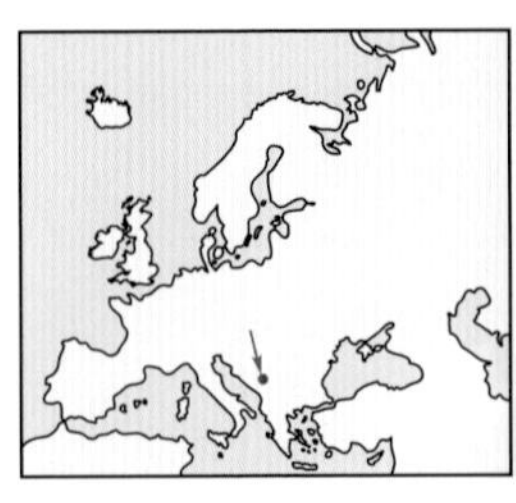

Picea omorika (Pancic) Purkyne
Serbian spruce

Description • A remarkably straight, narrow tree up to 30 m tall with a narrow crown only 3 m wide **1**. Perfectly adapted to shed snow in its native mountain environment, a branch modification retained in cultivation for several generations. Gradually however home-grown seedlings develop wider spreading branches. Stems seldom exceed 60 cm in diameter. The bark is orange-brown but is mostly obscured by the densely arranged branches. Evergreen 2–3 cm needles occur singly on woody pegs, all round leading shoots and facing upwards on side branches **2**. There are dark, almost black, hairs on the pale brown shoot, a helpful diagnostic feature. Also, unlike other European spruces, the needles are flat and not four-sided. Flowers are on previous year's side shoots. Males are tightly packed clusters of red anthers which shed copious amounts of yellow pollen when ripe. Females, mostly at the top of the tree, are like miniature red cones. They develop into fully grown, slender, purplish, pendulous, 5 cm long cones which ripen to pale brown but remain on the tree for several years **2**. **Habitat and Ecology** • A fragment of a once much wider distribution now almost pushed to extinction in the wild. **Similar species** • Several other spruces when the narrow environmental adaptation is reversed.

Natural range

Cultivated distribution
An excellent forest species when grown in dense, close spaced plantations on mountainous sites **3** or in lowland situations. The poles are straight, long and slender.

Picea orientalis (L.) Link
Oriental spruce

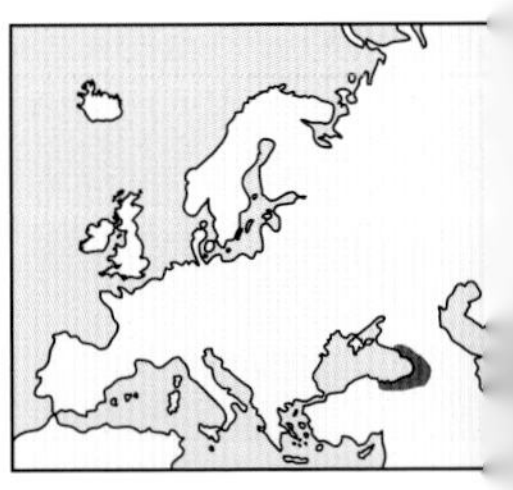

Description • Immediately identified by its exceptionally short 6–8 cm, four-sided needles **4**. Most specimens retain their picturesque, symmetrical outline even when fully mature and growing in isolation **5**. The largest known are almost 40 m tall with a straight, persistent stem. The bark is fairly smooth and reddish-brown; small peeling scales develop from the base **6** (here disguised by grey-green lichen). The foliage is very dense and always facing upwards on side shoots. Male flowers are in tightly packed, red clusters appearing in late spring. Female flowers are erect, maroon, cone-like structures developing into thin, 8 cm, pendulous cones that have rounded, leathery scales. **Habitat and Ecology** • Dense conifer forests on acid or alkaline soils. **Similar species** • Only *Picea mariana* (Mill.) B.S. and P. has such short needles but they are grey-green; the tree is smaller and rare in cultivation. Also *Picea obovata* Ledeb., Siberian spruce **7**, which is closely related to Norway spruce (p52) but has shorter needles and small cones.

Natural range

Cultivated distribution
An ornamental specimen or commercial timber tree that has potential for use on lime rich sites where rainfall is les than would normally be required to successfully grov Spruce.

1
2
3
4
5
6
7

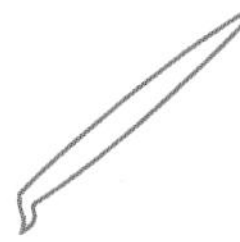

FAMILY Pinaceae

Picea glauca (Moench) Voss

White spruce

Description • One of the most hardy trees in the world but this species is quite variable and not easy to identify. Its range, the whole of sub-Arctic North America, means that considerable provenance differences are inevitable. Most confusing is the foliage colour, which may be green or glaucous-grey. It is a straight, conical tree with tiered branches **1**. The bark is smooth grey-brown eventually becoming scaly **2**. Twigs are orange-brown, glabrous and rough with abandoned needle pegs. Needles are around 1 cm long, pointed, square in section and packed tightly along the shoot. Some trees are blue-green especially when young **3**. Flowers are similar to Norway spruce developing into drooping, 4–6 cm, papery, flexible cones. **Habitat and Ecology** • Severe upland conditions; usually in dense, even-aged forests for mutual protection. **Similar species** • Several other northern forest spruces including Black spruce *Picea mariana* (Mill,) B.S. and P. from much the same natural range. In cultivation the other familiar 'blue' needled Spruce is *Picea pungens* Englm. the Colorado spruce, particularly the cultivars 'Glauca' **4** and 'Koster'. They have longer, 3 cm needles.

Natural range
Across North America from the Arctic tree line from Newfoundland to Alaska, south to Maine and west to Minnesota, only at high elevation in the south.

Cultivated distribution
Rare as an ornamental and only planted in experimental plantations until recently. Now in demand as a luxury Christmas tree.

Picea engelmannii (Parry) Engelm.

Engelmann spruce

Description • A rare tree in Europe capable of growing to over 25 m in height in forestry plantations. Young individuals are conical with short, tiered branches **5**. Stems are straight with greyish or purplish-brown, thin bark which eventually becomes scaly **6**. The twigs are rough with woody pegs and, unlike most similar looking Spruce species, they are hairy. Cones are 4–6 cm long with undulating toothed, papery, light brown scales. Some trees cone in profusion in a good year. **Habitat and Ecology** • In conifer forests and scattered clumps at high elevation and in a stunted form up to the tree line. **Similar species** • Several mostly obscure Alpine Spruces.

Natural range
Rocky Mountains mostly from British Columbia to Montana and Idaho, then as scattered populations high up in the mountains to New Mexico.

Cultivated distribution
Only an experimental forest tree in Europe and a rare ornamental, mostly represented by forma *glauca* Beissn. an attractive tree with sage-green young foliage **7**.

1
2
3
4
5
6
7

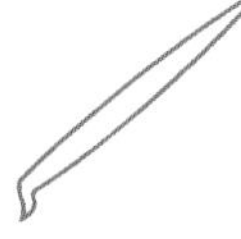

FAMILY Pinaceae

Picea sitchensis (Bong.) Carr.
Sitka spruce

Description • In the British Isles, this species became the most important component of twentieth century plantation forestry. Vast areas of poor upland grazing and grass moorland were planted with it; much to the delight of timber and pulp producers and the despair of many conservationists. This is a fast-growing, straight, clean-stemmed tree which has already exceeded 60 m in height in Scotland. Plantations grow evenly and become highly productive at an early age **1**. The bark is purplish or brownish-grey, thin and becoming scaly from the base upwards **2**. Some individuals are particularly scaly while adjacent stems may remain smooth. Vigorous young growth, up to 1 m per year, produces flat, sharp-pointed, blue-green, 2–3 cm needles arranged all round the stem **3**. The shoot is yellowish-orange or buff and consists entirely of short pegs each holding a solitary needle. Old shoots, when the needles have fallen off, remain very scratchy because of the persistent rough pegs (pulvini). Older side shoots have shorter more tightly packed greener needles which tend to face upwards with a parting on the underside. The buds are small, ovoid and light brown sometimes encased in translucent resin. The flowers ripen in May, males are crimson then yellowish and globular **4** while females, high up on the same tree, are brilliant crimson, shaped like miniature closed cones. The cones expand to about 7 cm long and become pendulous. They are pale green at first and ripen to the colour of straw, opening in dry autumn weather **5** to shed the seed. Each seed has an aerodynamic wing about four times its own length. **Habitat and Ecology** • A moisture loving, fairly hardy maritime tree resistant to salt spray but requiring high rainfall and adequate soil phosphate to thrive. On very wet ground it is extremely shallow rooted and may become unstable. **Similar species** • There are several spruces with 'blue' needles but none grow as rapidly as this. *Picea x lutzii* Little **6** is a natural hybrid with *Picea glauca* (p56). It combines the growth rate of Sitka spruce with the hardiness and frost tolerance of *Picea glauca.*

Natural range

A long narrow north–south strip down the North American Pacific coast from Kodiak Island Alaska to Mendocino County California. Confined to the coastal fog belt in the south.

Cultivated distribution

Discovered (by a European) in 1792 but not introduced to Europe until 1831. Planted on a huge scale after 1922 in British forestry plantations. It is an ideal species for the production of long fibre paper pulp. Increasingly it is becoming susceptible to disease and insect predation which is always a disadvantage with monocultures.

1
2
3
4
5
6

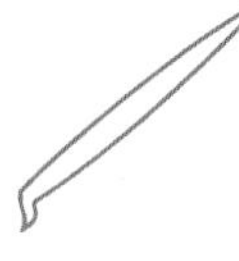

FAMILY Pinaceae

Cedrus atlantica (Endl.) Manetti ex Carr.

Atlas cedar

Description • The Cedars are evergreen trees bearing tufted needles on spur shoots and solitary needles on current and leading shoots. They form a homogenous group of geographic forms extending from Gibraltar to the foothills of the Himalayas. In cultivation, intermediates occur and precise identification is difficult. The old adage 'A (ascending) is Atlantic, L (Level) is Lebanon and D (drooping) is Deodar', a reference to the branch ends, is fine in the classroom but carries little weight in the field. Atlas cedar is a variable tree, several forms have adapted differently to the rigours of high elevation. An average tree will be around 20 m tall with a conical top which becomes increasingly rounded and spiky **1**. The main stem, or stems if it is forked, is vertical and straight with side branches going off more or less at right angles. The trunk is often impressive, well over 1 m in diameter with grey-brown, evenly spaced ridges and fissures **2**. Shoots are grey-brown with radially arranged needles on new growth then short spur shoots terminating in a cluster of needles **3**. All the spurs face upwards presenting 30 or so needles to the light. Flowers appear on the tips of mature spurs. Pale coloured males are 5–7 cm long produced in profusion in the autumn **4**. Females are less frequent and green, developing into 8 cm barrel-shaped deciduous cones, finally disintegrating and shedding the winged seed the following year. **Habitat and Ecology** • An alpine species growing up to 2100 m elevation where snow lies for several months in winter. In coniferous and Juniper forest at high levels and mixed with Holm oak (p292) lower down. **Similar species** • Other Cedars (see above).

Natural range
North Africa high up in the Atlas Mountains of Algeria and Morocco.

Cultivated distribution
Introduced to France in 1734 and grown as a commercial forest species in the south. Widely planted elsewhere in Northern Europe as an ornamental. It will withstand hot, dry, city conditions, calcarious soils and air pollution. The pale brown timber is strong, durable and fragrant. The heartwood is brittle but the sapwood is tough and stringy.

Cedrus atlantica forma glauca Beissn.

Blue Atlas cedar

Description • An alpine variant of ordinary Atlas cedar occurring naturally in the wild population. It is identical except for varying amounts of grey, waxy bloom on the foliage. Trees are equally as large as the species **5**. The flowers and cones are exactly like the species **6**, but more attractive as an amenity feature. **Habitat and Ecology** • Blue-leaved trees appear to be randomly distributed in the natural population and not confined to particular environments or climatic regions. **Similar species** • None, but from a distance some blue-needled Spruces (p56) may be confused with young trees.

Natural range
The Atlas Mountains in Algeria and Morocco.

Cultivated distribution
A favourite amenity tree on country estates or in urban open spaces where space permits. There is a pendulous form 'Glauca Pendula'. Nurserymen have also selected and named particular trees with the brightest blue foliage since 1845. All are now lumped together as the 'Glauca group' and not given individual cultivar names.

1
2
3
4
5
6

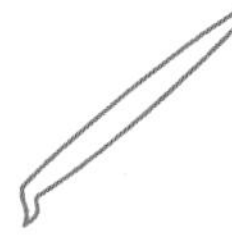

FAMILY Pinaceae

Cedrus libani A. Rich.

Cedar of Lebanon

Description • Isolated from the Atlas cedar (p60) only by desert and the Cypress cedar, *Cedrus brevifolia* Henry, by the sea this species has affinities with both of them. It is a massive tree with wide-spreading, tiered branches **1**. Often the bole is short but may exceed 2 m in diameter. The bark is grey-brown roughly fissured with scaly ridges **2**. The soft, dark green, 1–3 cm needles are in whorls on short upward pointing spurs **3**, but borne singly on current shoots **4**. Male and female catkins are yellowish-green appearing in the autumn. The following year females develop into barrel-shaped cones about 12 cm long. They are silvery-green at first then flushed with purple by the autumn **5**. After the winter they turn brown and gradually break up. Like the Atlas cedar some individual trees have a grey, waxy bloom on the foliage. **Habitat and Ecology** • Once extensive Cedar of Lebanon forests have been much depleted by exploitation and wars over a period of 50 centuries. The last natural grove on Mount Lebanon at 1890 m elevation is believed to be 2500 years old. **Similar species** • Other Cedars.

Natural range
Asia Minor and Syria to the Mediterranean coast. Mostly between 1400 and 2000 m elevation.

Cultivated distribution
Introduced to Britain in 1638 later there were massive plantings on country estates between 1760 and 1810. Probably because of its ultimate size, especially width, this tree is seldom grown for amenity now. Many ancient individuals have been severely disfigured in the past by snow damage. When upper branches fail under the weight of snow on the tiered foliage there is often a 'knock-on' effect righ down the tree.

Cedrus deodara (Roxb.) Don, G.

Indian cedar or Deodar

Description • Fortunately this species has a prominent identification feature that sets it apart from other Cedars; its needle length, about twice that of Cedar of Lebanon (above), which is up to 6 cm. In Northern Europe it is a majestic tree usually with a single stem and a columnar outline and slender side branches **6**. The foliage is pale green and pendulous on young trees **7**. The stem is straight with brown fissured and vertically ridged bark **8**. The flowers, on established spur shoots in the autumn, are erect catkins. Cones are 12 cm long, barrel-shaped, glaucous green then brown a year later. **Habitat and Ecology** • A mountain forest species well adapted to shed snow. **Similar species** • Other Cedars.

Natural range
Western Himalayas to 3000 m elevation and west into Afghanistan.

Cultivated distribution
Introduced to Northern Europe around 1831 primarily as a potential timber tree. Its value was already well known in Northern India. Forests established to supplement Oak for shipbuilding in Britain failed to produce material of the required quality. Occasionally grown an ornamental, there are als rather dubious 'golden' folia forms in cultivation.

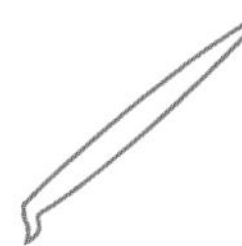

FAMILY Pinaceae

Larix decidua Mill.

European larch

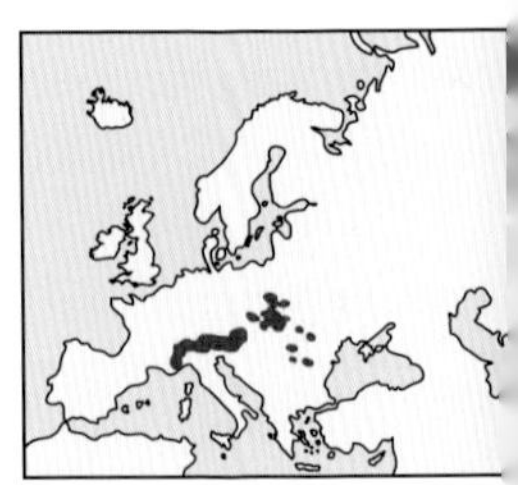

Description • This particular larch is recognized in winter by its slender, leafless, pale yellowish-grey shoots and in summer by its grass-green needles. It is potentially a big tree up to 35 m tall with a stem 1 m in diameter. Most trees likely to be encountered are smaller. The stem is fairly straight but noticeably less so than Silver firs (p40) and Spruce (p52). The outline is open and conical until the top becomes ragged in old age. Branches are horizontal leaving the stem, then bend downwards with an up-turned tip. Side shoots are often pendulous [1]. For a short time the bark is reddish-brown and fairly smooth but it soon becomes warty, scaly and rough eventually fissuring vertically and turning grey [2]. Lower moribund branches break off easily. Twigs are slender and lax, light yellowish-grey punctuated by short, stout, grey spur shoots. Dense rosettes of 3 cm green needles develop on the tips of these for several years. Soft, flat needles also occur singly in a spiral arrangement on current growth. Flowers are spectacular, appearing just before the leaves break. Males are numerous and are like small, 5 mm, upright, globose, yellow cones [3]. Females are rose-pink shaped like an 8 mm upright cone. All flowers face upwards even if the branch they are on is pendulous. Should anything change the angle of the branch, the flowers will turn to face the light once again in a day or two. Cones are 3–4 cm long, green, then light brown and leathery with rounded scales that are not reflexed. They also face upwards regardless of the angle of the branch [4]. The winged seeds are shed a small number at a time on dry days through the winter but the old cones stay on the tree for several more years. **Habitat and Ecology** • A forest tree always demanding good light. Often a pioneer species seeding freely on disturbed ground [5]. **Similar species** • There are around ten species of larch. The genus is distinctive but some of the individual species are not: morphologically variable provenances of European larch add to this problem. Hybrids and backcrosses are common in plantations grown from locally collected seed.

Natural range

Cultivated distribution
A native forest species in much of mainland Europe requiring only good management to keep it sustainable. In the British Isles, widely cultivated since around 1620 on good, well-drained soils especially in high rainfall areas. Markets for the excellent durable timber have declined so plantations are now less frequent. British foresters recognize four distinct provenance types – Alpine, Sudeten, Polish and Tatra. Some, mainly Alpine types, have completely failed due to die-back and canker. Sudeten larch has proved to be superior, disease and Aphid resistant, fast-growing and fairly straight stemmed [6].

1
2
3
4
5
6

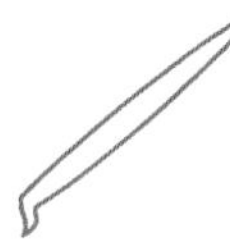

FAMILY Pinaceae

Larix kaempferi (Lamb.) Carr.
Japanese larch

Description • Unlike European larch (p64) this species has distinctive, reddish-brown winter shoots. Distant Japanese larch forest or plantations appear to have a haze of red spread across the tree tops. Stems are straight although vigorous young trees often 'ripple' along their length. Mostly they do not exceed 30 m in height with stems around 80 cm diameter. The outline is columnar with a pointed tip until the tree top flattens or grows out to one side. Bark is reddish-brown soon becoming fissured and flaky dividing into small, squarish, grey scales [1]. Needles, single on new growth and in tufts on short spur shoots, are 3–4 cm long and grey-green. Male flowers are small and yellowish [2]; females are erect, like miniature cones, and may be purple, pink or yellowish [3]. The mature cones have rolled back scales [4]. **Habitat and Ecology** • Rocky mountain sides and poor soils mostly in open coniferous woodland. **Similar species** • Other Larch species.

Natural range
Central Japan but occurring on a wide range of site conditions there.

Cultivated distribution
An important component of British forests. Planted as a deciduous fire break or an amenity feature. Autumn foliage colour is deep yellow.

Larix x marschlinsii Coaz. (Larix x eurolepis Henry)
Hybrid larch

Description • An artificial cross between Japanese and European larch (p64) originating in Scotland around 1904. The botanical characteristics are mid-way between the parents. This is a superb plantation tree [5] producing straight saw logs in around 30–40 years [6]. The vigorous foliage is sea-green [7] and the cones are glaucous. **Habitat and Ecology** • As for the parent species. **Similar species** • Other larches.

Natural range
None.

Cultivated distribution
Limited in forestry because cones collected from Hybrid larches result in inferior quality trees. Each new batch of seed must be taken from an original cross.

Larix gmelinii (Rupr.) Kuzeneva
Dahurian larch

Description • A medium-sized tree in cultivation, 30 m tall in the wild, with a ragged outline [8] often spoiled by unseasonal frost in the north. The stem is fairly straight with purplish-brown flaky bark [9]. Shoots are yellow with a brown side in full light and the soft 2–3 cm needles are light green [10]. Cones are 2–3 cm long with thin, leathery, rounded scales. **Habitat and Ecology** • Deciduous conifer forest. **Similar species** • European larch and several *Larix gmelinii* varieties extending into China, the Kurile Islands and Korea.

Natural range
South East Asia including Eastern Siberia.

Cultivated distribution
Not widely grown because it has no commercial timber value or ornamental merit in Northern Europe. In European climatic conditions it comes into leaf early and is often frosted.

1
2
3
4
5
6
7
8
9
10

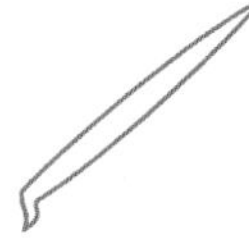

FAMILY Taxodiaceae

Metasequoia glyptostroboides Miki ex Hu and Cheng

Dawn redwood

Description • A deciduous conifer with distinctive light green foliage in summer and bare, orange-brown branches and twigs in winter. The outline is narrow with a conical top **1**. The bark is orange-brown and stringy but hard. Some old trees develop exaggerated fluting and deep depressions in the stem close to branch junctions **2**. Others produce a much more even trunk especially when grown in plantations **3**. Trees already exceeded 30 m in Europe less than 50 years after their introduction. The young, 10–15 cm shoots are green but these turn rusty-brown and fall off the tree more or less intact in the autumn. Leaves are mainly in two ranks in opposite pairs: individual flat needles are 2.5 cm long and about 2 mm wide **4**. They are pointed at both ends and soft to the touch. Cones are 2 cm long, ovoid or oval, with a pointed tip and set on a 3 cm woody stalk. **Habitat and Ecology** • A relic of a primitive form of vegetation now extinct except in the Hubei province of China. **Similar species** • Swamp cypress (below).

Natural range
A few isolated sites in China but obscured by a long history of cultivation, particularly around temples.

Cultivated distribution
This tree first appeared outside China in 1948 since when it has been planted all round the temperate world. It is the only living example of a common fossil genus in the northern hemisphere. As a forest tree it prefers wet sites and a cool climate.

Taxodium distichum (L.) Rich.

Swamp cypress

Description • A large coniferous tree up to 30 m tall with a buttressed stem ultimately around 80 cm diameter in Europe. Young trees in summer have pale green foliage **5**. In winter they take on a more spiky appearance after all the deciduous shoots and green foliage turns brown and is shed. This is a tree of watery places often found actually growing in shallow standing water **6**. To aid oxygen supplies to the roots in stagnant conditions hollow, woody 'knees' develop around the base of the tree projecting above the water level. The bark is reddish-grey, stringy but hard, often spiral round the tree **7**. The soft foliage consists of short deciduous opposite or alternate 5–10 cm shoots with needles twisted round to form two upward-facing ranks. Individual needles are under 2 cm long and only 1–1.5 m wide, with a pointed tip **8**. Cones are oval, around 3 cm long with short-spined scales. **Habitat and Ecology** • A wetland species which survives best in seasonally flooded areas. The seed requires wet conditions to germinate. **Similar species** • *Taxodium ascendens* Brongn. Pond cypress, a smaller tree rare in cultivation, also Dawn redwood (above).

Natural range
South Eastern North America extending north and west to Illinois, Oklahoma and Texas. Called Baldcypress in the United States.

Cultivated distribution
Grown in Europe as a curiosity and wetland feature. The wood is brittle and storm damage is frequent.

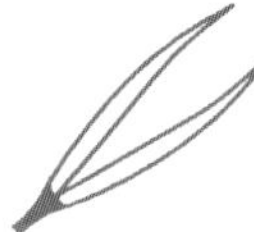

FAMILY Pinaceae

Pinus pinaster Ait.

Maritime pine

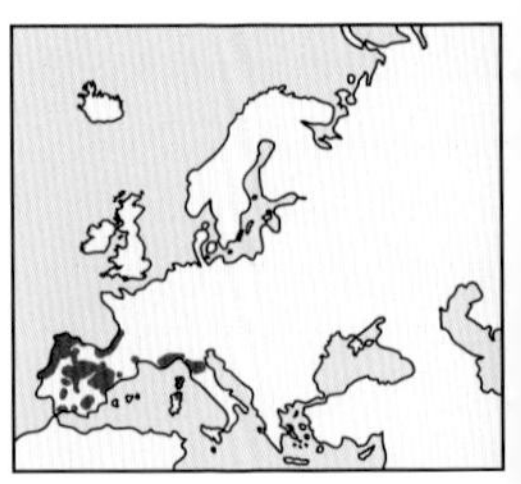

Natural range

Description • A fast-growing, large, long-needled pine tree often with coarse heavy branches and thick rough, but often brightly coloured bark. Typically this is a gnarled tree less than 15 m tall with a thick curved stem growing near to the coast. It may seem that winds off the sea cause these picturesque shapes to develop but trees growing inland are often exactly the same; usually because young saplings grow so rapidly that the root–shoot ratio gets out of balance. During the first critical five to ten years the top growth exceeds root development which is unable to hold the plant upright **1**. There is however a straight form, subspecies *atlantica* H. del Villar, from Portugal and the extreme west of the Natural range, which is a good productive forest timber tree **2**. This subspecies reaches 35 m with stems up to 1 m diameter. The bark is orange-brown or purplish-brown, deeply fissured into prominent squarish plates. These eventually bleach to pale grey in full sunshine **1**. Shoots are orange-brown or pink and glabrous. Buds are large with free-reflexed, brown papery scales. Needles in twos are stiff, dark grey-green, often around 15–20 cm long. Each pair is bound together at the base with a dark brown, 2–5 cm, persistent sheath. On newly emerging needles this sheath is white **3**. The flowers occur on the current shoots, males at the base **4** in dense clusters. Females near the apex usually in clusters of three to six developing into cones in rings round the shoots. In the first year these are small conelets, expanding in the second year to large ovoid cones 15–20 cm long **5**. They are reluctant to open and shed the seed, in fact they are often held on the tree for two or three more seasons before falling. A sprinkling of seed seems to be shed from time to time all year round so at least some of it has a chance of germinating. **Habitat and Ecology** • Sandy ground, from maritime sand dunes to dry inland heaths. **Similar species** • Without cones similar to Corsican pine (p74) and other two-needled pines but the needles are thicker and stiff.

Cultivated distribution
Maritime pine has a long history of use. It was formerly tapped for resin which produced pitch and tar after turpentine and rosin were extracted from it. Plantations, usually mixed with Corsican pine, have been established to fix sand dunes and for amenity in seaside towns but the tree sheds lower suppressed dead branches unpredictably. A lot of 'knotty pine' timber sold in DIY shops now is Maritime pine.

1

2

3

4

5

FAMILY Pinaceae

Pinus sylvestris L.

Scots pine

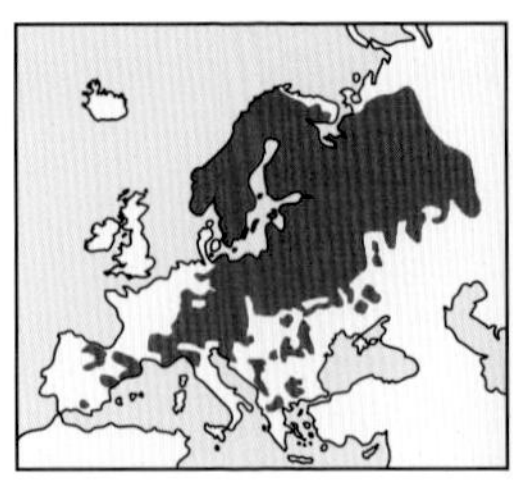

Natural range
Dense forests occur from Europe to the Caucusus, across Kazakstan and Russia almost to the Pacific and north into the Subarctic.

Cultivated distribution
Extensively used as a plantation tree and managed as semi-natural woodland for timber production. Re-introduced to the British Isles on a large scale from mainland Europe at an early date and widely grown in South and East England.

Description • A familiar native North European species, sometimes a 25 m tall forest tree, but also found as a stunted, fire-scorched landmark on heaths and moors or as a cultivated specimen in parks and gardens. The stem is usually straight but less so than Corsican pine (p74). The top is conical at first then columnar and untidy. Lower suppressed branches rapidly die and eventually fall off leaving a long, clear stem and a rounded or irregular billowing crown **1**. The bark is rough and grey-brown at the base with fissures and scaly plates **2**, but higher up it is distinctive pale orange with paper thin peeling scales **6**. Trees grow well in close company with each other to form dense but fairly light, airy woodland that supports a diverse ground flora **3**. The stiff, dark green needles are 5–7 cm long in pairs all round the shoot. Flowers, male and female on the same tree, consist of bunched, 5 mm, yellow male cones and single, tiny, crimson female flowers all on current shoots. In the first year, small, spiny conelets develop at or near the shoot tip. In the second year, these turn into woody, 4–7 cm, gently curved, downward pointing cones **4**. They are green all summer then turn glossy brown on ripening in the autumn. Sometime around midwinter they open and quickly shed the winged seed. Open, grey-brown, spent cones fall from the tree the following summer. **Habitat and Ecology** • Dry heathland and thin, acid, peaty moorland. Mostly in harsh Continental climatic conditions. **Similar species** • Scottish Scots pine (below).

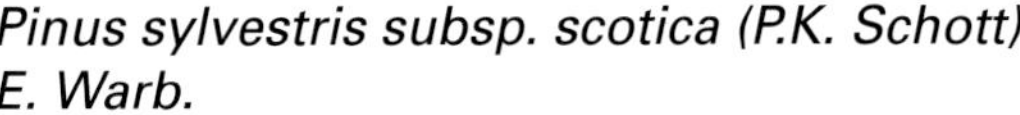

Pinus sylvestris subsp. scotica (P.K. Schott) E. Warb.

Scottish Scots pine or Caledonian pine

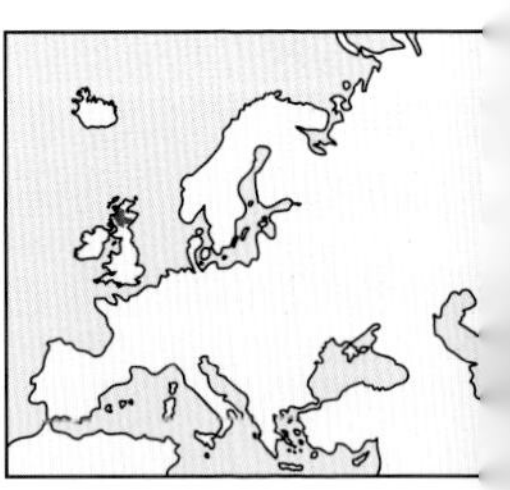

Natural range

Cultivated distribution
Exploited but never cultivate until the latter part of the twentieth century when the last remnants of the natural Caledonian forest were deemed to be threatened. Now genetically appropriate progeny are planted in and near to former forest sites.

Description • This is the native pine of Western Europe which once covered much of Britain in the pre-boreal period (9500 BP). It was subsequently pushed northwards by invasive broadleaved trees benefiting from climate change, to its present refuge in the Caledonian Forest. Although similar to the species the needles are more glaucous, shorter and tend to be more twisted **5**. This is a tree of monumental proportions, sometimes wide-spreading and very tall **6**. Specimens over 200 years old are known. The cones tend to be dark coloured with more pronounced scale bosses **7** than the species. Intermediate forms are common. **Habitat and Ecology** • The main component of an ancient woodland and moorland type which is a perfectly balanced ecosystem that has great biodiversity. **Similar species** • Other cultivated, two-needled pines selected for their glaucous foliage.

1

2

3

4

5

6

7

FAMILY Pinaceae

Pinus nigra subsp. laricio (Poir.) Maire

Corsican pine

Description • This form of Black pine (*Pinus nigra* Arnold) is usually straight and has annual rings of level branches evenly spaced out along its length. As the lower branches are gradually suppressed by dense foliage above they eventually drop off leaving a long clean bole. A mature tree will usually be around 30 m tall with a stem 1 m in diameter **1**. Most trees are in forest plantations **2**. The bark is deeply furrowed with flat, scaly ridges. These are dark grey and brown in plantations but pale grey, light brown and pink on old trees in open situations. Shoots are yellowish-brown turning more orange in the second year. Buds are large, 2 cm long and shaped like an onion, with free, red-brown, grey edged scales. Needles are in pairs, slightly twisted, 12–18 cm long and dull green **3**. Male flowers occur massed along new side shoots in clusters which are pale yellow with brown-tipped scales. Females are less frequent, deep pink and always close to the shoot tip. Woody cones take 18 months to ripen **3**. They are ovoid, around 7 cm long and green until they mature, shed seed during the autumn and fall off the following summer. **Habitat and Ecology** • A pioneer species seeding freely into sandy heathland, fixed sand dunes or any light, dryish disturbed ground, even surviving on thin soils over limestone or chalk. In Northern Europe, this species is well beyond its natural climatic range, so in cold, wet areas it will be liable to die back and even die owing to the fungus *Gremmeniella* (*Brunchorstia*) *destruens*. **Similar species** • *Pinus nigra* exists as a series of geographical forms. *Pinus nigra* subsp. *nigra* Arnold, the Austrian pine, has wide-spreading branches and a domed top **4**. The bark is dark grey, almost black and deeply fissured. Needles are 8–10 cm long and cones are ovoid-conic up to 8 cm long **5**. *Pinus nigra* subsp. *pallasiana* (Lamb.) Holmb., the Crimean pine, is a huge tree with multiple upswept limbs **6**. Stems, often exceeding 1 m in diameter have light pink, yellowish and grey scaly bark with dark vertical fissures **7**. The needles are hard, straight and stiff, up to 15 cm long, dark green with fine, grey lines of stomata and a yellow translucent point. Cones are narrowly-conic, 6 cm long, evenly tapered, light lustrous green with purplish-brown scale tips **8**. There are also Pyrenean and Dalmatian subspecies.

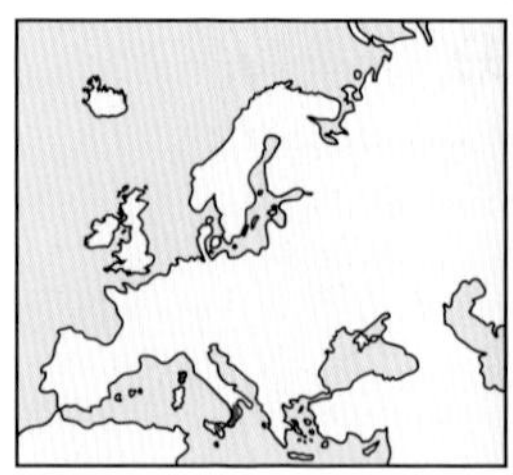

Natural range

Cultivated distribution
Corsican pine is a widespread commercial plantation species. Austrian pine has been used extensively as a shelter and wind-break tree especially in the late nineteenth century. Crimean pine is rare in cultivation and only found in specialist tree collections or on large private estates.

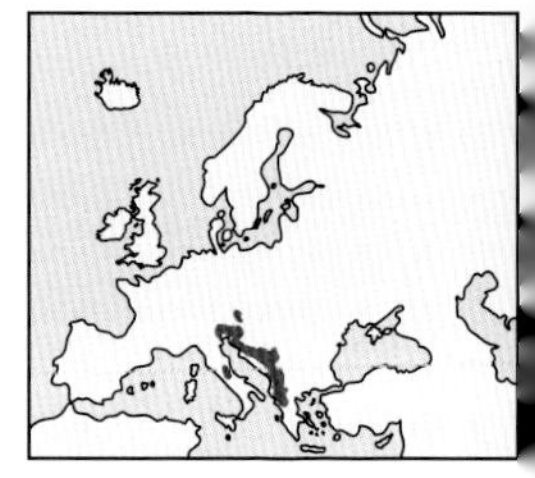

Natural range
subsp. pallasiana

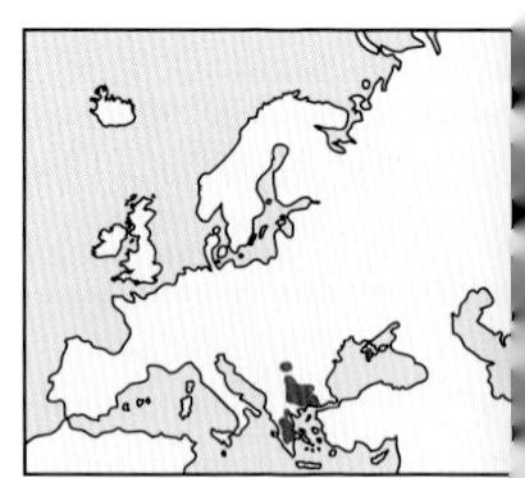

Natural range
subsp. nigra

1

2

3

4

5

6

7

8

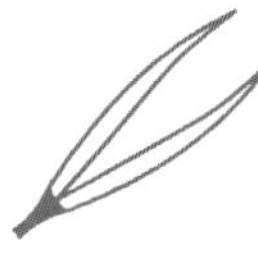

FAMILY Pinaceae

Pinus heldreichii var. leucodermis (Ant.) Markg. ex Fitsch.

Bosnian pine

Description • A straight evergreen tree, 12–18 m tall with spreading upturned branches **1**. Stems, up to 60 cm diameter, are grey-brown and smooth. The bark is only slightly roughened and peeling at maturity **2**. Shoots are light yellowish-grey with periodic bare patches where large clusters of male flowers have prevented needle growth. This interrupted foliage effect is a fairly good diagnostic feature **3**. The stiff, straight needles are in twos, tightly packed together and retained for many years. They are dark green with a hard, pointed tip. Male flowers are yellowish-brown and numerous at the base of each year's new growth. Females are infrequent and red. They develop into spiny conelets in one season then steel-blue cones the following year **4**. **Habitat and Ecology** • Dry hillsides in mild areas, especially on thin limestone soils. **Similar species** • Other two-needled pines including *Pinus nigra* Arnold (p74).

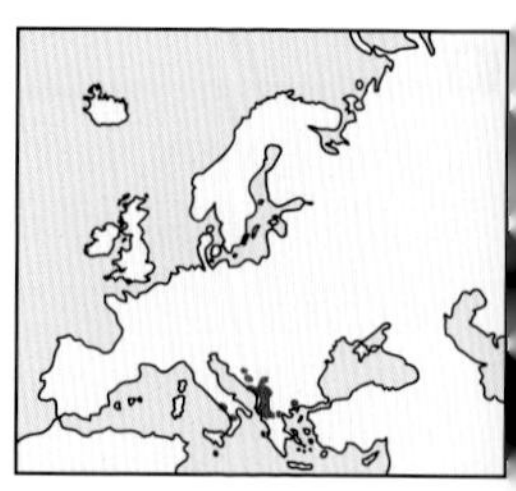

Natural range

Cultivated distribution
Rare in cultivation but some ornamental cultivars are available. As *Pinus leucodermis* Ant. around ten ornamental named cultivars are listed by nurseries.

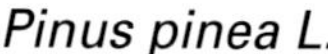

Pinus pinea L.

Stone pine

Description • Also called the Umbrella pine because of the shape of mature specimens **5**. A common sight close to the North Mediterranean coast. Ultimately 15 m tall, a good tree usually has a short stem up to 1 m in diameter. The bark is orange-brown at first becoming fissured and developing distinctive grey, buff and pinkish-brown, flat platy scales. Shoots are light brown and deeply grooved between pairs of 10–16 cm, stiff, grey-green needles **6**. Each pair is held together at the base by a loose, papery sheath. Juvenile foliage consists of soft, straight, 5 cm single needles: two- to four-year-old seedlings are sold as decorative Christmas trees in pots. Cones are spectacular woody structures, 16 cm long and 10 cm wide **7**. Seeds take three years to develop and are wingless. **Habitat and Ecology** • Limestone hills and hot, dry coastal sites. **Similar species** • Reminiscent of stunted Maritime pine (p70).

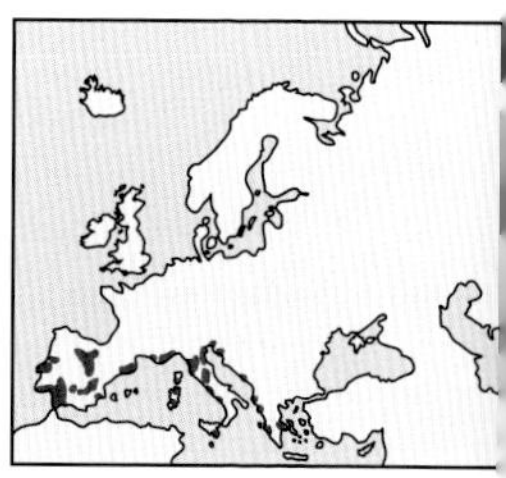

Natural range

Cultivated distribution
Rare in Northern Europe. A source of edible 'Pine nuts' in the south.

Pinus cembra L.

Swiss stone pine or Arolla pine

Description • Rare in Northern Europe beyond its native range and seldom characteristic when it is found **8**. The bark is dark grey developing vertical fissures and scaly ridges in old age. Needles are 8–10 cm long, in fives, gently curved and spreading thickly round the shoot **9**. Woody, 8 cm cones may be blue-grey or purplish-brown falling intact after 18 months with the wingless seed inside. **Habitat and Ecology** • A mountain side tree. **Similar species** • Other five needled pines.

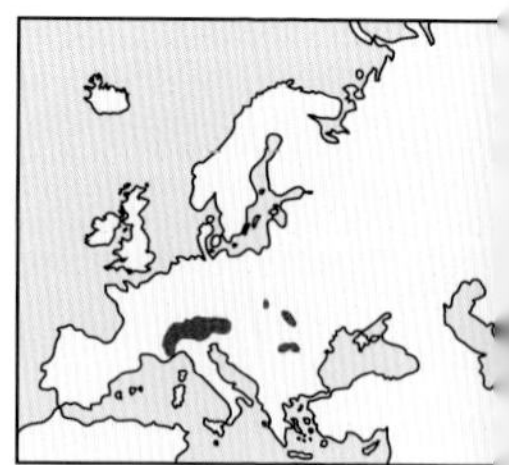

Natural range

Cultivated distribution
Introduced to Scotland in 17 by the Duke of Argyll but never widely planted. Occurs only in specialist collections and botanic gardens.

1

2

3

4

5

6

7

8

9

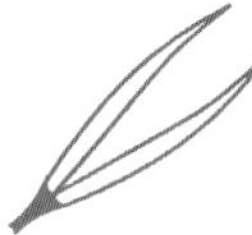

FAMILY Pinaceae

Pinus uncinata Mill. Ex Mirb.
Mountain pine

Description • European mountain pines are confusingly given two species names for what is essentially the same thing. *Pinus uncinata* is a 10–20 m tall tree with a single vertical stem **1** while *Pinus mugo* Turra has a similar sized stem, around 40–50 cm diameter, but it creeps about close to the ground often responding to the prevailing wind by growing away from it; an environmental adaptation to harsh mountain life. The bark of both species is dark grey soon becoming fissured and scaly. Shoots are flexible and yellowish-brown with resinous buds. The needles, in pairs, are 6 cm long, stiff and deep green with fine lines of grey stomata and a hard, pointed tip **2**. For two to three years they are held closely together by a grey-brown basal sheath. Woody 5 cm cones, produced over two seasons, are distinctively spiteful to touch, having a sharp inverted spine on the tip of each scale. They ripen dark purplish-green then pale brown. **Habitat and Ecology** • Tree line scrub and high elevation coniferous forest. **Similar species** • Other two-needled pines with small cones.

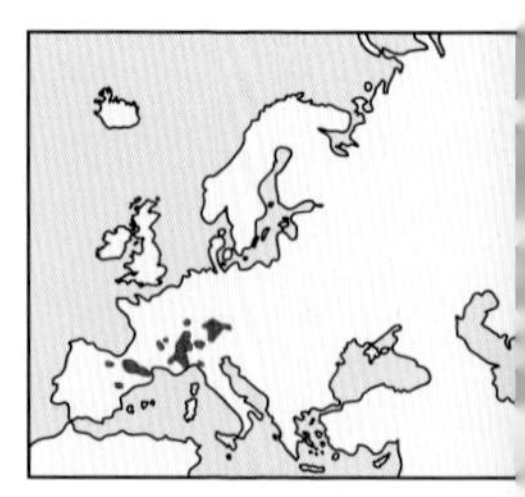

Natural range

Cultivated distribution
The dwarf form *mugo* has been used as a wind-break along the upper edges of exposed plantations. *Pinus uncinata* is seldom used at all in cultivation. It grows slowly and is not a viable timber producer.

Pinus peuce Griseb.
Macedonian pine

Description • A straight, monopodial evergreen tree up to 30 m tall with a mature stem diameter around 80 cm. The outline is conical for much of its life **3**. Plantations maintain a 'saw-tooth' skyline of conical tops **4**. The bark is distinctly smooth for many years, grey-green and resinous. Vertical cracks eventually appear between prominent rings of knots or suppressed branches **5**. The luxuriant foliage consists of soft, 10–12 cm, green needles in fives with distinctive, grey, longitudinal bands of stomata **6**. Pendulous cones, produced over 18 months are leathery, up to 15 cm long, containing 5 mm seeds each with a 15 mm membranous wing **7**. **Habitat and Ecology** • Mountain forests and moist, acid, peaty moorland. **Similar species** • Other five-needled pines with soft foliage.

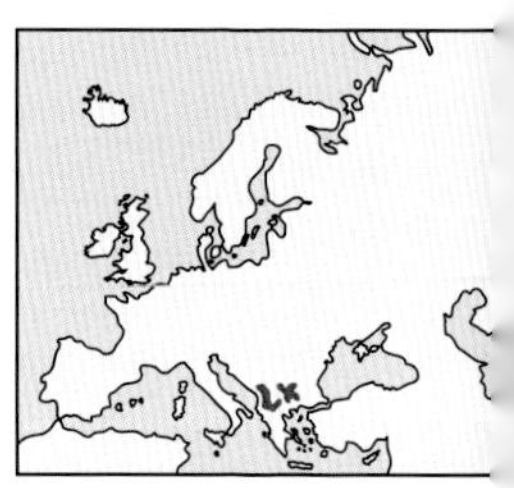

Natural range

Cultivated distribution
Unlike most pines this specie will thrive in cold, wet conditions, peaty soils and moderate to severe exposure making it a good alternative to spruce in commercial plantations. Particularly so where disease or predation b insects becomes a problem, to break up vulnerable or unsightly monocultures.

1
2
3
4
5
6
7

FAMILY Pinaceae

Pinus halepensis Mill.

Aleppo pine

Description • An evergreen tree around 15 m tall with a stem diameter ultimately around 50–60 cm. Branches and some stems are often contorted giving a generally rounded or domed outline **1**. The bark soon becomes deeply fissured into rugged vertical ridges. It is pinkish-brown becoming grey with age. Shoots are grey-green and resinous but always remaining relatively smooth for a pine. Needles are in pairs, sometimes threes, 6–9 cm long with a 1 cm basal sheath holding them in a forward pointing position along the shoot for the first year **2**. Woody cones are tapered to a blunt point, around 8 cm long, ripening to orange brown after 18 months. **Habitat and Ecology** • Hot, dry conditions on rocky hillsides and amongst upland pastures. **Similar species** • Other two-needled pines but the smooth shoots are distinctive.

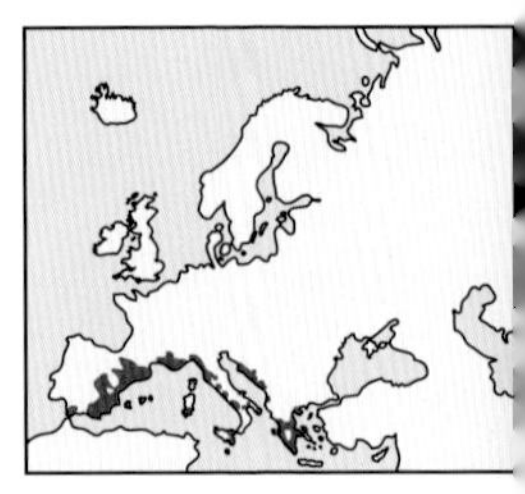

Natural range

Cultivated distribution
Rare in Northern Europe, planted in larger collections only as a curiosity.

Pinus contorta Doug.

Shore pine and Lodgepole pine

Description • The species itself (var. *contorta*) Beach pine or Shore pine is found along the entire Pacific coastal belt of North America. It is a fast-growing, bushy tree with substantial horizontal branches with up-swept extremities **3**. The bark is dark reddish-brown roughly fissured and ridged into squarish scales **4**. Foliage is bright, glossy, deep green and dense. Needles, in pairs, are 5 cm long and twisted to some extent, usually through about 90 degrees. Male flowers are abundant, tightly packed yellow or reddish along 5–10 cm sections of otherwise bare stem, shedding clouds of pollen in late winter. Female flowers are located near shoot tips: they are bright red. Cones are 4–5 cm long, woody, pointed, obliquely oval with short, sharp, recurved spines on the scales **5**. They ripen in 18 months, shed the winged seed and fall. Lodgepole pine, var. *latifolia* Watson, is the inland form. It is slower growing, light branched, but monopodial **6**, often growing in dense forests **7**. The needles are shorter, some provenances are yellowish-green. Cones are more numerous and first-year conelets have sharp spines **8**. This is a pioneer species able to set viable seed from about seven years of age. **Habitat and Ecology** • Harsh situations in a variety of different environments from sub-tundra to alpine rocky slopes, gravel banks, burnt-over ground, floodplains and the seashore. **Similar species** • Other two-needled pines.

Natural range
North America from Southern Alaska and Central Yukon south to the Sierra Nevada and Baja California. In the south as Sierra Lodgepole pine var. *murrayana* (Grev. and Balf.) Engelm. Inland Lodgepole pine grows up to 900 m elevation in the Northern Rocky Mountains and 3500 m in the extreme south.

Cultivated distribution
Grown extensively in twentieth century British forestry plantations mainly as an unproductive shelter species or a first tree crop on marginal land where little else would survive. The name recalls the Native Indian use of the poles for their teepees.

1
2
5
3
6
4
7
8

FAMILY Pinaceae

Pinus strobus L.

Weymouth pine or Eastern white pine

Description • A fast-growing, 25 m tall, smooth barked, straight stemmed pine tree with lax grey-green foliage **1**. The 10–15 cm needles are in fives with distinct grey lines of stomata and a basal sheath which soon disintegrates allowing them to flop around freely. The bark is grey-green with shallow vertical cracks and distinct whorls of knots or suppressed branches **2**. The pendulous leathery cones take 18 months to develop fully, shed seed and fall **3**. Each one is 10–16 cm long, light rusty-brown speckled with white dots of hardened resin. **Habitat and Ecology** • A forest tree thriving best in well drained sandy soils. **Similar species** • Several other five-needled pines.

Natural range
Eastern North America from Newfoundland to Northern Georgia then west to Manitoba and Northern Iowa. A segregate variety grows in Mexico.

Cultivated distribution
Introduced to Europe from Maine by Captain George Weymouth of the British Navy. This fine tree is now decimated by disease (White pine blister rust, *Cronatium ribicola*) in Europe and America whenever it grows close to Currant bushes.

Pinus x holfordiana A. B. Jacks.

Holford pine

Description • A rather coarse tree, fast-growing at first, then slowing down before reaching 18 m in height. The outline is conical then round topped but with long branches projecting unpredictably sideways or upwards **4**. Stems, up to 80 cm diameter, have closely fissured and ridged dark-brown bark which is often spotted and streaked with abundant, dry, white resin flecks **5**. The 8 cm needles in bunches of five are green with conspicuous white lines of stomata. The cones, often described as 'banana-shaped', are leathery and around 25 cm long. In their second summer they are pale green and pendulous **6**, quickly ripening to light brown with sticky encrustations of white resin **7**. By midwinter they have shed their winged seed and fallen to the ground. **Habitat and Ecology** • An entirely artificial hybrid. **Similar species** • The parents (below) and other five-needled pines.

Natural range
None, the parent trees are from different continents.

Cultivated distribution
Seldom planted and of curiosity value only, this hybrid occurred at Westonbirt Arboretum in 1906 when seed was collecte from one of the parent trees planted adjacent to the othe in 1852 (*Pinus ayacahuite* va *veitchii* (Roezl) Shaw, Mexican white pine x *Pinus wallichiana* A. B. Jacks., Bhutan pine from the Himalayas **8**.

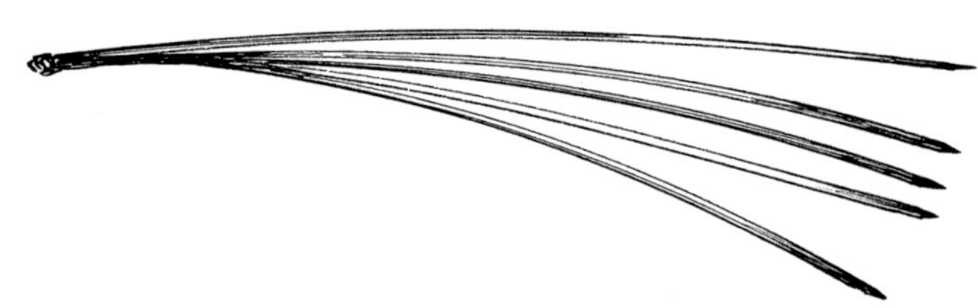

1
2
3
4
5
6
7
8

FAMILY Pinaceae

Pinus radiata D. Don
Monterey pine

Description • Almost pushed to extinction by post-glacial climate change in its native, hot, dry California this species has risen like a phoenix elsewhere in forests round the world as one of the most valuable, fast-growing and highly productive timber trees ever planted. It is probably better known in South Africa or New Zealand than it is in Northern Europe. A vigorous, brilliant green, three-needled conifer, 30 m tall in around 30 years. The outline is ragged at first **1** becoming round topped or developing tiered branches **2**. Stems are rapidly encased in craggy fissured bark **3**. Poles 40 cm thick have been cut in South West England only 15 years after being planted. Needles 10–12 cm long are soft, straight and tightly packed round the shoots **4**. A good diagnostic feature is the tree's tendency to hang on to its cones for about 20 years. Large, 15 cm, oblique, oval, wooden structures often remain in clusters lined up along branches. **Habitat and Ecology** • A coastal species **2** requiring great heat from the sun or fire to open the cones. **Similar species** • Other three-needled pines but the bright green colour is distinctive.

Natural range
California coast, San Mateo, Santa Cruz, Monterey and San Luis Obispo. Also on Guadalupe Island.

Cultivated distribution
Since its introduction to London in 1833 frequently planted in mild localities as a wind break and seaside amenity tree. Experimental plantations have been established where second generation home-grown seedlings appear to be the most hardy.

Pinus muricata D. Don
Bishop pine

Description • Like Monterey pine this species is now confined by post-glacial climate change to a limited range in California. Movement to a cooler environment is blocked by the Pacific Ocean. In Northern Europe the most frequently planted tree is the 'blue-needled form' which is fairly hardy. It is a strong branched, 20 m tall, spreading, conical tree at first **5**. Stems grow rapidly with prominent, annual nodal rings of branch stubs or knots often 1 m apart **7**. Needles are 10–15 cm long, in pairs with a persistent basal sheath. Cones are oblique-oval, solid and woody, about 9 cm long often in clusters all pointing back along the branch **6**. **Habitat and Ecology** • A pioneer species colonising burned or disturbed ground. Confined to coastal regions in its Natural range, often stunted by hot, dry conditions. **Similar species** • Unlike most other two-needled pines the retained cones hardly ever fall until a whole branch dies and comes down intact.

Natural range
Pacific coast of California, Santa Cruz and Santa Rosa Islands. Also Baja California and Mexico.

Cultivated distribution
Mostly imports from Humboldt and Mendocino Counties as possible potenti plantation species. First introduced to Europe in 183 but has little amenity merit.

1
2
3
4
5
6
7

FAMILY Fagaceae

Fagus sylvatica L.
Common beech

Description • A silver-grey stemmed, native forest and hedgerow tree throughout Northern Europe. The foliage is bright green in the summer months 1 then turns brilliant golden-brown in the autumn. Young trees and cut back stems (e.g. as hedges) retain some dry, rustling, brown dead leaves throughout the winter. Beech grows rapidly to a great size even on poor thin soils, trees 35 m tall are known. Stems may be as much as 1.8 m in diameter on old trees 2. An 'ancient' beech tree is unlikely to be over 250 years old (compared with 700 years for a similar sized oak). The bark is thin throughout the life of the tree. Twigs are brown with distinctive, prominent, alternate, narrow, golden-brown, sharp pointed, 1–2 cm long buds. The 7 cm leaves are oval to ovate with a rounded base and acute point. The undulating margins are gossamer-fringed at first then entire except for a slight point at the end of each parallel vein 3. Brown bud scales adhere to the base of the petiole for a time then cover the ground in late spring when they fall, accompanied by spent, globose, 1 cm male flowers. Female flowers are cup-like on short stalks each with four bracts covered with silky hair. They develop into hard spiky fruits 4 each containing two triangular, glossy brown, 'back to back' seeds. **Habitat and Ecology** • A shade-tolerant woodland tree able to regenerate in dense shade. Thrives on thin soils over chalk. **Similar species** • The bark may be confused with Common hornbeam (p172). Foliage is similar to Oriental beech (p88).

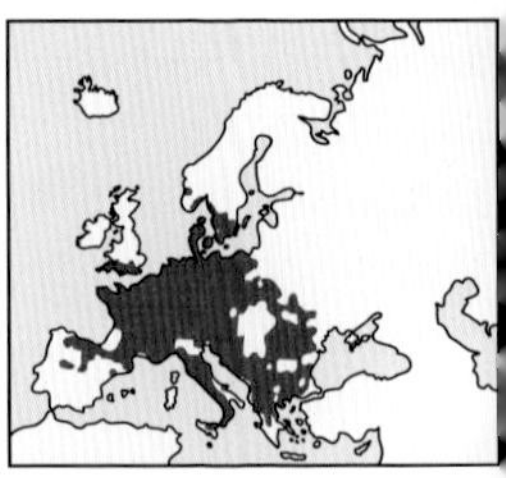

Natural range

Cultivated distribution
An important European timber tree. The wood is of high quality but not durable out of doors. As an ornamental it is most frequently seen as hedging or in one of its many ornamental forms.

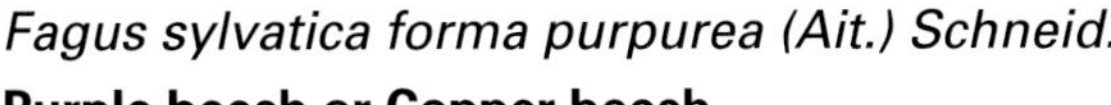

Fagus sylvatica forma purpurea (Ait.) Schneid.
Purple beech or Copper beech

Description • Occurs naturally and produces viable seed, some of which will have degrees of purple foliage. It is a large tree in every respect like Common beech 5 with brightest foliage colour in full light 6. The stem is silver grey and smooth 7. **Habitat and Ecology** • As Common beech (above). **Similar species** • There are numerous, purple-leaved trees and shrubs, none quite like Beech.

Natural range
Similar to Common beech a[s] an occasional spontaneous seedling in an otherwise green population.

Cultivated distribution
Grown usually as a vegetatively produced cultiv[ar] such as 'Riversii', 'Cuprea', 'Dawyck Purple' or 'Purple Fountain'. Nurserymen are always ready to select new 'improved' strains. There ar[e] upright and pendulous for[ms] in cultivation.

1

2

3

4

6

FAMILY Fagaceae

Fagus sylvatica L. forms
Green beech cultivars

Description • Weeping beech, although originally a natural form of Common beech (p86), is now almost exclusively represented in cultivation by the cultivar 'Pendula' originally produced in 1836. The branches are dramatically pendulous often extending from many metres up the tree down to ground level **1**. The stem, leaves, flowers and fruit are exactly like Common beech. The golden form 'Aurea Pendula' is a pretty tree if grown in good light but not in scorching sun where the leaves burn, or in deep shade where the foliage turns green. Most specimens are tall and slender **2** with branches held close to the stem. Another quite different tall, slender tree is the fastigiate beech 'Dawyck' **3** that originated in Scotland before 1850. **Habitat and Ecology** • Virtually unknown in the wild. **Similar species** • Weeping beeches are distinct, 'Dawyck' may be confused with Lomdardy poplar (p264) from some way off. See also cut-leaved beeches (p342).

Natural range
None.

Cultivated distribution
Grown in large gardens, parks and urban open spaces. Weeping beeches 'Pendula' require careful pruning and training. 'Dawyck' beech will grow anywhere and its full potential is not yet realised.

Fagus orientalis Lipsky
Oriental beech

Description • A big, deciduous, smooth, grey-barked tree up to 35 m tall, ultimately with a stem diameter around 1 m. In the open the outline is rounded with vertical upper shoots **4**. As a forest or plantation it grows closely spaced eventually producing good straight stems **5**. Shoots and buds are more or less like Common beech but the leaves are larger with up to ten pairs of veins: margins are entire but wavy **6** and **7**. Autumn foliage colour is yellow to rich brown. The fruit is a 2–3 cm woody cupule with soft curly spines containing a pair of triangular, glossy-brown, pointed seeds. **Habitat and Ecology** • A natural forest species in pure and mixed stands. **Similar species** • Common beech to the west in Europe and Asiatic Beeches to the east. In Western Europe where this species is always introduced it is seldom possible to separate it morphologically from well-grown Common beech with complete confidence.

Natural range
Iran, the Caucasus Mountain to 1800 m elevation, Bulgari Turkey and the Eastern Balkans. Interspecific forms occur where the range overlaps Common beech.

Cultivated distribution
Introduced in 1880 but rarel planted in Northern Europe and seldom recognized whe it is. It produces high-qualit timber and pannage for free- ranging domestic stock especially pigs.

1
2
3
4
5
6
7

FAMILY Rosaceae

Mespilus germanica L.

Medlar

Description • A bushy tree usually around 6 m tall and wide, often as a component of an orchard **1**. The bark is grey-brown, scaly and fissured. Shoots are grey pubescent with occasional woody spines. Leaves are more or less oblong, bright green and abruptly pointed. The usually entire margins are sometimes very finely toothed. Solitary white flowers in early summer are on terminal shoots **2**. These develop into distinctive brown 3 cm fruits with persistent, widely spaced sepals **3**. **Habitat and Ecology** • A woodland tree but usually found as a relic of past cultivation. **Similar species** • When not in fruit resembles many orchard species and some entire leafed thorns.

Natural range
Obscured by extensive cultivation and widely naturalized. Probably originating in south-east Europe, western Asia and Iran.

Cultivated distribution
Formerly grown for its edible fruit which is now out of favour because of its astringent taste. Over-ripe, frosted ('bletted') fruit is sweet but it will not keep or transport easily.

FAMILY Nyssaceae

Nyssa sylvatica Marsh.

Tupelo or Black gum

Description • A rough-barked tree up to 20 m tall with 5–13 cm leaves reminiscent of Medlar and Common quince **4**. Margins may sometimes be slightly toothed. The upper surface is shiny and glabrous **5**. This tree is most easily recognized in the autumn when the foliage briefly turns red and gold **6**. Insignificant greenish flowers appear in leaf axils in spring, male and female on separate trees. The fruit is a green then black 1 cm oval berry, sometimes in pairs, on a straight 5 cm stalk. **Habitat and Ecology** • Moist woodland. **Similar species** • Chinese Tupelo, *Nyssa sinensis* Oliv., which is a smaller tree.

Natural range
North America from Texas to Florida and north to Michigan and Maine.

Cultivated distribution
Widely grown as an ornamental in European gardens.

FAMILY Rosaceae

Cydonia oblonga Mill.

Common quince

Description • An old 6–8 m orchard tree that has declined in recent years along with the demand for its excellent fruit. A twiggy thicket may obscure the base **8**. The bark, where visible, is reminiscent of Sycamore (p362), scaly-grey randomly exposing pale orange-brown patches **7**. Shoots, leaves and developing pear-shaped fruit are all woolly at first and greyish green **9**. Solitary flowers are pale pink or white similar to Medlar (above **2**). Shoots become dark purplish-brown **10**, leaves become glabrous on the upper side and the fragrant fruits expand to 8–12 cm long. Bright golden-yellow with a persistent brown calyx and reddish stalk **10**. **Habitat and Ecology** • The wild origins have been forgotten after centuries of cultivation. **Similar species** • From a distance like orchard apples and pears.

Natural range
Unknown but probably West Asia.

Cultivated distribution
Once widely grown as an orchard tree. The excellent fruit can be made into jam which is reminiscent of marmalade. Now found as a relic of old orchards or naturalized in the landscape.

1
2
3
4
5
6
7
8
9
10

FAMILY Magnoliaceae

Magnolia spp.

Tree magnolias

Description • Several species and cultivars grown in Northern Europe qualify as trees, easily exceeding 6 m in height with a single stem. Magnolias often puzzle people trying to identify trees when there are no flowers to assist. However in winter they all have very large buds that are characteristically bristly or velvety and usually pale greyish-brown. The brightly coloured often large flowers set them apart from other trees with similar bold foliage. Towards the end of summer large seeds are produced in distinctive, often grotesque, distorted or cone-like pods. One of the most frequently seen species is *Magnolia x soulangeana* Soulange-Bodin, a hybrid between *Magnolia denudata* Desrouss. the Lilly tree, and *Magnolia stellata* (Sieb. and Zucc.) Maxim., a shrub with star-like flowers. *Magnolia x soulangeana* has many named cultivars. It is a substantial tree **1** that is most obvious when it flowers in profusion in late winter before the leaves appear **2**. In complete contrast *Magnolia wilsonii* Rehd., a 6–8 m tall tree, produces flowers with the young leaves later in the year **3**. Individual flowers always point downwards. They are followed by curious, bright pink, spiky seed pods **4** containing orange seeds **5**. *Magnolia denudata* is a large-spreading, 15 m tall tree with obovate, 12 cm pointed leaves tapering towards the base **6**. The fragrant white flowers are large and up to 15 cm across when fully open. Orange seeds are contained in 12 cm deformed pods **7**. Another substantial, fast-growing, 12 m tall tree is *Magnolia dawsoniana* Rehd. and Wils. It has 10–14 cm long, pointed oval leaves and huge, early spring flowers up to 20 cm across **8**. **Habitat and Ecology** • Partial shade provided by deciduous woodland encourages good growth and protection for early flowers but there are around 125 species so exact requirements vary considerably. Some will not tolerate lime in the soil. Most species are usually able to withstand gale force winds in Europe rather better than any other comparable sized trees. **Similar species** • There are numerous deciduous trees with oval pointed entire leaves but in *Magnolia* the petiole partially encloses the following year's bud and the leaf scar encircles the stem. Buds have a single outer scale which is often hairy.

Natural range
South East Asia and the Himalaya, also the southern States of America, through Central America and south to Venezuela.

Cultivated distribution
Extensively grown as a garden and park tree. The early flowering cultivars are frequently spoiled by spring frost and cold wind. When grown from seed the tree *Magnolias* usually take a long time, perhaps 25 years, to begin flowering. Seed from mixed collections can be of hybrid origin which may or may not produce a good new plant such as this *Magnolia campbellii* Hook. f. and Thoms. seedling which took 20 years to flower **9**, but was worth waiting for.

1
2
3
4
5
6
7
8
9

FAMILY Salicaceae

Populus tremula L.

Aspen

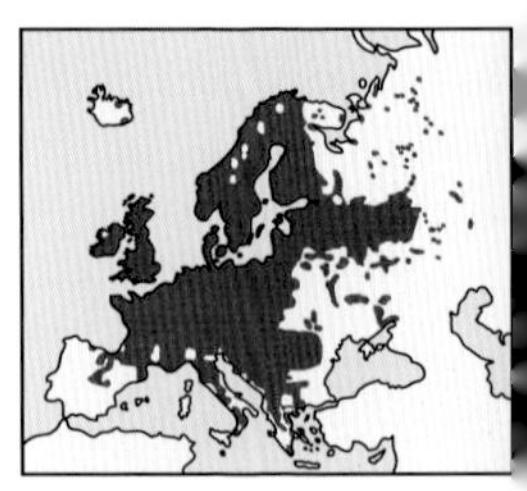

Natural range

Description • Aspen is recognized instantly in summer by its fluttering round leaves which tremble in the slightest breeze. Most individuals are not particularly large although trees 20 m tall with stems 40 cm in diameter do occur **1**. The bark is thin, greenish-grey and smooth when young. In very exposed places it is often bleached almost white **2**. As trees mature the stem develops rhomboidal brown spots that eventually expand into rough scars and ultimately deep furrows and ridges **3**. Although individual stems are relatively small and short-lived the tree itself may be hundreds of years old, continually rejuvenating itself by suckering from an ancient and extensive root system. A notable tree in South Wales has a root system in excess of one hectare with an estimated 1000 stems. Even small woodlands that have not obviously been planted are likely to consist entirely of suckers from a single ancient plant **4**. New trees are occasionally produced from seed but viability is measured only in hours and the right conditions for germination are critical. Furthermore, seed is shed in early spring when the weather is unpredictable. The glabrous leaves are round with wavy edges. They are held on long, unstable, flattened petioles **5**. Leaves on young sucker growth are completely different, distinctly pointed and pubescent **6**. Dense sucker regrowth is intolerant of shade so stems are forced to grow rapidly upwards and produce few side branches. Many potential trees die out in the process. Flowers appear on bare shoots in late winter, male and female on separate trees (often whole separate clonal woods). Males are 4 cm, grey-brown, pendulous catkins with deep red anthers. Females in clusters are pale grey-green and pink **7** soon becoming fluffy and shedding the wind blown seed. The minute seeds will only germinate in full light on the surface of the ground but they must not dry out. **Habitat and Ecology** • A pioneer species in upland or lowland areas on any kind of soil. **Similar species** • American aspen *Populus tremuloides* Michx. differs in its more finely toothed leaves and creamy-white young bark **8**. This feature however is usually less strong in Europe than it is in America. Vast stands of American aspen are a well known feature in the 'fall' when yellow foliage contrasts with numerous slender white stems. The soft wood is a favourite with American beavers for dam building.

Cultivated distribution

At present, hardly used commercially at all but its potential has been recognized. Small plantations for shelter and to fix sand dunes have been established **2**. It responds well to coppicing and benefits wildlife. Growth is rapid for 20–25 years and the wood produces very white, high-quality paper pulp. Once established it is naturally sustainable and can be harvested over and over again without damaging the environment.

1
2
3
4
5
6
7
8

FAMILY Salicaceae

Salix viminalis L.

Common osier

Description • A sprawling shrub or small tree, 6 m tall and immediately recognizable in summer by its long, narrow, toothless, silvery backed leaves. These are tapered to a fine point at each end and have undulating, smooth, rolled back (revolute) margins. On vigorous shoots leaves may be 18 cm long by only 1–2 cm wide **1**. In spring they are lustrous bright green **2** becoming duller by late summer before eventually turning yellow and falling. The underside has adpressed, silky white hairs which last all season. Petioles are short, generally less than 1 cm with or without basal stipules. Shoots are long, straight and pliable. Growth on annually cut coppice often exceeds 2 m in a single season. At first, stems are covered with dense, grey pubescence gradually becoming glabrous, yellowish green or olive brown. There are marked differences in shoot colour depending on the clone. In the traditional basket-willow osier industry there were at least 50 named clones of this species. If allowed to develop into a tree the trunk has greyish-brown bark which is fissured vertically. Clear stems are rarely seen because of frequent low erect branches and multiple stems **3**. Catkins appear in early spring before the leaves. Crowded towards the tips of the previous season's shoots males in particular provide a spectacular display of golden-yellow. Each sessile catkin points upwards regardless of the angle of the shoot. They are nectar rich and each flower has two free stamens **4**. Female flowers **2** on separate plants are subsessile, greenish-grey and densely tomentose. These develop very quickly, soon shedding fine seeds attached to copious amounts of fluff **5**. **Habitat and Ecology** • A wetland species thriving best close to standing water but not immersed in it for long periods. An important component of carr vegetation with alder and sedges initiating the transition between reed bed and damp woodland. **Similar species** • The only other narrow leaved and virtually untoothed osier is *Salix purpurea* L. the Purple osier **6**. It is much smaller, seldom ever a tree, with pea green, glabrous leaves which are unusual because they may be opposite or alternate even on the same shoot. Purple osier has also been extensively cultivated by the basket industry. It produces thin, lightweight rods in a range of colours from green to plum-purple.

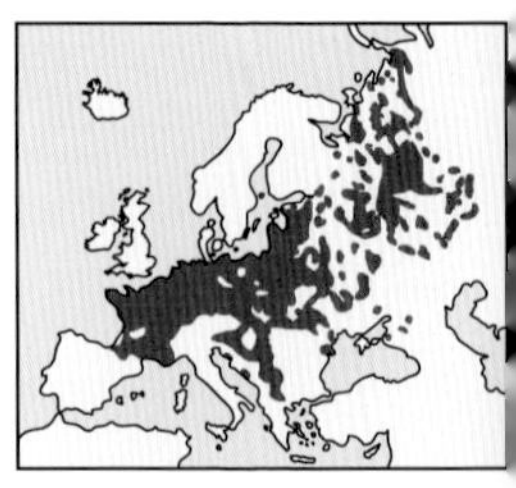

Natural range
Confused by extensive planting but considered by some to be native in East and Central England.

Cultivated distribution
Ancient cultivation of this osier for long, coarse basket rods used in agriculture and industry has disguised the real natural distribution of the species. It grows freely from cuttings and also from seed. The latter provides numerous opportunities for inter-specific cross-breeding. The rolled leaf margin occurs in many named *viminalis* hybrids.

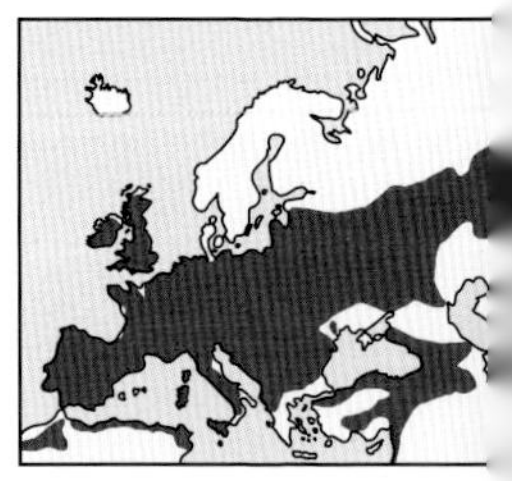

Natural range
Salix purpurea

1

2

3

4

6

FAMILY Salicaceae

Salix x smithiana Willd.

Description • An untidy, shrubby, often multi-stemmed tree up to 9 m tall. Shoots are grey-green then reddish-brown, densely grey, tomentose at first. Leaves are 5–10 cm long oblanceolate and acuminate dull grey-green **1**. Teeth are very small, indistinct or hidden by an undulating, slightly recurved margin. Petioles are 1–2 cm with a pair of ear-shaped basal stipules at first. Male plants are rare, the yellow catkins are ovoid-cylindrical, 2.5 cm long. Female catkins are longer, densely grey pubescent **2**. The red bud scales are distinctive. **Habitat and Ecology** • A common natural hybrid between *Salix cinerea* (p242) and *Salix viminalis* (p96). **Similar species** • Numerous named and unnamed spontaneous hybrid sallows.

Natural range
Widely distributed throughout Europe and lowland Britain particularly East Anglia. Native and cultivated populations are often confused.

Cultivated distribution
No longer in general cultivation but escapes contribute to floodplain protection from erosion. A potential short-rotation coppice plant.

Salix viminalis var. stipularis Leefe ex Bab.

Auricled osier

Description • Often described as a female clone 'Stipularis' or as a hybrid *Salix x stipularis* Sm., believed to involve *Salix aurita* L., *Salix viminalis* (p96) and *Salix caprea* (p240). An erect shrub or small tree with densely greyish pubescent foliage **3** with persistent stipules. Catkins appear before the leaves. **Habitat and Ecology** • Status uncertain but appears in several European countries. **Similar species** • Only larger stipules distinguish this plant from other *Salix viminalis* hybrids.

Natural range
None, except possibly in Russia.

Cultivated distribution
Believed to have been cultivated in Northern Britain as a tough basket osier.

Salix caprea L. var. sphacelata (Sm.) Wahlenb.

Scottish goat willow

Description • The more or less entire leaves distinguish this tree which otherwise resembles the species (p240). It becomes a tree over 10 m tall in favourable conditions **4**, but remains shrubby on high ground. The leaves are dark green, with soft grey pubescence on the underside, 3–7 cm long by up to 4.5 cm wide **5**. Flowers appear with the leaves, later than the species, but are similar in other respects. **Habitat and Ecology** • A tree of harsh northern regions through Scandinavia and Russia and at high elevation elsewhere in Europe. **Similar species** • Intermediates between this variety and *Salix caprea* occur at low elevation and hybrids with *Salix lanata* L. are found in extreme conditions.

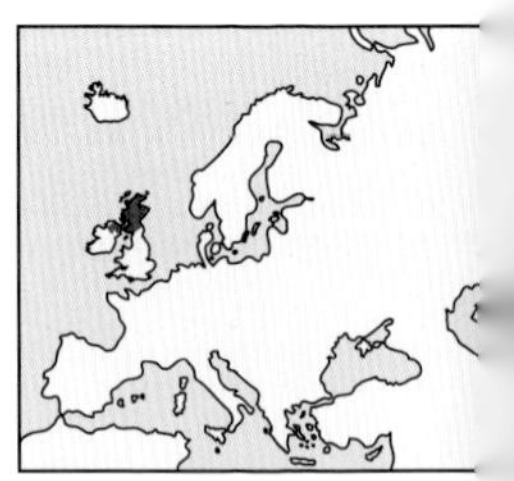

Natural range

Cultivated distribution
Not in commercial cultivation. It is doubtful whether any distinctive characteristics would be retained in cultivation.

1

2

3

4

5

FAMILY Elaeagnaceae

Hippophae rhamnoides L.

Sea buckthorn

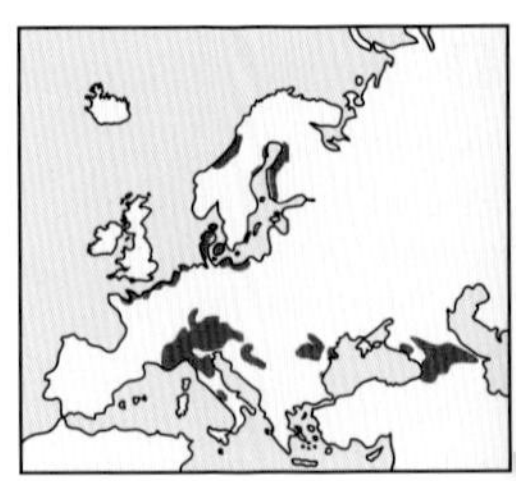

Natural range

Cultivated distribution
Grown as a shelter plant on exposed coasts and also to help fix moving sand dunes. An attractive, silver leaved tree widely planted in inland gardens **6**. The enduring berries are a feature in winter. Huge naturalized suckering clumps are a characteristic of neglected nineteenth century landscape planting.

Description • Most often seen as a tangled spiny cliff top **1**, or sand dune shrub close to the sea. However in sheltered situations it attains heights up to 12 m and a stem diameter of 20–30 cm **2**. The silvery grey deciduous foliage is distinctive in summer **3** and the pale greyish-orange berries in the autumn are unique to this species. In maritime or inland situations white stemmed suckers are frequent. These are well-armed with formidable spines set more or less at right angles to the shoot. The mature bark is dark brown with a thin, greyish, translucent skin becoming fissured on large stems. Winter buds are numerous but small and round, golden-brown with few visible scales. Leaves are deciduous but often remain on the tree into early winter. They appear to be pale grey-green because of a covering of minute silvery-white scales making them impervious to salt-laden air. Each one is linear-lanceolate, 4–5 cm long and tapered at both ends. Stellate glandular hairs on the underside show up as a faint rust coloured tint. The midrib, an extension of the 3 mm keeled petiole, is prominent below and recessed on the upper side. Flowers occur on separate male and female trees before the leaves. They are very small, yellowish, but in dense axillary clusters on second-year shoots. Racemes of female flowers often terminate in a protective thorn that develops as the fruit ripens **4**. The acidic berries are ovoid, about 7 mm long, each containing a single seed **5**. In their prime they are bright orange often occurring in profusion on female trees before the leaves fall. Seldom taken by birds they persist until midwinter gradually fading almost to white. **Habitat and Ecology** • Coastal sites particularly on blown sand on the landward side of the spring tide splash zone. Full light is essential for satisfactory growth. **Similar species** • May be confused with the foliage of some *Elaeagnus* (p104) in summer and superficially in winter with coastal blackthorn (p144).

1
2
3
4
5
6

FAMILY Leguminosae

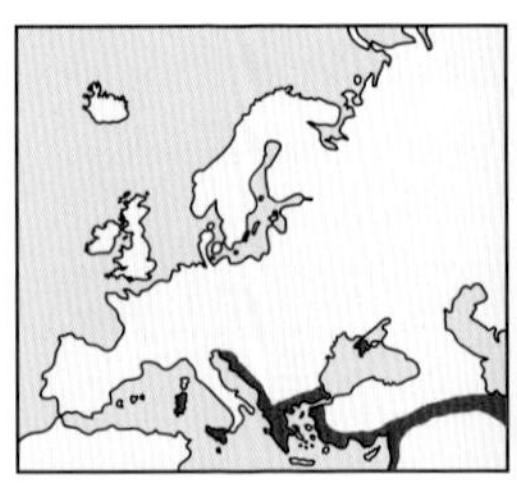

Cercis siliquastrum L.
Judas tree

Description • Originally from the south of Europe this small ornamental tree has become a firm favourite in northern gardens and parks, its profusion of pink flowers often appearing on bare branches before the leaves are fully expanded **1**. Each bloom is typical of the pea family, about 2 cm across on a 2 cm stalk **2**. Flowers often appear in clusters right on to the main stem **3**. The bark is fairly smooth, grey-brown eventually developing small squarish scales **4**. Fruits are green, flat, 10 cm pea-pods that ripen to brown in the autumn **5**. The round seeds are dark brown, glossy and also flat. The leaves are unlike most members of the pea family having entire margins and a rounded to heart-shaped 6–10 cm blade on a 5 cm petiole. **Habitat and Ecology** • Warm, dry, rocky hillsides. Not usually tolerant of heavy, poorly drained ground. **Similar species** • *Cercidiphyllum japonicum* (p280).

Natural range

Cultivated distribution
A popular garden tree or large shrub. Grown in the south as an urban open space tree, sometimes regularly pollarded to encourage the curious flowers on the bare branches.

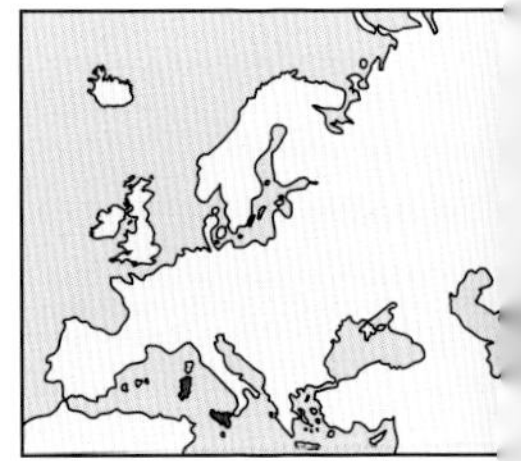

Genista aetnensis (Bivona) DC.
Mount Etna broom

Description • A typical Broom appearing to be leafless with numerous, straight, slender, mostly upright, green shoots, but this species is far larger than any other. Trees, albeit with multiple stems, can reach 6–8 m high and wide in Northern Europe **6**. The outline is rounded with no clear vertical stem. The bark is yellowish-grey becoming shallowly fissured. Plants are often partially blown over to form a sprawling thicket **7**. Shoots are slender and flexible, deep green with a grey sheen. Shallow grooves run along their entire length. The leaves are insignificant, like small bracts. Fragrant flowers appear in midsummer, they are pea-like, 2 cm across and bright yellow **8**. Fruits are small pea-pods each with two or three brown seeds. **Habitat and Ecology** • Hostile volcanic slopes in a hot, dry environment. **Similar species** • Other Brooms but none of them are as large.

Natural range

Cultivated distribution
Slightly tender in many northern areas so mainly confined to sheltered garden or near the sea. This is a salt-tolerant plant but when mature it tends to break up i[n] gale force winds. Some growers pollard or coppice plants regularly to limit this damage.

1

2

3

4

6

8

5

7

FAMILY Rosaceae

Cotoneaster frigidus Wall.

Tree cotoneaster

Description • A spreading deciduous or semi-evergreen, multi-stemmed or low branched tree around 6–8 m tall [1] with a stem up to 50 cm diameter [2]. Sometimes a cluster of stems much greater in total diameter. The shoots are pubescent at first soon becoming glabrous. The leaves are elliptic-oblong, broadly pointed at each end, 6–12 cm long with a short 8 mm petiole. The upper surface is leathery and deep green but the underside is persistently tomentose and pale green. Flowers are 8 mm across, creamy white in dense up-turned corymbs along the shoot [3]. Each one has five petals and numerous stamens. The fruit is a 6 mm red berry retaining a prominent black calyx [4] and containing two seeds. **Habitat and Ecology** • Lower mountain slopes and rocky ground. Forming thickets or as a component of mixed deciduous woodland. **Similar species** • In cultivation Tree cotoneaster has often been substituted by Waterer's cotoneaster, *Cotoneaster x watereri* Exell., a hybrid between it and possibly two other species. The original plant 'John Waterer' is a large, semi-evergreen, spreading shrub or small tree [5] with numerous upward-facing, cream flowers in dense corymbs [6] followed by heavy crops of berries [7]. Many nurseries sell seedlings that can be extremely variable. Various hybrids have escaped from cultivation and become naturalized.

Natural range
The foothills of the Himalayas.

Cultivated distribution
The plant is common in gardens and urban open spaces but its authenticity is increasingly in doubt as seedlings replace original plants.

FAMILY Elaeagnaceae

Elaeagnus angustifolia L.

Oleaster

Description • Most of this distinctive 'silver-leaved' genus consists of shrubs. Oleaster can make a small tree 6–8 m tall [8]. The outline is rounded usually with no single persistent stem. The leaves are narrow oblong, occasionally accompanied by sharp spines [9]. Small fragrant flowers occur in leaf axils in early summer. They are yellow but with minute, silver scales on the outer surfaces. Fleshy edible 1–2 cm fruits are yellowish-green also with silvery scales ripening to light brown. **Habitat and Ecology** • Mild, rocky hillsides in thickets or completely isolated. **Similar species** • Other *Elaeagnus* species but this is ultimately the largest.

Natural range
West and Central Asia in warm temperate conditions. Cultivated in Southern Europe.

Cultivated distribution
Less common in Northern Europe than other shrubby, broader leaved species such *Elaeagnus pungens* Thumb., particularly its ubiquitous variegated spiny cultivar 'Maculata'.

1
2
3
4
5
6
7
8
9

FAMILY Myrtaceae

Eucalyptus gunnii Hook. f.

Cider gum

Description • One of the easiest ways to identify *Eucalyptus* is to crush some leaves. But not this species as the characteristic smell associated with the genus is faint or absent. Morphological identification of *Eucalyptus gunnii* is never easy and often speculative. Juvenile leaves are orbicular and more or less opposite, bright bloomed, blue-green and under 6 cm long and wide **1**. Adult leaves are dull grey-green, lanceolate to sickle shaped, around 10 cm long and alternate. They tend to hang downwards from the shoot on a 2.5 cm petiole and are able to turn edgeways to the sun on a hot day. The foliage is evergreen and in Europe grows almost all year round. Stems may be huge 20–30 m tall and branching from near the base **2** or monopodial in plantations **3**. The subspecies *archeri*, widely recognised as a species, *Eucalyptus archeri* Maiden and Blakely, has been selected as a potential timber tree in Europe because of its exceptionally straight stem **4**. The young bark of Cider gum is smooth with an irregular pattern of grey-brown and paler greenish-grey as random patches exfoliate. There are also forms in cultivation with pale brown, stringy bark. The summer flowers are creamy-white **5**. They occur in umbels of three in leaf axils, each consisting of an urn shaped calyx-tube topped by a 1.5 cm dense cluster of stamens hiding the other parts of the hermaphrodite flower. The seeds are minute and numerous, like fine grains of sand. **Habitat and Ecology** • A high-elevation species in south east Australia and Tasmania on heavy, wet soils. In Europe, various soils suit it so long as ground water is not restricted. Growth is very fast and trees are generally wind firm. **Similar species** • Hundreds of other *Eucalyptus* (p108) particularly spontaneous hybrids from cultivated collections and gardens.

Natural range
Tasmania and South East Australia.

Cultivated distribution
Discovered in 1840 in high elevation swampland (1200 m) in Tasmania. Introduced to Europe in 1846, the first native Australian tree to grow out of doors in Britain. Recently the climate has warmed sufficiently to safely grow this species as far north as southern Scotland. The wood is heavy but not of particularly good quality: however a lot of it is produced very quickly. Due to the lack of eucalyptus smell browsing animals such as rabbits often damage young plants.

Buds

Fruit

FAMILY Myrtaceae

Eucalyptus pauciflora subsp. niphophila Johnson and Blaxell

Snow gum

Description • An alpine form of Snow gum which is confined to high elevation sites in South East Australia and Tasmania. Trees in cultivation are variable often with sinuous or multiple stems **2**. In Ireland specimens have exceeded 25 m in height but generally around 6 m may be expected. The bark is smooth, mostly brilliant white, with patches of light grey-green, pink or pale brown **1**. Adult leaves are 10–12 cm long, aromatic, waxy blue-green and lanceolate with distinct parallel veins. Young shoots are red **3**. Juvenile foliage is shorter, reddish-orange at first and the leaves are in opposite pairs. A thin, dark red margin is retained on some adult leaves. Flowers are in umbels of 7–11. This number is a diagnostic feature used to distinguish the various groups of *Eucalyptus*. Fruits are roundish, green capsules in a tight, short-stalked cluster, each with a flat top that eventually opens to shed numerous minute seeds. **Habitat and Ecology** • Alpine scrub woodland. **Similar species** • The subspecies is like the species except for more stunted growth and dramatic white bark.

Natural range
Mount Kosciusko region of the Snowy Mountains in New South Wales and Victoria. Also high mountain sites in Tasmania.

Cultivated distribution
Frequently grown in gardens as a bark feature.

Eucalyptus hybrids and exotic species

Description • Most second and subsequent generations of Eucalyptus grown and distributed in Europe are likely to be hybrids. There are over 500 species in Australia, but they only remain pure because of geographic isolation. As soon as they are mixed up, artificially compatible individuals hybridize. The purity of plants grown from seed obtained from exotic collections should always be suspect. Groups of newly planted seedlings quickly demonstrate variable foliage and bark characteristics **4**. There are an increasing number of species that will grow in Northern Europe as potential pulpwood or timber trees. For example, *Eucalyptus vernicosa* Hook., Varnish gum, which in Australia is little more than scrub but in Europe is a large tree **5**. *Eucalyptus subcrenulata* Maiden and Blakely is another promising 18 m tall tree **6**. *Eucalyptus nitens* (Deane and Maiden) Maiden, the Shining gum, is a huge tree, potentially 60 m tall **7**. *Eucalyptus delegatensis* subsp. *tasmaniensis* Boland has distinctive bark **8** unlike most other specimens.

Natural range
Australia and Tasmania.

Cultivated distribution
Hybrids are increasingly planted often in unsuitable places where their unpredictable size, spreading roots and excessive demands on water will cause damage. Authentic pure bred species, such as the examples shown, all growing in Scotland, are excellent timber trees. They do however require a fairly mild climate and copious amounts of rain to thrive.

2
3
4
5
6
7
8

FAMILY Ericaceae

Arbutus menziesii Pursh

Madrona or Pacific madrone

Description • A large, 15–25 m evergreen tree with remarkable bark, at first olive green with a cinnamon to red skin which peels off in sheets **1**. In old age the stem becomes rugged and flaky but remains distinctively red-brown. Large areas continue to peel away amongst the branches, revealing dramatic sheets of orange-red underbark **2**. The outline of the tree is unpredictable because it is tender in much of Northern Europe and dies back or breaks up. Early frost damage causes many specimens to be multi-stemmed, an amenity advantage usually. The 6–15 cm thick, leathery leaves are more or less oval with a blunt point and wedge-shaped base extending down the partially winged, 4 cm petiole. The upper side is deep shiny green while the underside is pale coloured. Margins are virtually entire or with microscopic teeth. Juvenile leaves and coppice re-growth are visibly toothed. Flowers are like bell heather, about 6 mm long, dull white and in open clusters (panicles). Round fruits about 1 cm across ripen in the autumn and often remain on the tree until the following year's spring flowers appear. **Habitat and Ecology** • Occurs in hot, mountain country at low elevations. Cultivated in Europe but not common. **Similar species** • Other *Arbutus* (below and p140).

Natural range
Western North America from Vancouver Island Southern California; also Sierra Nevada and Santa Cruz Island.

Cultivated distribution
Grown only as an ornamental tree in Europe where it will tolerate limestone soils but prefers acidity and adequate moisture. The fruit is edible but not particularly pleasant.

Arbutus andrachne L.

Greek strawberry tree

Description • A small evergreen tree or large shrub similar to Madrona (above). The outline is often ragged **3** and the stem twisted in a sinuous or procumbent shape **4**. Young shoots are cinnamon-brown, very smooth with a matt-finish. The leaves are oval to elliptic with an abrupt point and rounded or wedge-shaped base **5**. They are 5–10 cm long, dark shiny green above and pale glaucous green below. Like all Arbutus they are stiff and leathery. Margins appear to be entire although under a lens minute teeth may be detected. The 3 cm petiole is grooved along the upper side. Flowers appear late in the spring, in terminal clusters on second-year shoots, dull green, shaped like bell heather and around 6 mm long. Rough, round, 2 cm fruits are orange and remain on the tree for a long period. **Habitat and Ecology** • Rocky sites and open woodland especially on dry limestone. **Similar species** • Madrona (above) and the hybrid *Arbutus x andrachnoides* (p140).

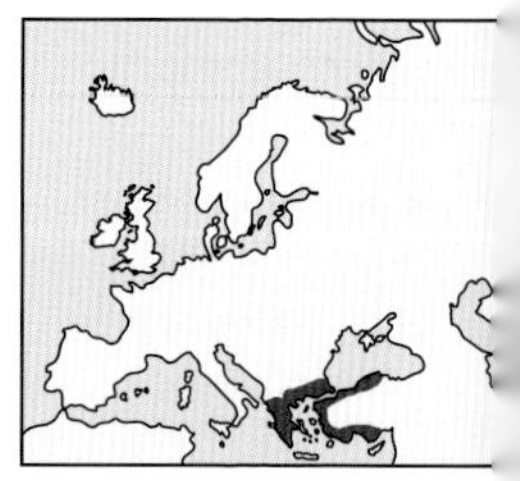

Natural range

Cultivated distribution
Rare in cultivation in Northern Europe where it is tender. Only found in sheltered gardens and some tree collections and often on as a shrub **6**.

FAMILY Pittosporaceae

Pittosporum tenuifolium Gaertn.

Kohuhu

Description • A small evergreen tree with distinctive waxy crinkled leaves. Before 1960 it only survived in mild coastal districts in Northern Europe. Now, in response to recent climate change, it thrives in sheltered gardens as far north as Central Scotland. At first the outline is ovoid **1** becoming more rounded at maturity. The bark is very dark brown, almost black, on young shoots, grey-brown on branches and dull grey on the main stem. Pale green leaves are 2–4 cm long, obovate to oblong with a blunt pointed tip and narrow rounded base **2**. Margins are wavy and the midrib is light coloured. The flowers, in pairs, appear in leaf axils in spring. They are brownish-purple, sweetly scented, each with five 1 cm petals. Fruits are green capsules divided into three. They turn black when ripe. **Habitat and Ecology** • Sandy soils, hot, dry areas or close to the sea. **Similar species** • There are many exotic species and cultivars available now in garden centres.

Natural range
New Zealand.

Cultivated distribution
A popular garden shrub and foliage plant for florists. Outstanding are 'Silver Queen' and 'Purpureum' which has striking almost black leaves and young shoots.

FAMILY Lauraceae

Umbellularia californica (Hook. and Arn.) Nutt.

Californian laurel or Headache tree

Description • An evergreen, resembling the Bay tree (p118), which should be avoided whenever possible. The scent of the foliage will bring on a severe headache on a hot day. This is a small- to medium-sized, 8–16 m tall tree with an informal rounded outline **3**. The bark is smooth and dark brown eventually becoming scaly and greyish. The leaves are oblong **4** or lanceolate **5** and pointed at both ends, about 8–10 cm long and leathery. Flowers are in terminal umbels and leaf axils. Flower buds are formed almost a year before they bloom. In a good season they occur all over the tree in summer transforming the whole plant from sombre green to bright yellow **6**. Fruits are round berries ripening from green **5** to almost black. **Habitat and Ecology** • Moist valleys usually in the shade of larger deciduous trees. **Similar species** • Bay tree and some Laurel cultivars (p116). *Osmanthus decorus* (Boiss and Bal.) Kasap. and *Illicium anisatum* L.

Natural range
Oregon and California.

Cultivated distribution
Rarely grown in cultivation, quite unsuitable for public parks and urban open spaces. A curiosity in some collections in the same way as the Toothache tree *Zanthoxylum americanum* **7**

1
2
3
4
5
6
7

FAMILY Rosaceae

Prunus lusitanica L.

Portugal laurel

Description • Usually an evergreen shrub but sometimes a small tree. Rarely as much as 12 m tall and with stems usually under 60 cm diameter. Always a bushy plant, eventually with spreading branches making it wider than high. When suckers occur a very extensive shrubbery develops covering a large area of ground. The bark is dark brownish-grey and smooth except on very old stems **1**. On young plants and large branches it is almost black. Shoots are green but tinted purple on the sunlit side. Buds are purplish-brown and distinctly pointed. The 8–10 cm leaves are oblong with a slender point, glossy green above and paler below, and distinctly undulating, which enhances the shiny effect **2** and hides the irregular teeth. Although margins are finely round-toothed they appear entire from a distance. Petioles are red and do not have glands, unlike most other cherry species. The crushed foliage does not smell, unlike Common laurel (p116) or the similar looking Bay tree (p118). The summer flowers are spectacular, slender racemes around 20 cm long held stiffly outwards beyond the line of the foliage **3**. Each fragrant flower is about 1 cm across with five white petals. Fruits develop in late summer, green at first **4** then deep red and finally purplish-black. They are 1 cm globose cherries now in much depleted racemes that are soon taken by birds. **Habitat and Ecology** • Originally from hot, dry limestone areas in Southern Europe but now frequent as a planted species further north. Often found in the countryside on estates and in urban areas as an escape from cultivation. Many such individuals have become invasive by suckering. **Similar species** • The Bay tree is superficially similar but quite different on close inspection. There are also various cultivated forms. Subspecies *azorica* (Mouillef.) Franco, is virtually indistinguishable.

Natural range
North West Spain and Portugal, Maderia and the Canary Islands.

Cultivated distribution
Introduced to Northern Europe in 1648. Immediately favoured in gardens as a screen and hedging plant and as a hardy visual substitute for Bay. It was used for game cover and found to be superior to Common laurel for this in exposed places. It tolerates alkaline soils and is still popular with gardeners today. There is a variegated form with white and pinkish leaf markings.

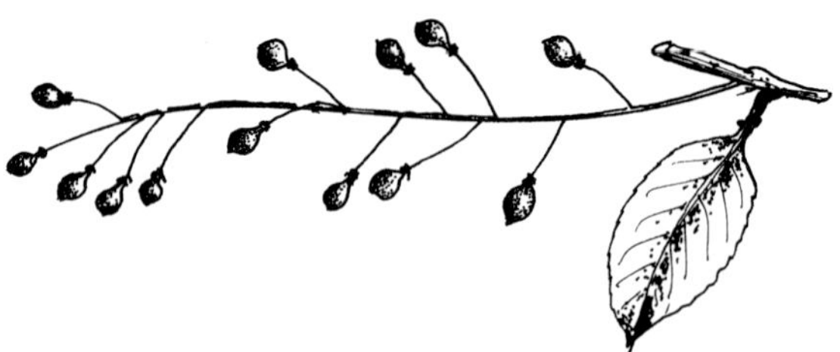

FAMILY Rosaceae

Prunus laurocerasus L.

Common laurel

Description • Although widely thought of as a shrub or hedging plant this species can exceed 6 m in height with stems 30 cm in diameter. It usually has several trunks growing up from ground level **1** where it has been repeatedly cut back and re-grown, something it does very well. The outline is open and rounded, unmistakable from some way off **2**, particularly in winter. Leaves are leathery, like patent leather, with a very glossy upper surface. They are ovate and pointed at both ends, up to 18 cm long and about 6 cm wide with eight parallel veins. The margins are finely serrated but this is not immediately obvious because they are also revolute. Often the whole leaf is rolled downwards towards the edge. Flowers appear in spring briefly transforming the plant from deep shining green to white. They are in erect racemes, 10–15 cm long, each containing around 60 flowers. Individual flowers have five petals arranged in a funnel shape filled with 20 yellow stamens **3**. The flowers are strongly scented so at this time plants are invaded by bees and other nectar-feeding insects. Shoots are green and glabrous at first becoming grey then dark grey. The bark on main stems remains fairly smooth and almost black under the shade of the dense foliage **4**. The fruit is a globose, glossy cherry turning from green to red and finally black **5**. An alternative common name for this tree is Cherry laurel, which is an unfortunate choice of name because it implies edible cherries, but in fact they are poisonous. The leaves are also extremely dangerous: they contain prulaurasin which on fermentation liberates hydrocyanic acid. **Habitat and Ecology** • A component of deciduous forests in hot and arid regions. Often an understorey to Beech woods on mountain sides. **Similar species** • Common laurel is fairly unique but there are a large number of cultivated forms of it with very indistinct characteristics. In some circumstances it can be mistaken for rhododendron.

Natural range
Romania, Bulgaria, Northern Greece and Turkey along the Black Sea coast to Georgia and the Caucasus.

Cultivated distribution
First recorded in Europe in 1574. Brought to Vienna from Constantinople (Istanbul) by the botanist Clusius. It was used medicinally, probably until the time its toxicity was fully realised in the eighteenth century. Popular on shooting estates for game cover and feeding pheasants. Also widely grown in urban situations for hedging because it is able to survive hostile, hot, dusty city conditions and regular clipping. There are at present around 30 named cultivars in the nursery trade.

1

3

2

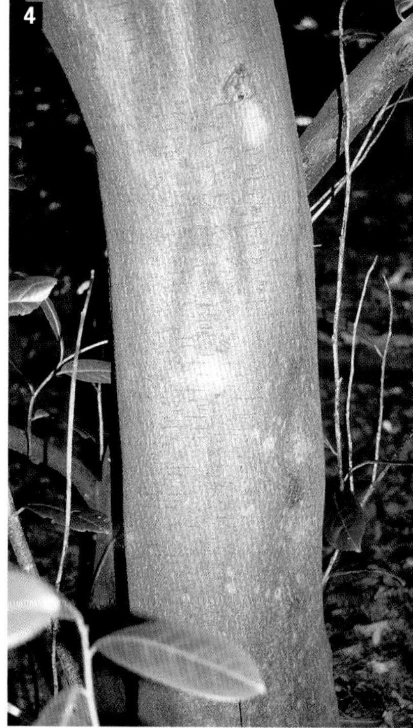
4

FAMILY Magnoliaceae

Magnolia grandiflora L.

Bull bay

Description • Although this is a free-standing tree in its native America it is most often seen in Europe trained up the side of a house or wall **1**. Ultimately it grows to around 12 m tall (30 m in America). It has a strong extensive root system and is very wind resistant. The glossy, 12–24 cm evergreen leaves are oval to obovate tapering towards the base and having a short point. The underside has distinctive, rusty-brown pubescence in the first year which subsequently wears off. Flowers are few and far between on terminal side shoots in late summer. They are large, creamy-white and fragrant **2**. **Habitat and Ecology** • Withstands exposure very well, the wind may tear the leaves but trees usually remain stable. **Similar species** • Reminiscent of Laurel (p116) except for the rufous-backed leaves. There are many other evergreen *Magnolia* species and only specialists in this genus can separate them with confidence. Some exotic *Rhododendrons* also have orange- or brown-backed leaves.

Natural range
North America, from North Carolina to Texas and Florida

Cultivated distribution
Extensively grown in Europe against house walls. There are several outstanding cultivated selections. 'Exmouth' has reddish-brown backed leaves and very fragrant flowers and 'Goliath' is potentially a large short-stemmed tree with big 25 cm flowers.

FAMILY Lauraceae

Laurus nobilis L.

Sweet bay

Description • Familiar as a shrubby pot herb in many gardens this plant is capable of becoming a substantial 20 m tall tree in a sheltered, mild area **3**. Stems in excess of 60 cm diameter are known. Past frost damage dictates that many old individuals have multiple stems **4**. The bark is dark grey and smooth except on old trees. Leaves are glossy evergreen, 6–12 cm long, lanceolate to narrow oval and pointed at each end. Margins are entire but evenly crinkled at first **5**. They are aromatic if crushed. Flowers appear in early spring on previous season's shoots. They are creamy-yellow and in small clusters **6**. **Habitat and Ecology** • Hot, dry hillsides in a mild climate. Thriving further north now in response to current climate change. **Similar species** • The smell of the foliage is unique. Superficially the leaves resemble Portugal laurel (p114).

Natural range

Cultivated distribution
The fresh or dried leaves ha[ve] been used in kitchens since ancient times. In Greece an[d] Rome laurel wreaths were made from this species, wo[rn] by heroes, poets and triumphant sportsmen, a custom revived in the 2004 Olympic games in Athens.

1
2
3
4
5
6

FAMILY Ericaceae

Rhododendron arboreum Sm.

Tree rhododendron

Description • It is relatively easy to recognize a rhododendron bush or tree straight away, but naming the cultivar or even the species is much more difficult. *Rhododendron arboreum* is a tree often with a substantial stem or cluster of stems **1**, up to 1 m in diameter. The leathery evergreen leaves are 10–20 cm long × 3–6 cm wide elliptic, pointed at the tip and tapering towards a rounded base. They are dark lustrous green above, paler green beneath, with light brown or whitish hairs at first. The margins are rolled downwards. Clusters of flower buds develop in the autumn. Flowers appear in the following spring. Some trees are red, others are pink **2**, and white-flowered specimens are known. Rhododendron specialists have split the species into subspecies depending not on different flower colour but on the colour of the hairs on the underside of the leaf. **Habitat and Ecology** • Lower mountain slopes where the climate is cool and wet, on acid ground with water in good supply but not stagnant; often in dense woodland. **Similar species** • It is nearly impossible to identify tree rhododendrons when they are accompanied by other cultivated arboreal hybrids **3**, many of which have originated from this species.

Natural range
Kashmir to southern China, in the Himalayas and also southern India and Sri Lanka.

Cultivated distribution
Seldom planted now, replaced by cultivated hybrids. A few old plants from nineteenth century collections do still survive.

Rhododendron ponticum L.

Rhododendron

Description • Although not generally thought of as a tree this ubiquitous plant can reach 10 m in height but more often forms a massive tangled bush **4**. The evergreen leaves are dark glossy green with a pale, duller yellowish underside. They average about 15 cm long by 4 cm wide, elliptic and pointed towards the tip and base. Current shoots and the prominent over-wintering buds are pale green. Second and subsequent years' shoots are distinctly rust brown. The familiar late spring flowers **5** are usually prolific. The purple colour is tempered by orange spots inside the upper lobe of the flower. **Habitat and Ecology** • Acid, usually peaty, soils determine the habitat of this plant. It is strongly invasive by seeding and layering. **Similar species** • Many cultivated rhododendrons, evergreen *Magnolia* (p118) and Laurel (p116) may appear to be superficially similar.

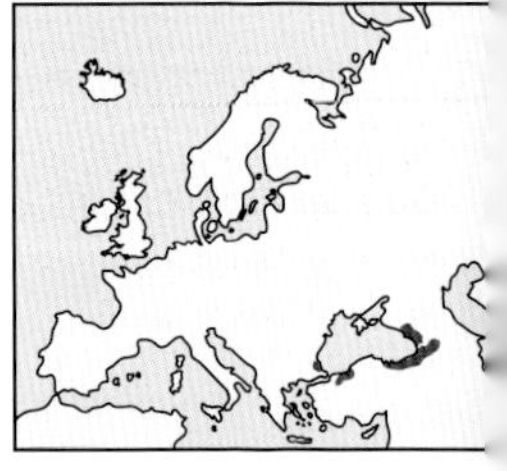

Natural range
Extends eastwards to Turkey through Bulgaria to the Caucasus and the Black Sea Coast.

Cultivated distribution
Widespread in gardens and naturalized or invasive in open countryside where the soil is sufficiently acid. Often failed scions allow rootstock of *Rhododendron ponticum* to invade ornamental collections.

1

2

4

3
5

FAMILY Buxaceae

Buxus balearica Lam.
Balearic Islands box

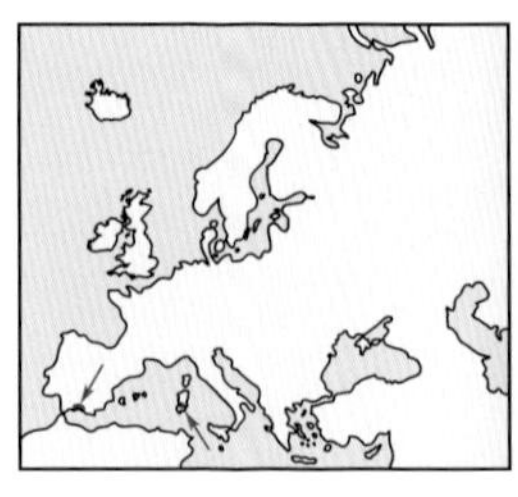

Description • A spreading shrub or erect tree up to about 6–8 m tall **1**. The brilliant, evergreen, glossy leaves are around 4 cm long, oval with a short rounded or notched point and twisted tapered base. In most respects the foliage is like Common box but the leaves are larger, lighter and more luxuriant **2**. The bark is pale pinkish-brown and slightly rough. Stems are usually around 20–30 cm diameter. The flowers in early spring are in the axils of second year leaves **3**. **Habitat and Ecology** • Damp woods especially as an underwood species in partial shade. **Similar species** • Common box, particularly strong-growing cultivars of it such as 'Handsworthensis' and the 'Latifolia' segregate group.

Natural range

Cultivated distribution
Rather overshadowed in cultivation by exotic forms of Common box, many of which are more hardy than this species. Positive identification is also difficult.

Buxus sempervirens L.
Common box

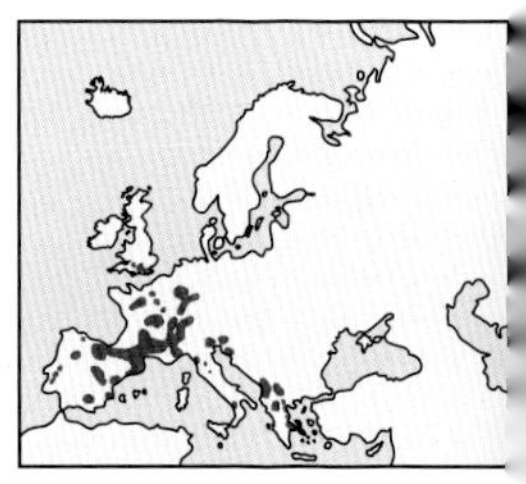

Description • This familiar plant is more often seen as hedging than as a full-grown tree. It can however develop a good stem some 20–30 cm in diameter **5** and reach heights of around 8 m, like those at Box Hill in Surrey **4**. The wood is sought after and is so valuable that trees have been cut down many times and encouraged to regrow as coppice. The bark is pale, yellowish-brown with small fissures, ridges and scaly plates eventually forming an intricate almost geometric pattern **5** and **4**. In semi-shade, this tree's preferred environment, stems are often mossy and green with microscopic epiphytes. Young shoots are dull green and more or less square in cross section. In a year or two they become pale brown. Most of the small oval leaves are in flat sprays facing up to the light. Very dark, glossy green above and pale, dull green below. Buds are slender 3–5 mm long running parallel to the shoot. The foliage has a distinctive smell reminiscent of tom cats. Male flowers in second year leaf axils are in yellow clusters **3** exactly like Balearic Islands box. Female flowers occur on or close to secondary shoot tips developing in one season into pale green, three-horned capsules containing glossy black, 5 mm seeds. When ripe some seeds are expelled with great force while others seem to get stuck and left behind for another year. **Habitat and Ecology** • Shady woodlands or open countryside. For an evergreen this is a very hardy, frost-tolerant species **6**. **Similar species** • Cultivated forms and Balearic Islands box (above).

Natural range
The status of Common box in Britain remains uncertain. Local populations on chalk and limestone south of the River Thames may be native but Neolithic introductions cannot be ruled out.

Cultivated distribution
Nurtured in the past for its valuable timber. Numerous cultivated garden forms have been developed for hedging, topiary and parterre.

1

2

3

4

5

6

FAMILY Bignoniaceae

Catalpa bignonioides Walt.
Indian bean tree

Description • The best-known of a valuable genus of deciduous amenity trees with large, paper thin leaves, bold, frilly summer flowers and curious fruit like runner beans. It is around 10 m tall and wide **1**. The bark is pinkish-brown, smooth at first then developing a network of shallow ridges **2**. Leaves are up to 25 cm long and around 16 cm wide, broadly ovate with a slender point and rounded truncate base. Petioles are 15 cm long protecting a tiny, almost black bud. Flowers are tubular in open terminal panicles up to 30 cm long. They are about 4 cm across, mainly white with red and purple markings **3**. Soon clusters of long, pendulous seed pods develop **4**. **Habitat and Ecology** • Open, moist woodlands, clearings and road sides. **Similar species** • Other *Catalpa* species (below).

Natural range
South East USA, Georgia and Florida to Mississippi.

Cultivated distribution
Widely grown in Europe as a city amenity tree. Withstands dust and dirt and thrives on the moist soil under paving.

Catalpa ovata G. Don
Yellow catalpa

Description • A shapely tree up to 10 m tall with a stem rarely larger than 50 cm diameter **5**. The 20 cm leaves are broad ovate with three to five small abrupt points. The underside is hairy with floral nectaries in the vein axils. Buds are small and purplish brown. Terminal, 25 cm panicles of flowers appear in mid- to late summer **6**. Each individual tubular flower is creamy white with yellow and purple markings. Bean-pods are 25 cm long, green tinged with purplish-brown **7**. **Habitat and Ecology** • Damp woodlands. **Similar species** • Other *Catalpa* species.

Natural range
China.

Cultivated distribution
This tree is less likely to shed branches than Indian bean. The cultivar 'Flavescens' has superior, deeper yellow flowers; an ideal garden tree where space permits.

Catalpa fargesii Bureau
Farges catalpa

Description • A 10 m tree with up-swept branches, a straight stem **9** and thin, grey, flaky bark. The leaves are ovoid with a drawn out pointed tip and rounded base. Occasionally there are one or two additional points or small lobes half way along the margin **8**. Flowers in terminal panicles are pale pink marked with brownish-red and yellow. Seed-pods are often flushed with purplish-brown. **Habitat and Ecology** • Cultivated since ancient times in China. **Similar species** • The hybrid *Catalpa x erubescens* Carr., which has similar foliage, is more vigorous and will rapidly outgrow its space **10**.

Natural range
Western China.

Cultivated distribution
Rare in cultivation in Europe then often represented by forma *duclouxii* (Dode) Gilmour, which has more distinctly lobed leaves.

1
2
3
4
5
6
7
8
9
10

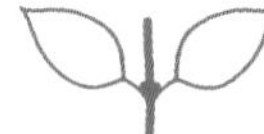

FAMILY Cornaceae

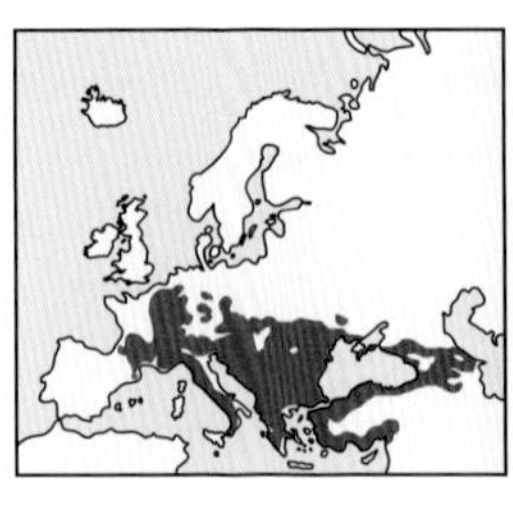

Natural range

Cultivated distribution
A common winter flowering garden plant, often intended to be a shrub but outgrows its allotted space very quickly. In dry areas the leaves tend to wilt in summer.

Cornus mas L.
Cornelian cherry

Description • A distinctive, rounded tree or large shrub with angular, often tangled, low branches reaching the ground. Stems may be up to 30 cm diameter **1**. The bark is pale brown to grey becoming coarsely ridged into scaly plates reminiscent of an old Pear tree (p214). The angular shoots are deep green at first turning light purplish-brown in one season **2**. The 6 mm flowers, the best identification feature, begin to appear in late winter on completely bare branches. They are yellow with four bracts and four stamens in clusters of up to 15 all emerging from a single bud **2**. The 6–10 cm leaves, which appear after the flowers, are oval with an abrupt point and rounded, sometimes a subcordate base on a short petiole. They each have five pairs of prominent curved main veins **3**. The fruit, although large, 2–3 cm long, is seldom noticed during the summer amongst the green foliage but towards the autumn it turns brilliant, glossy scarlet and is difficult to miss **4**. It is cherry like with a 2–3 cm stalk and a single seed. **Habitat and Ecology** • Scrub woodland, clearings and on disturbed ground. In nature, several individuals often combine to form a continuous thicket. **Similar species** • Other cultivated Dogwoods in summer when flowers are absent.

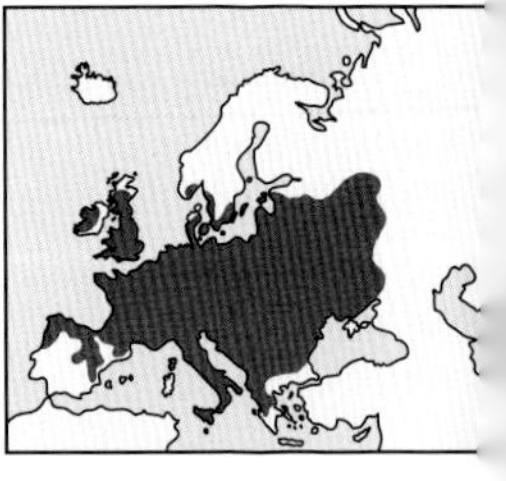

Natural range

Cultivated distribution
Not usually cultivated but generally encouraged in the countryside for its environmental benefits. The hard wood was formerly use to make skewers and good-quality charcoal. An oil was once pressed from the berri for lamps.

Cornus sanguinea L.
Common dogwood

Description • Native in Northern Europe this plant is usually a shrub or part of a field hedge. However, given space and time it will make a small, upright tree. The shoots are reddish-black and show up as distinctive red sections in late winter hedgerows. Leaves are oval with a short, blunt point and small, marginal teeth on some vigorous growth. They have distinctive curved main veins, usually three, in pairs or slightly staggered. Flowers are pale green with four bracts **5**. They are followed by clusters of black berries **6**. The autumn foliage colour is very dark radiant purple. **Habitat and Ecology** • Hedgerows and waste ground particularly on lime-rich sites. **Similar species** • Other Dogwoods including *Cornus alba* L., also some black fruited *Viburnum*.

1
2
3
4
5
6

FAMILY Oleaceae

Syringa vulgaris L.

Common lilac

Description • Seldom seen as a wild plant in Northern Europe but very common as a cultivated garden plant. It is a large, vigorous shrub or small, suckering tree up to 7 m tall with multiple stems and a more or less rounded outline **1**. Escapes from cultivation are frequent and Lilac often appears to be naturalized in the countryside **2** and in many areas forms a distinctive component of hedgerows. Most occurrences can be traced to abandoned shrubberies and dumped garden rubbish. Individual stems over 20 cm diameter are rare. The bark is grey-brown, mostly smooth but very old stems become fissured. Shoots are slightly angular with ridges running between plump, bright green buds **3**. Terminal buds are often in pairs and squarish in cross-section. The shoot itself is brown with a thin, deciduous, silvery skin that gives it a greyish sheen. Leaves are thin textured, glabrous ovate to round, with an acute point and cordate base, about 9 cm long and entire **4**. Petioles are 3 cm long. Larger, luxuriant foliage occurs on plants that have recently been cut back and re-grown. Flowers are characteristic, dense terminal, 15–25 cm panicles of numerous small flowers which appear with the young leaves in spring. The wild form is light mauve and scented. Cultivated plants range from deep reddish-purple to white. The fruit is 2 cm long, flat and green, eventually splitting to release seed. **Habitat and Ecology** • Mountain sides and deep valleys, thriving in a relatively harsh continental climate and tolerant of alkaline soils. **Similar species** • This is a large genus of trees and shrubs many of them are very similar in appearance. The cultivars of the species *vulgaris* are strong, erect shrubs and trees which can only be identified safely when in flower. Many old plants eventually revert back to something resembling the wild form.

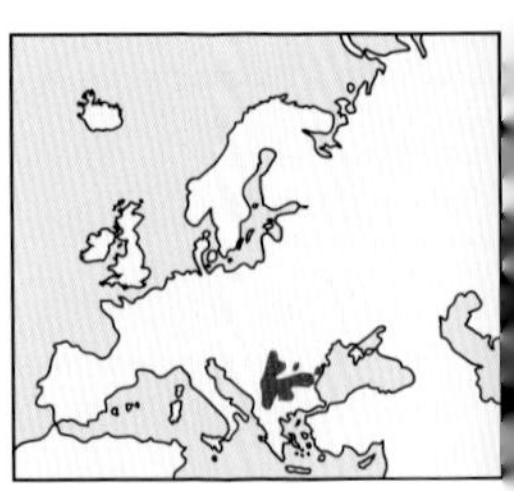

Natural range

Cultivated distribution
Seldom grown as a wild species but often found as a naturalized seeding or reverted escape. It was introduced to Northern Europe in the sixteenth century. In the early twentieth century, many named forms were distributed especially by French nurserymen. Over 30 named cultivars have existed, distinguished only by the colour of the single or double flowers. Cultivar propagation is a complicated procedure, traditionally by root cuttings on Privet (p132).

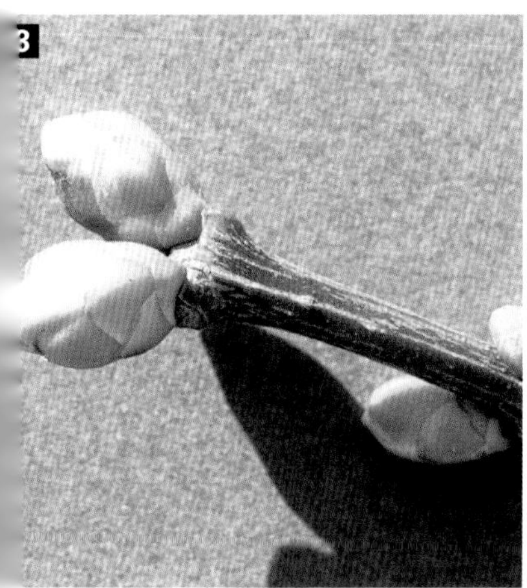
3

4

FAMILY Celastraceae

Euonymus europaeus L.

Spindle tree

Description • This native species in Northern Europe is a small tree seldom over 6 m tall with a 25 cm maximum diameter stem [1]. In the open it develops a neat, rounded outline but most often it is an understorey shrub in deciduous woodland so its shape is dictated by the amount of light and space available. It is probably at its best round the edge of clearings, along field sides and adjacent to open sunny rides. Good specimens can also be found in overgrown hedgerows. The bark is pale grey-brown, slightly fissured and ridged. Shoots are dark green and distinctly four-angled. Vigorous shoots develop thin, pale brown, corky ridges along the four corners. Brown and green buds are 2–3 mm long in opposite pairs held flat against the shoot. The leaves are more or less ovate with an acute point and wedge-shaped base. Margins have regular, blunt, rounded teeth [2] and a short 1 cm petiole. Some individual plants sheltered from the wind colour well in the autumn, turning very pale yellowish-green flushed with pink and red. In the open, leaves usually blow away before colouring. The late spring flowers in small clusters completely cover some trees [3]. Each individual flower has four pale yellow, 8 mm petals and four short stamens with brownish-purple anthers [4]. The main characteristic feature of Spindle is its late autumn and early winter ripe fruits. They are a brilliant, artificial looking pink [2]. If this were not enough the four segments eventually split to reveal orange-skinned 5 mm seeds [5]. Fruits and seeds cling on to the shoots for some time after the leaves have fallen. **Habitat and Ecology** • A long-established component of the lowland agricultural landscape. **Similar species** • Superficially when not in fruit reminiscent of Blackthorn (p144) in hedgerows, but quite different on close inspection.

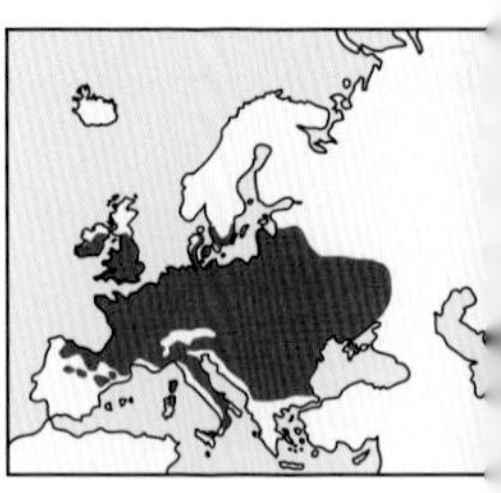

Natural range

Cultivated distribution
Probably never cultivated bu certainly managed in the wil in the past. The very hard wood had several important uses in the rural economy such as skewers and spindles hence the name. The dried powdered fruits were used tc treat lice. Today it is frequently included in urbar amenity planting schemes especially along trunk roads, partly on its own merit as ar autumn colour feature and partly to satisfy a political requirement to plant native species. The whole plant is poisonous.

1
2
3
4
5

FAMILY Oleaceae

Ligustrum lucidum Aiton f.

Chinese privet

Description • A 15 m, billowing evergreen tree **1** when growing on a sheltered site. A species noticeably benefiting from current climate change to warmer conditions in Northern Europe and the artificial heat generated by cities. The generally straight, pale grey stem remains smooth for many years, eventually developing sinuous extended buttresses. Buds are 2 mm long in opposite and decussate stalked pairs. The 7 cm oval, very glossy leaves are entire with a pointed tip and tapered, pointed or rounded base on a 1–2 cm long petiole. When crushed they have a distinctive privet smell most noticeable when a privet hedge (*Ligustrum ovalifolium* Hassk.) is being clipped on a hot day. The small, tubular, off-white, four-petalled flowers occur in prominent terminal panicles in summer **2**. In a good year, numerous clusters of 1 cm, bloomed, purplish black berries are produced. **Habitat and Ecology** • A woodland species, but tolerant of open conditions if not exposed. **Similar species** • *Ligustrum vulgare* L. Common privet is a native European species barely large enough to be regarded as a tree **3**. It has smaller leaves that in severe winters are semi-evergreen. Tough woody stems seldom exceed 10 cm diameter **4**, but they form a tangled mass which is useful to wildlife and provides shelter, even near the sea. The white, nectar-rich flowers **5** attract numerous insects. Another close relative of the privet genus is *Olea europaea* L., the olive from southern Europe **6**.

Natural range
Central China, but obscured by cultivation over centuries.

Cultivated distribution
Chinese privet is widely planted world-wide as an ornamental tree but remains infrequent in Britain.

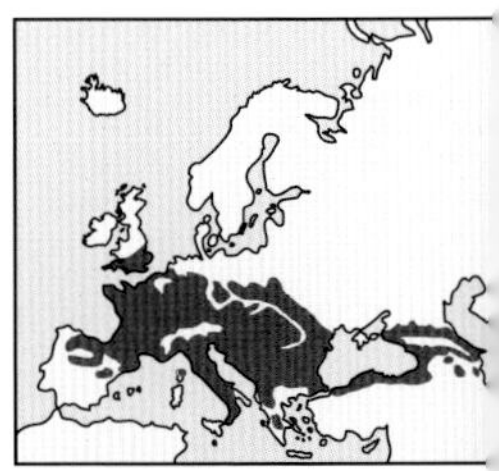

Natural range
Common privet

FAMILY Myrtaceae

Myrtus luma Mol. (Luma apiculata (DC) Burret)

Orange-barked myrtle

Description • A decorative little tree seldom over 8 m tall **7**. With distinctive orange, pale brown and cream coloured peeling bark **8**. The opposite evergreen leaves are dark and glossy. Only 2–3 cm long, oval to elliptic with an abrupt point and tapering base. The short petiole is yellowish-pink. Fragrant, four-petalled, 1–5 cm flowers are white sometimes tinted pink. Numerous stamens fill the cup formed by the petals **9**. Fruits are 1 cm, fleshy, dark purple berries. **Habitat and Ecology** • Cool, wet forest. **Similar species** • Superficially like box (p122) or *Phillyrea* (p282) when not flowering. The stems resemble some *Arbutus* species (p110 and 140) and *Stuartia pseudocamellia* Maxim.

Natural range
Chile and Argentina in temperate rain forests.

Cultivated distribution
Limited to gardens in mild damp areas in Northern Europe mostly towards the Atlantic coast. Also grown a a conservatory plant.

1
2
3
4
5
6
7
8
9

FAMILY Fagaceae

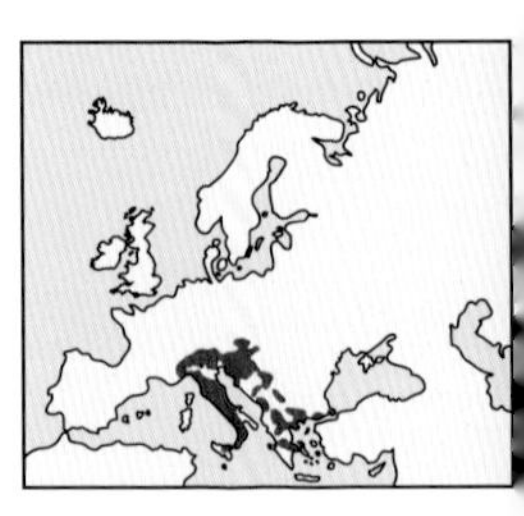

Castanea sativa Mill.

Sweet chestnut

Description • A large, or very large, tree often with a massive stem up to 2 m diameter. It grows rapidly to around 20 m then some individuals in the right environment continue to greater heights. A tree 36 m tall has been recorded in Scotland. The outline is rounded or tiered with several subordinate domed sections **1**. In woodland it produces long, straight, clean stems **2**. Very old trees tend to break up and become picturesque, or grotesque **3**. Individuals over 700 years of age are known. By this time they usually consist of a jumble of layered reclining branches and very little of the original tree. The bark is light brown or purplish-grey and smooth for 30–50 years developing cracks from the base which eventually turn into deep ridges and furrows. These spiral (either way) or run vertically up the stem **3**. The foliage is deep green in summer and affords good shade. Individual leaves are distinctive, like thick paper and slightly leathery, 20 cm long, broadly elliptic with about 20 prominent parallel veins. Each of these terminates in a pronounced softly spined 'saw' tooth. Petioles are yellow, about 3 cm long and joined to a stout, angular, brown often slightly bloomed twig. In early summer flowers appear sometimes in great profusion **4**. They consist of slender, stiff catkins that usually support a few female flowers near the base and male flowers towards the tip **5**. All female trees are known. Heavily flowering trees have a strong, rather overpowering unpleasant smell. Fruits are green, four-sided, heavily spined husks up to 6 cm across usually occurring in clusters **6**. Each husk contains one or more familiar, glossy brown, edible chestnuts **7**. **Habitat and Ecology** • A tree of moist, well-drained acid ground forming thickets and open woodlands. Often managed in the past as coppice on a 10–70 year cycle. **Similar species** • A few mostly obscure Chestnut-leaved oaks such as *Quercus pontica* K. Koch, the Armenian oak.

Natural range

Cultivated distribution

The early history of this tree is uncertain. Its range appears to have been extended northwards by the Romans who are credited with its introduction to Britain 2000 years ago, probably for the edible nuts. The Greeks may have introduced the species to Rome in the first place. In addition to nuts, Sweet chestnut provides cleft or round poles of every size that are extremely durable out of doors and in contact with the ground. The timber is fairly straight grained over short lengths and as strong as Oak but it is difficult to produce in large sizes without cracks and shake defects. The best fruit-producing trees are growing in the south of Europe.

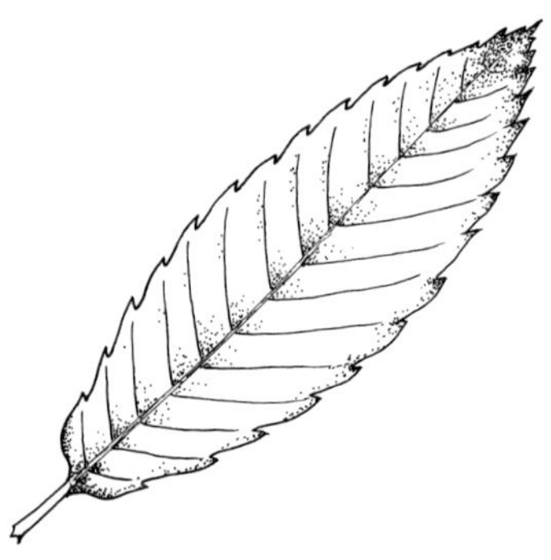

1
2
3
4
5
6
7

FAMILY Fagaceae

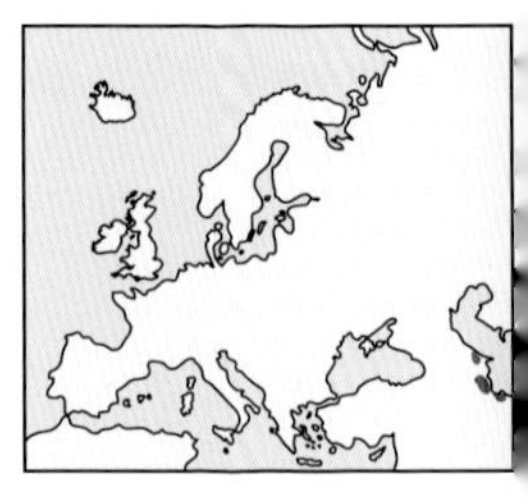

Quercus castaneifolia C.A. Mey.
Chestnut-leaved oak

Description • An elegant tree up to 25 m tall with long branches and an open uneven outline **1**. The stem is greenish-brown, smooth at first, gradually becoming lightly fissured showing pale orange-brown under bark in the cracks **2**. Old trees become rougher with grey scaly ridges. Shoots are slightly hairy at first becoming glabrous in a single season. The leaves are distinctive but not typically like oak. They are oblong, up to 16 cm long with 8–12 pairs of triangular lobes **3**. Each glandular point is positioned at the end of a parallel vein. The almost sessile acorns are 2–3 cm long, half enclosed by the cup which has recurved scales. **Habitat and Ecology** • Woodland in hot, dry regions and on mountain slopes. **Similar species** • There are several 'chestnut-leaved' oaks including *Quercus variabilis* Blume.

Natural range
Iran and the Caucasus Mountains.

Cultivated distribution
First cultivated around 1840 but never widely planted. Closely related to Turkey oak (p302) so the quality of the wood may be suspect.

Quercus trojana Webb.
Macedonian oak

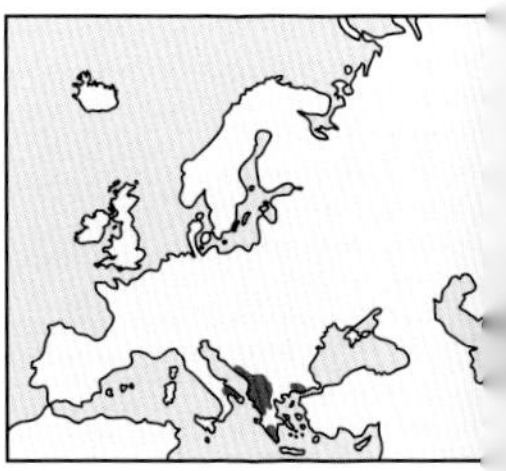

Description • A semi-evergreen 'Chestnut leaved' oak around 15–20 m tall with a thick stem up to 80 cm diameter **4**. The bark is reminiscent of an old Ash tree (p408) with flattish, grey, vertical ridges and pinkish-orange young bark showing along the base of shallow fissures. The leaves are oblong, 5–9 cm long with 6–10 pairs of triangular lobes each with a sharp bristle tipped point at the end of a straight, parallel vein **5**. The acorns are sessile around 2 cm long almost concealed inside the distinctive scaly cup **6**. **Habitat and Ecology** • Open, mixed woodland often growing below larger deciduous trees. **Similar species** • *Quercus libani* Oliv., Lebanon oak. *Quercus coccifera* L., Kermes oak, which is smaller in all its parts and completely evergreen **7**. The leaves are variable, some resemble spiky holly, others are flat and less spined. This species is seldom more than a stunted bush but it is environmentally valuable in its native habitat.

Natural range

Cultivated distribution
Rare in cultivation except in specialist oak collections. There appears to be various provenance types affecting performance and size in Northern Europe.

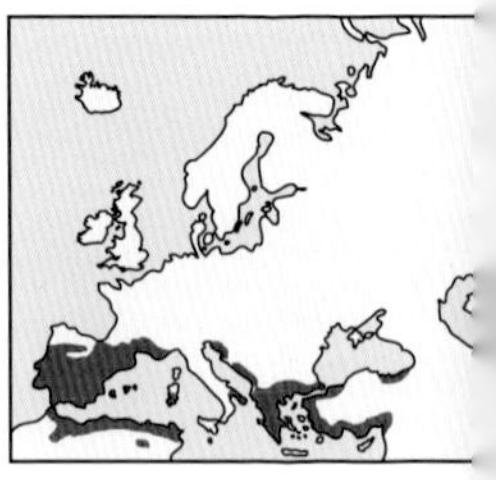

Natural range
Quercus coccifera

1
2
3
4
5
6
7

FAMILY Ulmaceae

Zelkova carpinifolia (Pall.) K. Koch

Caucasian elm

Description • Ultimately a massive 30 m tall tree usually developing an unmistakable crown consisting of huge, multiple, erect stems **1**. The bark is smooth and grey reminiscent of Hornbeam (p172) **2**. Shoots are slender, greenish then glossy, stiffly angled between the alternate, dark brown buds. Leaves are rough to the touch like Elm but less hairy. They are oval with a blunt point and rounded, slightly oblique base **3**. Each one is 6–9 cm long with around nine pairs of evenly spaced, parallel veins leading to the point of a prominent, rounded tooth. Petioles are very short, often less than 5 mm long. Flowers are indistinct but males may be numerous in young leaf axils. Females are less frequent and develop in one season into 6 mm stout, ovoid nutlets borne near to the shoot tips. **Habitat and Ecology** • Mixed broadleaved forest. **Similar species** • Some Elm species and superficially *Nothofagus nervosa* (p198).

Natural range
Eastern Turkey, Iran and around the Caspian Sea.

Cultivated distribution
Uncommon as an ornamental tree. Requires a huge amount of space and has oblique branch forks that give the impression of being unsafe, even if they are not. Sometimes catches Dutch Elm Disease.

Zelkova serrata (Thumb.) Makino

Keaki

Description • Like Caucasian elm but slightly smaller in height and stem diameter. The branches are less vertical but equally numerous. The bark is smooth and grey on young trees **4**, but with age random fissures develop and eventually a few, small isolated scales exfoliate revealing distinctive patches of orange inner bark **5**. These are never frequent and always widely spaced even on a very old tree. The shoots are red-brown, very slender and lax. Buds have red outer scales. Leaves are ovate or oblong-ovate up to 12 cm long, sharply serrated with a narrow, acute tip and rounded or subcordate base **6**. There are 8–14 pairs of more or less parallel, pale coloured veins. Flowers and fruit are insignificant. **Habitat and Ecology** • Mixed deciduous woodlands. **Similar species** • Other *Zelkova* species and some Elms but mature bark is distinctive.

Natural range
Japan, Korea and North East China.

Cultivated distribution
Not common in cultivation, the scaly bark is of minor interest. Susceptible to Dutch Elm Disease.

1
2
3
4
5
6

FAMILY Ericaceae

(see also p110)

Natural range

Cultivated distribution

This is a plant that is clearly benefiting from current climate change to warmer conditions. Increasingly grown in gardens, especially the cultivar 'Rubra', which has pink flowers and abundant fruit.

Arbutus unedo L

Strawberry tree or Killarney strawberry tree

Description • A beautiful small evergreen tree 7–10 m tall, rarely more, with a rounded or billowing outline usually on a short stem **1**. The bark, unlike other more colourful Strawberry trees growing in Northern Europe, is rough and scaly, dull pink at first then grey-brown **2**. Old trees may be dark brown particularly when wet with rain. Young shoots are pale pink on the sunlit side and greenish on the shaded side, glandular hairy for a short time then glabrous. Leaves are dark green, stiff and leathery, oval to elliptic and pointed at both ends. Size varies greatly between 5 and 10 cm long. Margins are distinctly toothed **3**, although occasionally some leaves are entire. The heather-like, 6 mm, white or blushed pink flowers in clusters of up to 20 appear from late summer until the first winter frosts **3**. The 2 cm round fruits from the previous year's flowers also appear at this time **4**, and are a distinctive feature of this tree. They are green, ripening to orange and red. These 'strawberries' are edible but unpleasant as the name unedo implies 'you only need one'. **Habitat and Ecology** • Inhabits mild, wet places in Ireland but also hot, dry, open scrub in Southern Europe. **Similar species** • Other *Arbutus* and the leaves of some *Photinia* (p210) and *Osmanthus delavayi* Franch.

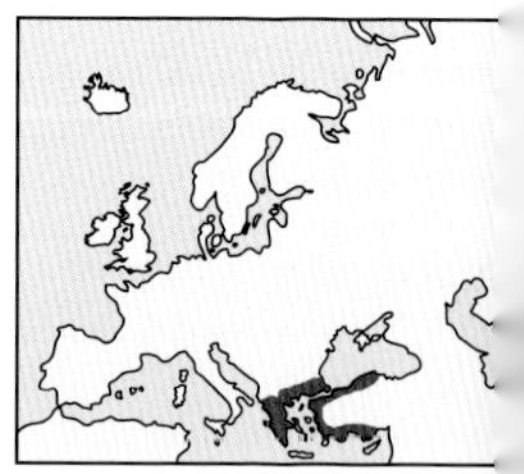

Natural range

Cultivated distribution

Seldom recognized in cultivation because it is easily confused with either of its parents.

Arbutus x andrachnoides Link

Hybrid strawberry tree

Description • A spontaneous cross between the Strawberry tree (above) and the Greek strawberry tree (p110). A variable hybrid with entire or toothed leaves. Most features are intermediate between the parents and vary from tree to tree. Height is around 10 m, bark is brightly coloured and peeling **5**. Leaves are oval to elliptic usually with pointed teeth or almost entire; sometimes with a flanged petiole. The flowers are white in clusters with distinctive pink stalks **6**. They appear in spring or autumn or both. Fruits are smaller than Killarney strawberry tree and not so rough. They turn from green to orange in the summer. **Habitat and Ecology** • Warm, dry, limestone hillsides typically in Cyprus and Greece. **Similar species** • Other *Arbutus*. Difficult to positively identify.

1
2
3
4
5
6

FAMILY Rosaceae

Prunus avium L.

Wild cherry or Gean

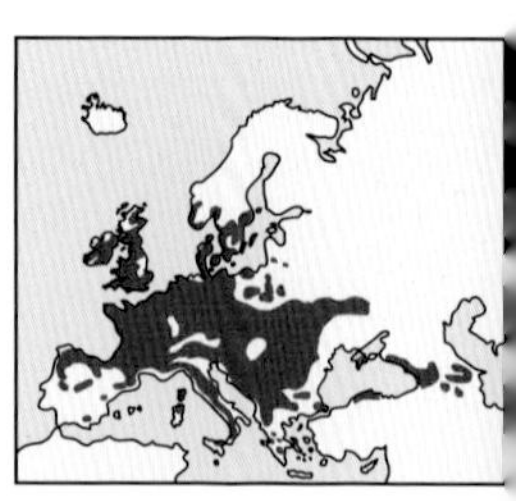

Natural range

Description • The alternative name Gean used in Scotland comes from an Italian name Guina, a local variety of cherry. This is the largest cherry tree in Europe, specimens 30 m tall are known and stems often exceed 60 cm diameter. It has an untidy outline with spreading branches **1**. Where there is no vegetation control, such as cattle grazing, it suckers freely from the shallow roots. In the space of 20–30 years a single tree will become a copse or small wood all consisting of one original clone **2**. Cherry bark has distinctive horizontal bands of purplish-brown and pinkish-brown. At first it is lustrous, then lines of corky lenticels develop and finally the stem becomes craggy, grey and slightly peeling around the edges of broad, flat plates **3**. If damaged the stem or main branches may exude clear yellowish gum, a defence against airborne disease. Buds are reddish-brown, oval and pointed, alternate along the stem and clustered at the tip. The elliptical leaves have distinct teeth, a drawn out point and rounded base. The slender petioles have one or two distinct glands. In the autumn, for a brief period, the whole tree turns crimson-purple before the leaves fall. In spring, clusters of pendulous flowers appear on spur shoots with the new, fresh green leaves **4**. Each individual flower on a long stalk is 2 cm across with five white petals and numerous yellow stamens. Fruits are familiar but small cherries, about 1.5 cm across with a relatively large stone. They are sweet when ripe but do not contain very much that is edible **5**. Birds quickly strip the trees bare usually before the fruit is ripe. Stones that pass through birds are said to germinate quickly the following spring. **Habitat and Ecology** • Generally a tree of fairly rich, fertile agricultural land although it can be found on hillsides and in moderately exposed conditions. Some woods that have originated as suckers from a single plant are self-sterile. **Similar species** • Out of flower the double form ‘Plena’ is identical **6**. Some other ornamental cultivars are similar looking and some revert to this species when they are grafted on to wild cherry rootstocks.

Cultivated distribution
The early history of this tree in cultivation is interesting. Its taxonomy was only finally sorted out in 1940. Some authorities consider it to have been wild only in West Asia and introduced to Europe by early man. It has been ‘improved’ for fruit and for ornament over many years. The timber is highly decorative. It is in great demand for good-quality furniture and musical instruments. It burns with ‘perfumed’ smoke and formerly smokers used to cherish their cherrywood pipes.

FAMILY Rosaceae

Prunus spinosa L.

Blackthorn or Sloe

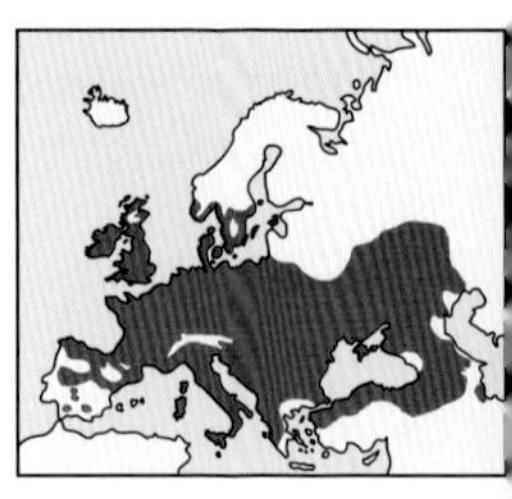

Natural range
Extends from Europe into Northern Asia.

Cultivated distribution
Not usually cultivated but existing trees are managed in some areas. Straight sucker stems 5–10 years old make excellent walking sticks. Sloes are harvested to flavour gin and also make 'hedgerow' jelly. Blackthorn is an ancestor of domestic plums. As a hedge species it makes a good barrier but is more difficult to manage than Hawthorn (p328). If not properly cut the bottom soon opens up enough to let stock through, suckers also invade field margins.

Description • An abundant small tree 6m tall, or a low sprawling shrub or a thicket. Suckers are produced freely so a single plant can in time become a tangled wood or overgrown hedge **1**. Crooked stems and strong woody thorns bind branches and twigs together into an impenetrable barrier. The bark is reddish-black, smooth at first with orange lenticels then peeling into thin, curly scales and eventually becoming rough and fissured **2**. Stems are seldom straight although vigorous young suckers do often grow vertically for a time. New sucker shoots are deep green whereas young growth on the tree itself is brown with thin, peeling, transparent, silvery skin. Flowers appear in profusion in early spring before the leaves **3**, but not quite so early as Cherry plum (p148). Each 1.5 cm short stalked flower has five white petals and white stamens with deep crimson anthers. The stigma is pale yellowish-green. The calyx is light red **4**. Some of the flowers produce fruit, the sloe, a globose plum about 1.5 cm across with juicy, astringent pulp round a single, light brown stone. The outer skin is purplish-black bloomed with white like a black grape **5**. The leaves are obovate to narrowly oval with a blunt point and a broad, wedge shaped base. Margins have small, evenly spaced, soft teeth. The upper side is dull dark green and reticulate while the underside is lighter and slightly shiny. The foliage is pubescent at first but all trace of hairs will be gone by the end of the summer. In the autumn some trees produce good orange autumn colour **6**. **Habitat and Ecology** • A native North European species providing dense, low-level cover for wildlife on woodland edges, where woody plants are invading grassland and on sea cliffs. Totally hardy, windfirm and moderately salt resistant. **Similar species** • Frequently confused with Cherry plum and Damson (p150).

1
2
3
4
5
6

FAMILY Rosaceae

Prunus padus L.

Bird cherry

Description • A native European tree around 17 m tall, often much less, with a stem up to 80 cm diameter but usually consisting of multiple stems in one place surrounded by a scattering of spaced out suckers which, if left alone, eventually become a substantial thicket **1**. Occasionally single stems do occur **2**. The bark is dark, glossy red-brown at first, becoming progressively more grey with age but usually remaining smooth. A diagnostic feature is the pungent and rather unpleasant smell when young bark is scratched. It is reminiscent of Common buckthorn (p278). Branches are ascending then pendulous at the extremities on mature trees. The alternate buds are sharply pointed and pressed against the shoot. Leaves are 6–10 cm long elliptic or obovate with a very short point, rounded base and finely toothed margin. There are 10–12 pairs of main veins that are impressed into the upper surface and prominent below. The upper side in particular has a leathery texture, it is dark dull green. The underside is pale green. The 2 cm petiole has two or more distinctive glands close to the leaf blade. A feature shared with most deciduous Cherry species. Flowers appear with the young leaves in spectacular 7–14 cm racemes which are upright in bud and lax when in full flower **3**. Individual flowers are white with five petals up to 15 mm across. They are strongly scented like almonds and attract numerous flying insects. Fruits develop from only a few of the original 15–35 flowers, well spaced out along the stem of the inflorescence **4**. They ripen to purplish-black but remain astringent to taste. Birds relish them so they are taken off the tree as soon as they ripen. **Habitat and Ecology** • Woodland edges and in pure thickets or small woods of the tree's own making. Occasionally found in hedgerows but usually grubbed out by cereal farmers to prevent the spread of disease into cornfields. This species tolerates cold exposed conditions and thrives in the far north of the region. **Similar species** • There are several exotic Cherries with a similar flower arrangement. Most of them are rare. Also there are several cultivated forms of Bird cherry. 'Watereri' in particular is an outstanding shapely tree **5**, regularly flowering in great profusion **6**.

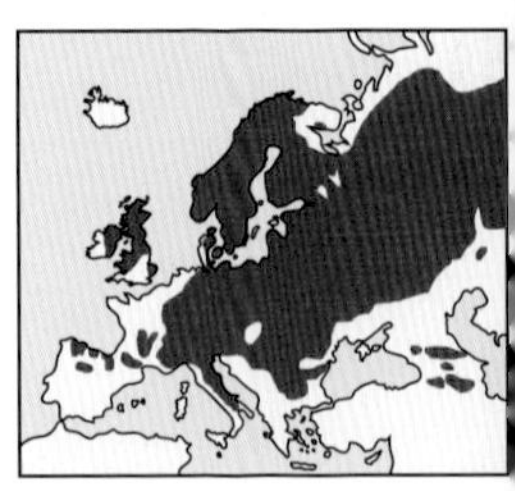

Natural range

Cultivated distribution
The wild species has probably never been cultivated, generally in rural areas it has been discouraged. The variety *commutata* Dipp. is an Asiatic form first cultivated in Western Europe in 1880. It forms a larger spreading tree usually with a single stem. A double-flowered form appeared in 1892 and a pink-flowered form 'Colorata' was found in Sweden in 1953.

1
2
3
4
5
6

FAMILY Rosaceae

Prunus cerasifera Ehrh.

Cherry plum or Myrobalan plum

Description • Often mistaken for Blackthorn (p144) in late winter when it comes into flower [1], this 8 m tall tree is probably much more common than it seems. The blossom actually appears 2–3 weeks before Blackthorn. Stems seldom exceed 30 cm in diameter. The bark is dark purplish-brown, smooth at first becoming rough with horizontal ridges then developing scaly, vertical ridges and fissures [2]. Light orange-brown under bark shows up in the cracks. Shoots are slender often tangled and angular with short horizontal spurs but not sharp spines. The leaves are oval or ovate 4–6 cm long and pointed at both ends. Flowers are 2 cm across with five white petals mostly on spur shoots [3]. Fruit appears in late summer, consisting of 3 cm, single-stoned edible plums ripening through yellow to red [4]. The subspecies *divaricata* is similar except that it only has yellow fruit [5]. **Habitat and Ecology** • Only found now in a semi-wild state as a relic of old orchards and homesteads. It thrives in open country on field margins and along woodland edges. **Similar species** • The whole plum and Damson group of the genus *Prunus.*

Natural range
Considerably obscured by past cultivation. The subspecies divaricata is native in the Balkans and Black Sea coastal areas.

Cultivated distribution
Unfortunately neglected as a orchard tree in the modern age. It is a perfectly hardy, deliciously edible fruit, cast aside in favour of mass-produced, imported plums. There are ornamental forms in cultivation (below).

Prunus cerasifera 'Pissardii'

Purple-leaved plum

Description • A striking tree up to 8 m tall with stems around 40 cm diameter at maturity. In winter it is exactly like the species but in early spring copious amounts of pale pink blossom appear [6]. Over a period of 2–3 weeks bright, copper coloured leaves unfold, interspersed amongst the flowers. This is a superb little tree in blossom [7] and in leaf [8]. Individual flowers are 2–3 cm across with five pink petals and a carmine red centre [9]. **Habitat and Ecology** • A rare sport of the species occupying a similar environment. **Similar species** • Superficially like Copper beech (p86) and various other purple leaved shrubs.

Cultivated distribution
Frequently planted, often recently as a fashionable hedge. There are also superic ornamental clones. 'Nigra' h almost black leaves and stem 'Vesuvius' is probably the same thing, dating back to 1916. 'Diversifolia' has lobed or misshapen leaves. 'Rosea' has superb deep pink flower and bronze leaves which gradually turn green throug the summer. The foliage can be spiny.

1
2
3
4
5
6
7
8
9

FAMILY Rosaceae

Prunus domestica L.

Plum

Description • How this tree is managed affects its ultimate size and shape. Orchards are usually intensively pruned and harvested so trees are rarely more than 6–8 m tall **1**. In a semi-wild situation individuals over 12 m tall are known, with a 30–40 cm diameter stem. It is probably impossible to identify a truly wild plum now, although the Damson (below) comes close to it. The bark is grey-brown becoming fissured in old age. Leaves are 5–10 cm long, elliptic or oval, toothed with an acute point and rounded or wedge-shaped base. The underside is distinctly grey-green with prominent, pale pubescent veins. Petioles are grooved along the upper side with a pair of glands close to the leaf blade. Flowers on bare branches in spring are single, white, about 2.5cm across on a 2 cm stalk. In wet or windy weather they are fleeting and in a poor year fail to pollinate. Edible fruits are 5–7 cm long, globose, ripening to yellow, red or purple depending on the cultivar **2**. The almost smooth, hard pointed stone is pale brown, flattened-oval with sharp edges. **Habitat and Ecology** • Wild plums or escapes from abandoned orchards often occur in hedgerows. They spread by producing root suckers especially when the roots are severed by agricultural machinery. **Similar species** • Damson and Cherry plum (p148) particularly when in flower.

Natural range
Probably The Caucasus. The original domestic orchard plum is believed to be a hybrid between Blackthorn (p144) and Cherry plum (p148).

Cultivated distribution
Grown throughout the temperate world and represented by hundreds of selections made over thousands of years.

Prunus domestica subsp. insititia (L.) Poir.

Damson

Description • Similar in many respects to the orchard plum, 6 m trees are usually seen as a suckering thicket **3**, often marking the site of an abandoned homestead. The flowers are indistinguishable from Plum **4**, but the smaller 3–4 cm, purple, subglobose fruit is distinctive **5**. Stones are more rounded. **Habitat and Ecology** • A woodland tree creating its own cover by suckering. **Similar species** • Cherry plum (flowers) and Blackthorn (dark purplish-brown stems and sometimes slightly spiny). This subspecies is also confusingly called Bullace.

Natural range
Uncertain because of extensive cultivation but probably Europe through South West Asia.

Cultivated distribution
Seldom grown as an orchar crop now, less so than the closely related *Prunus domestica* subsp. *italica* (Borkh.) Aschers. and Graebn., Greengage **6**.

1
2
3
4
5
6

FAMILY Rosaceae

Prunus dulcis (Mill,) D.A.Webb
Almond

Description • A small tree with a rounded or untidy outline and willow-like foliage. Trees 10 m tall are known but most are much less. The bark is dark grey-brown eventually with shallow cracks and ridges. Shoots are green at first with 5 mm, brown pubescent buds. Finely toothed leaves are lanceolate to narrowly oval with an acute tip and rounded base **1**. The short petiole is glandular. Flowers are 4–5 cm across, pale pink with five petals in early spring **2**. Fruits are characteristic light green and felted **3**. Inside the husk is a single, hard-shelled, familiar almond nut which contains one or sometimes two edible kernels. **Habitat and Ecology** • Almost always cultivated. Best in hot, dry places. **Similar species** • The fruit is unique. In winter the tree may be confused with some other cherries.

Natural range
West Asia and North Africa extending into South West Europe but confused by ancient cultivation.

Cultivated distribution
Widely cultivated round the Mediterranean for fruit and in Northern Europe as an ornamental tree. The nuts are poisonous if eaten in excess. Often infested by aphids that defoliate the shoots and spoil the nuts.

Prunus persica (L.) Batsch
Peach

Description • In Northern Europe peach trees are usually trained onto south facing walls or grown in conservatories. Climate changes recently however have encouraged Peaches to flower and fruit outdoors further north than ever before **4**. The shoot is angular and ridged, buds are brown. Evenly toothed leaves are glossy green, 12 cm long, lanceolate with a tapered point and slightly rounded base. The short petiole is glandular. Flowers on bare shoots before the leaves are spectacular, almost 4 cm across and pale pink **5**. There are also deep pink flowering cultivars. **Habitat and Ecology** • Cultivated for so long that any natural habitat has been long forgotten. **Similar species** • Out of fruit the foliage is reminiscent of *Salix triandra* (p254). Often grown alongside *Prunus armeniaca* L., the Apricot, which has broad leaves **6**, and fruit which is not velvety **7**.

Natural range
Peach is from Northern China and Eastern Asia. The Apricot is probably from a similar area but extends into cooler areas.

Cultivated distribution
Only grown for edible fruit with difficulty in Northern Europe. There are several ornamental flowering forms that are perfectly hardy in sheltered places. Like most plants on the edge of their climatic range these species suffer disease in cold summers. Peach leaf curl, *Taphrina deformans* can be debilitating and even fatal. Infestations of aphids cause similar looking unsightly damage to young foliage in early summer.

1
2
3
4
5
6
7

FAMILY Rosaceae

Prunus mahaleb L.

St. Lucie cherry

Description • A small-spreading deciduous tree with a rounded outline **1** and copious, scented spring blossom at maturity. The bark is smooth and dark grey-brown at first soon developing horizontal bands of rough, light coloured lenticels, a distinctive feature that used to be the 'trade mark' of a cherry wood tobacco pipe. The leaves are 6 cm long, oval, with a short point and rounded base. The 2–3 cm petiole has two very small, indistinct glands. Flowers, in racemes sometimes consisting of only three or four blossoms, are white, 2 cm across each on its own 2 cm slender stalk. Fruits are black when ripe, up to 1 cm across and bitter. Most of the cherry is taken up by the hard-shelled stone. **Habitat and Ecology** • Hedgerows, woodland edges and thickets in agricultural countryside. **Similar species** • Bird cherry (p146).

Natural range
From South and Central Europe to The Ukraine and Southern Russia.

Cultivated distribution
Formerly cultivated for cherry wood pipes and walking sticks. There is also a French ornamental pendulous form.

Prunus serrula Franch.

Tibetan cherry

Description • A small, rounded tree usually around 6–8 m tall **2**. The foliage is deciduous, bright green, luxuriant at first **3**, but tends to thin out and curl up by mid-summer. The flowers, in small clusters, are fairly insignificant. Fruit, although seldom seen, is a red cherry 1 cm in diameter. The chief diagnostic feature of this tree is the unique, shining, mahogany-red, peeling bark **4**. **Habitat and Ecology** • Mixed hill forests. **Similar species** • Except for the bark the form of this tree is like an Almond (p152).

Natural range
China, the western part of Sichuan and adjoining Yunnan.

Cultivated distribution
Extensively grown in gardens and parks as a bark feature.

Prunus subhirtella Miq. 'Autumnalis'

Winter cherry

Description • A small cultivated tree with slender, tangled branches derived from a plant that is unknown in the wild. It has no particular features that mark it out from the species except that the small flowers appear out of season in the autumn and persist through most of the winter **5**. A more floriferous cultivar is 'Autumnalis Rosea', the spring cherry **6**, covered in late winter with shell pink blossom from a young age **7**. **Habitat and Ecology** • Possibly bred from *Prunus incisa* Thumb. the Fuji cherry, a Japanese hill cherry. **Similar species** • No other ornamental cherries flower so early.

Natural range
None. Produced artificially from a plant of unknown origin.

Cultivated distribution
Mostly represented by these two cultivars and a range of pendulous forms. Also 'Stellata' which has pretty, star-shaped flowers.

1
2
3
4
5
6
7

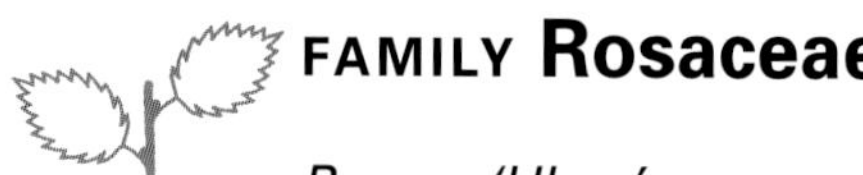

FAMILY Rosaceae

Prunus 'Ukon'

Description • Japanese flowering cherries, given the species name *lannesiana* by Ernest Wilson in 1916 (a name used again now by Japanese horticulturalists), are a complex group. Western taxonomists often refer to them as *speciosa* or *serrulata* species or (as here) simply by a cultivar name on its own. Few Japanese cherries can be accurately identified by the non-specialist without access to planting records. 'Ukon' in flower is perhaps an exception as it is the nearest thing in cherry blossom to yellow. It is a low-spreading tree **1** with large semi-double almost translucent flowers in big, pendulous clusters **2**. In cultivation it is a good foil to 'Kanzan' (below). **Habitat and Ecology** • None. **Similar species** • None.

Prunus 'Kanzan'

Description • The most flamboyant of all pink cherries, popular in Europe ever since it was introduced in 1913. An urn shaped, 6–8 m tree with up-swept branches covered in spring with dense clusters of double, sugar-pink blossoms accompanied by emerging copper-coloured leaves **3**. **Habitat and Ecology** • An artificially raised plant. **Similar species** • There are many pink flowering cherries. Some of the finest have arisen from *Prunus sargentii* Rehd. **4**, which produces masses of single flowers. 'Rancho' is a narrow, upright form ideal for street planting. The most outrageous cultivar is 'Amanogawa' **5**, which may exceed 6 m in height when only 1 m across.

Prunus 'Shirotae'

Description • The white flowering equivalent of 'Kanzan' is 'Shirotae' meaning 'Snow white' in Japanese. It is a flat-topped tree able to spread widely. Dense clusters of big fragrant, semi-double flowers hang down from the horizontal branches **6**. During its rapid establishment stage some of the flowers may only be single. The emerging leaves are green expanding to 12 cm long and deeply incised. **Habitat and Ecology** • An artificially raised plant, around 1905. **Similar species** • 'Mount Fuji' is indistinguishable from 'Shirotae'.

Cultivated distribution
In Japan cherries have been cultivated for thousands of years in temples and palaces. They have now spread all round the temperate world. The 'Sato Zakura' are the largest group which includes 'Ukon', 'Kazan', 'Shirotae' and many more. Most Sato Zakura cherries are small trees, some are particularly delicate depending upon the species originally selected for breeding them – *Prunus incisa* Thumb. the Fuji cherry, for example **7**. Some plants that closely resemble 'Sato Zakura' cherries are not – 'Kursar', for example, was bred by the Englishman Captain Collingwood Ingram **8**. A wide range of soil types are tolerated by flowering cherries. They should not be pruned at all if possible, or in late summer if it is unavoidable, because of disease problems. Original cultivars often suffered from graft incompatibility. Some rootstocks would develop at a faster, or slower, rate than the grafted scion producing an unsightly lump or fat stem above or below the graft, occasionally causing failure.

1
2
3
4
5
6
8

FAMILY Betulaceae

Corylus colurna L.

Turkish hazel

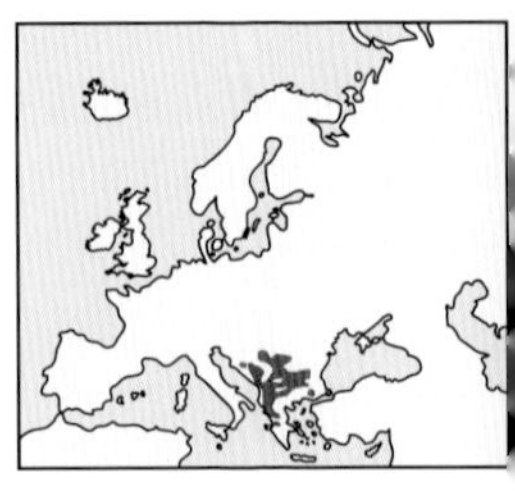

Natural range

Cultivated distribution
Before it became popular as an amenity tree Turkish hazel was cultivated for its fine-quality, pinkish-brown timber. The decorative grain of root wood was particularly prized for inlays and cabinet decoration. It was introduced to Northern Europe around 1580, and is now extensively planted as a street and park tree in Europe and America. It withstands heat and dust in the city environment.

Description • A large, symmetrical, 15–20 m tall tree with a straight stem ultimately 1 m in diameter **1**. The crown is often conical but not particularly narrow at maturity **2**. Young specimens have short branches and a single, persistent, yellowish-grey stem **3**. The bark is smooth and lightly peeling at first developing into a fissured, light brownish-grey, corky surface in old age. Shoots are glandular hairy at first soon becoming glabrous and maturing from light green to brown. Buds are light brown, flower buds noticeably larger than leaf buds especially in late winter. Leaves are variable, vaguely oval or nearly round 7–12 cm long and wide with an uneven, wavy, irregular toothed margin, cordate base and abrupt point **4**. The six to ten main veins are prominent and nearly parallel. Both surfaces of the leaf are thinly pubescent and lustrous. Petioles are pubescent and slightly sticky, pale green or tinged with pink. The male flowers (in 7 cm drooping catkins) are spectacular, appearing in early spring long before the leaves, mostly in multiple clusters of at least three. They are brown until dusted with yellow pollen at maturity. Female stigmas extend from the tip of a modified bud: they are bright red. The nuts, similar in size to common hazel (p160), occur in clusters of between three and ten. The involucre protecting each nut is pale green, deeply divided, recurved and frilly **5**. When ripe the fruit is warm brown with glandular hairs. **Habitat and Ecology** • The considerable environmental and wildlife benefits of hazel are shared by this species. It is a woodland tree that grows out of the shrub layer usually associated with hazel. The nuts in warmer areas are a valuable food source. **Similar species** • A hybrid between this and common hazel exists (*C. x colurnoides* Schneid.) but is rare. The almost identical eastern extension of the species into the Himalayas, formerly a variety, is now *Corylus jacquemontii* Dcne.

1
2
3
4

FAMILY Betulaceae

Corylus avellana L.
Hazel

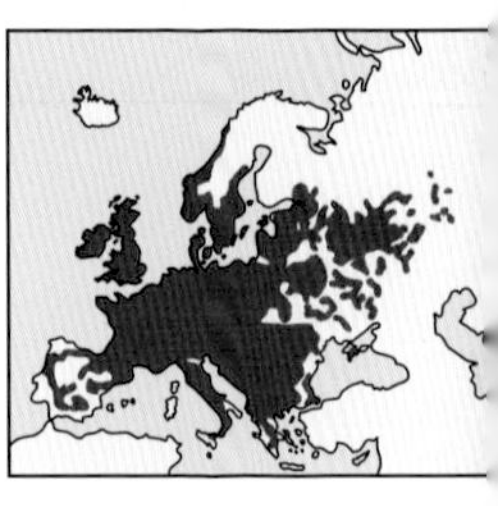

Description • Arguably a shrub but in the right conditions reaching 6–8 m with a similar amount of spread **1**. Stems are hardly ever single. The outline is rounded in the open, rather more drawn up as underwood. The bark is mottled light and medium brown peeling slightly when young. Old bark is hard, grey-brown but remains thin. The shoot is pale green then light brown, glandular hairy becoming glabrous in the second year. Greenish buds are obovoid and pointed. The 5–10 cm leaves are approximately round with uneven teeth, a blunt point and cordate base. At first stiffly pubescent above and beneath especially along the prominent veins. Autumn foliage colour is yellow. Male flowers in pendulous catkins **2** on second year shoots extend with the first mild days of late winter. About 7 cm long and yellow, catkins occur singly or in bunches of two or three. The only visible part of the female flower consists of two or three crimson stigmas projecting from an occasional enlarged bud **3**. They develop into hard, pale green, ovoid nuts held in a ragged involucre **4**. The whole fruit ripens to golden brown. **Habitat and Ecology** • An indicator of ancient woodland usually growing under the shade of oak. **Similar species** • Other hazel species and cultivars.

Natural range

Cultivated distribution
Widely cultivated (encouraged to grow in a semi-natural state) as coppic **5** to produce pliable sticks formerly vital to the rural economy for thatching pegs, hurdles, fencing, etc. Regular coppicing increases the life span of hazel at least tenfold.

Corylus maxima Mill.
Filbert or Cobnut

Description • A similar looking bush or small woodland tree to hazel **6**. The 7–14 cm leaves have irregular double teeth sometimes exaggerated into small lobes. One distinguishing feature is an extended involucre completely covering the developing nut **7**. Mature nuts are larger than wild European hazel and very hard shelled. The variety *purpurea* (Loud) Rehd. has deep purplish-black leaves and nuts **8**.

Natural range
Eastern Europe the Balkans and Asia Minor.

Cultivated distribution
Grown for the edible nuts i the southern part of Northern Europe and throughout Southern Europ

var. purpurea fruit

1
2
3
5
6
4
8
7

FAMILY Betulaceae

Betula pendula Roth.

Silver birch

Description • Usually a slender, flexible, elegant tree with a light branched open top and fluttering foliage. The silvery peeling stem is its most distinctive feature **1**. Young stems and most branches have golden-brown bark **2**. In middle age this becomes the characteristic and familiar Birch bark, white punctuated by dark brown, almost black, patches around the base of branches or where suppressed twigs have fallen off. Ultimately, starting at ground level, mature stems become encased in hard, rough, deeply fissured bark **3**, which is to some extent fire resistant, a valuable asset on heathland where ground fires were once common. The twigs are thin, flexible and resinous, covered with rough almost scratchy warts – a diagnostic feature when comparing this species with White birch (p164). At the top of the tree new shoots usually point upwards, but lower down they stick out randomly then as trees age, they become pendulous. This is a light-demanding species, so closely spaced woodlands grown from naturally sown seed often consist of long-stemmed trees racing up to the light with hardly any side branches. The leaves are triangular or more or less heart-shaped, 4–6cm long with prominent uneven teeth, exaggerated into lobes on vigorous shoots. Deciduous stipules are often present at the base of the 3 cm petiole. Separate wind-pollinated male and female flowers are borne on the same tree. Males are groups of pendulous catkins on side shoot tips **4**. The smaller females are located further down the stem **5**. These develop into plump, seed-bearing, cone-like catkins **6**, which disintegrate over several months in the autumn and winter, ensuring that at least some of the windblown seeds will fall in ideal growing conditions. **Habitat and Ecology** • A tree of sandy heaths and mountain slopes. A short-lived, shallow-rooting pioneer that seeds freely on to any disturbed or burnt ground. It thrives on derelict urban sites and proliferates in the wake of natural disasters and ground-breaking human activities far beyond its Natural range. **Similar species** • White birch (p164) and several other exotic ornamental species and cultivars. Hybrids occur where exotic and native birches are planted in close proximity. In the nursery trade they are sometimes taken to be genuine Silver birch.

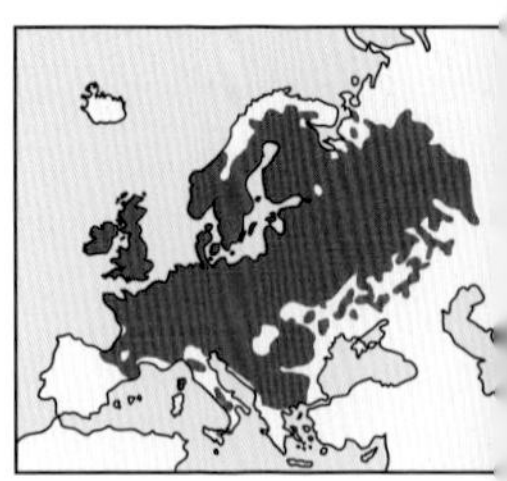

Natural range

Extends from Europe across Asia almost to China and throughout Russia into the subarctic.

Cultivated distribution

Valued as a timber tree particularly in northern lands where less hardy hardwood species have never been available or where such trees need the shelter of birch to establish themselves. There are numerous traditional uses for the wood, bark and twigs. Cultivated forms of Silver birch include various cut-leafed trees: also the purple leaved 'Purpurea', an elegant tree **7**, produced in 1872 with glossy blackish-green leaves **8** and weeping cultivars such as 'Youngii' **9**

Rough shoot

1
2
3
4
5
6
7
8
9

FAMILY Betulaceae

Betula pubescens Ehrh.

White birch

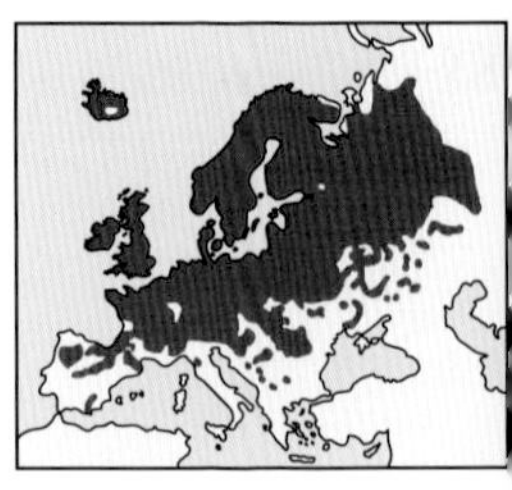

Natural range
Extends through the whole of the 'Old World' subarctic and south to Central Asia.

Cultivated distribution
This species is not generally cultivated, but its timber, bar and twigs are used in the same way as other Birches in areas where it is the only species available. Plants resen being moved long north-south distances. For example Arctic trees planted further south respond to changed da length by coming into leaf early and suffering frost damage. Trees moved from south to north may not survive the intense cold.

Description • This is the characteristic Birch of wild moorlands, heaths and boggy ground, but it is not confined to such locations and may appear almost anywhere. Its size and shape is influenced by where it is growing. Trees 25 m tall are known but some populations are never more than stunted bushes. Young trees have brown and grey stems and a columnar outline softened by lax foliage **1**. Very old trees, which are not common, develop spreading branches **2**, a dull greyish-white 30–40 cm stem with black burrs and various other irregularities **3**. Exceptionally old stems are a mass of cavities, epicormic shoots and become excessively fluted **4**. The young shoots are thin, flexible and covered with soft, downy white hairs, an important diagnostic feature when comparing this species with Silver birch (p162). The leaves are 4–6 cm long, more or less oval, with a rounded or wedge-shaped base and coarsely toothed margins **5**. They turn yellow and gold in the autumn. Flowers are in separate male and female catkins on the same tree. Males are pendulous and in clusters, usually of three. They appear tightly closed on shoot tips in winter then extend to 5–7 cm long as the leaves emerge in spring **6**. Females are smaller in adjacent leaf axils, developing into green, fruiting, cone-like catkins which ripen in the autumn then gradually disintegrate through the following winter. It is not uncommon to see catkin debris and seeds scattered on top of snow. Seeds are yellowish-brown, about 2 mm long and flat with a pair of minute, fin-like membranous wings. They blow away on the wind and can also float on water. **Habitat and Ecology** • A subarctic species, able to survive in severe conditions, even growing over permafrost but extending south into the natural range of Silver birch. A crucial shelter and food plant for wildlife, often the only tree in the habitat. **Similar species** • Some individuals and populations resemble Silver birch, and there are intermediate forms of both species but genuine hybrids seem to be rare and are usually infertile. In cultivation some other exotic Birches also have hairy shoots.

Hairy shoot

FAMILY Betulaceae

Betula nigra L
River birch

Description • An uncommon tree in cultivation that is worthy of much wider use on wet sites. The main diagnostic feature is the constantly peeling, pinkish-grey or brown curly bark, which is not shed in great sheets like some other Birches but stays on the tree until it builds up into thick layers. Some stems are very dark **1**, others are pale **2**. The tree in Europe is usually under 10 m tall with a spreading top. The leaves are ovate to almost diamond-shape with coarse, irregular teeth like small lobes on vigorous growth **3**. Twigs are pubescent and reddish. Male catkins are pendulous and females are small, greenish and upright, developing into tightly packed, cone-like clusters of deciduous, hairy scales and two-winged seeds which mostly overwinter on the tree. **Habitat and Ecology** • A wetland pioneer species preceding other hardwoods into treeless flood plains, sedge beds and swampy ground. **Similar species** • Other birch species but the bark is distinctive. *Betula lenta* L. also has dark bark but it is not shaggy.

Natural range
Eastern and Central North America south of Connecticut and north of Florida, extending west to Eastern Texas.

Cultivated distribution
Confined to specialist collections and plantsman's gardens.

Betula papyrifera Marsh.
Paper birch or Canoe birch

Description • Not an easy tree to identify in Europe for two reasons. Firstly, since its introduction in 1750, seed has often been collected from home-grown horticultural specimens planted adjacent to other Birches, so hybrids have inevitably occurred. Secondly, the vast Natural range of the species in North America results in considerable provenance variation. A typical tree has almost horizontal branches with drooping extremities **4**. The 5–10 cm leaves are ovate with a drawn out point and irregular teeth **5**. There are up to nine pairs of main veins, a characteristic of just a small number of Birches. Twigs are slender, glabrous and reddish-brown. Bark is variable in colour but usually forms a continuous peeling skin round the tree with numerous horizontal, buff-grey bands of lenticels **6**. Flowers are similar to River birch (above) but the seeds are shed earlier in the autumn. **Habitat and Ecology** • A pioneer tree exploiting seed-beds created by natural disasters or human earth-moving activities. It survives in the north of its range in harsh sub-arctic conditions. **Similar species** • Other birch species with multiple pairs of leaf veins (e.g. *Betula costata* Trautv., *Betula ermanii* Cham., *Betula albo-sinensis* (p170), *Betula alleghaniensis* (p170) and *Betula lenta* L.).

Natural range
North America, from the Atlantic Ocean to the Pacific on either side of the USA–Canada border and north to Hudson Bay and Alaska.

Cultivated distribution
Frequently planted but in Europe there is a lot of dubious stock in cultivation Mainly grown as a curiosity because of the reference in the name to Native Indian canoes.

1
2
3
4
5
6

FAMILY Betulaceae

Betula utilis D. Don
Himalayan birch

Description • A vigorous, 10–20 m tall tree with a stem diameter up to 60 cm **1**. Columnar at first gradually becoming rounded with irregular branches. The bark is variable in colour but peels in substantial sheets. Some individuals are pinkish-white **2**, and some are red-brown but they all have rough dark brown or black patches around knots which expand and join up in old age. The foliage is luxuriant. The relatively large 6–10 cm leaves are ovate with a rounded or subcordate base. There are 9–12 pairs of parallel veins and prominent uneven forward-pointing teeth. The tip comes to a short point, a kind of final enlarged tooth **3**. Male flowers are arranged in long, 8–12 cm, pendulous, slender catkins expanding before the leaves in spring **4**. Female catkins are small, 2–3cm long, green and solitary, developing into cone-like pendulous or semi-erect, tightly packed clusters of small, hairy bracts and winged seeds which are shed in the autumn and early winter. **Habitat and Ecology** • A mountain-slope species in some areas forming the tree line. From a diverse natural habitat so there are considerable provenance variations in cultivated specimens. **Similar species** • *Betula ermanii* Cham., a rather variable Himalayan tree sometimes almost indistinguishable from *Betula utilis.*

Natural range
Nepal, Tibet, Northern Burma and the Yunnan and Sichuan Provinces of Western China.

Cultivated distribution
The typical species is rare in cultivation, but varieties and cultivars are frequently planted. The varieties *occidentalis* and *jacquemontii* (below) are usually represented by vegetatively reproduced selections.

Betula utilis var. jacquemontii (Spach) Winkl.
Himalayan white birch

Description • Also described as a species, *Betula jacquemontii* Spach, this tree has distinctive creamy-white bark. It was originally distributed in Britain as a cultivar named 'Silver Shadow' **5**. It also has pure, very white, thinly peeling bark **6**. This variety is a 15 m tall tree with slender, green shoots which have silky hairs as well as rough, glandular warts. The leaves are ovate with a tapered point and rounded base and the margins are unevenly toothed. There are 10–12 distinct parallel veins reminiscent of Hornbeam (p172) **7**. Flowers and fruit are similar to the species (above). Most planted trees are selected named clones such as 'Inverleith' or 'Jermyns'. **Habitat and Ecology** • Lower mountain slopes on moist, rocky ground; in mixed or pure woodlands. **Similar species** • The stems are unique.

Natural range
Eastern Afganistan to West Nepal in the foothills of the Himalayas.

Cultivated distribution
Widely cultivated in its man forms in parks and gardens. Young trees have brilliant white bark, later it becomes green with algae or black wi soot or traffic fumes until th top layer peels off.

1
3
2
4
5
6
7

FAMILY Betulaceae

Betula alleghaniensis Britt. (B. lutea Michx.)

Yellow birch

Description • In its native America a large, 25–30 m tall tree, but in Europe usually much less. This is one of two Birches with strongly aromatic foliage, the other being *Betula lenta* L. When a young shoot is scratched there is a diagnostic smell like oil of wintergreen. Young trees are finely branched and elegant **1** with pale yellowish-grey, slightly peeling bark **2**. The leaves are relatively large for a Birch, up to 13 cm long on young, vigorous growth. They are narrowly ovate to elliptical with a short point, rounded base and sharp, irregular, marginal teeth. There are about ten more or less parallel veins most prominent on the underside. In the autumn, the foliage turns to golden yellow before falling. Male flowers are in drooping yellow catkins and females are green, short and erect, and they develop into tight, upright, cone-like clusters of winged seeds and hairy scales, which mature in the autumn then slowly disintegrate. **Habitat and Ecology** • A mountain-slope forest tree growing in deep ravines by streams and lakes. **Similar species** • Superficially like several other Birches, but the bark colour is distinct.

Natural range
Eastern North America from the Atlantic coast of Newfoundland, Maine and New Hampshire, then sporadically to North East Georgia and west in a broad band all round the Great Lakes to North East Iowa.

Cultivated distribution
Rare in cultivation in Northern Europe. One of the most productive timber-producing Birches in America.

Betula populifolia Marsh.

Grey birch

Description • A small, bushy tree with thin, flexible branches and an open, conical then spreading top. The shoot tips and foliage are distinctly pendulous. Frequently medium-sized or even small trees tend to snap off at or near ground level producing a cluster of new stems. Height seldom exceeds 8 m and individual stems over 30 cm are rare. The dark green leaves are rounded triangular with a long pointed tip and irregular teeth **3**. The leaf tips usually point downwards and after rain each one holds a droplet of water for a time. Autumn foliage colour is pale yellow. Bark is smooth chalky-white or greyish punctuated with darker, rough patches. The surface skin only peels very slightly and in small amounts **4**. Twigs are glabrous and rough with warty glands, very slender and reddish-brown. Flowers are similar to Yellow birch (above) and the seeds are shed from autumn to early winter. **Habitat and Ecology** • Woodlands and thickets on dry, acid, sandy uplands. **Similar species** • *Betula pendula* (p162).

Natural range
Eastern Canada and the North Eastern Atlantic states of the USA, north to Cape Breton Island.

Cultivated distribution
Rarely cultivated as it has no commercial or particular amenity value. In horticulture Birches are mostly grown for their ornamental bark, for example, *Betula albo-sinensis* var. *septentrionalis* Schneid **5**

FAMILY Corylaceae

Carpinus betulus L.

Common hornbeam

Description • Characteristic smooth, pale grey, fluted bark persists even in old age **1**. Mature trees seldom exceed 20 m in height with a 1 m bole, but ancient pollards have larger diameter stems **2**. Young shoots are slender with white pubescence and pointed, 6 mm, brown buds. Like beech (p86) the outer bud scales are shed in great profusion when the young leaves appear. At this time, male catkins, concealed all winter, emerge **3**. Female flowers are green appearing at the end of short shoots. They develop into pendulous 6–10 cm chains of small, winged nuts. Each fruit consists of a central, papery, 3–4 cm, irregularly toothed wing with two shorter basal lobes forming a 'fleur-de-lis' pattern with the exposed seed at its centre **4**. Leaves are 3–5 cm long, oblong-ovate with angular but soft teeth **5**. There are light brown tufts of hairs confined to the 10–15 parallel, vein axils on the underside. The leaves are bright green all summer then golden brown before they fall. **Habitat and Ecology** • Open countryside and low elevation woodlands especially on heavy clay soils. Stems managed as pollards for hundreds of years are exceptional wildlife refuges **6**. **Similar species** • Foliage is like beech except for the toothed leaves. Also *Ostrya* (p174), *Nothofagus* (p198) and *Zelkova* (p138) which are less often seen. An unexpected Hornbeam 'look-alike' is *Acer carpinifolium* Sieb. and Zucc. but the leaves occur in opposite pairs.

Several varieties of Common hornbeam have an important role in ornamental and urban arboriculture. The Weeping hornbeam 'Pendula' seldom exceeds 10 m in height and width **7**. It is not usually infested with insects and provides pleasant shade. Conversely the upright form 'Fastigiata' **8** is a valuable street and park tree with upright branches and light foliage. An even tighter narrow crowned tree is 'Columnaris' produced in 1891, but it is slower growing and ultimately smaller than 'Fastigiata'. A Dutch equivalent is 'Frans Fontaine'. There are also various cut-leaved forms with exaggerated toothed margins to the leaves. 'Incisa' has deeply toothed leaves but it is said to revert to the species very readily. 'Variegata' has creamy-white variegation but it too is unstable and likely to revert.

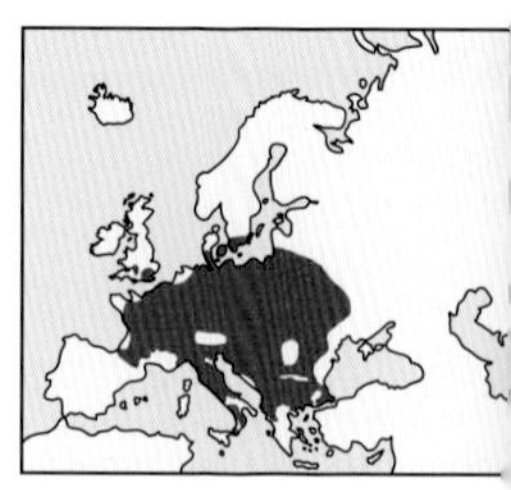

Natural range

Cultivated distribution
Traditionally pollarded for hard, heavy timber or fuel wood and managed in conjunction with grazing domestic stock. Although thi[s] the bark resists chewing by animals. Much used for hedging and ornamental pleaching.

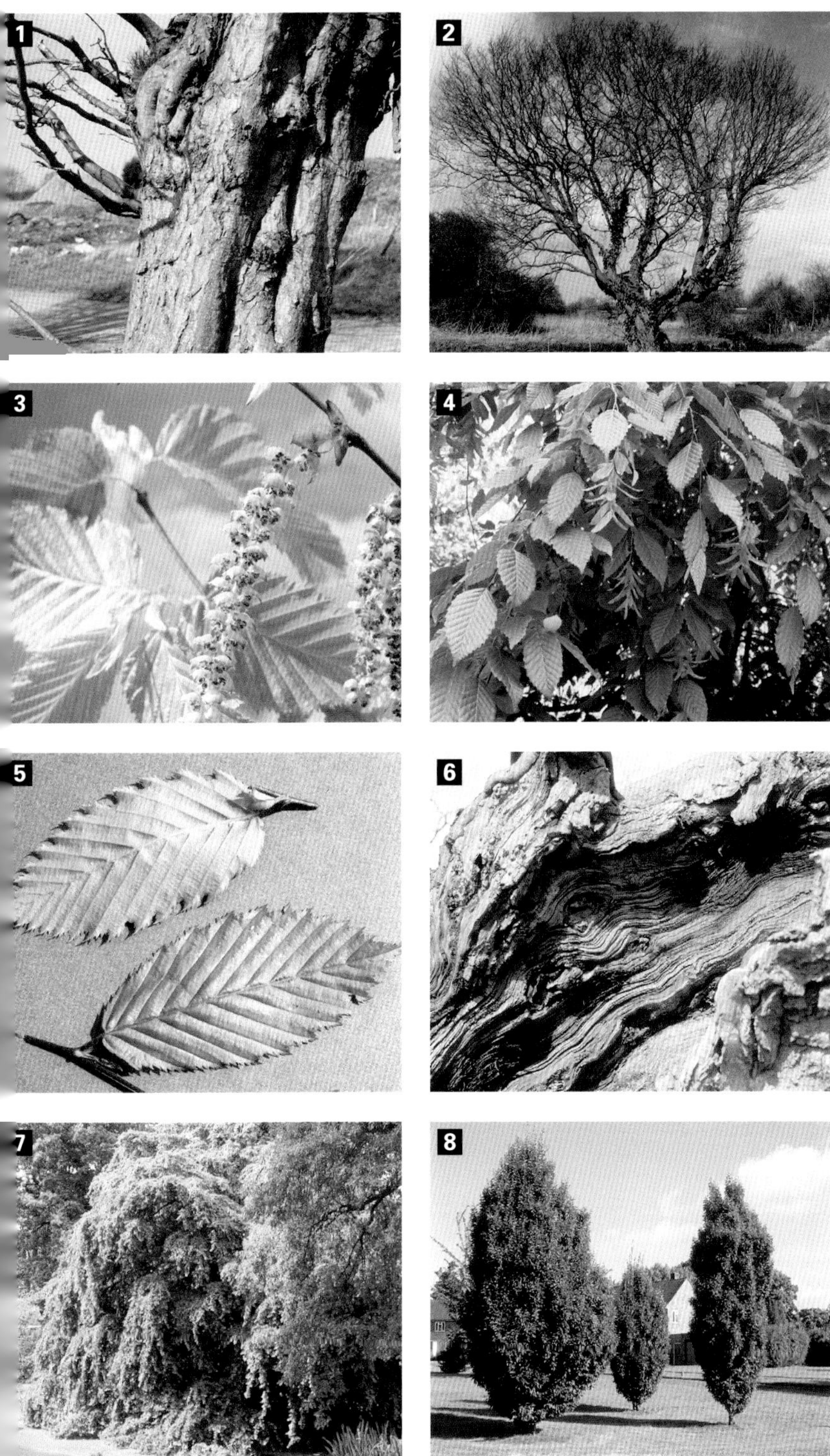
1
2
3
4
5
6
7
8

FAMILY Betulaceae

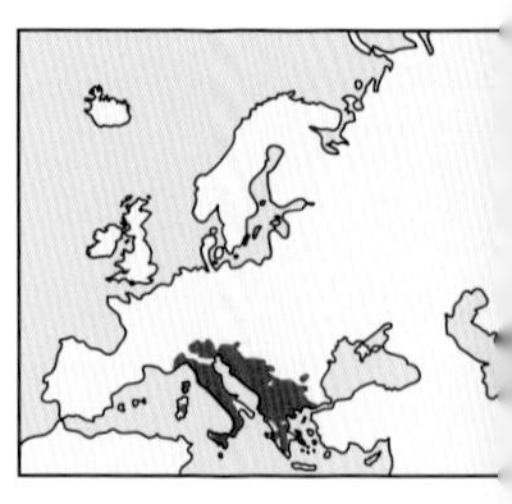

Ostrya carpinifolia Scop.
Hop hornbeam

Description • A spreading tree sometimes over 15 m tall with a mature stem diameter around 60 cm. Young trees have a conical outline usually with a straight, short stem **1**. The bark is greenish-brown at first becoming grey-brown and developing a flaky surface and long, fluted, vertical ridges **2**. The leaf is reminiscent of Hornbeam (p172), 8–12 cm long with 12–15 pairs of veins **3**. When the new foliage appears there are narrow stipules at the base of each petiole. Tightly closed male catkins appear on the tree in early winter. In spring they become pendulous, 7–10 cm long, and turn bright yellow in clusters, usually of three. Female flowers are found on the tips of side shoots, they are insignificant at this stage but soon develop into characteristic Hop-like papery fruits **4**. These ripen to light brown in the autumn **5**. Each bladder-like scale contains a smooth, flat, 3 mm seed. **Habitat and Ecology** • A shade-tolerant woodland tree in mild conditions. **Similar species** • Hornbeam, except that unlike hornbeam the male catkins are visible throughout the winter and the fruits do not have extended wings. There are about ten species of *Ostrya* in cultivation most of them are fairly obscure. Botanists have placed the genus in various families including Carpinaceae, Hornbeam and Corylaceae the Hazels.

Natural range

Cultivated distribution
Infrequent in parks and gardens but present in most specialist tree collections. Th[e] golden autumn foliage is attractive and the fruits are a[n] interesting curiosity.

Ostrya virginiana (Mill.) K. Koch
Ironwood

Description • A smaller, slower growing tree than Hop hornbeam with glandular hairs on the young shoots. The branches are spreading so open grown specimens are often as wide as they are tall, ultimately about 8–12 m. The leaves are rich green, ovate to elliptical, with a short point and rounded or subcordate base **6**. Margins are finely double-toothed and have about 14 pairs of parallel veins. The bark is light brown then grey-brown **7**, eventually fissured and divided into thin scaly plates which curl at the edges but rarely fall off. Male flowers are 4–6 cm, reddish-brown, drooping catkins, female flowers are small and green tinted with red. The papery Hop-like fruits are light red. **Habitat and Ecology** • Usually an understorey species in deciduous woodland on damp or wet, but well-drained, soils. **Similar species** • Other *Ostrya* species and Hornbeam.

Natural range
Eastern North America from Cape Breton Island to Manitoba then south to Eastern Texas and Northern Florida.

Cultivated distribution
Rare in Europe and then often mistaken for Hop hornbeam (above). It is call[ed] Ironwood because of its incredibly hard timber, reminiscent of Common hornbeam wood (p172). In America it has been used fo[r] tool handles and fence posts

1
2
3
4
5
6
7

FAMILY Ulmaceae

Celtis australis L.
Nettle tree

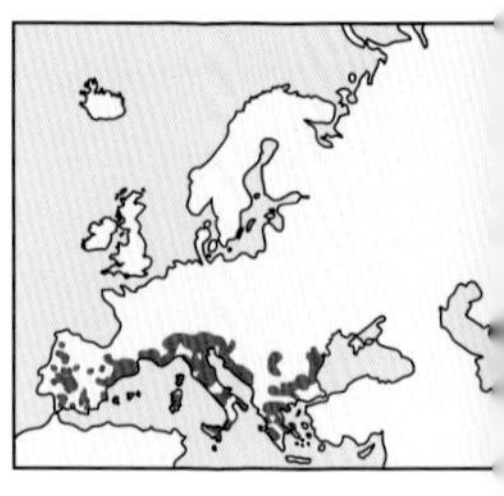

Description • This genus is one of the most difficult to identify without close inspection of the foliage. There are many species but the differences between them are minimal. Although not common, the Nettle tree is one of the most frequent in cultivation. It is a 15–20 m tall tree with a stem up to 80 cm in diameter. The bark is smooth and grey with faint ridges and fissures eventually developing on old stems **1**. Shoots, like elm (p182), are slender, reddish with zigzag alternate buds. The 8–14 cm, rough, nettle-like leaves are narrowly oval, each with a long, tapered point and rounded, slightly oblique or flat base. The prominent venation is distinctive (for the whole of this genus). There are three forward-pointing, main veins running from the base of the leaf towards the tip **2**. Margins are coarsely toothed and the petiole is short, 2 cm. Flowers are green and insignificant in the leaf axils. Fruits are 1.2 cm, globular, stalked berries with a single, hard, shelled seed. They turn from green to yellowish-brown, red and finally black. **Habitat and Ecology** • Open woodland, best in hot, fairly dry conditions. **Similar species** • Other *Celtis* species, some Elms and some *Zelkova* species (p138).

Natural range

Cultivated distribution
First cultivated in England in the sixteenth century but has never been popular and remains confined to obscure specialist collections.

Celtis occidentalis L.
Hackberry

Description • A medium-sized tree up to 20 m tall with a stem less than 60 cm diameter. The outline is rounded but uneven, said to be prone to witches' brooms. The bark is light grey and yellowish-brown with corky ridges on the main stem and major branches **3**. Shoots are slender, green at first then dark brown with light coloured lenticels, reminiscent of Elm (p182). The 12 cm leaves in two ranks are narrow-ovate with a distinct point and evenly toothed margin. The base is oblique-rounded and the slender petiole is around 2 cm long **4**. Mature leaves are dark green on the upper side and grey-green with raised veins on the underside. Both surfaces have stiff hairs that are rough to the touch. The 3 mm spring flowers in some leaf axils are green and insignificant followed by single, 10 mm fruits on slender stalks. These are yellow, eventually turning greenish-black **5**. **Habitat and Ecology** • Open woodlands, river valleys and lower mountain slopes to 1500 m elevation. **Similar species** • Other *Celtis* species.

Natural range
A vast area of the East and Central United States and Southern Canada, from the Atlantic to Oklahoma, North Dakota and Southern Manitoba.

Cultivated distribution
Infrequent in Northern Europe as an ornamental and not used as a commercial timber tree. In America it is used for furniture as well as other low-grade timber products, boxes, crates and plywood. A good species to attract game such as pheasants.

1

3

2

4

5

FAMILY Ulmaceae

Ulmus glabra Huds.

Wych elm

Description • Although now much depleted in Northern Europe by Dutch Elm Disease, Wych elm has fared rather better than some other species, probably because of its inherent genetic diversity. Mature and semi-mature trees can still be found **1**. Individuals 30 m tall are known, with a stem diameter up to 1 m. The bark is smooth and grey for many years like the bark on young Lime trees (p224). Then it develops an intricate pattern of vertical and diagonal fissures and ridges **2**. Shoots are slender, pale green at first then golden brown and silky haired with dark brown, distinctly alternate, pointed buds. The leaves are characteristic, amongst the largest of any Elm. The shape varies from narrow to broad obovate with an oblique base and small, abrupt point **3**. Sometimes vigorous leaves produce two or three distinct points or small forward-pointing lobes. Margins are double-toothed giving a ragged appearance. The upper surface is rough with bristly hairs. There are 16–20 straight parallel pairs of veins leading from the midrib to the edge. Flowers appear before the leaves in spectacular profusion covering the tree in late winter with lime-green clusters of colour **4**, a feature only matched by Norway maple (p360). Each individual flower rapidly develops into a 5 mm, flat seed held more or less in the centre of a 12 mm, round membraneous wing. These turn light brown when ripe in summer and are quickly shed. The seed is usually fertile. **Habitat and Ecology** • Woodlands, agricultural field margins and hillsides, often surviving in very exposed situations and in close proximity to the sea. **Similar species** • Other Elms. The leaves superficially resemble *Corylus* (p158).

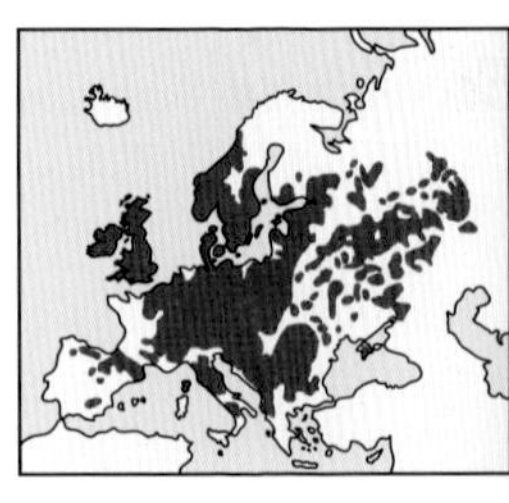

Natural range

Cultivated distribution
Not cultivated deliberately now but greatly encouraged in former times to provide green fodder for domestic stock. The inner bark was used for cordage or cut into strips for woven chair bottoms, etc. The tough, rot-resistant wood was valued fo cart wheel hubs, water pipes, pumps, piles and coffins. Thi species grows easily from see or by vegetative propagation.

Ulmus glabra x Ulmus minor

Hybrid elm

Description • Hybrids between Wych elm and Smooth-leaved elm (p180) are locally common in some regions notably East Anglia in the British Isles. Trees vary in size, most are cut back as hedges, but may reach 20 m in height. The bark is rougher than Wych elm with yellowish-brown and grey, vertical ridges **5**. Leaves are intermediate between the parents **6**. **Habitat and Ecology** • Hedgerows and woodland. Moderately resistant to Dutch Elm disease. **Similar species** • Other forms and subspecies of *Ulmus minor* and some regional types of *Ulmus glabra*, for example, a smaller-leaved type frequent in Central Ireland.

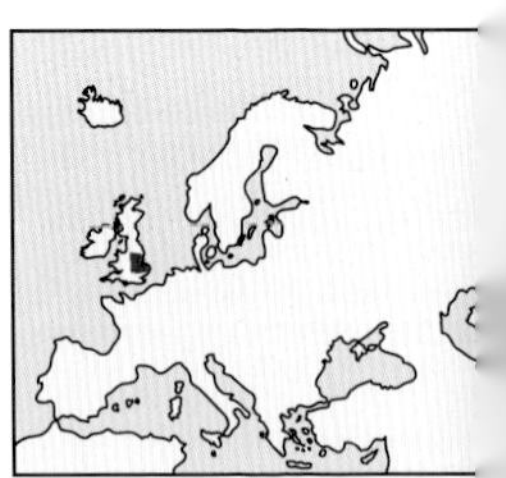

Natural range

Cultivated distribution
Not deliberately cultivated now but utilized for the sam purposes as other Elms whe this hybrid mainly represen the genus.

1
2
3
4
5
6

FAMILY Ulmaceae

Ulmus minor Mill. subsp. minor (Ulmus carpinifolia Suckow)

Smooth-leaved elm

Description • Once a common tree but now much reduced in numbers by Dutch Elm Disease. Trees 30 m tall have been recorded with huge stems around 1.5 m diameter. Anything approaching this size is now rare **1**. The branches spread widely supporting a tall, domed crown. Bark is pinkish-grey with vertical fissures revealing traces of pale orange inner bark **2**. In old age, stems become rough, scaly and grey. Shoots, buds and the upper side of the leaves are distinctly shiny **3**. Individual leaves are ovate, 5–10 cm long, with 10–12 pairs of straight, parallel veins leading from the midrib to the double-toothed margin. The tip is pointed, the base is oblique, one side is rounded, the other wedge-shaped and emerging further up the midrib. Petioles are yellow and 5–10 mm long on the shortest side. Flowers appear in late winter in dense, purplish-red clusters developing rapidly into lime-green seeds each surrounded by a flat, papery, oval wing 15 mm long with a notched tip **4**. They ripen to straw colour and soon blow away in the wind. **Habitat and Ecology** • This was the common field Elm in parts of Europe growing along hedgerows and around settlements, but now much reduced by disease. Cultivation has also disguised its natural habitat over centuries. **Similar species** • Modern Elm nomenclature suggests that many Elms previously described as species should now be varieties or cultivars of this species. Cornish elm, *Ulmus minor* var. *cornubiensis* (West.) Richens, was once a familiar sight locally in Cornwall planted in rows and looking like a giant clipped hedge on the skyline **5**. Stems are grey and fissured, foliage is light **6**. Individual leaves are 4–8 cm long, shiny on the upper side with distinct teeth and a drawn out point **7**. The Jersey elm (or Wheatley elm) subsp. *sarniensis*, is a hybrid between *minor* and x *hollandica* (p184). It has dense foliage **8** with individual leaves double- or triple-toothed **9**. The tree outline is columnar often tapering towards the top. Bark is coarsely fissured and ridged showing pale orange inner bark in places **10**. Other similar species include English elm (p182) and the *Ulmus glabra x Ulmus minor* hybrids (p178).

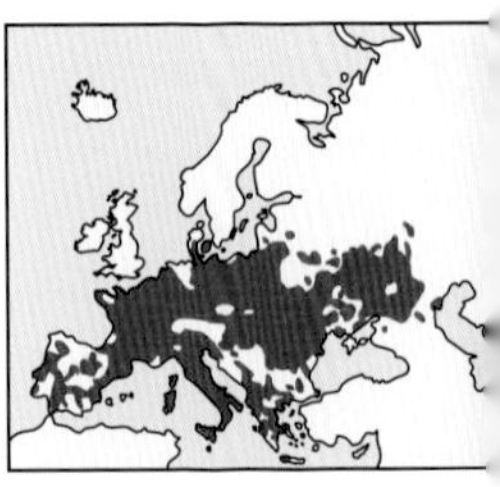

Natural range

Cultivated distribution
Many forms of Smooth-leaved elm were transported and cultivated by Iron Age farmers as green summer fodder and boundary hedge plants. They have since been allowed to spread in a semi-natural state, often by suckering, far beyond their original range. In recent tim[e] selections have been made f[or] urban planting and for ornament (e.g. 'Dicksonii' and 'Louis van Houtte', whic[h] have golden-yellow foliage).

Natural range
var. *cornubiensis*

Natural range
subsp. *sarniensis*

1
2
3
4
5
6
7
8
10

FAMILY Ulmaceae

Ulmus minor var. vulgaris (Ait.) Richens (Ulmus procera Salisb.)

English elm

Description • This once common tree is now much depleted by Dutch Elm Disease which swept through the English population in the 1960s. Potentially this is a 30 m tall tree with a stem in excess of 1 m **1**. The typical shape of English elm, a great straight-stemmed tree with a domed top and a series of lower subordinate domes creating an inverted pear shape, is seldom seen now. It was once part of the accepted view of the English countryside. The bark is fissured, grey and craggy on mature trees but younger stems have exaggerated, pale brown, corky ridges **2**. The leaves are ovate with a short point and oblique base. The surface is rough to the touch and the margin double-toothed **3**. Leaves vary considerably in size from 5–8 cm in length, smallest at the base of the shoot. Petioles are short, often hidden on one side by the uneven oblique leaf base. The foliage on trees infected by, or recovering from, Dutch Elm Disease is often stunted **4**. Young shoots die back in midsummer and typically the wilted tips bend over at the end like a shepherd's crook. An entire hedgerow or cluster of trees may exhibit similar symptoms. This is because trees are almost always suckers growing on a vast, ancient, spreading, common rootstock. Some individuals produce flowers **5**, but as most are single-sex clones seed is hardly ever produced. **Habitat and Ecology** • Introduced by Neolithic farmers and planted around homesteads and as hedges to confine domestic stock, often spreading away from original locations by suckering. **Similar species** • Various subspecies and slightly different clonal populations. The cultivar 'Jacqueline Hillier' is a small tree **6** with foliage like English elm but on a smaller scale **7**. It appears to be resistant to Dutch Elm Disease.

Natural range
Uncertain.

Cultivated distribution
Thought to have been brought to England by Neolithic farmers from Sout East Europe probably by way of Spain. It was grown vegetatively for green cattle fodder in late summer when grass was usually scorched and dry. Green shoots were cut from annually sprouting (lammas) growth on the stems. The timber was also used, in much the same way as Wych elm (p178), but thi source was more sustainable As soon as a tree was cut down a new one started to grow from the existing, long established root system. Extant trees today are often the same genetic material th has been in situ for thousan of years.

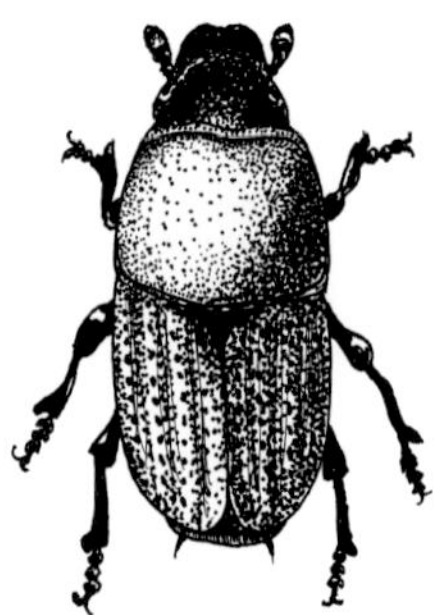

Large elm bark beetle (Scolytus scolytus). Carrier of the Dutch Elm Disease fungus.

1
2
3
4
5
6
7

FAMILY Ulmaceae

Ulmus x hollandica Mill.

Dutch elm

Description • A complex natural and artificially produced hybrid that can only be identified reliably by named cultivars and only then before they have been parted from their cultural notes or labels. The most often seen example in Britain is 'Vegeta' the Huntingdon elm. A vigorous 30 m tree with stems around 1 m in diameter **1**. The leaves are large, 10–15 cm long, elliptic with an oblique base and long pointed tip. It arose at Huntingdon, England in 1750, an *Ulmus glabra x Ulmus minor* and possibly *x Ulmus plotii* cross. In this area of Eastern England most Elms have broadly the same origin and many set fertile seed. Several fashionable Dutch Elm Disease resistant clones of *Ulmus x hollandica* have been developed, for example, 'Commelin' and 'Groenveldt' **2**. They have subsequently proved to be less resistant than was first thought and are likely to disappear quite soon. As clones they lack genetic diversity and actually cause the disease to spread rapidly. **Habitat and Ecology** • Probably a natural hybrid in woodland and hedgerows. **Similar species** • Wych elm (178).

Natural range
Widespread in Western Europe particularly Eastern Britain and the Low Countries.

Cultivated distribution
Extensively cultivated for centuries and more recently as a possible Dutch Elm Disease resistant, urban, open space tree. A project which has so far largely failed.

Ulmus plotii Druce (Ulmus minor var. lockii (Druce) Richens)

Plot's elm or Lock's elm

Description • Clearly from the muddled taxonomy this is a complex tree as difficult to identify as it has been to name. As a cultivar, the original 'Plot's elm', it could be named, but as a variety growing in the wild state it has affinities with Cornish elm (p180) and other types of *Ulmus minor*. Potentially it is a large tree with up-swept, top branches and rather thin, lax shoots **3**. The stem is usually straight with vertically ridged and fissured, pinkish-grey bark **4**. Foliage is glossy but rough textured on the upper side and has long pendulous side branches **5**. The leaves are 3–7 cm long, ovate to elliptic with an oblique base. There are seven to ten pairs of straight lateral parallel veins running from the midrib to the double-toothed margin. Flowers appear in spring before the leaves, followed by winged seeds in summer. **Habitat and Ecology** • Hedgerows and thickets along field margins and round settlements. **Similar species** • Most forms of *Ulmus minor*.

Natural range
Endemic in Central and Eastern England.

Cultivated distribution
The natural variety has not been recently cultivated but clonal selections have been made from the population, for example, Plot's elm clone for amenity and urban, open space planting.

1
2
3
4
5

FAMILY Ulmaceae

Ulmus pumila L.

Siberian elm

Description • A deciduous or occasionally semi-evergreen tree up to 18 m tall usually with a straight stem and wide-spreading, rounded crown. This is not an easy tree to identify morphologically and provenances vary considerably. The foliage has a glossy appearance, shoots are yellow and pubescent in the first year then light brown **1**. The bark is evenly fissured somewhat like a Common oak (p298), brownish-grey with flecks of pale orange-brown where small scales occasionally flake off **2**. Leaves are 5–8 cm long, oval to ovate with around ten pairs of prominent parallel veins. The point is not sharp and the base is more or less rounded and only occasionally oblique **3**. Margins are distinctly but evenly double-toothed and petioles are stout. **Habitat and Ecology** • A variable range covering numerous diverse land types. Said to be tolerant of harsh cold or dry conditions. **Similar species** • A large number of trees and shrubs have similar looking foliage.

Natural range
A vast area including regions of Siberia, Mongolia, China, Korea and parts of the Himalayas.

Cultivated distribution
Rare or not identified in cultivation, some specimens from diverse parts of the range contradict any general group description.

Ulmus laevis Pall.

European white elm

Description • Potentially a large, 30 m tall tree with widely spreading often sinuous branches and characteristically fluttering flowers and fruit when the wind blows. Stems over 1 m in diameter are known. The bark is smooth at first becoming grey-brown with dark, deep, vertical furrows **4**. Shoots are purplish-grey, pubescent at first then glabrous and pale grey-brown. The 5–10 cm leaves are broadly oval, double-toothed with an indistinct point and rounded, often oblique base. There are up to 18 pairs of parallel veins but they are less prominent than most other related Elms, but the yellow 1–2 cm petiole is distinctive **5**. Flowers on relatively long stalks appear before the leaves, followed by flat seeds enclosed in the centre of a thin, flat, obovate, 1 cm, membraneous, ciliate-edged wing. **Habitat and Ecology** • Woodlands and lowland agricultural field margins. **Similar species** • Other elms except when flowers and seeds are present.

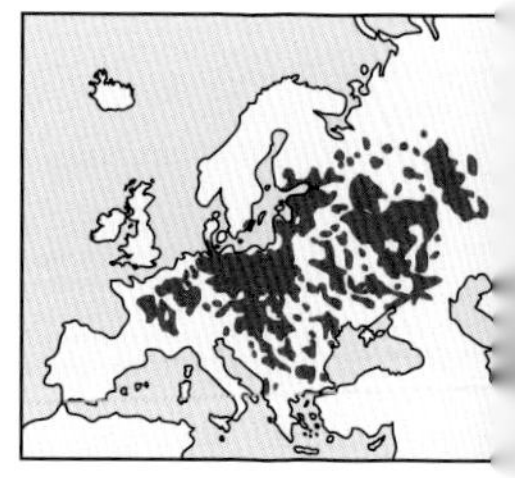

Natural range

Cultivated distribution
Seldom cultivated beyond its natural range. A valuable timber species in the past. Only a curiosity now in collections of limited ornamental value and susceptible to Dutch Elm Disease.

1

2

3

4

5

FAMILY Davidiaceae

Davidia involucrata Baill.

Handkerchief tree

Description • For two weeks in late spring this tree flowers, and during that period it is easy to identify, for the rest of the year it is difficult. The flowers are unique and very striking **1**. It is impossible not to spot them because in the slightest breeze they constantly move. In the strict botanical sense it is not the true flower (a 2 cm round cluster of tightly packed stamens) that is obvious, but the accompanying pair of white, pendulous, pointed, oval bracts that protect it. These are unequal in length, typically 20 cm and 12 cm, off balance and unstable in the wind. Mature trees are around 15–20 m tall with a stem up to 75 cm in diameter. The bark is pale brownish-grey, finely fissured then becoming rougher in old age **2**. The leaves are relatively large, 10–15 cm long, ovate and pointed with a cordate base and evenly spaced, bristle tipped teeth. The 10 cm petiole and midrib are pale green and prominent. There are six to eight forward-pointing main veins which fork in a characteristic way several times **3**. Fruits are oval, 3 cm long, green in summer **4**, turning purplish and eventually brown, each containing a hard nut divided into five compartments. **Habitat and Ecology** • In the wild a mixed woodland species in deep mountain valleys and along stream sides. **Similar species** • The variety *vilmoriniana* (Dode) Wanger, which has pubescence on the underside of the leaves, is as common as the species in cultivation.

Natural range
China.

Cultivated distribution
Occasionly found in large gardens and ornamental tree collections. Seedlings take 12–20 years to flower.

FAMILY Tetracentraceae

Tetracentron sinense Oliver

Spur leaf

Description • A rather gaunt tree in cultivation with dark grey bark, upright branches and sparse foliage. Leaves in tufts on short spur shoots are ovate and cordate up to 10 cm long. The five to seven main veins radiate from the end of the petiole to the margin supporting a characteristic reticulate framework **5**. The inflorescence is a slender, 15–20 cm, pendulous catkin bearing small, yellow flowers without petals in midsummer. Fruits in clusters of four contain whitish oily seeds. **Habitat and Ecology** • A relic of an ancient vegetation type which has water-conducting cells in the wood reminiscent of the conifers. **Similar species** • None.

Natural range
Central and Western China, parts of Burma, Tibet and Nepal.

Cultivated distribution
A botanical curiosity with little ornamental merit other than the long catkins. Introduced from China in 1901 but rarely planted. There appears to be some debate concerning plants from Eastern Nepal which are now thought to be a distinct variety, *himalense* Hara and Kanai.

1

2

3

4

5

FAMILY Rosaceae

Sorbus aria (L.) Crantz
Whitebeam

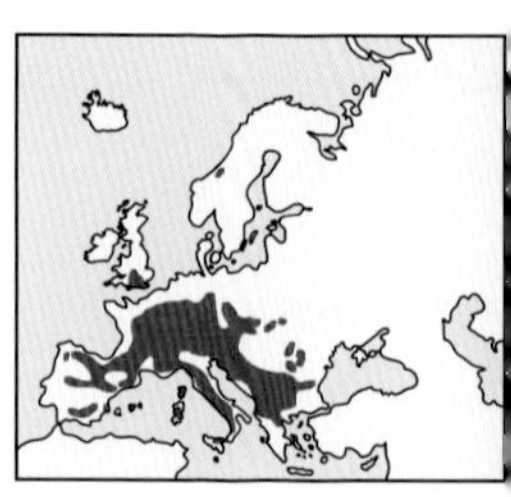

Natural range

Cultivated distribution
Wild trees are not used for any particular purpose although their status in landscape amenity is high: they also provide cover and other environmental benefits for wildlife. There has been limited experimental planting for forestry and widespread use in urban situations such as street planting, parks and gardens. In some areas, notably hot dry places, this species is not a good amenity tree. It sheds leaves from midsummer and is susceptible to fireblight (*Erwinia amylovora*).

Description • A small or medium-sized deciduous tree depending on the region or environment in which it is growing. It is also genetically variable and appears to be closely related to some other named microspecies of *Sorbus* (p196 and below). Most specimens seldom exceed 15 m in height with stems less than 75 cm diameter. Often they stand out visually on limestone hillsides and chalk downland as pale grey spheres of foliage reaching from ground level, or a sheep grazing line, to a domed top. This effect is enhanced if they are accompanied by dark green Yew (p50) which thrives in a similar habitat. This species is by no means confined to limestone hillsides. Good trees can be found on woodland edges **1**, and even in plantations on mountain slopes **2**. Here trees take on an entirely different greener appearance. The grey bark is smooth for many years becoming scaly and rougher in old age. Shoots emerge densely covered in white tomentum which eventually rubs off. Leaves are 8–12 cm long, ovate to round **3** with approximately 12 pairs of parallel veins leading from the midrib to the coarsely toothed margin. The upper side is dull green after being densely hairy at first. The underside is persistently white felted, a good diagnostic feature. Spring flowers, appearing with the new leaves, are in broad terminal corymbs on side branches. Individual flowers are 12 mm across with dull, creamy-white petals and reddish then yellow anthers. Fruits are scarlet and ovoid, 1 cm long, in clusters **3**, becoming prominent as the autumn leaves colour yellow and brown before falling. **Habitat and Ecology** • Limestone countryside but thrives in any light open or scrub woodland conditions. **Similar species** • Part of a large group of species within *Sorbus* containing many exotics; microspecies including *Sorbus rupicola* (Syne) Hedl., a shrubby 4–6 m tree on limestone in the British Isles **4**; and *Sorbus hibernica* E. Warb. the Irish Whitebeam, which replaces *Sorbus aria* in Central Ireland. Its leaves are broadly ovate and lustrous deep green on the upper side **5**, and brilliant white on the back **6**. Irish whitebeam thrives in Ireland but tends to grow poorly elsewhere in less moist, cool conditions.

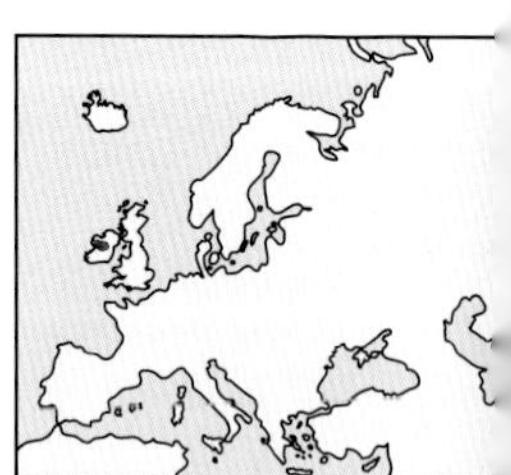

Natural range
Sorbus hibernica

1
2
3
4
6

FAMILY Rosaceae

Sorbus intermedia (Ehrh.) Pers.

Swedish whitebeam

Description • What is not immediately obvious from observing this tree in a southern town street or shopping centre is just how tough and cold resistant it really is. In the north this is one of the last broadleaved trees to survive the Arctic cold. In northern areas that are exposed to the sea (e.g. Orkney), it may be the only broadleaved tree able to exceed 6 m in height. Normally it is a shapely specimen up to 12 m tall with a clear, straight (often pruned in cultivation) stem up to 50 cm diameter. The outline is columnar or rounded **1**. Bark is grey or light purplish-brown with rough, grey, horizontal lines of calloused lenticels. It becomes slightly fissured upwards from the base at maturity **2**. Shoots are green at first becoming purplish-brown with a white coating of fine tomentum. Leaves are oval with five to seven pairs of rounded, forward-pointing, toothed lobes. The largest close to the base then decreasing in size towards the tip, almost merging with the adjacent prominent marginal teeth **3**. The upper surface is glossy green with strongly textured, impressed veins. A dense covering of short, white, woolly tomentum covers the whole underside. This remains more or less intact all season. The flowers are off-white with light red anthers appearing in dense, terminal corymbs with the leaves **4**. Flower stalks are distinctly grey and woolly. Fruits often in dense clusters start off grey-green and felted but soon shed all hairs and ripen, eventually turning bright orange-red with tiny, yellow, spaced out lenticels and the persistent remains of a grey-brown calyx. **Habitat and Ecology** • Cold northern forest fringes and thickets often bordering and protecting Beech woods. Widely naturalized in many lowland areas further south. Although this tree is probably of hybrid origin it comes true from seed because it is apomictic. **Similar species** • Other shrubby microspecies, members of the *intermedia* group including *Sorbus minima* (Ley.) Hedl. and *Sorbus arranensis* (p196), Mougeot's whitebeam, *Sorbus mougeotii* Soy-Willem and Godron, which is a very similar tree in most respects. It has a greater number of more triangular lobes on the 10–12 cm leaf. The fully ripe fruits are brighter red with fewer lenticels **5**. It occurs from the Pyrenees to the Austrian Alps.

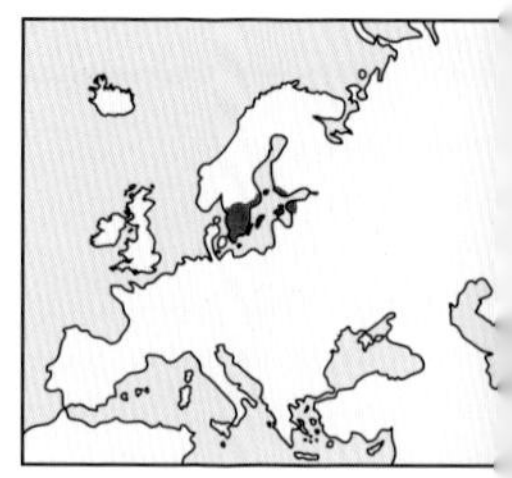

Natural range

Cultivated distribution
One of the most widespread trees in urban streets and public open spaces **6**. Introduced far beyond its original northern native habitat but appearing to cop[e] with changed climatic conditions very well. It is probably not resistant to fireblight. Experimental plo[ts] have been successfully plant[ed] beyond the usual northerly limits of where broadleaved trees of any sort might be expected to grow.

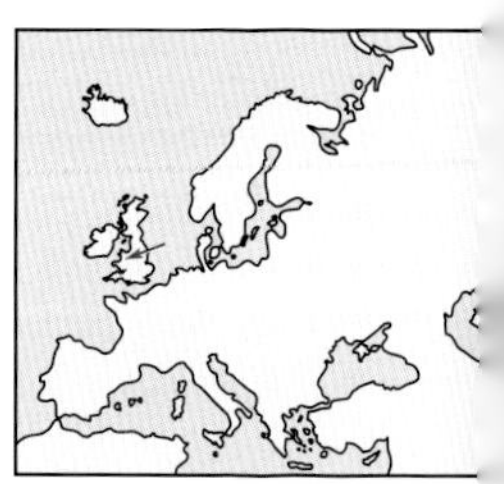

Natural range
Sorbus minima

1
2
3
4
5
6

FAMILY Rosaceae

Sorbus latifolia (Lam.) Pers.

Broad-leaved whitebeam

Description • Also occurs in a cultivated form known as the Service tree of Fontainebleau, but both trees are always difficult to identify. As an aggregate species *Sorbus latifolia* includes several named microspecies (below and p196). Specimens from Fontainebleau show very constant features probably because this is an apomictic species which produces viable seed without the need for sexual fusion. They have 12 mm, globular, edible, twin-seeded fruits that ripen reddish-brown with prominent, scattered, light brown lenticels. *Sorbus latifolia* as part of the wild aggregate is somewhat different, a 10–15 m tall rounded tree with light, open foliage **1**. The stem is smooth and greyish-brown bleaching to pale grey and cracking vertically with age **2**. The leaves are broadly oval and pointed with slightly more exaggerated lobes than Whitebeam (p190) **3**. A form of Whitebeam crossed with *Sorbus torminalis* (p324) is believed to be the origin of this group of plants. Flowers in small corymbs appear in late spring. They are 15 m across, creamy-white with five petals, two styles and numerous stamens. The orange fruits are smaller than the Fontainebleau selection. **Habitat and Ecology** • Open woodlands and hedgerows. Much confused by ancient cultivation **4** and subsequent abandonment, but presumed to be broadly similar to the parents. **Similar species** • There are at least seven named microspecies including *Sorbus bristoliensis* Wilm., a bushy, orange berried tree often with multiple stems **5** clinging to carboniferous limestone in the Avon River gorge in South West England. The leaves are glossy above and felted white on the underside **6**. Another is *Sorbus devoniensis* E. Warb. a tree up to 15 m tall with a substantial stem **7**. The foliage is similar **8** with individual leaves reminiscent of Whitebeam but with more pronounced lobes **9**. The fruits are orange-brown, closer to *Sorbus torminalis* (p324).

Natural range
Confused by past cultivation, *Sorbus latifolia* probably cam originally from South East Europe but is naturalized in many areas including England and Central Scotland. *Sorbus bristoliensis* is endemic in a limited part of Western England and *Sorbus devoniensis* is endemic in South West England, the Isle of Man and parts of Ireland.

Cultivated distribution
The use of Service trees, of various sorts, for food or making a harsh kind of alcoholic cider has largely died out. Orchard trees have spread out into some parts o the landscape. The rare endemic microspecies are n in general cultivation but ca be found in conservation an research collections in botanic gardens.

S. bristoliensis

S. devoniensis

S. latifolia

1
2
3
4
5
6
7
8
9

FAMILY Rosaceae

Sorbus decipiens (Bechst.) Irmisch. (Sorbus x decipiens (Bechst. Hedl.)

Broad-leaved whitebeam

Description • Part of the *Sorbus latifolia* aggregate (p194) this can be a substantial tree around 10 m tall. It usually has a straight stem eventually with rugged, furrowed bark **1**. Shoots are green at first then purplish-brown. The leaves are more or less oval and pointed at each end. The margin is finely and coarsely toothed **2**. There are also about 12 distinct, pointed lobes each directed forward, the largest near the base of the leaf. The flowers and fruit are similar to *Sorbus latifolia*. **Habitat and Ecology** • Rocky limestone hillsides. **Similar species** • Other *Sorbus* microspecies in the *Sorbus decipiens* group, notably *Sorbus croceocarpa* Sell., which may grow to a larger size and has less indented, lustrous green foliage (upper side of leaves) **3**. The stem is smooth, purplish-grey **4**. *Sorbus subcuneata* Wilm. has foliage intermediate between these two.

Natural range
Sorbus decipiens originated in Central Europe. The origin of *Sorbus croceocarpa* is unknown and *Sorbus subcuneata* is native only in South West England, North Devon and South Somerset.

Cultivated distribution
The regional integrity of thes[e] microspecies depends on their not being widely distributed. They occur in botanic gardens reference collections.

Sorbus anglica Hedl.

Description • Part of the *Sorbus intermedia* aggregate (p192) this is a shrubby tree generally because of the difficult terrain in which it grows. Multiple stems often occur with smooth, purplish-brown bark. Leaves are ovate with a narrow, tapered base and toothed margin with a series of shallow, forward-pointing lobes **5**. These decrease in size towards the rounded or cuspidate leaf tip. Flowers and fruit are similar to *Sorbus aria* (p190). **Habitat and Ecology** • Woodlands and hillsides often in ravines and between rocky crags. Mostly on carboniferous limestone. **Similar species** • Other *Sorbus intermedia* group microspecies, including the very rare *Sorbus leyana* Wilm. **6**, *Sorbus minima* (Ley) Hedl. from Mid Wales and *Sorbus arranensis* Hedl. which is endemic on the Isle of Arran, West Scotland.

Natural range
Very local on limestone in Wales, South West England and County Kerry. A form from Wales with very narrow leaves may be a separate microspecies.

Cultivated distribution
Not in general cultivation b[ut] *ex situ* specimens are retaine[d] by botanic gardens.

1
2
3
4
5
6

FAMILY Fagaceae

Nothofagus nervosa (Phil.) Dim. and Millano

Southern beech (Rauli)

Description • A large, fast-growing, straight tree up to 30 m tall often with a stem over 80 cm in diameter. Reminiscent of a well-grown hornbeam (p172) at first. As a plantation species in western Britain 15 m has been reached in nine years **1**. Branches are light and ascending with pendulous shoots eventually developing. Slender new growth has a tendency to zigzag between buds. The leaves are oblong-ovate and rounded at each end with about 18 parallel veins **2**. Male flowers are in small, globular heads **2**, females are very small in vein axils. **Habitat and Ecology** • Forest species. **Similar species** • Hornbeam (p172).

Natural range
Central Chile and adjacent parts of western Argentina.

Cultivated distribution
Grown as an ornamental in Europe (as *Nothofagus procera*) since 1913. Also as a potential broadleaved plantation tree.

Nothofagus obliqua (Mirbel) Blume

Roble beech

Description • A craggy tree superficially like oak **3** with a domed crown up to 25 m tall. Bark is smooth at first becoming fissured and scaly, grey-brown with age **4**. To some extent the timber resembles Common oak. The leaves **5** are around 7 cm long, colouring to good red and yellow in the autumn. **Habitat and Ecology** • Forming extensive forests below Monkey puzzle (p6) on mountain slopes. **Similar species** • *Nothofagus nervosa* but less graceful and more hardy.

Natural range
Central and southern Chile and Argentina, along the Pacific coast and into the foothills of the Andes.

Cultivated distribution
Introduced to Europe in 184 and again in 1902, 1914 and 1926. Not all provenances (regional types) have been successful. Testing as an alternative European plantation species is still underway.

Nothofagus dombeyi (Mirbel) Blume

Evergreen southern beech (Coigüe)

Description • Occasionally up to 20 m tall with a stem over 1 m diameter **6**. Trees have a compact, rounded outline with upswept branches and dense, twiggy shoots **7**. The lustrous, deep green leaves are oval, around 3 cm long with an acute point and tapered base. The margin is double-toothed. Flowers are insignificant on two-year-old wood, followed by a toothed cupule containing three small seeds (nuts). **Habitat and Ecology** • Temperate rain forest and ancient woodland on moist uplands. **Similar species** • Superficially like *Phillyrea* (p282).

Natural range
Chile and central southern Argentina.

Cultivated distribution
Introduced to Britain in 191 Occasionally grown as a par and garden ornamental and tried as a plantation species **8**, but potential for timber production seems to be limited.

1
2
3
4
5
6
7
8

FAMILY Aquifoliaceae

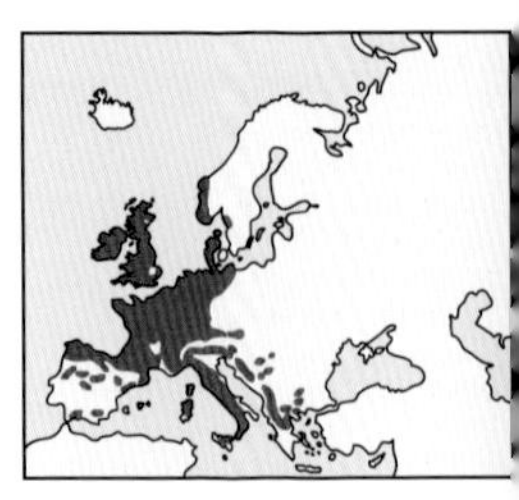

Ilex aquifolium L.

Common holly

Description • A familiar, small, slow-growing evergreen tree usually 15 m or less tall, frequently many-stemmed with a dense, spreading crown. Ancient trees develop craggy stems around 75 cm diameter **1**. It seeds freely and suckers in the semi-shade of large deciduous trees **2** sometimes forming an extensive evergreen understorey. Young branches are glabrous, green often purplish in full light, stems are silvery-grey and smooth. The distinctive leaves are stiff, waxy, lustrous, glabrous and ovate. Up to 7 cm long with extended, irregular, spiny teeth between deep, rounded sinuses: upper leaves are less well armed. Male **3** and female **4** flowers on separate trees are white with four 5 mm petals. They are short stalked and fragrant, produced in clusters in late spring. Fruit, the familiar glossy red berry **5** containing four hard nutlets, is globose, 8 mm long, on 5–8 mm stalks produced annually in clusters between second year leaves. The berries ripen in early winter and attract birds such as thrushes, blackbirds and fieldfares. Seeds pass unharmed through the birds' digestive systems and germinate freely, most often below well-used roosts. **Habitat and Ecology** • Hedgerows and woodlands both as a monoculture and an underwood species. Thrives on a range of neutral to acid soils. Cold, wind, salt and pollution tolerant. Holly is also good cover and food for game and wildlife. Leaves are browsed by deer, hares, rabbits and domestic stock. The timber is hard and heavy, greenish white, easy to work and takes an excellent finish (stain or polish). Dyed it is used as a substitute for box or ebony. **Similar species** • There are numerous variegated leaf forms, such as 'Handsworth New Silver' **6** and berry colours from orange to yellow. Other spiny leaved evergreen trees include *Olearia macrodonta* Baker, *Osmanthus x fortunei* Carr. and *heterophyllus* (G. Don) P.S.Green.

Natural range

Cultivated distribution
Extensively cultivated since ancient times for bold winter foliage and Christmas berries can also be clipped as an effective, decorative thorny hedge. Pollution, drought resistance and small size mak this a good, urban, open space tree. There are no serious diseases exclusively associated with Common holly.

1
2
3
4
5
6

FAMILY Aquifoliaceae

Ilex x altaclerensis (Hort. ex Loud.) Dallim.

Highclere holly

Description • An entirely artificial plant raised at Highclere House (Alta Clera in Latin) in Southern England. Sometime around 1800 tender *Ilex perado* Ait. trees, which were grown in ornamental tubs and moved into the conservatory each winter, hybridized with Common holly (p200). The resulting progeny which exist today as individually named hybrids in the nursery trade can be substantial, vigorous trees around 10 m tall [1] with large leaves. Spines are few and far between or absent. The cultivar 'Wilsonii' produced in the 1890s is cited here as typical. It is a female tree with 8–12 cm, glossy, oval leaves [2]. Stems are up to 60 cm diameter and have fairly smooth, grey bark [3]. The shoots are bottle-green and the flowers are white with four petals, about 1 cm across and fragrant [2]. They occur in the leaf axils on previous season's growth and are followed by glossy, scarlet berries often hidden away in the foliage [4]. One of the best male trees, comparable in all other respects with 'Wilsonii', is 'Mundyi' produced in the English Midlands in 1898. It also has green shoots and large, glossy leaves. The white flowers are scented. Another example is the Irish clone 'Hendersonii', one of the earliest named plants. It has dull, green leaves, many of which bear no spines. The berries are brownish in midwinter [5], but do eventually go red in early spring [6]. 'Camelliifolia' is a female clone with entire spineless, glossy leaves and purple shoots in full light. In addition to green-leaved forms several variegated clones are available. 'Lawsoniana' is a sport of 'Hendersonii' with large more or less spineless leaves with tricolour variation, yellow in the centre then lime green with deep green towards the margin [7].
Habitat and Ecology • This tree has no natural habitat. Although one parent is tender in Northern Europe the plants at present in cultivation are hardy. They thrive best in partial shade. **Similar species** • Common holly: some cultivars appear to be morphologically similar (e.g. 'Balearica' formerly *Ilex aquifolium* var *balearica* Hort.).

Natural range
An artificial hybrid first produced in England.

Cultivated distribution
A popular garden shrub or tree in many forms. Originally it came about because *Ilex perado*, the Madeira holly, would only bear berries in England if it was artificially pollinated wit common holly when the Madeira hollies were wheeled outside for the summer. Seed were grown at Highclere, at first to raise more Madeira holly plants and not in the hope of discovering a new hybrid.

1
3
2
4
5
6

FAMILY Rosaceae

Malus sylvestris (L.) Mill.

Crab apple

Description • The common or wild crab apple is difficult to distinguish from escaped or naturalized orchard apples. The botanical characteristics are not strikingly obvious. If a tree is growing by a road or abandoned railway line it is unlikely to be a genuine crab apple. If it is deep inside semi-natural woodland further examination is justified **1**. Fully grown trees seldom exceed 10–12 m in height with a stem, or sometimes a cluster of stems, 40–50 cm in diameter **2**. The bark is smooth purplish-brown on young trees becoming fissured and more or less scaly in old age. Shoots are generally less hairy than orchard apples soon becoming glabrous, red-brown with distinctive orange lenticels. Stiff woody spur shoots are common, frequently terminating in a sharp point. Leaves are 5–7 cm long **3**. The petiole is grooved along the top and slightly downy with a hint of deep red extending from the base turning to pink and extending along the midrib. Flowers, in umbels of four to seven are around 4 cm across, carmine pink in bud then fading to white as they mature. Blossom time coincides with the spring flush of new leaves so the effect is less dramatic than in orchard apples which mostly flower slightly earlier (p207, **2**). Fruit is produced on individual trees without the need for cross-pollination. The apples are globose, green with minute white dots, ripening to yellowish-green with russet patches and a hint of brownish-crimson on the sunlit side when over-mature **4**. They are juicy, sour if eaten raw but excellent cooked particularly as crab apple jelly. In former times they were cultivated for animal fodder, especially for pigs, and some extant trees may have originated from this practice. It may be that before orchard apples were perfected wild crab apples were grown for food or cider making. Seeds, usually in fives, are 5 mm long, flat and lustrous brownish-black, mostly fertile although germination may take 18 months. Crab apples can, and frequently do, hybridize with orchard apples. **Habitat and Ecology** • Extremely valuable as a food source and shelter tree for wildlife. Good for bees in spring. Well armed with thorny shoots especially on lower branches providing small birds with some protection from raptors. A tree of open woodland and scrub. **Similar species** • Subspecies *mitis* (p206), which does not have thorns, also some domestic orchard apples and ornamental crabs. Introgressive hybridization and backcrossing with compatible cultivated individuals is common

Natural range
Frequent throughout Europe and the British Isles but exact distribution is confused by naturalized populations and problems with identification.

Cultivated distribution
Rarely cultivated today but relics of former cultivation for food and drink may remain. Trees also appear in neglected orchards where crab apple rootstocks have been used and scions have subsequently failed.

1

2

3

4

FAMILY Rosaceae

Malus domestica Borkh.

Orchard apple

Description • A familiar cultivated tree probably of hybrid origin with no wild predecessor. Frequently found in a semi-wild situation grown from discarded apple cores, sometimes naturalized and forming thickets. In orchards the shape and size is usually influenced by pruning to encourage fruit on horizontal or down-turned branches **1**. In the natural state the crown fills out to a smooth, rounded outline **2**. Bark is light grey, brown, smooth at first then fissured, reminiscent of oak, or flaking a little like an old sycamore. Shoots and buds are woolly pubescent at first and not thorny. Leaves are 5–10 cm long, elliptic-ovate with a rounded base and short, often twisted, point. The margins are evenly toothed. Hermaphrodite flowers, which often require cross-pollination by another tree, occur in small corymbs on short side shoots have five, usually pink, petals **3**. Fruit is edible and varies widely in size, colour and taste according to variety **4**. **Habitat and Ecology** • Probably originated several thousand years ago by selection and breeding from *Malus sylvestris* subsp. *mitis* (below), *Malus dasyphylla* Borkh. from China, *Malus sieversii* (Ledeb.) Roem. from Asia and the Siberian crab *Malus baccata* (L.) Borkh. **Similar species** • Crab apple (p204) and some ornamental crabs.

Natural range
Probably of hybrid origin with various parent species from outside Europe.

Cultivated distribution
World-wide in temperate regions. Over 1000 forms have been named but sadly the modern trend is to only cultivate a small number of good-looking rather than good-tasting varieties.

Malus sylvestris subsp. mitis (Wallr.) Mansf.

Description • Similar to *Malus sylvestris* (p204) but having larger leaves and no spines. Flowers are pale pink **5**, the fruits are yellowish and sour **6**. Thought to be involved in the parentage of some forms of orchard apples by some botanists. However other authorities suggest *Malus sylvestris* played no part in the development of the orchard apple. **Habitat and Ecology** • Probably introduced, naturalized in hedgerows and on waste ground. **Similar species** • Crab apple (p204). Some authorities consider this subspecies to be the same as *Malus domestica*. It is also mistaken in the field for *Malus sylvestris*. The whole subject of apple identification in the countryside has been confused by so many feral seedlings growing from discarded apple cores.

Natural range
Unknown.

Cultivated distribution
No longer cultivated in its natural state but used as an artificial parent of some orchard apples.

1
2
3
4
5
6

FAMILY Rosaceae

Malus sp. and cvs.

Ornamental crab apples

Description • Ornamental crab apples are a common and popular component of gardens and urban, open space planting schemes. In some areas they are widely used as street trees. Up to 25 species qualify as ornamental crabs but many more have been developed artificially by cross-breeding and subsequent selection of the best cultivars. Plant breeding has been directed in two ways: firstly the production of white, pink and carmine flowers; and secondly the development of coloured, sometimes edible, fruit. At the flowering stage in mid- to late spring crab apples can be distinguished from flowering cherries (with which they are most often confused) by the presence of two to five styles and not just one. There are also many more stamens, up to 50, in each flower. *Malus floribunda* Sieb. ex Van Houtte from Japan and cultivars bred from it produce a great profusion of small, single flowers often completely obscuring the emerging foliage. Deep pink flowered forms are known as the *purpurea* group. Well-known examples are 'Eleyi' **1** and 'Royalty' which has very deep pink flowers accompanied by purplish black leaves **2**. It makes an excellent small garden tree **3**. Semi-double flowers and strongly scented blossom are features of other selected cultivars such as *Malus coronaria* (L.) Mill. Crab apple fruit is a particularly ornamental and durable feature. Some cultivars, the ubiquitous 'Golden Hornet', for example, retain numerous, 3 cm spherical, yellow apples on its leafless branches until midwinter **4**. 'Butterball' **5** has similar fruit that develops a rosy orange flush on the sunlit side. A group of crab apples bear fruit that superficially resembles cherries, notably the translucent, red fruited Chinese species *Malus hupehensis* (Pampan) Rehd. and *Malus toringoides* (Rehd.) Hughes **6** that also has occasional lobed leaves. **Habitat and Ecology** • Apples grow best in full light on sheltered fairly fertile ground. Ornamental species come from a diverse range of sites and climate types. **Similar species** • In fruit the long-stalked, red, cherry-like fruits of *Malus hupehensis* are particularly difficult to designate. In blossom, several other crab apple cultivars superficially resemble flowering cherries.

Natural range
Malus species selected for their ornamental properties occur in temperate regions world-wide. The Siberian crab *Malus baccata* (L.) Borkh., for example, has fragrant flowers and small fruit. It is particularly hardy. *Malus coronaria* (L.) Mill. from Eastern North America has shell pink flowers: some cultivars of it are double flowered. The Japanese crab *Malus floribunda* Sieb. ex Van Houtte is early and very floriferous. *Malus yunnanensis* (Franch.) Schneid. and its varieties are well-known for brightly coloured fruit.

Cultivated distribution
Extensively grown for a wide range of flower colours and ornamental fruit. Where disease problems with flowering cherries are rife crab apples may be a good alternative.

1
2
3
4
5
6

FAMILY Rosaceae

Photinia serratifolia (Desf.) Kalkman
Giant photinia

Description • A large evergreen tree up to 20 m tall with a stem 40–60 cm in diameter. The outline is usually fairly compact. Bark is grey-brown, smooth except for raised horizontal lines of calloused stomata, eventually it becomes slightly scaly. Leaves are oval, around 15 cm long, leathery, with a finely toothed margin and short, abrupt point **1**. Young growth is bronze becoming green then turning brown or red again in small numbers, usually after three to four years, before falling. Flowers are small, off-white and produced in dense, flat, terminal corymbs. Berries, around 5 mm across, are red ripening in the autumn but they are soon taken by birds. **Habitat and Ecology** • An underwood species in mixed deciduous forests. **Similar species** • *Photinia davidiana* (Decne.) Cardot. is a smaller, more familiar tree with a compact, rounded outline **3** and substantial, short stem **4**. The leaves are less persistently evergreen, narrower and brightly coloured prior to falling **5**. This is a much more frequently planted tree in Northern Europe, usually on acid soils.

Natural range
South and West China and surrounding countries, also Taiwan.

Cultivated distribution
As a species quite rare but crossed with *Photinia glabra* (Thunb.) Maxim. it has produced several very good spring foliage feature garden plants such as *Photinia x fraseri* Dress 'Red Robin' which has spectacular, brilliant red young growth **2**.

FAMILY Styracaceae

Halesia monticola (Rehd.) Sarg.
Mountain snowdrop tree

Description • Only easily identified when in flower, this is a 15 m tall (30 m in America) deciduous tree with a stem around 50 cm diameter **6**. The bark is pale grey and soon becomes fissured and rugged (photographed here in deep shade) **7**. The 6–10 cm leaves are ovate or oval tapering to a point at each end. Margins have very fine hooked teeth. The upper surface is matt green and the underside is glaucous. Flowers appearing after the new leaves in late spring are in delicate, pendulous, thin-stalked clusters. Each one is 25 mm long, white, like a half open bell with four rounded lobes and 10–16 yellow stamens inside **8**. The distinctive 3 cm fruits are light green with four longitudinal wings **9**. **Habitat and Ecology** • A woodland species also occurring in mixed deciduous upland forests. **Similar species** • Carolina silverbell, *Halesia carolina* L. which is a smaller tree. The flowers resemble the 'Snowbell' (*Styrax*), an unusual genus of exotic ornamental trees and shrubs.

Natural range
North America, from North Carolina and Tennessee to Georgia.

Cultivated distribution
Grown in parks and gardens as an ornamental curiosity but infrequent. Introduced around 1897.

FAMILY Rosaceae

Pyrus pyraster (L.) Burgsd.

Wild pear

Description • A plant of uncertain status because of the confusion between it and *Pyrus communis* (p214). It is considered here to represent wild pear stock from which, in part, domestic orchard pears have been developed. A medium-sized tree seldom over 12 m tall with a bushy top and heavy, multiple branches from low down on the stem or even ground level. Individual stems over 50 cm diameter are unusual. Short spur shoots are frequent often terminating in dead woody spines. A feature less common in cultivated pears. The bark is smooth at first **1** becoming rugged with old age **2**. Long new shoots and older spur shoots develop into a dense compact crown with billowing or rounded outline. Flowers appear before the leaves in spring. In a good year, the whole tree will be transformed into a white cloud of blossom. In a poor season, flowers will be limited to isolated clusters. The flowers **3** are 2–2.5 cm across with five-clawed, white petals and numerous reddish anthers. Flowers are arranged in racemes which are so compact they resemble umbels. The fruit **4** is more rounded than pear-shaped, less than 6 cm long, hard, barely edible, and contains numerous grit-cells. The seeds are dark brown, almost black when fully ripe. The leaves are rich glossy green, ovate to almost round, with an acute pointed tip and fine, evenly spaced marginal teeth. If damaged they turn almost black. Black is the ultimate autumn colour after briefly turning fiery red. Pear wood is heavy, tough and fairly durable. It is yellowish brown with fine grain and texture often with a decorative mottled figure. **Habitat and Ecology** • With little commercial value wild pears have been left to waste places and hedgerows at low elevation. Although rare they provide a valuable habitat for wildlife. They are susceptible to and may spread Silverleaf disease (*Chondrostereum purpureum*). **Similar species** • Wild pear is easily confused with orchard pears and also the Plymouth pear *Pyrus cordata* Desv., a rare British native species confined to southwest Britain, western France and Portugal. It has reddish fruit. Wild pear was formerly used as a common rootstock for ornamental, orchard and perry pear trees. Failed scions or re-growth from a root will often produce a wild pear tree in a totally unexpected situation, even under a neglected espalier **5**. Modern orchard pears are generally no longer grown on *Pyrus pyraster* stocks.

Natural range
Difficult to define because o[f] the affinity this species has with *Pyrus communis* p214.

Cultivated distribution
As such this species has no cultivated distribution but as part of the *Pyrus communis* complex it has a long history of cultivation in Europe (p214).

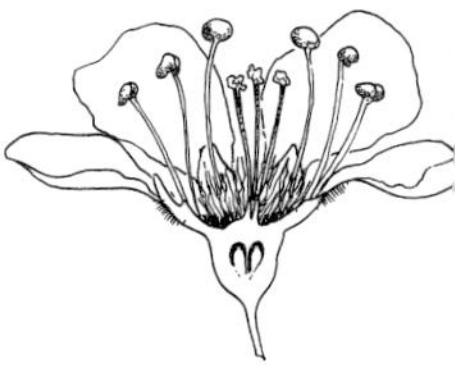

Cut away pear flower

FAMILY Rosaceae

Pyrus communis L.

Common pear

Description • Medium-sized trees up to 15 m tall although many cultivated, listed orchard varieties are considerably smaller. Some modern cultivars grafted onto dwarfing rootstocks are little more than bushes. According to the Hillier nurseries in England over 1000 cultivars are known. The most obvious feature of a pear tree in summer is its glossy green leaves. In autumn the shining foliage turns crimson, edible pears ripen to golden yellow or russet brown. Superb eating varieties such as ‘Conference’, for example **1**. Stems seldom exceed 50 cm in diameter, although some individuals grow much larger, for example, the ‘Robin’ pear **2** in Eastern England. Very old trees develop hard, craggy, dark grey-brown bark divided into small but prominent angular plates **3**. Some individuals have a tendency to sucker. As may be expected from its confused ancestry, the outline of the tree does not conform to any particular pattern. Nevertheless, in winter, trees have a spiky appearance, long arching limbs and tightly packed bunches of short shoots. New growth is glabrous or slightly pubescent and glossy brown, darkening and developing into fruiting spurs in subsequent years. The glossy leaves are broadly ovate, about 7 cm long with an acute tip and rounded or subcordate base **4**. The margin is finely toothed. Petiols are yellowish, up to 4 cm long. Single, 3 cm flowers, in dense corymbs, have five white petals and reddish anthers. They appear before the leaves on slender 5 cm stalks **5**. The juicy, gritty fruits are pear shaped to subglobose, yellowish with russet patches in varying amounts. Minute, darker lenticels cover the skin. Seeds are lustrous dark brown to almost black. Like wild pear the timber is of high quality. But fruit trees are usually so valuable as fruit producers that little sound pear wood is ever cut. Perry pears, in particular, produce long, straight stems. **Habitat and Ecology** • Similar to wild pear (p212) which was formerly treated as a variety of this species. The most ecologically useful specimens occur in old mixed woodland or hedgerows where the fruit is particularly valuable for wildlife. Most trees today in a semi-wild situation have originated from discarded cores or naturalized from a nearby cultivated orchard or garden. **Similar species** • Identification of individual cultivated pears is a specialist skill. It often relies more on good historical information than botanical expertise.

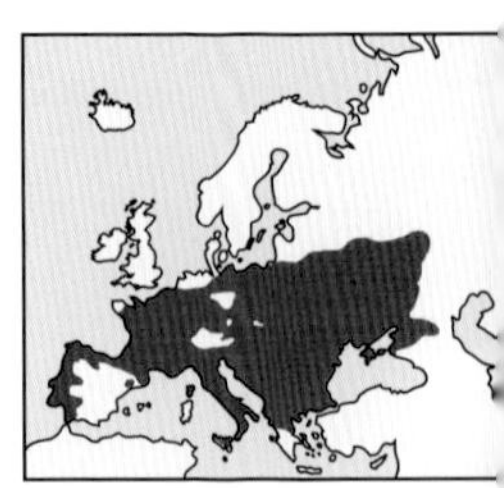

Natural range

Cultivated distribution
Distribution is world-wide. Today cultivars in the southern hemisphere supply out of season fruit to the north. Records show pears of some sort in Sennacherib’s garden in 700BC. Earliest named varieties were listed in the reign of Henri III in France and around 1611 in England.

1

4

5

2

3

FAMILY Rosaceae

Pyrus nivalis Jacq.

Snow pear

Description • The tomentose, silvery-grey backed foliage is the colour of white poplar (p290) but clearly this is a fruit tree. Small and thornless, eventually 15 m tall on a favourable site [1]. The single, white flowers which appear with the leaves are in compact corymbs and have prominent, red anthers [2]. Leaves are elliptic to obovate turning to greyish-red with a pink underside. The subglobose, upright, 5 cm fruit is yellowish-green on a long stalk [3]. **Habitat and Ecology** • Open, dry woodland in full sun. **Similar species** • Oleaster-leaved pear *Pyrus elaeagrifolia* Pall., *Pyrus nivalis* var. *austriaca* (Kern.) Schneid. and Sage-leaved pear *Pyrus x salviifolia* DC. are very similar. Willow-leaved pear (below) may be confused with it.

Natural range
An extensive area of Souther Europe from Italy to Romani and the Black Sea coast.

Cultivated distribution
Widely available in the horticultural trade but infrequently planted in the past.

Pyrus calleryana 'Chanticleer'

Description • An upright selection of a species from southern and central China. A narrow-headed tree up to 12 m tall with semi-fastigiate branches. The foliage flushes out covered in deciduous, white tomentum. White flowers occur at the same time. By midsummer the whole tree becomes completely glabrous. In autumn the leaves turn deep carmine red and finally very dark brown. **Habitat and Ecology** • Although an entirely artificial tree this cultivar does much to improve the urban environment [4]. It is usually planted as a street tree because of its narrow shape. Eventually stems become substantial, 30 cm diameter in 40 years [5]. **Similar species** • The original thornless selection of *Pyrus calleryana* called 'Bradford' was made in 1918. New developments concentrating on outstanding autumn colour have been made resulting in cultivars such as 'Autumn Blaze', 'Trinity' and 'Red Spire'.

Natural range
This cultivar was developed artificially in the United States, using a 1908 introduction from China.

Cultivated distribution
Extensively planted in city streets and squares in Europ and North America. Resistan to dust, air pollution and disease. The branches do not impede traffic or obscure street lights.

Pyrus salicifolia Pall.

Willow-leaved pear

Description • A small, slightly pendulous tree seldom reaching 8 m in height. The bark is silvery brown eventually becoming rough and dark. Shoots are white at first bearing grey-green, elliptic, 4–8 cm leaves mostly pointed at the base and tip. Dense, white corymbs of flowers usually occur freely on the species [6], but not in such profusion on the more commonly grown form 'Pendula'. The dark red anthers show up as a distinct, red spot in the centre of the flower [7]. Small, short-stalked, 3–4 cm, green pears with tiny, brown lenticels follow. **Habitat and Ecology** • Open woodlands often on harsh, dry, cold mountain sides. 'Pendula' is a garden tree tolerant of air pollution. [8]. **Similar species** • Willow-leaved pear resembles white willow (pp234–7) superficially.

Natural range
The Caucasus Mountains, Siberia and Asia Minor.

Cultivated distribution
Introduced to horticulture i 1780 but now almost completely replaced by 'Pendula', one of the finest, grey leaved, small, weeping trees available to gardeners.

1

2

3

4

5

6

7

8

FAMILY Moraceae

Morus alba L.

White mulberry

Description • A small, spreading tree on a short, often stout, stem. Usually growing in an orchard or cultivated garden environment **1**. The bark is variable but always pale coloured. Some trees are distinctly pinkish-grey. Old stems develop deep, irregular fissures which expose younger, reddish-brown layers. Shoots are slender, pubescent at first and pale grey-green. The paper thin leaves, around 15 cm long by 5–10 cm wide, are variable in shape from ovate to one to three or occasionally five-lobed. The tip may be acute, short-acuminate or rounded. The base can be cordate, curved or straight. Sometimes the midrib and two main lateral veins extend beyond the leaf blade to join the petiole a short way down its length **2**, which may be 2–6 cm. The bright green leaves are bristly on the upper surface but look smooth and glossy **3**. The underside is paler green with prominent pubescent veins. Margins have coarse but blunt rounded teeth. Flowers, which appear with the leaves **4**, male and female on the same tree, are small drooping catkins developing by late summer into white and then red fruits **2**. These are swollen, fused, fleshy petals and sepals forming a juicy, berry-like drupe held in a cluster. Like a blackberry or raspberry in appearance. Although edible they are insipid and probably harmful in large quantities. **Habitat and Ecology** • Known to have been cultivated since 2967 BC so any natural habitat or range has been totally obscured. **Similar species** • The variable nature of this tree has encouraged nurserymen to select extreme forms for cultivation. Although originally described as varieties most of these are now regarded as cultivars. 'Laciniata' ('Skeletoniana') is a cut-leaved form with leaves divided almost to the midrib and main veins. 'Macrophylla' has large 18–22 cm lobed leaves. 'Pendula' **5** has long, slender, weeping shoots and a large proportion of lobed leaves. Brilliant green foliage and neat shape make this an outstanding decorative garden tree. In a good year the fruit is an additional attraction.

Natural range
Originated in China, Japan and the Philippines.

Cultivated distribution
Few trees have such a well-documented history of cultivation. White mulberry has been used in China to feed silkworms for thousands of years. The root, leaves and fruit have also been used as medicines and as a vitamin C tonic. Ancient Chinese texts suggest that white mulberry is an indispensable aid to good health.

1

2

3

4

5

FAMILY Moraceae

Morus nigra L.

Black mulberry

Description • Most specimens seldom exceed 10 m before they fall down or need propping up in some way. This does not reduce their ability to fruit: it probably improves it. An intact tree develops a rounded top often supported by substantial, low branches **1**. The bark is orange-brown, bleached in the open by sun and rain to grey-brown and vertically fissured like oak **2**. Burrs and protruding calloused splits or breakages are common on old trees. The shoots are stiff and relatively thick, pubescent, greyish or pinkish-grey soon developing a pale lattice pattern of shallow fissures. Winter buds are stout and shiny red brown. Heart shaped leaves around 10 cm long by 7 cm wide are luxuriant and prolific. Margins are coarsely but evenly toothed except occasionally for a pair of lobes, or just a single lobe on either side. The upper surface is rough like sandpaper covered in short bristles. The underside is also rough and hairy especially on the prominent veins. Petioles up to 2.5 cm long are grooved and pubescent. The leaf blade is often supported by the petiole in such a way that rain water runs down the midrib and drips off the tip. Few trees can match the brilliant, summer green of Black mulberry leaves **3**. Flowers appear in the leaf axils in late spring. They are in short, greenish catkins, in tight clusters but not conspicuous. The sexes are separate but occur close together. Female flowers develop through the summer into 2–3 cm ovoid clusters of 30–50 rounded drupes made up of swollen sepals. White at first then red **4**, and finally black, juicy and edible. Ripe fruit is soft like a large raspberry and will usually squash when picked. It has been used medicinally for soothing coughs and sore throats, also as a laxative. The bark was once used to expel tapeworms. The unripe berries are astringent. **Habitat and Ecology** • Only cultivated trees are known. They provide an abundant food source for birds (if birds are not discouraged) in the autumn. **Similar species** • White mulberry (p218) and Paper mulberry *Broussonetia papyrifera* (L.) Vent. A small tree from Asia, naturalized in the United States, which has a greater proportion of lobed leaves and the fruits are orange.

Natural range

Black mulberry has been cultivated for so long that its Asiatic origin has become obscure. In biblical times it was taken from Iran to Southern Europe.

Cultivated distribution

Grown throughout the temperate world for centuries for its fruit. It is the 'Sycamine tree' of the Bible, where there is a reference to its permanence and ability to grow after falling down. Although thought to have been introduced to Northern Europe in 1548 records of cultivation go back to the eleventh century. It is known that mulberries were popular with the Romans, who dedicated the tree to the goddess Minerva. Linnaeus first published the name (*Morus foliis cordatis feabris*) in 1753 based upon specimens growing in Italy.

FAMILY Rosaceae

Amelanchier lamarckii Schr.

Snowy mespilus

Description • There are several species and obscure cultivars of *Amelanchier* in cultivation, mostly shrubs but one or two that look like trees. It may exceed 10 m in height but it is more likely to be under 6 m tall with a rounded outline and several stems **1**. In summer the foliage turns from coppery-brown to green. The bark is grey-brown and smooth and very old stems become slightly fissured. The leaves are elliptic to oval with a short point and more or less rounded base, margins have fine, forward-pointing teeth. In the autumn foliage colours are characteristically brilliant red and orange. New foliage, which accompanies the flowers in spring, is coppery-brown. The flowers, usually in great profusion, are white **2** in loose racemes 7–10 cm long. Each 3 cm flower has five prominent narrow petals, a brown stalk and sepals and greenish-yellow stamens and stigma **3**. The fruits, in depleted clusters, are round or oval 1 cm berries with persistent erect blackish sepals. They turn orange and red then finally purplish-black. **Habitat and Ecology** • An understorey or shrub layer of deciduous acid woodland wherever there is good water availability in the soil. **Similar species** • *Amelanchier canadensis* (below) and other species. Out of flower it is like some *Cotoneaster* (p104) and Cherry species (p154). Flowers vaguely resemble the Bird cherry group (p146).

Natural range
Unknown.

Cultivated distribution
The most widely cultivated *Amelanchier* in Western and Northern Europe. Probably a hybrid between two East North American species. It is apomictic so will come true from seed.

Amelanchier canadensis (L.) Medikus

Serviceberry

Description • Many plants in cultivation are labelled *Amelanchier canadensis*, but few are this actual species. It is a small tree up to 6 m tall with many stems and mostly upright branches **4**. Often it is confused with Snowy mespilus (above) or *Amelanchier laevis* Wieg. The flowers are white in short, upright racemes followed by red fruits **5**. Leaves are bronze-green at first then dark green with paler backs. **Habitat and Ecology** • A lowland and coastal plain thicket-forming species on sandy soils with good water availability. **Similar species** • Other *Amelanchier* species with upright flowers including Downy Serviceberry, *Amelanchier arborea* (Michx. f.) Fern **6** that some authorities in America regard as synonymous with *Amelanchier laevis* Wieg.

Natural range
Eastern North America from South West Quebec through Maine and the Atlantic States to Georgia and Alabama.

Cultivated distribution
Because of years of dubious naming this species is probably less frequent in Northern Europe than was once thought.

1

2

3

4

5

6

FAMILY Tiliaceae

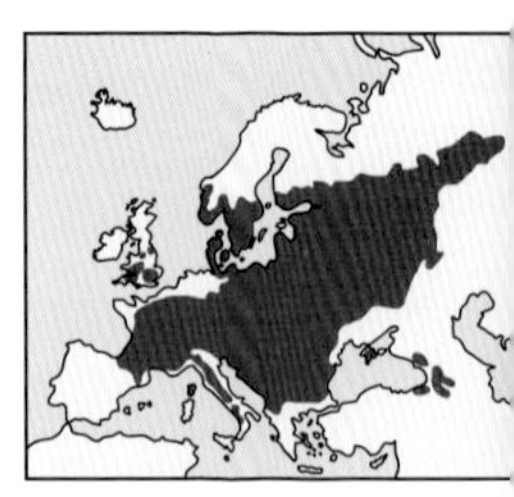

Tilia cordata Mill.

Small-leaved lime

Description • In prehistory this species was the most common tree in parts of lowland Western Europe. Now it has only sporadic distribution with a few remaining local strongholds. Until recently in Britain, for example, climatic changes have not favoured its expansion. Before the late twentieth century some individual trees had not set seed for a 100 years. Current climate change has reversed this situation and now trees covered in nectar rich flowers are commonplace **1**. This is an elegant tree up to 40 m tall with upswept branches and a rounded top **1**. In old age it becomes craggy and monumental **2**, but few trees have ever been allowed to develop an old superstructure. The species has a long history of being coppiced so most 'old' trees are actually misshapen regrowth in neglected coppices **3**. Young poles were traditionally cut while the bark was still smooth and unblemished at around 20 years of age. The bast or inner bark was removed to make coarse fabric and cordage. The root or stool lived on and some are considered to be thousands of years old **4**. The bark is grey-green and never particularly rough, although woodpeckers sometimes cause a dramatic reaction in the form of raised horizontal lines of blemishes at certain times of year, by sucking the sweet sap **5**. Side branches, if not managed, will sweep down to the ground and layer. Some specimens also sucker freely. The heart-shaped 4–7 cm leaves are more or less glabrous with even teeth and a short point. The petiole is yellowish and about as long as the leaf blade. In dry weather the foliage droops and the leaves curl up showing their pale green backs. Flowers appear in midsummer in clusters of five to ten on a long stalk attached to the centre of an elliptical pale yellow bract. Fruits are pale green **6**. **Habitat and Ecology** • Very much a cultivated tree but seldom planted. It has ancient origins and in many places is still growing from original postglacial wild roots. Small-leaved lime woods are mostly classified as ancient woodlands in the strict sense. The associated biodiversity has never been lost even if the wood has always been traditionally managed for coppice. **Similar species** • Other limes especially some forms of the hybrid Common lime (p226).

Natural range

Cultivated distribution
One of the few fibre producing plants available in Europe before jute and hemp were discovered and imported. The wood too had many traditional uses it is light and has no taste (so could be used in contact with food). Charcoal was used by artists and for gunpowder. Most famously of all it was used for decorative carving, notably by Grinling Gibbons Its cultivars are used for modern amenity planting.

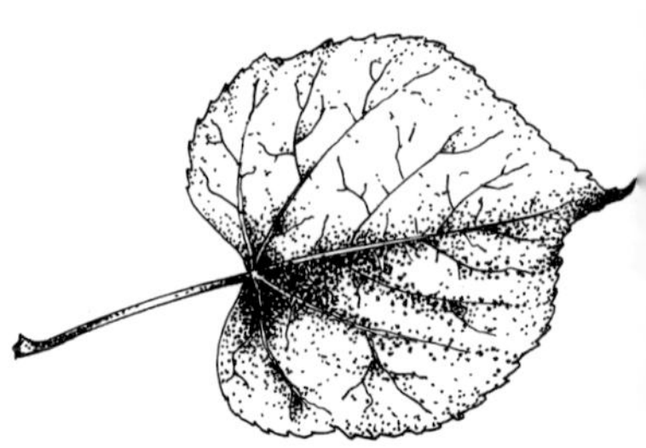

1
2
3
4
5
6

FAMILY Tiliaceae

Tilia x europaea L. (T. x vulgaris Hayne)

Common lime

Description • Invariably in Northern Europe, on an estate, town park or whole region, this will be the tallest deciduous tree. Truly a monumental structure ultimately around 45 m high on a favourable site, with a discontinuous forked stem and columnar or rounded outline **1**. Buttressed trunks 2 m in diameter are known but most trees stick at 1.5m **2**. Often these great stems are hidden by a jungle of epicormic, twiggy shoots **3**. On some individuals these extend like great bird's nests into the crown of the tree, a diagnostic feature that holds good in winter from a long way off. The bark is dull grey, very smooth on branches and young stems becoming vertically fissured and ridged. Where domestic stock have access to the trees a distinctive level grazing line develops as the edible leaves are removed **2**. Fortunately the bark on the main stem is not usually damaged by animals. Young zigzag shoots are glabrous and green becoming grey-brown in the second year. Prominent, alternate buds are oval with a blunt point, light green, tinged with red on the sunlit side. Leaves are variable in size, 8–15 cm long, more or less round with a short point and truncate, asymmetric or subcordate base. Margins have soft triangular teeth. The underside has prominent veins with distinctive light brown tufts of short hair in the acute angles formed at each junction. The petiole, about half as long as the leaf blade, is green, glabrous and round in cross-section. The midsummer scented, nectar rich flowers arc yellowish-white in clusters of around seven on a long slender stalk attached to a lanceolate papery bract **4**. Some specimens reliably flower in great profusion, a valuable resource for bee keepers **5**. Fruits are 8 mm round, green, slightly ribbed spheres in small clusters **6**. **Habitat and Ecology** • Never a woodland tree, always found in cultivated, or previously cultivated and now neglected, situations. Traditionally used as an avenue tree and planted in lines for landscape amenity. In cities it is notorious for the 'rain' of sticky honeydew expelled by aphids sucking sap from the foliage. In time this substance becomes infested with a black mould which itself becomes a characteristic of identification. **Similar species** • This hybrid between Small-leaved lime (p224) and Large-leaved lime (p228) is variable and may be confused with either parent. Several exotic limes have similar looking foliage but none is as large.

Natural range
Spontaneous hybrids have occured but most trees are artificially produced.

Cultivated distribution
The exact origin of this hybrid is uncertain. It has been in cultivation for several hundred years. For a long time nurserymen have been cultivating it vegetatively from easy to obtain basal, epicormic shoots. By so doing they have proliferated a type of tree that has this unsightly feature. A narrower German form 'Pallida' with light green foliage is fashionable at the moment.

1
2
3
4
5
6

FAMILY Tiliaceae

Tilia platyphyllos Scop.

Large-leaved lime

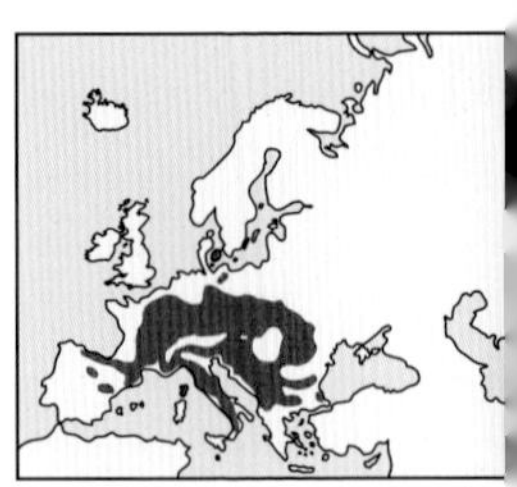

Natural range

Cultivated distribution
A native species occurring in woodlands and managed in that situation for amenity an conservation but seldom deliberately planted as a horticultural specimen. It is rather large and spreading fo normal urban use. There are several cultivated forms most importantly 'Rubra' the Red-twigged lime, favoured for avenues and street planting especially when periodically pruned to encourage the ruby-red new shoots **5**. Because it is propagated vegetatively trees are uniform in growth rate, size and shap

Description • Usually a large tree often with a wide-spreading, rounded top. Heights up to 40 m are known, with stems in excess of 1 m diameter. In open situations this is a much smaller tree with a more irregular outline **1**. It grows well in a woodland situation and may produce a straight, clean, branch-free bole **2**. Usually though it has large branches from low down on the stem **3**. Sometimes a few epicormic shoots are also produced. The bark is grey and relatively smooth only developing irregular cracks and ridges in old age. Shoots are green for a short time turning reddish by the second year. On some individual trees shoots are very hairy on others they are less so. Buds are oval with a rounded point, darkish-green with only two or three visible scales. The leaves are hairy, a good diagnostic feature. Some are velvety on both sides others have stiff pubescence mainly confined to the underside for most of the summer. They feel completely different to the somewhat clammy leaves of Common and Small-leaved limes (previous pages). An average leaf is around 12 cm long with a slender point and oblique subcordate base **4**. There are uneven, forward-pointing, soft teeth round the margin and about ten pairs of veins that are prominent on the underside. There is considerable variation in leaf size and hairiness which depends to some extent on the particular subspecies being examined. The most common (and most hairy) in Northern Europe is subspecies *cordifolia* (Besser) C. Schneider. Flowers are in clusters of three to six: they develop into 1 cm round-ribbed, light greenish-brown fruits. **Habitat and Ecolo gy** • A woodland tree of great potential size, moderately shade tolerant at first. Prefers moist, relatively fertile soils. **Similar species** • Other Limes but few have such distinctly soft, pubescent foliage. Confidence in field identification may sometimes be undermined because some trees do not have the otherwise most reliable identification feature – the velvety pubescent leaves. These are likely to be the introduced subspecies *pseudorubra* Schneid., the southern form originating in the Ukraine, Romania and Bulgaria. Intermediates occur between northern and southern types.

1

2

4

3

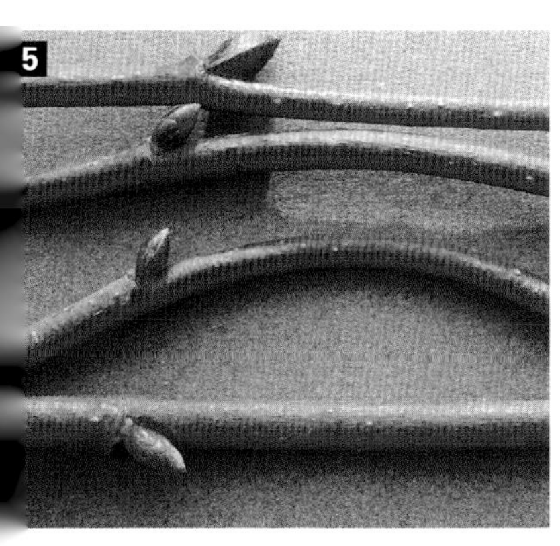
5

FAMILY Tiliaceae

Tilia x euchlora K. Koch

Caucasian lime

Description • A compact tree often less than 15 m tall with a rounded outline [1]. The ascending branches arch over at the extremities and on mature specimens may weep down to the ground. The bark is grey and usually smooth. Parkland trees are sometimes grafted at the base on to much coarser Common lime (p226). Stems are otherwise straight and up to 80 cm thick. The dark, glossy leaves are toothed, more or less round, 6–12 cm long with a short tip and oblique rounded or subcordate base [2]. Summer flowers are in clusters of five to seven on a slender stem joined to the centre of a narrow bract. Fruits are ovoid about 7 mm long, slightly tapered at both ends. **Habitat and Ecology** • A hybrid with obscure origins and parentage. **Similar species** • Other small limes but none is as glossy leaved or pendulous.

Natural range
Probably originated naturally in the Crimea. Thought to be a cross between *Tilia dasystyl* Steven subsp. *caucasica*, and Small-leaved lime (p224).

Cultivated distribution
Widely grown in parks and a an urban open space tree. It does not attract aphids but the flowers are narcotic to some bees.

Tilia tomentosa Moench 'Petiolaris'

Silver pendent lime

Description • A huge, 35 m tall tree with cathedral-like ascending and arching limbs rising up into a mass of white-backed foliage. The outside of the tree has a greener appearance [3]. Stems are pale grey and have shallow furrows and slightly rough ridges [4]. They are often grafted some way above the ground and the scion is invariably more vigorous than the rootstock causing an ugly discrepancy. The leaves are more or less round or heart-shaped with uneven teeth, some of which are prominent like small lobes. There are six pairs of parallel veins. The underside is brilliant white giving the whole tree a light appearance on a windy day [5]. In dry weather leaves tend to droop downwards under their own weight [6]. Flowers are strongly scented, pale yellow in clusters of four to eight. Fruits are roundish, grooved and glandular. **Habitat and Ecology** • Thought to be a hybrid of *Tilia tomentosa* but of unknown origin. **Similar species** • *Tilia oliveri* Szyszlowicz, and superficially the leaves of the Handkerchief tree (p188).

Natural range
Uncertain but probably Sout West Russia.

Cultivated distribution
Not common probably because of its expensive and lengthy nursery top grafting treatment. Seeds do not germinate without special preparation. Flowers are narcotic to some bees, but aphids are not attracted to th foliage in summer. Weak branch forks, potential large size and the incompatible graft union make this plant unpopular with arboriculturalists.

1

2

3

4

5

6

FAMILY Salicaceae

Salix babylonica L. 'Pendula'
Chinese weeping willow

Description • The true species *Salix babylonica* is tender in much of Northern Europe. This pendulous form is slightly more hardy, but is seldom seen now because it is replaced in cultivation by various other weeping willows (p262). It is a strongly weeping, graceful tree seldom exceeding 10 m in height **1**. The narrow leaves are lance-shaped with fine, tapered points and small, evenly toothed margins. Their slightly glaucous backs give the foliage a shimmering light green effect. Shoots are glabrous olive green to pale brown. Most cultivated individuals are female. Yellowish catkins appear with the leaves in early spring, they are slender, 3 cm long and sessile with two or three small leaves at the base. **Habitat and Ecology** • A wetland tree in open situations. **Similar species** • Other weeping willows particularly the *Salix x pendulina* (p262) group. *Salix matsudana* 'Pendula' appears to be synonymous with *Salix babylonica* 'Pendula'.

Natural range
Widespread in river valleys in China, North West India and Tibet.

Cultivated distribution
Probably introduced to the Middle East at an early date giving some credibility to biblical willow references although the real 'willows of Babylon' are thought to be *Populus euphratica* Oliv.

Salix babylonica L. (matsudana) 'Tortuosa'
Corkscrew willow or Dragon's claw willow

Description • A familiar plant in cultivation often under its now invalid name *Salix matsudana* 'Tortuosa'. The tangled and contorted twigs **2** are olive brown, glabrous and glossy. Stems and branches grow rapidly, up to 1 m per year, but tend to split easily under their own weight. Leaves too are misshapen and contorted but bright green. Catkins are late to appear amongst fully formed foliage. Stems often over 30 cm diameter are greyish and orange-yellow becoming vertically fissured. **Habitat and Ecology** • No natural habitat is known. Cultivated plants seem to prefer wet ground. **Similar species** • Only *Salix x erythroflexuosa* Rag., which is a hybrid of this species, looks similar. Its twigs are bright red when growing vigorously. The cultivar 'Crispa' formerly 'Annularis' is another peculiar aberration of similar origin with curled and contorted leaves. It is a weak plant seldom surviving for long **3**.

Natural range
Unknown in the wild but originated somewhere in Northern China.

Cultivated distribution
Introduced to France in the early 1920s and now widely planted all round the temperate world.

2

3

FAMILY Salicaceae

Salix alba L.

White willow

Description • A tree up to 25 m tall with smooth, ascending, grey-green branches supporting thin, lax foliage **1**. Mature bark has vertical fissures becoming rugged with old age **2**. Huge stems over 2 m in diameter are known. Unlike Crack willow (p248) large branches do not break off easily so neglected pollards remain intact for longer **3**. Nevertheless large willow limbs do become brittle and eventually succumb to storm damage. Young trees are often narrow crowned, silvery green and elegant. Good clones with these attributes have long been selected and reproduced vegetatively for urban amenity planting. Twigs are flexible and silky pubescent when young, later glabrous, lustrous and olive-brown. They do not crack off easily at a joint like Crack willow (p248). Leaves are narrow, 5–10 cm long and only 1–2 cm wide, slender pointed at each end and finely toothed. The overall colour is silvery green **4**. There are silky-white, adpressed hairs above and below but most numerous and persistent on the underside **5**. The petiole is short, not more than 1 cm, with four to six small, dark glands close to the leaf. Stipules when present are small, 5 mm and narrow. Catkins appear with the leaves in late spring. Males are up to 5 cm long, densely pale yellow flowered. Each individual flower has two stamens. Female catkins are shorter and pale grey-green. Seed capsules are flask-shaped ripening in midsummer and shedding minute seeds amongst copious quantities of white fluff. The seed is viable for only a short time and carries no reserves of food so rapid contact with damp ground is essential for germination. The seed fluff carrier can hinder this unless it is soon flattened by heavy rain. **Habitat and Ecology** • A vital component of floodplain woodland but requiring open, light conditions to thrive. Natural distribution and even the exact genetic nature of native plants have been masked by centuries of cultivation. Local populations are often clonal particularly if they are naturalized or planted. Vegetative propagation is easy but natural regeneration by seed is not. **Similar species** • Of the tree willows, this species has superior grey-green or silvery foliage. There are however greyish forms of *Salix x rubens* (p250) that resemble it. Similar coloured and shaped leaves occur on Willow-leaved pear (p216).

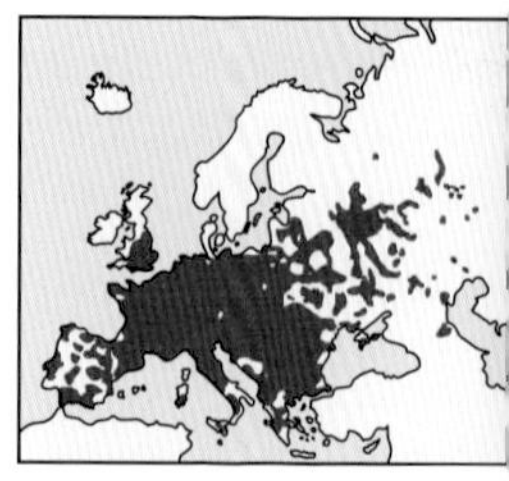

Natural range

Cultivated distribution

Selected since ancient times for its soft pliable wood. Ideal for turnery, dry cooperage especially barrel hoops, domestic utensils, mill work, charcoal for gunpowder and even treated weather-boarding. The bark was once highly valued for tanning and the foliage for its medicinal qualities.

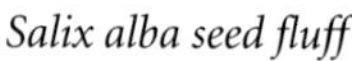

Salix alba seed fluff

FAMILY Salicaceae

Salix alba L. var. caerulea (Sm.) Sm.

Cricket-bat willow

Description • Also called blue willow because of the distinctive blue-grey sheen emanating from the summer foliage. Potentially a very large tree, 30 m tall but mostly grown in plantations and harvested before ultimate height is reached. If not pruned to produce cricket-bat material this tree is very like white willow (p234), an erect, branching pyramidal or loosely rounded specimen. Sometimes mature pollards are seen which have originated as failed commercial trees or where cuttings have been established and cut back in hedgerows close to commercial plantations. The translucent leaves are slightly larger than ordinary white willow but otherwise similar in shape. They lose the silvery hairs from the young growth quite quickly and become dull bluish-green above and paler and glaucescent below **1**. The favoured and original clone selected for bat manufacture is female but the variety now includes several different cultivated individuals of both sexes. **Habitat and Ecology** • Similar in most respects to *Salix alba* (p234)although not known in the wild state. The exceptional vigour has led some authorities to suggest hybrid origin possibly involving Crack willow (p248). It prefers wet ground especially sand and gravel adjacent to freely running streams. It tolerates open woodland conditions **2** provided there is full light on all sides of the crown. Best growth occurs on fertile mineral soil. Intensive management involves wide planting distance (10 m), early stem pruning (pinching out buds) to form a clean bole **3**, and clearance of competitive ground vegetation. Most trees are felled on a short rotation. **Similar species** • *Salix x rubens* (p250) is a polymorphous group of hybrids some of which closely resemble this variety. The backcross (formerly var. *albescens* Anderss) to *Salix alba* differs only in 'having more spreading branches', an impossible attribute to quantify.

The bacterial disease of Cricket-bat willow *Bacterium salicis* Day (Watermark disease) causes wilting of foliage in early summer and bacterial slime on the stem. The infected wood becomes discoloured and unsuitable for the manufacture of cricket bats.

Natural range

Eastern England and adjacent areas of Europe, although confused nineteenth century taxonomy undermines any certainty about the trees proper identity. Whether cricket-bat willow trees originally selected were wild or introduced is unknown.

Cultivated distribution

James Crowe an English surgeon of Norwich found a female plant 'wild' in Suffolk, in the parish of Eriswell in 1803. The variety was known locally before that date. A tree of this clone in Essex 30 m tall was cut down in 1899. It is said to have contained enough wood to make 1179 cricket-bats. Plantations and escaped trees are still common in South-eastern England.

2

3

FAMILY Salicaceae

Salix alba L. var. argentea Wimm.

Silver-leaved white willow or Silver willow

Description • Also known in cultivation as *Salix alba* var. *sericea* Gaud. and var. *splendens* Schneid. The most brilliantly silver leaved forms of white willow are included here. There are obviously variants selected by different people some of which are distributed as horticultural clones. Usually var. *argentea* is a small tree less than 8 m tall with a spreading crown **1**. The foliage is dazzling white in early summer **2**. **Habitat and Ecology** • A wetland tree like *Salix alba* (p234). **Similar species** • Amenity selections (e.g. 'Belders Clone'). There is a narrow-leafed form 'Argentea Elegantissima'. Also Willow leaved pear (p216).

Natural range
Within the range of *Salix alba* but only as a rare variant.

Cultivated distribution
Widely grown as a small ornamental tree in parks and gardens. Completely hardy in Europe even close to the sea.

Salix alba L. var. vitellina (L.) Stokes

Golden-twigged willow

Description • Similar to the species but having golden yellow current shoots, a feature disguised by foliage in summer but striking in winter. Trees 10–15 m tall are known **3**. In an uncultivated state the stem colour is confined to short, new growth which becomes greyish yellow in the second year then simply grey **4**. In cultivation as annually cut coppice, brilliant yellow shoots grow four to five times longer **5**. **Habitat and Ecology** • Said to be unknown in the wild but degrees of yellow bark occur in *Salix alba* and *Salix fragilis* (p284) populations. **Similar species** • A whole range of dubiously named yellowish clones exist. Also *Salix x rubens* nv. *basfordiana* (p250).

Natural range
Unknown in the wild.

Cultivated distribution
Widely grown for amenity as a winter shrub feature. Formerly used as a basket osier with the bark kept on. One parent of golden weeping willow (p262).

Salix alba L. var. chermesina hort.

Scarlet willow

Description • A cultivated form of var. *vitellina* with brilliant orange-red current shoots. An alternative trade name is 'Cardinalis' the Cardinal willow. It makes a 6 m, red-twigged tree if left alone with attractive summer foliage **6**. The effect is more stunning if it is coppiced or pollarded annually and treated as a winter feature. **Habitat and Ecology** • A horticultural selection of *Salix alba*. **Similar species** • There are a confusing range of nursery cultivars including 'Chrysostela' **7** and 'Britzensis'. Also *Cornus alba* L. the Red-barked dogwood when regularly coppiced.

Natural range
Unknown in the wild.

Cultivated distribution
Widely grown as clumps of coppice in winter gardens and parks.

1

2

3

4

5

6

7

FAMILY Salicaceae

Salix caprea L.

Goat willow

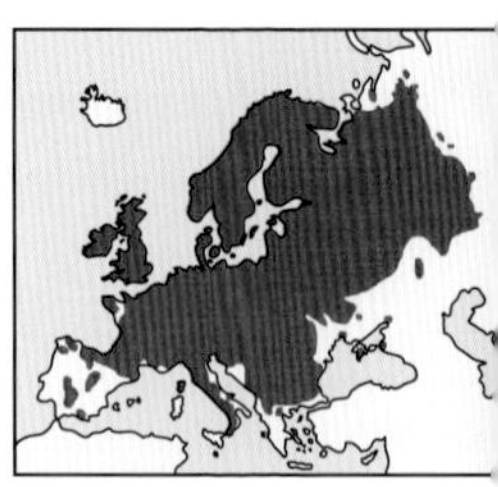

Natural range

Cultivated distribution For a short time it was fashionable to include Goat willow in urban tree planting schemes. Unfortunately half the seedling plants were female and their seed fluff was regarded as a nuisance. Nurserymen successfully growing Goat willow from male hardwood cuttings found that they were not growing Goat willow at all.

Description • Great sallow as it was once known is not specifically a wetland species. In the north and at high elevation it is frequently represented by the variety *sphacelata* (p98). Like most willows it is dioecious so there are individual male and female trees. Each generation of seedling progeny has therefore to involve two trees, and as so many sallows are sexually and phenologically compatible hybrids are frequent. Precise identification, or even the definition of 'pure' Goat willow, has now become a matter of some speculation. To add to the problem the tree will not reproduce vegetatively in nature by growing from winter twigs forced into soil or mud as most other willows do. Its lineage depends almost entirely upon seeding (which it is very good at) so the species is in a constant state of evolution. The illustrations here depict trees that are as 'average' as possible. It is a large shrub or small, rounded tree, 6–8 m tall **1**, most obvious when in flower **2**. Male catkins are bright yellow after emerging silky white and often completely covering the tree before the leaves appear. Female catkins are slightly larger but grey-green **3**. Stems may exceed 80 cm in diameter often divided into two or more stems at the base **4** with brownish-grey bark, irregularly fissured and ridged **5**. Twigs may be greenish-brown, brownish-red or on some individuals almost black all with red-brown buds which only have one visible scale. The underlying wood on young 2–3 cm thick shoots is, except for bud scars, entirely without striae, short, vertical ridges common on most other sallows. The leaves are broad, bright green and reticulate on the upper surface **6**. Densely woolly and grey on the underside **7**. Margins are irregularly wavy with occasional rounded, glandular teeth. On vigorous young shoots there are ear shaped stipules on either side of the base of the 2–3 cm petiole **6**. Male flowers each have two stamens, female flowers are flask shaped with long, silvery hairs **3**: both sexes are rich in nectar. **Habitat and Ecology** • Hedgerows, woodland clearings, margins and gravel road alignments or other newly disturbed ground where the seed can quickly germinate. There is an apparent preference for lime rich soils. **Similar species** • *Salix caprea* var. *sphacelata* and other broad-leaved sallows. Confused mostly with the wide range of spontaneous hybrids it generates itself.

Male flower

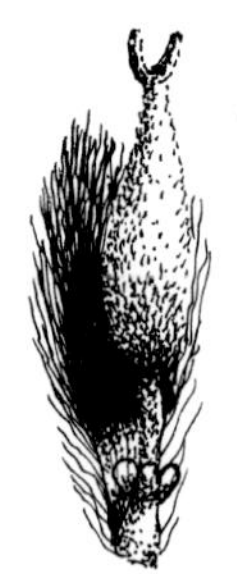

Female flower

1
2
3
4
5
6
7

FAMILY Salicaceae

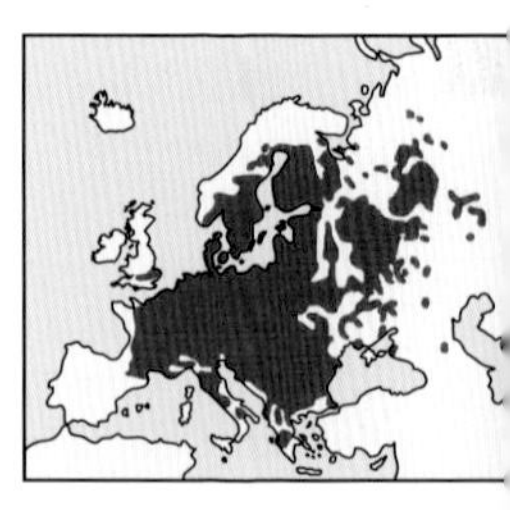

Salix cinerea L. subsp. cinerea
Grey sallow

Description • Grey sallow is divided into two subspecies. They are distinct in theory but hybrids between them produce many confusing intermediate forms. Subspecies *cinerea* is a Continental type that extends into Eastern Britain. It is a tree or large shrub seldom over 6 m tall usually with several or many main stems **1**. The largest of these is unlikely to be over 20 cm diameter. Trees larger than this tend to break up or fall over and begin to regrow from branch material pushed into wet ground **2**. The bark is grey-brown becoming fissured with age. Shoots are grey-green then reddish-brown and densely pubescent in the first year. The leaves are variable in shape and size but uniformly hairy and grey-green **3**. Generally they are larger than subsp. *oleifolia* (below) with an undulating margin and indistinct teeth. On vigorous growth there are large, persistent stipules. The young wood is distinctly striated. **Habitat and Ecology** • Freshwater bogs, marshland, fens, riversides and by open water. **Similar species** • Other Sallow willows especially the hybrid *Salix x reichardtii* (p244) **4**.

Natural range

Cultivated distribution
This species and subspecies have never been cultivated fc basket osiers, amenity or any other purpose. It is a valuabl fast-growing, easily established plant for erosion control having a dense fibrous root system.

Salix cinerea L. subsp. oleifolia Macreight
Common sallow

Description • A bushy shrub or small tree with a single trunk or a number of main stems. In the open it develops a compact outline **5**, but as a thicket or in a carr situation it is a shapeless spreading plant constantly collapsing and being rejuvenated vegetatively **6**. Shoots are dark brown with weak striations on the wood under the bark. Leaves are narrowly ovate, pointed or rounded and with a wedge-shaped or rounded base. When viewed obliquely they have stiff hairs on the grey underside that are rusty-brown, a diagnostic feature, but not immediately obvious until late summer or when the leaves are viewed square on. The upper surface is dark green. Vigorous growth has deciduous ear-shaped stipules. Flowers occur before the leaves. Male trees produce yellow catkins, they flower well but less conspicuously than Goat willow (p240). Female flowers are pale grey-green **7**, soon producing copious amounts of seed fluff **8**. **Habitat and Ecology** • Similar to subspecies *cinerea* (above) but also thrives on drier ground, hillsides and lower mountain slopes. **Similar species** • Hybrid sallows and *Salix aurita* L. in upland areas.

Natural range
The subspecies occupies the western extremeties of the species.

Cultivated distribution
Never cultivated commercially or even described as a distinct supspecies until 1837. Its environmental value is recognized, so existing semi natural plants enjoy some degree of protection.

1
2
3
4
5
6
7
8

FAMILY Salicaceae

Salix x reichardtii A. Kern.

Hybrid sallow

Description • This large shrub or small tree is a hybrid between *Salix caprea* L. (p240) and *Salix cinerea* L. (p242), a common cross often repeated on waste ground, railway tracks and forest rides **1**. The shoots are grey, pubescent at first then glabrous and olive-brown. Underbark striae are infrequent or absent. The foliage is variable, dense in full light but sparse in the shade **2**. Leaves are mostly obovate with felted, grey-green backs showing a network of prominent veins **3**. This is a polymorphic hybrid linking the parents in an unbroken series of intermediate forms produced by continuous crossing and backcrossing. It also seems probable that both subspecies of *Salix cinerea* (p242) are represented as parents. **Habitat and Ecology** • Hybrid swarms take on the identity and environmental requirements of the parent species. *Salix caprea* requires dryish ground, *Salix cinerea* grows anywhere including swamps and the margins of stagnant water. Millions of seedlings are produced and those best suited to a particular location survive. **Similar species** • The parents and other broadleaved sallow species and hybrids.

Natural range
Common within the ranges of the parent species but native status is uncertain.

Cultivated distribution
Not cultivated but encouraged in some nature reserves because of the immense environmental benefits for wildlife. Often replaces Goat willow in cultivation, probably by mistake.

Salix x sericans Tausch ex A. Kerner

Description • A spreading bush or branchy tree up to 8 m tall. Twigs are orange-brown after grey pubescence on new growth wears off. Stems are generally only 10–20 cm in diameter but almost always multiple. Often outer shoots have no place to grow except outwards, forming an extensive thicket **4**. Peeled twigs have no striae. Leaves are ovate-lanceolate, up to 12 cm long with silvery pubescence on young growth for a short time **5**. Later the upper surface becomes dull green and glabrous but the underside remains grey tomentose and is soft to the touch like the *Salix caprea* parent **6**. Margins are variable, sometimes recurved like the *Salix viminalis* (p96) parent, sometimes glandular toothed and undulating, often a mixture of both. Male and female catkins in profusion on separate plants resemble those of *Salix viminalis*. **Habitat and Ecology** • Natural in wet places, gravel beds, etc. also escaped from osier beds or still in cultivation. **Similar species** • Many *Salix viminalis* hybrids and commercial osiers, especially *Salix x smithiana* (p98).

Natural range
Similar to the parent species but obscured by centuries of cultivation.

Cultivated distribution
Occasionally grown as a basket willow. Also tried as a potential short rotation biomass plant to produce renewable energy. It grows readily from winter cuttings, an attribute entirely inherited from the *Salix viminalis* parent.

1
2
3
4
5
6

FAMILY Salicaceae

Salix x calodendron Wimm.

Description • An erect shrub **1** or small tree seldom over 10 m tall with multiple stems not more than 25 cm in diameter **2**. Shoots are velvety at first becoming glabrous by the end of the first year. The wood at three years of age has long, distinctive striae suggesting *Salix cinerea* (p242) in the parentage. The foliage is dark and grey-green when seen from a distance. Leaves are leathery textured, around 10 cm long with prominent veins on the grey, pubescent underside **3**. Margins are partly recurved and partly glandular toothed. The most vigorous growth seems to be more distinctly toothed. New growth also has conspicuous, ear-shaped stipules at the base of the short 1–2 cm rigid petiole. Catkins appear before the leaves from almost every bud towards the top of terminal shoots. This causes distinctive lengths of bare shoot which remain leafless later on in the year. Only female trees are known: the flowers are tightly packed together in a 5 cm catkin with silvery-green bracts at its base. Seed does not appear to develop even when this willow is planted close to other sallows. **Habitat and Ecology** • Almost certainly an escape from cultivated osier beds which thrives best in wet boggy ground. **Similar species** • A vast number of hybrid willows in the 'cap-cin-vim' (see below) category.

Natural range
None, but some affinity with *Salix aegyptiaca* L. from West Asia is suggested.

Cultivated distribution
Formerly grown as a heavy basket osier but now usually found as an escape from cultivation.

Salix x dasyclados

Description • This invalid scientific name is included here to represent a vast group of hybrid sallows in Northern Europe with 'cap-cin-vim' (*Salix caprea x Salix cinerea x Salix viminalis*) parentage. There are numerous plants in the wild that exhibit characteristics of these parents but at present there is no authenticated binomial designation for them. They are variable, vigorous, upright bushes or small, multi-stemmed trees around 8 m tall **4**. Confusingly there is a species, *Salix dasyclados* Wimm., in Central Europe and Russia which is, it is claimed, altogether unlikely to be a feral hybrid or a complex of diverse hybrids. However plants of this species grown in Britain from Russia appear to have much in common with the 'cap-cin-vim' hybrids **5**. **Habitat and Ecology** • A multiple hybrid of three (or more) species occurring in neglected fairly wet places. **Similar species** • Numerous 'sallow hybrids', the most appropriate designation for plants of this sort found in the semi-wild state.

Natural range
Unknown for the hybrid. Th species extends from Poland to Siberia north to the fores tundra belt.

Cultivated distribution
The only published referenc suggests *Salix x dasyclados* is represented in cultivation b the male clone 'Grandis', originally 'Aquatica Grandis In fact this is probably Wimmer's 1849 species *dasyclados* from Silesia.

FAMILY Salicaceae

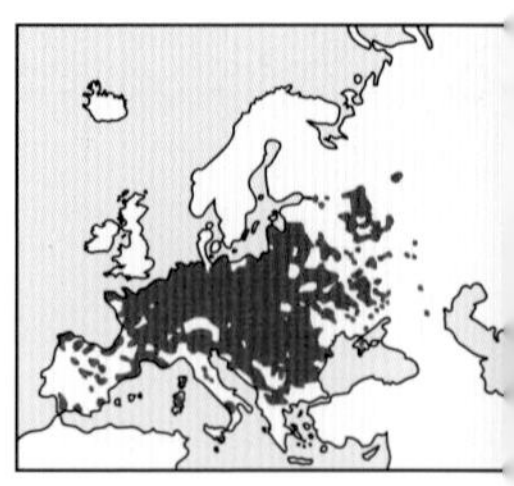

Salix fragilis L.
Crack willow

Description • A large tree with a ragged outline as major limbs crack off. Often pollarded and developing a large girth stem [1]. Botanically the status of this tree is uncertain as the name is usually broadly applied to a complex group of tree willows. In the strict sense the name should refer to the single variety (*Salix fragilis* L. var. *fragilis*) usually represented by a clonal population reproduced vegetatively along river sides [2]. It is generally a small tree, 15 m tall, which readily falls to pieces [3] and produces characteristic 'water roots' [4]. The brittle twigs are glossy olive brown. Mature shoots crack audibly at the point of attachment to second or third year wood if pushed gently downwards. Leaves are glossy green with glaucous undersides becoming completely glabrous. Margins are distinctly glandular toothed. Around 12 cm long and 2.5 cm wide, pointed at both ends on a short, glandular petiole. Deciduous stipules are present on young vigorous growth and coppice. Flowers appear with the leaves, male and female on separate trees. Male catkins 5 cm long are pale yellow with stamens in pairs, sometimes threes: female flowers are pale green. Most clonal populations are all female. **Habitat and Ecology** • Riparian (riverside), nectar rich and good for early bees and other insects. **Similar species** • *Salix x rubens* (p250) and *Salix triandra* (p254).

Natural range

Cultivated distribution
Seldom cultivated. Not suitable for basket osier beds. Often found in hedgerows when living stakes have been used for fencing and hedge repairs.

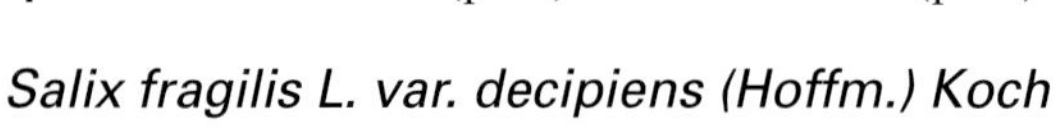

Salix fragilis L. var. decipiens (Hoffm.) Koch
White Welsh willow

Description • A typical Crack willow but generally smaller, 10–12 m tall with coarsely fissured bark [5]. First-year shoots are yellowish and lustrous. The 10 × 2–3 cm leaves are finely toothed [6]. Male catkins are 3 cm long, rather slender and erect on the stem appearing with emerging leaves. Female flowers, which are rare, on separate plants, are slightly larger. **Habitat and Ecology** • A wetland tree seldom found wild but frequent as an escape. **Similar species** • Other Crack willows, *Salix alba* var. *vitellina* in winter (p238) and *Salix triandra* (p254).

Natural range
Native status uncertain because of extensive cultivation.

Cultivated distribution
The common name, more correctly White Welsh osier, was used in Norfolk and Cambridgeshire for the bask rods.

Salix fragilis L. var. russelliana (Sm.) Koch
Bedford willow

Description • A large Crack willow tree 25–30 m tall, frequently pollarded [8]. The foliage is luxuriant green [7], less glaucous than other varieties. Leaves are 12–15 cm long and up to 3 cm wide, glossy green with distinct glandular teeth and petiole. In vigorous growth petiole glands may be subfoliaceous like *Salix triandra*. Young shoots are polished yellow then olive-brown. Slender female catkins 4 cm long occur with the leaves. Male trees are unknown. **Habitat and Ecology** • Like the rest of the *Salix fragilis* aggregate. Grows very easily from cuttings so appears on a wide range of sites. **Similar species** • *Salix fragilis* var *fragilis*.

Natural range
Uncertain but may occur naturally in central England and Holland.

Cultivated distribution
Extensive, first introduced t Woburn Abbey before 1795 and named in honour of the owner, the 5th Duke of Bedford.

1
2
3
4
5
6
7
8

FAMILY Salicaceae

Salix x rubens Schrank

Description • A complex variable hybrid between *Salix alba* (p234) and *Salix fragilis* (p248). A wide range of intermediates occur from *Salix alba* to *Salix fragilis* (var. *decipiens*). It is tempting, and usually acceptable in Europe, to assume that any tree which is not quite one or other parent can be assigned to this group. At its best it is a vigorous spreading tree up to 25 m tall with vertically fissured bark **1**. In isolation it develops a broadly rounded crown **2**, especially if it has been pollarded in the past. In woodland it is drawn up to the light and produces long, slender stems **3**. Shoots are thinly pubescent at first soon becoming glabrous glossy and often brightly coloured olive-brown to yellowish. Leaves are 9–15 cm long, lanceolate with adpressed white pubescence at first, soon becoming glabrous above, but variable depending upon the origin of the population. Catkins are spreading, narrowly cylindrical, up to 6 cm long occurring with the young leaves. Males are fairly lax and bright yellow. Females, on separate trees, are shorter, grey-green with flask shaped flowers. Fertile seed is produced and backcrossing with the parent species is possible. Once established on wet ground from seed populations reproduction is usually vegetative. Natural clonal carr woodlands and plantations of distinct regional types are common. **Habitat and Ecology** • Selected in the past for low-grade but high-volume wood production, fencing, charcoal and fuel. Used in place of white willow on poor wet ground when the true species was not readily available locally. Of little or no value as a basket willow. **Similar species** • In its most intermediate form very like cricket-bat willow but bats made from it are inadequate. Coloured twig forms are frequent, most are usually replaced in horticulture by recognized red and yellow forms. Nothovar *basfordiana* (Scaling ex Salter) Meikle is the best known. Its shoots are brilliant red at the tip merging into orange then yellow at the base **4**. If allowed to develop into a tree it reaches 10–15 m but the winter twig colour is confined to the extremities of the crown. When cut annually as coppice it gives a fine display of orange and red winter colour **5**. Less often planted is forma. *sanguinea* Meikle possibly brought into cultivation from the forests of the Ardennes. It is also found wild or naturalized in the British Isles and is reminiscent of a red-twigged form of *Salix fragilis*.

Natural range
There is a wide range of variants within this series of hybrids. Extensive cultivation has made it difficult to determine authentic native status.

Cultivated distribution
In the past this hybrid was cultivated vegetatively as a wetland and carr plantation tree. It will grow reasonably well in open forest but subordinate individuals are soon suppressed and die. Plantations, most of which are no longer managed, are usually clonal and single sex. The best-quality produce comes from variants close to *Salix alba*.

1

2

3

4

5

FAMILY Salicaceae

Salix daphnoides Vill.
Violet willow

Description • Most specimens encountered are shrubby bushes, seldom exceeding 5 m in height. This species is rare as a wild plant because its distribution has been confused by past cultivation. Mature bark is smooth and grey. Branches are dark purplish-red and variably pruinose, with waxy, grey bloom. Leaves are narrowly obovate and around 10 cm long **1**: dark green and glossy on the upper side and glaucous below. Margins have evenly spaced glandular teeth and for a time there may be toothed stipules at the base of the pale coloured petiole. Single-scale buds are large and purplish-red turning almost black just before being forced off the catkin or developing leaves **2**. Flowers are showy, in pearly white upright catkins in late winter before the leaves appear. Males become yellow each with two stamens, females are pale green on separate trees. Flowers are mainly on weak side shoots **3**: on coppiced osiers they crowd dramatically along second-year main stems. **Habitat and Ecology** • Mainly an upland species thriving along mountain streams and on scree or gravel banks. **Similar species** • *Salix irrorata* Anderss is a North American counterpart. Most examples planted in Europe appear to be exceptionally pruinose **4**.

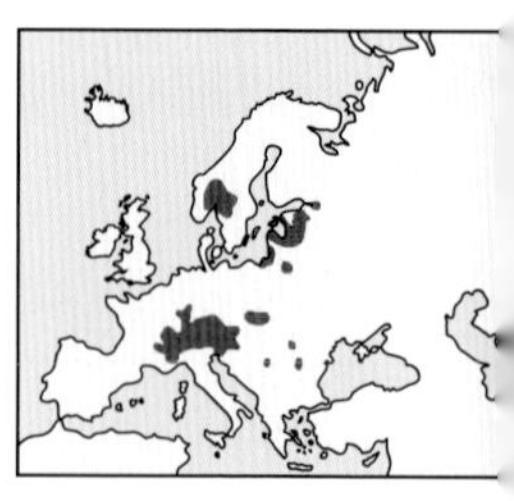

Natural range

Cultivated distribution
Seldom grown as the true species. The ornamental clon 'Aglaia' has become very popular as a garden plant. It i a vigorous, floriferous, 6 m tree but the shoots are less purple. There are also a few, rare, brilliantly coloured basket osiers such as 'Oxford Violet' and 'Continental Purple' surviving in specialis collections.

Salix myrsinifolia Salisb.
Dark-leaved sallow

Description • Occasionally a small tree but usually a spreading bush **5**. This is an ecologically important upland species but it is not common and easily confused with other sallows. A curious characteristic is that dead leaves turn black (not brown). Twigs are greenish at first then dark brown or almost black. Leaves are obovate, thin textured, 4–6 cm long, dark lustrous green above and glaucous below. Petioles are 1 cm long with deciduous, variable stipules. Catkins appear with the leaves. **Habitat and Ecology** • Wet flushes at high elevation or exposed reed beds. **Similar species** • The foliage is like *Salix phylicifolia* L., Tea-leaved willow **6**, but dead leaves of this species turn brown.

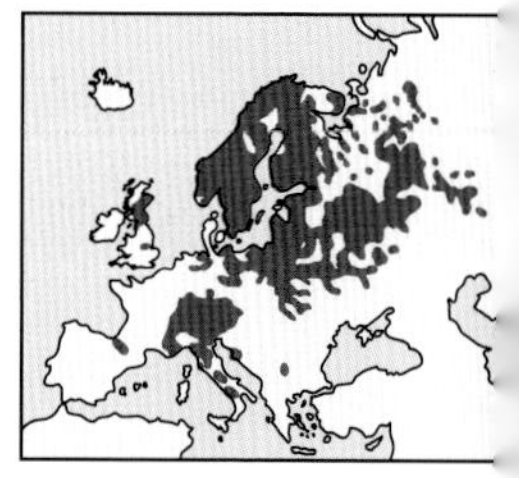

Natural range

Cultivated distribution
Not generally cultivated although a few commercial osiers are known mostly under the name *Salix nigricans* Sm. They have almost black young bark.

1

2

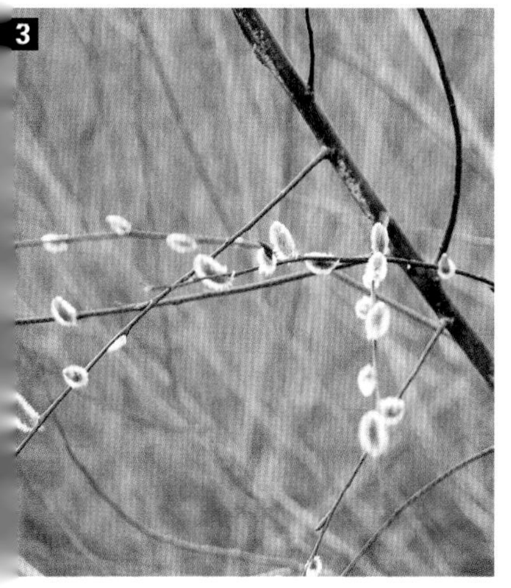
3

4

5

6

FAMILY Salicaceae

Salix triandra L.

Almond willow

Description • A shrub or small, rounded tree seldom over 10 m tall [1]. The bark can be distinctive when it flakes off in thin plates to reveal smooth patches of orange-brown [2]. This however is a variable feature. Young shoots are briefly downy then glabrous, sometimes angular. The 5–10 cm leaves [3] are oblong-ovate to oblong-lanceolate, finely and evenly toothed with an acute point. There is some variation between clonal types and subspecies in cultivation but the foliage is always bright green, shiny above and lustrous but paler below [4]. Petioles have two or three glands at the top and a pair of persistent stipules at the base. Trees cut back as coppice or pollards grow very strongly producing a mass of distinctive, exceptionally shiny, green foliage [5]. Normal catkins appear with or just before the leaves often in profusion. Males are bright golden yellow, 3–5 cm long [6]. Females on separate plants are denser and greenish. On some clones flowers may be produced sporadically throughout the summer. The ornamental cultivar 'Semperaurescens' [7] is known for this. Unfortunately it has the ability to cross with many other *Salix* species resulting in the phenological differences in flowering, that keeps some species distinct, from being bridged. Recent increased horticultural use of 'Semperaurescens' has aggravated this delicate balance of nature. **Habitat and Ecology** • Although doubtfully wild anywhere now, this species prefers wet, low-lying sites on rich mineral soil. Hedgerow and riverside escapes add much to the diversity of lowland countryside. **Similar species** • Although it has much in common with other tree willows, especially *Salix pentandra* (p258) and *Salix daphnoides* (p252), Almond willow can be positively identified by the distinctive piquancy of the young bark which tastes of roses or rosewater. Even hybrids (p256) containing *Salix triandra* usually contain this valuable marker. This species is compatible with the huge *viminalis* osier group when flowering early. The resulting progeny tend to flower during the 'time gap' that normally keeps the species separate. They also backcross with the parents causing taxonomic confusion and real identification problems.

Natural range
Frequent throughout Europe and Asia but not in extremes of cold in the north or heat in the south.

Cultivated distribution
This is one of the most important basket-willows in cultivation annually producing heavy, straight rods often in excess of 3 m. A long history of commercial use has disguised natural population boundaries. Many clones have traditional osier names such as 'Black Maul' and 'French Purple'.

Salix triandra. Male flower.

1
2
3
4
5
6
7

FAMILY Salicaceae

Salix x mollissima Hoffm. Ex Elwert

Description • This hybrid between *Salix triandra* (p254) and *Salix viminalis* (p296) is important because it transgresses the genetic boundary between the subgenera *Salix* (tree willows) and *Caprisalix* (sallows) which other willows do not. Plants occur on river banks, wetland thickets or in hybrid swarms wherever both parents are present **1**. Often their occurrence is associated with old cultivated or abandoned osier beds, both species have been, and still are, used as basket-willows. The hybrid itself has been cultivated for this purpose, represented by two nothomorphs or varieties (below).

Nm. *hippophaefolia.* A vigorous rambling shrub up to 5 m tall if not managed as an osier. The leaves resemble those of *Salix* viminalis **2**, up to 13 cm long by 1.5 cm wide, linear-lanceolate, pointed at each end. Margins are sub-entire, minutely glandular toothed, sometimes undulating. At maturity they are shiny dark green, duller and paler below and glabrous. Small stipules persist at the base of the petiole only on young shoots. Catkins 3 cm long occur with the young leaves in spring. Male flowers are yellow with brown-tipped scales and two or three stamens. Female flowers can sometimes be found amongst the males which is unusual in willows. Female catkins, usually on separate trees, are slender, grey-green and densely pubescent. One old name for the osier is 'Sarda'.

Nm. *undulata* (Ehrh.) Wimm. A tall, 5 m shrub or small tree with spreading branch tips. The shoots are green at first then glossy red or olive-brown. With age the bark becomes flaky like *Salix triandra.* Leaves are lanceolate or linear-lanceolate, 10–12 cm long, at first slightly pubescent then becoming glabrous with distinct, glandular teeth. Colour and texture is reminiscent of *Salix triandra* **3**. There are fairly persistent stipules at the base of the petiole. In addition the leaf-blade is often subtended by a pair of small, stipule-like, glandular pointed auricles **4**. Female catkins are erect, narrow, 3–4 cm long, cylindrical and less hairy than *hippophaefolia.* Male trees are unknown. **Habit and Ecology** • The status of this plant in the wild is uncertain. Almost all specimens can be related to past or present osier beds. Nm. *undulala* appears at present to be a single clone. **Similar species** • Easily confused with either parent. In the past thought to be in some way related to *Salix alba* (p234).

Natural range

The complex nature of this hybrid, which is split into at least three varieties, dictates that the exact location of natural populations is vritually impossible. Cultivation has added further confusion.

Cultivated distribution

Rarely used now as a basket-willow, so distribution is more or less limited to the vicinity of redundant osier beds. *Salix x mollisima* appears to have hybridized with *Salix cinerea* (p242) in the vicinity of Bristol, giving rise to further taxonomic and genetic confusion.

1

2

3

4

FAMILY Salicaceae

Salix pentandra L.

Bay willow

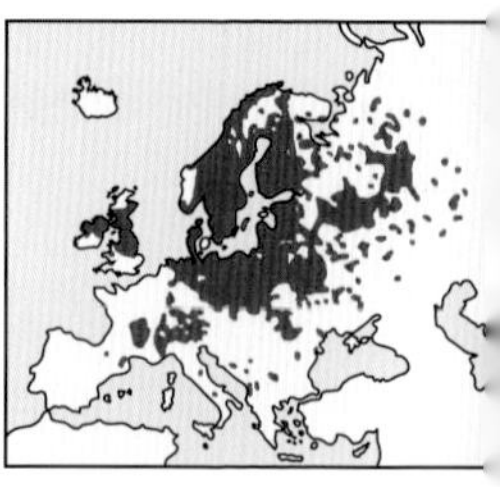

Natural range

Cultivated distribution
Grown as selections of the species and its hybrids for the basket industry. Valued for it glossy bark and pliable rods. Crossed with *Salix triandra* it produces very strong, heavy rods. Increasingly used as an ornamental park and garden shrub or tree. Responds well to coppicing and grows reliably from winter cuttings. Very hardy in cold districts.

Description • A large shrub or small, single-stemmed tree, 7–10 m tall. Very old specimens in favourable wet conditions may reach 17 m with a bole over 70 cm thick **1**. The bark is deeply fissured on old trees. In the open, mature bay willow becomes rounded in outline. The twigs are glossy green ripening to brown or reddish-brown in a season. As a basket-willow the one-year-old rods are very pliable and valued for their decorative glossy bark. The distinctive leaves are ovate, acutely pointed and broader than most other tree willows, around 8 cm long by 4 cm wide **2**. The margins are finely glandular-serrate. If pressed hard for a few days between sheets of white paper an oily, balsamic scented, yellow excretion from each tooth will trace the precise outline of the leaf on the paper. In summer the waxy, shining green foliage colour gives the impression of an evergreen but in the autumn the leaves turn yellow and fall. Petiols are short, 5–8 mm, and stout with small, sessile glands mostly close to the leaf blade. Stipules are minute and soon deciduous. Catkins appear after the leaves have expanded usually on weak, lateral shoots. Males are cylindrical up to 5 cm long, dense-flowered and bright yellow **3**. There are 5 stamens (rarely 8 or up to 12) on each individual flower. Female catkins are shorter and greenish-yellow. **Habitat and Ecology** • Still to be found in a more or less natural state independent of cultivated osier beds. Wet meadows in mountainous areas are tolerated but trees become stunted at high elevation. The largest specimens occur in fens and wetland hedgerows sometimes as pollards **4**, or in open woodland **5**. **Similar species** • In North America *Salix lucida* Muhl. the Shining willow appears to be identical but it is rare in Europe. Cultivated osiers (e.g. 'Patent Lumley') also occur in cultivation. Bay willow will cross with White willow (*Salix x ehrhartiana* p260) and Crack willow (Salix x meyeriana p260) and also the complex hybrid between them. Hybrids with *Salix triandra* (p254) have been developed as commercial osiers (e.g. 'Black Hollander').

Salix pentandra. Male flower.

1
2
3
4
5

FAMILY Salicaceae

Salix x ehrhartiana Sm.

Description • This is a hybrid between *Salix pentandra* (p258) and *Salix alba* (234). A small, elegant tree seldom more than 10 m tall with deeply fissured bark and lustrous, finely toothed leaves (10–18 points per cm) intermediate between those of the parents **1**. Shoots are pubescent at first then glabrous, pale brown or olive brown, slightly less glossy than bay willow. An interesting cultivated form, possibly of French origin, with pale clay-coloured twigs was once used as a basket-willow **2**. Male catkins appear after the leaves. They are longer than bay willow and slender, up to 6 cm by less than 1 cm wide on weak side shoots. The flowers have five or more stamens. The female tree is probably absent from Britain but is found in Scandinavia. Catkins are similar to those of female white willow. **Habitat and Ecology** • A rare tree in Britain almost always escaped from cultivation particularly in south-east England and Cumbria. Spontaneous plants may have originated in Scotland and Northern Europe. Trees grow on a wide range of soils. **Similar species** • May be confused with some forms of bay willow and *Salix x meyeriana* (below).

Natural range
Natural distribution is uncertain.

Cultivated distribution
Seldom grown now as an osier or in horticulture probably because positive identity is so difficult. Several trees with this name in collections appear to be wrongly labelled. The clay coloured coppice plant from the Long Ashton Research Station, Bristol has considerable ornamental merit.

Salix x meyeriana Rostk. ex Wlld.

Pointed-leaved willow

Description • A hybrid between *Salix fragilis* (p248) and *Salix pentandra* (p258). A beautiful and under-rated small tree or large, vigorous shrub with polished, rather brittle, brown twigs and shiny, deep green foliage **3**. The 6–12 cm leaves are longer than *x ehrhartiana*, five times as long as wide, abruptly narrowed to a long, fine point. Margins are evenly serrulate with six to nine points per cm. The deep green upper surface is glabrous and glossy, the underside is pale green with a slightly darker network of veins **4**. Catkins are narrow and cylindrical, male flowers mostly have four stamens. **Habitat and Ecology** • Infrequent but not rare in the wild but only on damp open sites where seed can quickly germinate. Once established, plants subsequently grow from brittle cuttings strewn along river banks and on flood plains after inundation. **Similar species** • *Salix pentandra* and *fragilis*, also confused with *Salix daphnoides* (p252) in cultivation.

Natural range
Frequently occurs as a seedling in a natural situation but the exact range of native trees cannot be defined with certainty.

Cultivated distribution
A superb ornamental plant. Clones were traditionally used as basket-willows.

FAMILY Salicaceae

Salix x pendulina Wend. var. elegantissima

Weeping willow

Description • This more or less disease-free weeping willow tree up to 12 m tall is an artificial hybrid between *Salix babylonica* (p232) and *Salix fragilis* (p248) **1**. Some clones have long, slender shoots trailing downwards **2**. Others are less pendulous with features more reminiscent of *fragilis*. The strongly weeping form is sometimes wrongly listed as var. *blanda* (below). The deep green, glossy, lanceolate leaves, up to 12 cm in length, have long, slender points. Margins are finely but irregularly toothed. Veins are ascending (descending in situ). Petioles, up to 1.5 cm long, have a few small glands near the apex. Twigs are shiny olive-brown and glabrous developing into vertically fissured, grey-brown bark **3**. Catkins like those of *Salix fragilis* occur with the leaves on weak side shoots. Most trees are female but sometimes androgynous flowers are produced. **Habitat and Ecology** • Always planted as an ornamental tree, usually on damp ground. **Similar species** • Other weeping willows (below).

Natural range
An artificial European hybrid using Chinese and native European parents.

Cultivated distribution
The original cross was first described and distributed in Marburg, Germany, in 1831. At least three nineteenth century variants were subsequently cultivated. First described in 1871, var. *elegantissima* is now the most widely used in the British Isles because of its exceptional weeping habit. The variety *blanda*, known as Wisconsin weeping willow, although of German origin, is widely used in America.

Salix x sepulcralis Simonk. nv. chrysocoma (Dode) Meikle

Golden weeping willow

Description • Yellow shoots immediately distinguish this tree from other weeping willows. Up to 10 m tall, it has strongly descending branch tips **4**. Yellow twig colour shows up best in winter. There is also a brief yellow, autumn foliage colour period **5**. Leaves are narrowly lanceolate, 7–12 cm long with acuminate points, pubescent at first then glabrous. Margins are finely and evenly toothed. Catkins are often androgynous. This tree is believed to be a hybrid between a golden twigged white willow (p238) and *Salix babylonica* (p232). The bright yellow form appears to be clonal in western Europe. It is very susceptible to disease caused by *Marssonina salicicola*. *Salix x sepulcralis* (*Salix babylonica salamonii* Carr.) is a straight cross between *alba* and *babylonica* without yellow shoots **6**. **Habitat and Ecology** • Always planted in Northern Europe, usually by water. **Similar species** • The yellow twigged form is distinct.

Natural range
Occurs naturally where the species overlap in central Asia. The yellow twigged form has no Natural range.

Cultivated distribution
The original hybrid was first cultivated in France around 1850. The nothovar *chrysocoma* was first listed in a Berlin nursery in 1888. Invasive roots and disease problems make it unpopular.

1
2
3
4
5
6

FAMILY Salicaceae

Populus nigra L. 'Plantierensis'

Description • A large, fastigiate male Black poplar which arose at Metz in France in the nineteenth century. Branches are distinctly fastigiate. A characteristic of 'Plantierensis' is the density of summer foliage it carries **1**. The shoots are bright green with bristly, deciduous pubescence on new growth. Leaves remain on the tree late in the year particularly the topmost branches. Catkins are pendulous and deep red. **Habitat and Ecology** • Requires deep, moist, fertile soils preferably in a moderately sheltered lowland site. **Similar species** • 'Afghanica' (*Populus nigra* var. *thevestina* Dode) is a female clone also with pubescent shoots and a fastigiate outline **2**. In nature (as the variety) it covers much of the Near East and into Africa surviving in hot, dry conditions. The winter bark on young stems and branches is distinctly silvery-white.

Natural range
None ('Plantierensis').

Cultivated distribution
Said to have largely replaced Lombardy poplar in Britain because of its superior dense foliage but this is not certain.

Populus nigra L. 'Italica'

Lombardy poplar

Description • Planted for screening and amenity this slender tree is universally well-known. It is a male clone with deep red spent catkins in spring before the leaves appear. The outline is fastigiate but rather more irregular then 'Plantierensis' (above), reaching in excess of 30 m in height **3**. Stems over 1 m diameter occur with tightly packed branches usually emerging almost from ground level **4**. The green shoots are entirely glabrous as if coated with transparent glossy varnish. This clone is very susceptible to *Marssonina* leaf blight especially if the tops are pruned out to reduce its height. **Habitat and Ecology** • Probably a sport of a riparian *Populus nigra* (p266) in Italy before 1750. **Similar species** • A female form 'Italica Foemina' ('Gigantea') is a broader, more open-topped tree **5**. Enormous diameter stems are known **6**.

Natural range
None.

Cultivated distribution
Extensively cultivated in the past but now frequently replaced by disease resistant cultivars (above). A bold statement in the landscape providing windfirm shelter.

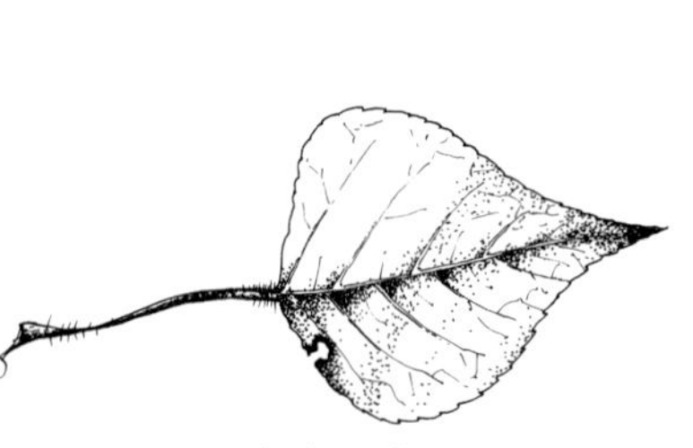

Black poplar

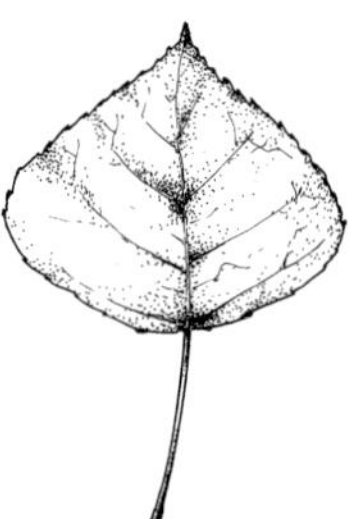

Lombardy Poplar

1
2
3
4
5
6

FAMILY Salicaceae

Populus nigra L.

Black poplar

Description • A large, heavily branched, rounded tree ultimately about 30 m tall with a thick stem in excess of 1 m diameter [1]. Long, arching branches are characteristic, especially of the western subspecies *betulifolia* (Pursh) W Wettst. [2]. In summer this massive structure is disguised by shining green foliage [3]. The leaves are deltoid-ovate, up to 10 cm long with an elongated point. Margins are bluntly toothed and slightly translucent [4]. The 7 cm petiole is compressed so the leaf blade becomes unstable and flutters freely in the wind. Except in late autumn there are no distinctive glands at the junction of the petiole and leaf. A diagnostic characteristic for identifying this species when compared to Hybrid black poplars (p268). Shoots are clay coloured at first with some bristle hairs on this subspecies, but glabrous on the continental subspecies (*Populus nigra* subsp. *nigra* Meikle,) becoming grey after two or three years. Bark becomes deeply fissured and dark grey. Old trees frequently develop large, rough barked swellings and burrs. Buds are sticky and smell of balsam in late winter. Male catkins on separate trees begin to expand before the leaves appear [5]. They are 5 cm long, with multiple crimson stamens [6]. Female catkins are slender and pale green [7]. Female trees are infrequent (see Cultivated distribution). Seed capsules are 5–6 mm long and more or less ovoid. They develop rapidly and split open to shed copious, white seed fluff carrying minute seeds in early summer. Viability is measured only in hours so conditions are seldom exactly right for germination. Furthermore, windblown pollen can travel considerable distances so cross-pollination from compatible cultivated Poplars in most areas is likely. Black poplar grows easily from hardwood cuttings: in nature from fallen branches or in severely storm damaged individuals by suckering. **Habitat and Ecology** • A wetland tree in thickets along woodland edges. This species is light-demanding and will not tolerate heavy shade. Many trees lean at a slight angle, probably because of shoot to root size incompatibility when young on soft ground. **Similar species** • There is much debate about the true identity of this species. Morphological characteristics, especially of *Populus nigra* subsp. *nigra*, are precariously close to Hybrid black poplar (p268).

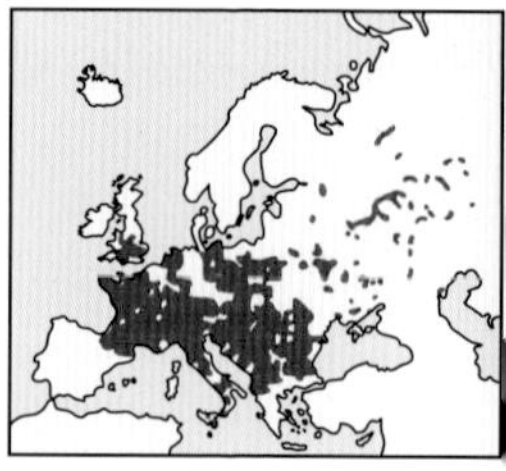

Natural range

Cultivated distribution

Most if not all extant trees are relics of past cultivation. This tree provided 'pre-formed' massive curved timbers for low-status, 'cruck framed' buildings such as barns, etc. Also its fire resistant wood was used for industrial flooring in maltings and oast houses. Female trees were not cultivated because of the nuisance the seed fluff caused to agricultural crops, notably strawberries.

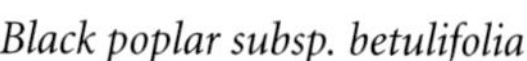

Black poplar subsp. betulifolia

1
2
3
4
5
6
7

FAMILY Salicaceae

Populus x canadensis Moench

Hybrid black poplar

Description • This species does not really exist in a general sense. Each individual tree is the product of a particular artificial cross. In the majority of cases the parents' identity has been forgotten. It is said that over one million Poplars were bred using the European and American Black poplar species, *Populus nigra* (p266) and *Populus deltoides* Marsh, the Eastern cottonwood. Before the hybrid was made in the early 1700s both parents had already been 'improved' in cultivation by selection. The best, most productive, hybrid progeny were originally selected in Europe notably Italy. The objective was to produce trees that would grow faster. Much of the research was on behalf of the paper pulp industry. Soon it became clear that disease resistance also had to be a prime objective. Clonal monocultures are particularly prone to bacterial and fungal diseases. With the exception of a few, well-known named cultivars (p270) it is impossible for the casual observer to identify this tree beyond its hybrid designation. Almost always it is a fast-growing individual reaching 30 m in 15–30 years **1**. Stems are light grey or grey-green, smooth at first then evenly fissured, often reminiscent of Oak **2**. The leaves are deltoid, between 8 and 15 cm long, with rounded glandular teeth. There are one to three exaggerated glands at the base of the leaf on one or both sides of the petiole, something which aids identification when comparing this with Black poplar. The petiole, which is flattened, makes the leaf unstable so it blows about in the lightest wind. Characteristically leaves 'slap' together particularly just ahead of a rain squall **3**. Male trees produce reddish catkins before the leaves. Female trees have yellowish-green catkins which produce copious amounts of seed fluff in early summer, hence the name Cottonwood in America. In identifying clones, the colour of the unfolding leaves is said to be important. Some start off green, others have degrees of bronzing while some are coppery-bronze. One of the most frequently encountered trees today 'Serotina' is this sort. Its late flushing leaves are orange-brown **4**. The name *Populus x canadensis* was proposed in 1785 to describe this clone. It is one of the largest Poplars, routinely 36–40 m tall **5** with a rough, scaly barked stem **6** often in excess of 1 m in diameter. **Habitat and Ecology** • Cultivated plantations or escapes from them. **Similar species** • As described.

Natural range
The hybrid has no Natural range but the European parent was originally *Populus nigra* subsp. *nigra* (p266). The American parent was *Populus deltoides* that has a huge range across North America from Alberta to Southern Quebec then south just into Florida and west to Montana and Texas.

Cultivated distribution
Extensively cultivated, under the botanically invalid name *Populus x euramericana*, for matches, plywood, packaging and pulpwood until the 1950s, then mostly replaced by new clones involving more productive hybrids between Eastern cottonwood *Populus deltoides* Bartr. ex Marsh and Black cottonwood, *Populus trichocarpa* (p272) *Populus x generosa* (p274).

Populus 'Serotina'

1
2
3
4
5
6

FAMILY Salicaceae

Populus x canadensis Moench
Hybrid black poplar cvs.

Description • In the twentieth century over one million Hybrid black poplar clones were produced in Europe. An early success was 'Eugenei' which arose spontaneously in a nursery near Metz in France in 1832. It was imported to Britain in 1888 and became a key component of the British Poplar timber industry. Lombardy poplar (p264) was probably the male parent and *Populus x canadensis* 'Marilandica' the female parent. It has an ascending crown but a good straight stem **1** and will grow on drier sites than most other Hybrid black poplars. Another old but valuable clone was 'Gelrica' a Dutch tree selected in 1865. The bark is particularly light coloured, reminiscent of Birch when young. With age, stems tend to become fluted which is an unusual characteristic in Poplar. It is exceptionally fast-growing, stems 60 cm in diameter may be expected in less than 20 years on a good site. This is a male clone producing numerous red catkins in spring before the leaves emerge **2**. 'Robusta' was perhaps the most widely planted cultivar in Britain and Western Europe in the twentieth century. There are several different clones of it, all appear to be male and they differ very little. The male parent is unknown but the female is *Populus deltoides angulata* (*P. angulata* Hort.) the Carolina poplar, apparently raised at Kew in 1789. In addition to commercial plantations 'Robusta' has frequently been used for avenues, single lines along road sides and as shelter-belts. The foliage is particularly dense and healthy. It is one of the first Hybrid black poplars to come into leaf. The young foliage is bronze-red turning to deep glossy green in about three weeks **3**. Stems are relatively straight and although not shade tolerant it will survive in open plantations **4**. The bark is grey-brown, horizontally and diagonally ridged **5**. Stems 50 cm in diameter may be expected in 25 years on a good site. **Habitat and Ecology** • Artificial trees usually grown in plantations or on a limited scale for amenity. They all require good light to survive so wide spacing traditionally 18 feet (5.5 m), frequent pruning and regular thinning out are essential. **Similar species** • Botanical differences are often too slight to permit reliable identification. The date of leafing and colour of new growth in spring together with sex can be useful indicators. Good planting records are more helpful. As a last resort DNA comparison can be made with authentic material.

Natural range
Artificially produced in France and Holland.

Cultivated distribution
These three cultivars accounted for well over half of the Poplar planting throughout the temperate zones of the world in the mid-twentieth century. They became more important and widespread than the parent trees. The object of Poplar cultivation was the production of large, straight grained, evenly shaped, non-tapered, blemish free logs for veneering and for the production of paper pulp.

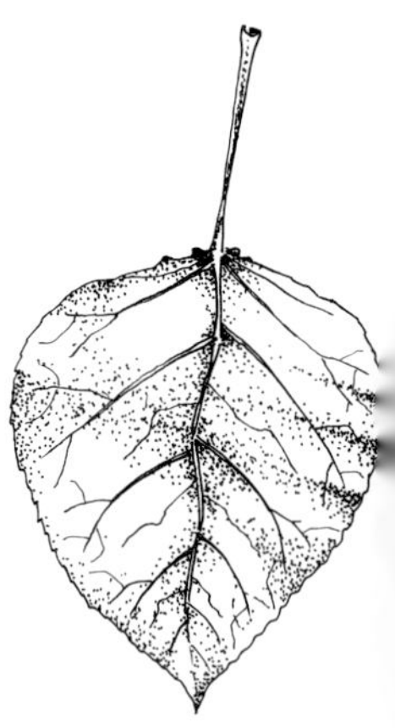

Populus 'Eugenei'

1

2

3

4

5

FAMILY Salicaceae

Populus trichocarpa Torrey and Grey ex Hook.

Black cottonwood

Description • In Northern Europe Black cottonwood, or Western balsam poplar, is seldom seen except as a selected clone or a component of a cross between it and another species. In its native Western North America it is the largest broadleaved tree, up to 60 m tall. In the British Isles it can easily reach 30 m in 20 years but usually breaks up or slows down dramatically after that. It has a fairly persistent, straight stem and upswept branches [1]. Lower branches are light and short-lived (usually pruned off) revealing silvery-buff, smooth bark which fissures slightly and bleaches grey from the base [2]. The foliage is fresh green and balsamic at first [3]. Leaves are eventually dark green on the upper side and glaucous below with a distinctive, long drawn out point [4]. The male flowers, on separate trees, are spectacular. Fat, crimson, pendulous catkins appear in late winter before the resinous, butter yellow leaf buds break [5]. Female catkins are light green, rapidly developing into strings of 'cotton'-producing fruits by early summer. Trees can often be located by fragments of white fluff blowing on the breeze. Seed is minute and short lived. **Habitat and Ecology** • Wet mountainous sites down to sea level. An aggressive pioneer on gravel banks and disturbed ground. **Similar species** • Hybrids with Balsam poplar (below).

Natural range
Western North America from Southern Alaska to Oregon and Western California also inland from British Columbia to Montana and Idaho up to 1800 m elevation.

Cultivated distribution
Able to withstand more shade and drier ground in plantations than Black poplars. Used in artificial breeding trials with many other species.

Populus balsamifera L.

Balsam poplar or Tacamahac

Description • A variable trans-Canadian species that is not generally successful in Europe because of its susceptibility to bacterial canker. Its strong balsam smell when the leaves emerge in spring or during summer rain is striking. It may reach 20 m in height with upswept branches but often develops ugly, cankerous swellings and lesions. Sucker shoots frequently occur [6]. The bark is smooth at first becoming furrowed into scaly ridges. Ovate leaves have a short point and subcordate or rounded base [7]. They are shiny green above and almost white on the underside. Petioles are round. Flowers in 6–10 cm long catkins occur on separate male and female trees. Males are red [8] and females are green and yellow [9]. **Habitat and Ecology** • A pioneer species on moist ground often forming pure seedling or suckering forests. **Similar species** • Many hybrids and cultivated clones including Balm-of-Gilead, *Populus candicans* Ait.

Natural range
Canada from the Pacific to the Atlantic coasts also south into Pennsylvania, Iowa and parts of Colorado.

Cultivated distribution
Mostly failed as a forest tree in Europe but grown in gardens in spite of its invasive suckers and disease problems. A common ornamental clone frequently planted was *Populus candicans* 'Aurora', a strikingly variegated pink, white and green leaved form.

1
2
3
4
5
6
7
8
9

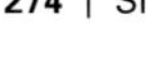

FAMILY Salicaceae

Populus x generosa Henry
Hybrid poplar

Description • The name *Poplus x generosa* is the botanical equivalent of the Dutch horticultural designation *Populus interamericana*, which includes all hybrids between two distinctly different North American species. *Populus trichocarpa* (p272) a balsam poplar (Black cottonwood) and *Populus deltoides* Bartr. ex Marsh. the Eastern cottonwood, a black poplar. The hybrid can occur spontaneously where the Natural ranges of the species overlap, a limited part of Alberta, Montana and Wyoming. Trees imported directly from the natural population have not been promising in Europe. However in the 1980s and 1990s Belgian researchers began a programme of artificial hybridisation. Trees were produced using disease resistant individuals of Populus trichocarpa, some from the Mount St. Helens region of Washington State. They grow extremely rapidly reaching harvestable size in under 20 years **1**. Stems are straight but have to be pruned from about three years of age **2**. The bark is smooth, grey-green becoming slightly scaly. The leaves are large, 15–25 cm long, more or less heart-shaped with rounded teeth. The upper surface is deep green and the underside is very pale green. One of the first clones resulting from modern research was named 'Rap' grown from a female *Populus trichocarpa*. It had phenomenal rates of growth in field trials. On soft ground shoot to root imbalance caused instability so trees had to be staked. It soon became apparent however that 'Rap' was susceptible to bacterial canker and it is no longer grown. More successful is the later clone 'Beaupre' **3**. It will grow 3 m in one year as short rotation coppice **4** and can be harvested as biomass for generating electricity in just three years **5**. **Habitat and Ecology** • A fairly insignificant natural hybrid which has been artificially improved to a high state of perfection and seems likely to replace most other species in Poplar plantations. **Similar species** • The new clones are distinctive, older hybrids may be confused with the parents but they are becoming rare in cultivation.

Natural range
North America where the parent species overlap (see left).

Cultivated distribution
The first artificial cross was made at Kew in 1912 to produce the original cultivar called 'Generosa'. New hybrid were introduced for forestry in Britain in 1974. Some included *Populus nigra* (p266 as a substitute parent for *Populus deltoides*. The best clone 'Oxford' produced veneer logs on trees in experimental plots almost 30 m tall in 11 years **6**. 'Oxford' subsequently becam infected with bacterial canke and was never released to commercial timber production. Poly-clonal mixtures to reduce the risk o total losses from disease and climatic extremes are being tested.

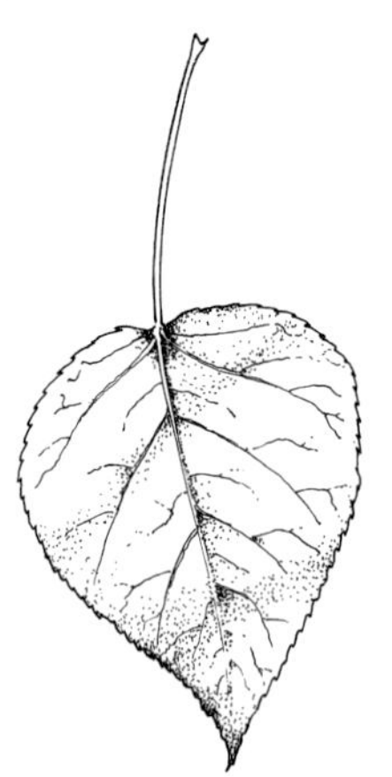

Populus x generosa 'Beaupr

1
2
3
4
5
6

FAMILY Betulaceae

Alnus cordata Desf.

Italian alder

Description • A medium to large fast-growing but fairly short-lived tree with a broad or narrow outline, 15–30 m tall, immediately distinguished from other alders (p336) by its bright, glossy-green, evenly toothed heart-shaped leaves, straight single stem and great vigour [1]. The bark is grey-green with vertical cracks that reveal a light red-brown underlayer [2]. Young bark is smooth, often with small blisters reminiscent of Abies (p30) but not resinous. Young shoots are green with pinkish lenticels, turning brown with a silvery translucent almost bloomed waxy deciduous skin in one season. Ovoid 5–7 cm buds are stalked, greenish-white with only two visible outer scales. Winter leaf buds are accompanied by embryonic male and female flowers. Leaves appear early and stay on the tree late in the season. They are heart shaped, to 10 cm long with or without a point according to the provenance (the origin of the seed). Corsican plants have smaller, 3–7 cm leaves without distinct points. Margins have small, evenly-spaced, shallow teeth. The upper surface is lustrous green with pale veins, and the underside is paler green with minute tufts of orange hairs in the vein axils. Both surfaces are otherwise glabrous [3]. Flowers consist of long, 10 cm, drooping, late winter male catkins with short, brownish-yellow, 1 cm female catkins close by [4]. During the summer, dark green, 2.5 cm egg-shaped 'cones' are produced, each containing numerous winged seeds. These persist on the tree for another season gradually turning brown and then black before shedding the seed [5], which is adapted to float in water and geminate on riparian mud banks. Away from open water, seeds are distributed by the wind. **Habitat and Ecology** • A pioneer species of damp woodlands and river banks on mineral soils. Attractive to numerous insect species as a food plant. **Similar species** • At first sight like an orchard pear (p214) but the 'cones' are distinctive.

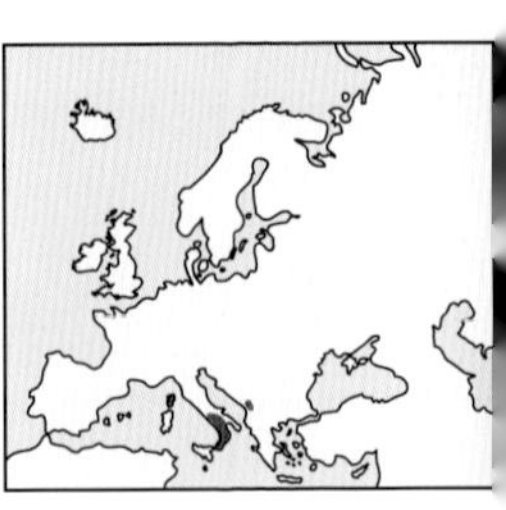

Natural range

Cultivated distribution
Supposed to have been introduced to Britain in 1820 but an earlier date is possible. It is both ornamental and useful as a plantation species for shelter and rapid, low-grade wood production. Proximity to water is not essential. Stems over 1 m in diameter are known but unusual. Poor soils planted with this species benefit from nitrogen enrichment (p336).

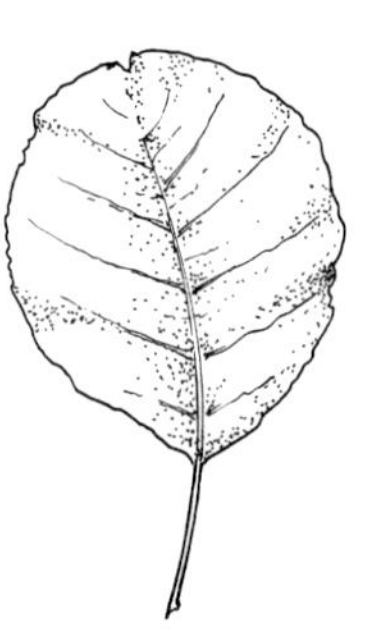

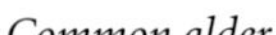

Common alder

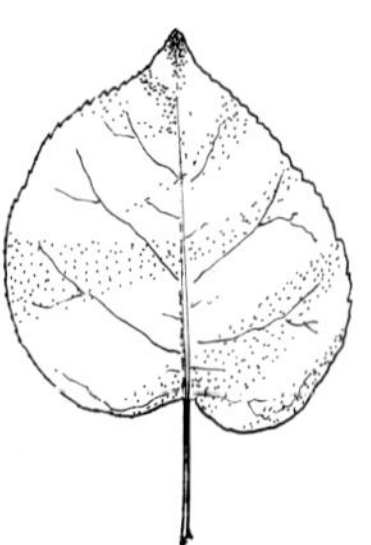

Italian alder

1

2

4

3

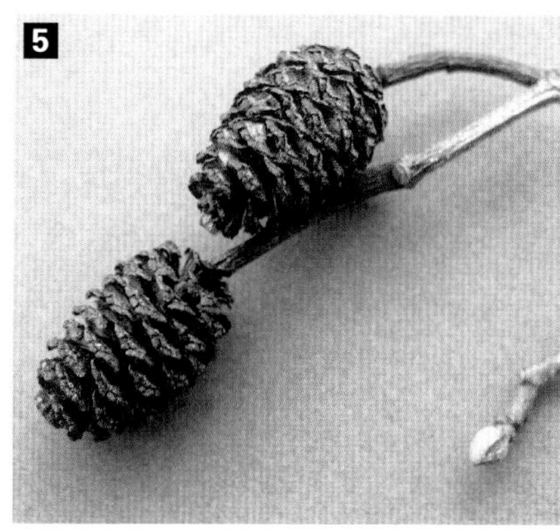
5

FAMILY Rhamnaceae

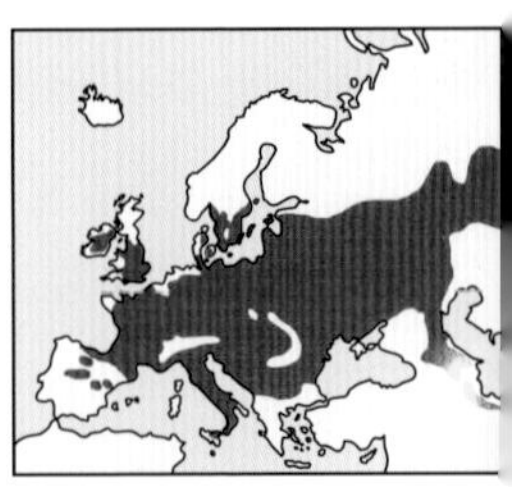

Rhamnus cathartica L.
Common buckthorn

Description • Buckthorn is a fairly widespread tree native to much of Northern Europe but generally it goes unnoticed. This is partly because it is often only seen as a hedgerow shrub, or it is only able to develop to its full potential as a tree on rare occasions in wild or wet places. This is a small, rounded tree up to 8 m tall **1** with spiny foliage. Stems are often forked from the base. Very old trees may exceed 80 cm in total diameter although individual trunks are usually under 50 cm **2**. The bark is dark brown with a silvery bloom at first and eventually scaly but not excessively so. Where scales break off the underbark is orange-brown, on twigs it is bright yellow and has a strong pungent smell. Although listed here as opposite-leaved this tree also has buds that are clustered and out of step with each other, not alternate in the accepted sense though. Twigs and branches are distinctly opposite, held almost at right angles to the stem. Thorns, which are infrequent, also project outwards from the stem, at the tip of some short spur shoots. A common but indistinct characteristic is a small, needle-like spine that persists in between pairs of opposite spur shoots. This is where an original spined spur has reverted to active growth by producing new shoots half way along its length. Young healthy plants also produce long, thin, flexible glabrous shoots. Buds are distinctly dark brown, sharply pointed, 5–10 mm long with distinct, minutely fringed scales reminiscent of Wild cherry (p142). The 5–8 cm leaves are ovate to round with a short point and rounded or subcordate base. Margins are finely and evenly toothed. The upper surface is bright lustrous green while the underside is paler with two pairs of prominent parallel but curved veins which follow the shape of the leaf margin from the midrib and converge towards the tip **3**. Flowers are pale green, 4 mm across and fragrant, held in dense clusters on spur shoots. By late summer these produce smaller clusters of green then black, juicy, 8 mm berry-like fruits **4** that are purgative if eaten. **Habitat and Ecology** • Mostly lime-rich sites, hedgerows, woodland edges and fens. **Similar species** • Winter buds are like Wild cherry, the strong-smelling, scratched shoots are like Bird cherry (p146). Often confused, probably only because of the similar common name, with Purging buckthorn, *Frangula alnus* Mill., an upright shrub or small tree with entire leaves unlike Common buckthorn in almost every botanical detail.

Natural range
Extends into Russia and Central Asia.

Cultivated distribution
Probably never cultivated deliberately but existing semi natural trees were formerly managed and highly valued. The wood is hard and heavy, of high quality but generally only available in small sizes. The largest trees are said to come from Siberia. Its calorific value is high and the charcoal is outstanding. Muc[h] favoured for the manufacture of gunpowder.

Buckthorn 'thorns'

FAMILY Cercidiphyllaceae

Cercidiphyllum japonicum Sieb. and Zucc.

Katsura tree

Description • The most distinctive feature of this tree cannot be seen. It is the ephemeral, sweet smell of burnt sugar or caramel associated with the autumn foliage. A smell that wafts around the tree but is less obvious at close quarters. Katsura can reach 20 m in height with up-swept acutely forked branches. Stems over 70 cm diameter are known. The outline is uneven or pyramidal but always graceful with thin downward pointing twigs and open, light green, glaucescent backed foliage **1**. Bark is pinkish-grey and smooth at first, later becoming roughly fissured and ridged **2**. Multiple stems often occur in cold areas where young plants have been repeatedly cut back by frost in their youth. Shoots are slender between opposite pairs of prominent pointed buds. They are bright green at first becoming greyish-purple. The leaves are very regular, all much the same size (8–10 cm) and heart shaped. More or less round with a short point and cordate base. In spring they flush out brownish-bronze before turning green. In texture they are papery thin with an intricate net pattern of veins **3**. Margins are finely and evenly toothed. Petioles are 2–3 cm long, slender, green usually with a pink sunlit side. Autumn foliage is pale cream and pink but fleeting in severe weather or following a summer drought. In those circumstances the leaves quickly screw up and turn brown. Flowers occur on separate male and female trees in late winter before the leaves. They are bright red but very small, located on short spur shoots or from axillary buds. Females develop into many-seeded, 2 cm pods which remain green all summer and tend to curve and twist slightly giving heavily seeding trees a peculiar appearance, as if infested with caterpillars. **Habitat and Ecology** • A monumental tree in the wild, 40 m tall in sheltered, mixed woodlands. Requires protection from gales, severe frost, hot summer sun and drought. **Similar species** • The foliage resembles the Judas tree (p102).

Natural range
Southern Japan and parts of China.

Cultivated distribution
Introduced to America in 1865 and Europe in 1881. Grown as an individual ornamental specimen or in groves to ensure that both sexes are represented. A larger leaved Japanese tree 'Magnificum Nakai' is a particularly good autumn colour tree and the cultivar 'Pendulum' is a popular weeping curiosity.

3

FAMILY Oleaceae

Phillyrea latifolia L.

Phillyrea

Description • A neat evergreen tree not exceeding 10 m in height, but often almost as wide, with a stem up to 30 cm diameter [1]. The bark is pinkish-grey appearing almost black under the deep shade of the dense canopy [2]. It is rough with very small ridges and shallow fissures developing into small, squarish plates. Shoots are fawn with tiny prominent lenticels, slender and lax. Subordinate shoots, like the leaves, are in opposite pairs [3]. Buds are 2–3 mm long and pale green. The thick leathery leaves are narrowly oval to elliptic, 2–4 cm long with well-defined, forward-pointing rounded teeth. The upper side is brilliant, deep glossy green when mature, the underside is only slightly paler and less glossy [4]. On both surfaces the midrib is conspicuously yellow. Flowers occur in late winter from axillary buds. They are insignificant, about 2 mm across, with pale yellowish-green petals and yellow stamens [5]. The fruit, a blue-black, round, 8 mm berry, ripens the following autumn in small clusters. **Habitat and Ecology** • Evergreen scrub woodland or individual clumps of trees on hot, dry, rocky sites especially close to the sea. **Similar species** • *Phillyrea angustifolia* L., a beautiful, compact, bushy species with narrower leaves and fragrant, pale yellow, early summer flowers. Also *Euonymus japonicus* (below).

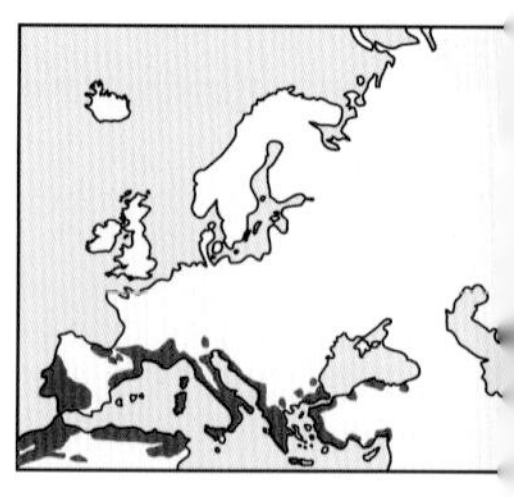

Natural range

Cultivated distribution
A widely grown garden specimen and hedge plant. More of a tree than Privet bu smaller and more manageabl than Holm oak (p292). *Phillyrea angustifolia* is a goo ornamental alternative for olive in cooler northern gardens.

Euonymus japonicus Thunb.

Japanese spindle tree

Description • Often mistaken for *Phillyrea latifolia* in cultivation because it is frequently grown in similar places such as seaside town gardens and esplanades. This is an evergreen Spindle which is most easily recognized as such when in flower [6] and when the four-segmented fruits appear. These do not have the striking colour of *Euonymus europeans* (p130) but ripen to pinkish-green and expose orange seeds in the winter. Although frequently clipped this species can make a shapely, dense evergreen tree up to 8 m tall [7]. The trunk may be 25 cm diameter or consist of a clump of smaller stems [8]. These often break under the weight of foliage but the plant usually lives on. Glabrous leaves are 2–4 cm long, oval, with toothed margins. They are thick and leathery, very glossy green on the upper side and paler beneath. There are five pairs of parallel veins. **Habitat and Ecology** • A dense, bushy plant very resistant to wind and salt laden air. **Similar species** • Other obscure evergreen *Euonymus* species and cultivars.

Natural range
Japan.

Cultivated distribution
Since being introduced to Northern Europe many cultivated forms have been developed. They are popular ornamental shrubs and hedging plants. The species survives hot sun, maritime gales and sea spray.

1
2
3
4
5
6
7
8

FAMILY Magnoliaceae

Liriodendron tulipifera L.

Tulip tree

Description • A fine, upright, 25–30m tall tree with an even outline and vigorous, bold summer foliage **1**. In time it becomes more uneven but is always ascending with a high domed top and usually a straight stem **2**. The bark is grey and smooth at first then an intricate, diagonal lattice pattern of ridges gradually develops **3**. The prominent leaves emerge from bloomed, leafy buds, they are uniquely shaped, as if the top third has been cut cleanly off **4**. In the summer, they are pea-green and glabrous with a silvery sheen on the underside. In the autumn, the foliage turns to clear yellow and golden-brown. The twigs are also glabrous green at first then brown and stout. The nodal scars are characteristic of this tree and reminiscent of Horse chestnut or some poplars. In its native America it is called Yellow poplar. The flowers in late spring are spectacular. Shaped like tulips, and about the same size, they have six greenish-yellow, erect petals each with a blotch of pale orange on the lower half. The centre of the flower is filled with long, creamy-yellow stamens **5**. The fruit consists of narrow, overlapping, 4–6 cm winged seeds held in a tight bunch like a cone with a short, upright central stalk. They break up in early winter and are dispersed by the wind. **Habitat and Ecology** • Wet but well-drained ground produces the best trees. In the wild this is an aggressive, light-demanding pioneer; widely spaced stands occur but subordinate individuals soon die out. **Similar species** • Chinese tulip tree, *Liriodendron chinense* (Hemsl.) Sarge. is difficult to distinguish from the American tree. It is said the former has a leaf tip with a 'V' notch cut down into it while the latter is cut more or less straight across. In fact both species usually have some leaves of both types on them. Since 1970 a hybrid between the two has also been in cultivation.

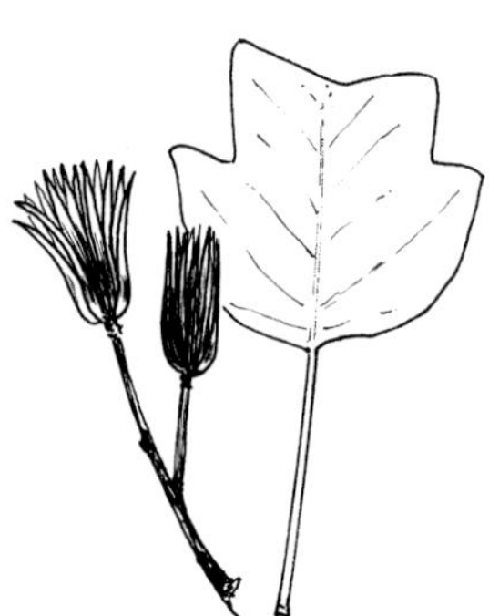

Tulip tree fruit

Natural range
The eastern half of the United States and South East Canada but not Northern Ontario or Southern Florida.

Cultivated distribution
This is a valuable timber tree with pale, cream coloured, easily worked wood that has a beautiful 'satin sheen', radial grain finish. It has been extensively harvested in America and re-established itself after logging. American Indians made lightweight dug-out canoes from large trunks. It is cultivated mainly as an ornamental in Northern Europe. There are yellow and green variegated leaf forms. It is not an easy tree to transplant but grows readily from seed.

1

2

3

4

5

FAMILY Platanaceae

Platanus orientalis L.

Oriental plane

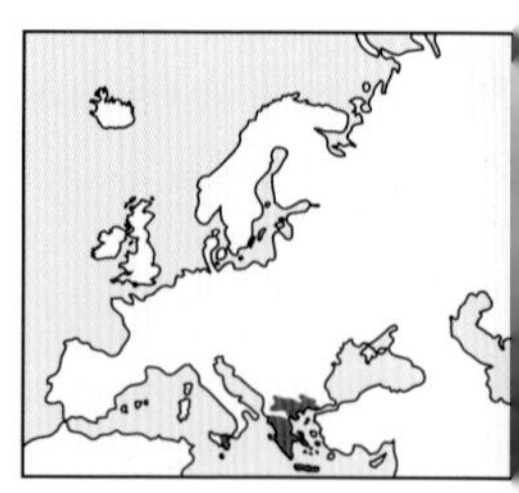

Natural range

Cultivated distribution
Introduced to Italy from Greece as a shade tree around 390 BC then to Northern Europe in 1562. Used to good effect in city open spaces and country estates ever since. It is less satisfactory as a street tree because of its spreading nature. The variety *insularis* A. DC. Cyprian plane is a smaller tree more suitable for gardens and urban use. It has deeply divided leaves. 'Digitata' is similar.

Description • Plane trees are immediately recognized by their attractive, dappled, exfoliating, cream, grey-green and buff bark. The Oriental plane is a huge, 20–30 m tree often wider than tall. In cultivation it usually lacks the single, long, clear trunk of London plane (p288). Usually it has a short bole and huge, lower, sinuous branches often resting on the ground and layering **1**. Main stems regularly exceed 1 m in diameter. In the wild state, narrow crowned trees also occur. Leaves are leathery, 10–20 cm wide and palmate like maple **2**. Some individuals produce deeply cut leaves. The five main lobes are further sub-divided into occasional acute points but in the strict sense the margin is not toothed. The upper surface is glabrous and dark green at maturity. Veins on the paler green underside are prominent and pubescent. Winter buds are completely obscured by the swollen base of the 5–7cm petiole. Autumn colour is coppery brown and the leaves take a long time to decompose on the ground. Flowers, male and female on the same tree, are arranged in clusters on 5–8 cm pendulous stalks. At maturity, two to five globose, 3 cm spheres containing numerous seeds develop **3**. A distinctive feature is the retention of these ripe seed clusters hanging on the leafless tree in winter long after the leaves have fallen **4**. **Habitat and Ecology** • In the wild this tree requires plentiful ground water. This enables it to thrive in an open situation where summer heat is considerable, often exacerbated by drying, dust laden wind. **Similar species** • *Parrotia* (p314) has similar bark. Some maples have superficially similar leaves but maple leaves are always opposite. *Liquidambar* (p332) has similar shaped leaves but they are smaller, not leathery and do not conceal the winter bud. There is often real confusion between some specimens of London plane and this species (p288). A shallowly cut leaf form of Oriental plane is indistinguishable from a deeply cut leaf form of London plane. The best feature for field identification is the stem persistence and form of the tree.

1

2

3

4

FAMILY Platanaceae

Platanus x hispanica Mill. ex Muenchh.

London plane

Description • A huge deciduous tree frequently exceeding 30 m in height with straight stems ultimately over 1.5 m diameter **1**. Branches are wide-spreading with pendulous extremities **2**. The thin bark exfoliates in large patches in response to the rapid expansion of growing wood beneath. After a good year, sheets of grey-green or yellowish material are shed and large areas of pale greenish-white are revealed. In full vigour stems replace their outer bark every four to eight years providing the most obvious characteristic of the tree **3**, and good defence against city grime. Leathery leaves are 15–25 cm wide, even larger on pollarded re-growth, with three or sometimes five pointed, triangular lobes **4**. They are glabrous on both sides when mature having been tomentose at first like the young shoots. The rounded sinuses seldom cut deeply into the leaf, unlike Oriental plane (p286). Petioles are 5–10 cm long with a swollen base which hides the developing bud. Flowers develop into hanging strings of seeds tightly packed in compact 2.5 cm spheres **4**. The exact origin of this tree and hence precise identification remains in some doubt. The first herbarium specimen is in Oxford dating back to the late seventeenth century. This may have originally come from Southern Europe. Some authorities regard London plane as a variety of Oriental plane (p286) which is native there. Alternatively, since 1996, it has been generally considered to be a hybrid between Oriental plane and *Platanus occidentalis* L. the American plane. Although hardy in Eastern North America the latter does not thrive in Northern Europe, a point that casts some doubt on the hybrid origin theory. **Habitat and Ecology** • Similar to Oriental plane. Such a large tree has a dramatic impact on its habitat which may be good in a city but visually and ecologically damaging in a semi-natural situation. **Similar species** • Oriental plane.

Natural range
Some authorities suggest variety status within the natural range of Oriental plane (p. 286).

Cultivated distribution
A ubiquitous city tree world-wide, planted in urban open spaces and along streets. The foliage and bark is resistant t dust, air pollution and heat. Adequate moisture is generally found under hard surfaces of concrete and tarmac and the spreading roots are capable of exploitir this. Lopping on a regular basis is tolerated but this costly practice is less commo now. The extremely high-quality timber (Lacewood) is often overlooked in favour o the living trees amenity valu

1
2
3
4

FAMILY Salicaceae

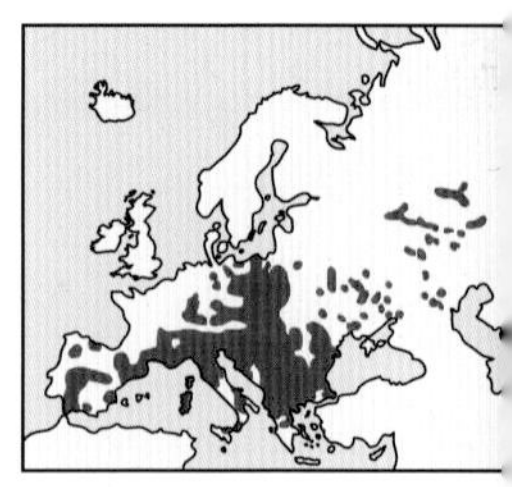

Populus alba L.

White poplar

Description • White poplar is a variable tree from a huge and diverse range in Europe and Asia. This is a suckering species so clonal thickets and small woods occur that all share a common root system. The white-backed leaves and white shoots give the tree a very pale appearance in summer **1**. Stems are usually unstable, and branches are crooked and forked in a distinctive way **2**. Young, smooth bark is very light olive-green becoming horizontally banded with dark grey, erupting lenticels which gradually develop and increase in size until a total covering of rough fissured, nearly black bark is formed. The leaves are palmate on long shoots and palmately-rounded on side shoots. Petioles and leaf undersides have thick, brilliant white tomentum on them **3**. Catkins appear in spring before the leaves. Males are pendulous, whiskery, 8 cm long and crimson. Females are shorter and pale green. They produce copious white fluff which carries away the tiny seeds on the wind. **Habitat and Ecology** • Introduced to Western Europe and the British Isles at an early date and naturalized in many places. A suckering pioneer on waste ground and coastal sand and shingle. **Similar species** • Grey poplar (below), cultivated forms, and imported Asiatic species.

Natural range

Cultivated distribution
The Chinese are researching canker resistant White poplars. The commercial value of selected forms is likely to be high. The soft, lightweight, fire resistant wood can be used for industrial and domestic construction and flooring. There are also ornamental selections. 'Richardii' is a small tree with white-backed yellow leaves.

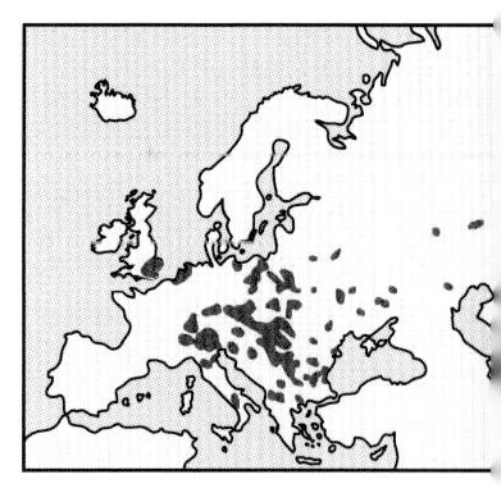

Populus x canescens (Ait.) Sm.

Grey poplar

Description • A large tree, 20–30 m tall, with a stem up to 1 m in diameter **4**. The bark is reminiscent of White poplar (above), pale silvery-grey with horizontal bands of blackish lenticels that gradually expand and merge together as the stem enlarges to form rough fissured bark **5**. The dark green leaves are vaguely palmate on vigorous shoots but the lobes are rounded and irregular **6**. Sucker foliage is completely different, toothed and pointed like Aspen (p94). Tomentum on the underside of the leaf is pale grey, much of it is rubbed off by the end of the season. Male catkins are whiskery, 4–9 cm long, brown and green with deep red anthers. Female trees are rare, their catkins are slender, 5 cm long, yellow and pale pink. **Habitat and Ecology** • Grey poplar is probably a hybrid between Aspen and White poplar. It is capable of producing viable seed. Because the majority of trees are male it is presumed to have been introduced in most areas. **Similar species** • White poplar.

Natural range

Cultivated distribution
Potentially a valuable timber tree already much 'improved' by clonal selection to obtain straight stems and vigorous growth. It is less site demanding than commercial Balsam and Hybrid black poplars.

1

2

3

4

5

6

FAMILY Fagaceae

Quercus ilex L

Holm oak or Evergreen oak

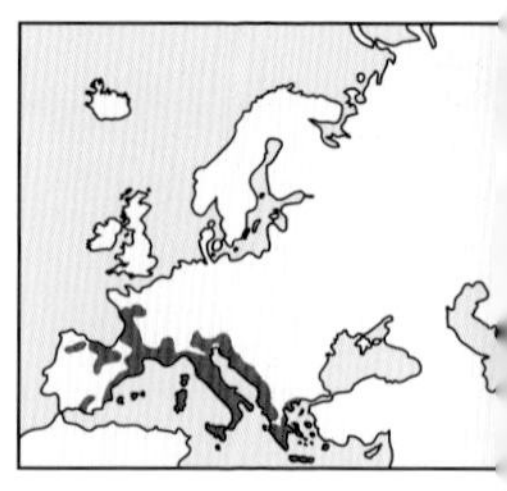

Natural range

Cultivated distribution
Planted in shelter-belts and gardens, usually facing the sea, since 1581 in England. Italian provenances appear to adapt to northern conditions rather better than Spanish.

Description • A large, distinctive tree with dark, heavily fissured, hard bark **1**. One of the largest diameter evergreen trees in Northern Europe **2**, often exceeding 25 m in height. The outline is compact and rounded **3**. The young foliage is covered with buff felt in the first year **4**. Male catkins are the same **5** giving trees an overall light brown look in spring. The leathery leaves are variable in shape from oval to almost lanceolate with entire margins and nought to ten rather inadequate, forward-pointing teeth. Young plants do produce more distinctly spined leaves reminiscent of Holly until they are above browsing height. The male catkins are pendulous and threadlike **6**. Females, on the same tree, are insignificant in small clusters. They produce green then brown, 1–2 cm acorns in one season, each held in a deep, grey-green to straw coloured cup **4**. **Habitat and Ecology** • Grows best on warm, sandy soils particularly close to the sea in Northern Europe. Severe winter weather or exceptional drought in summer can cause complete temporary defoliation. Snow damage can also be a serious problem if upper branches snap and cause a knock on effect as they fall. **Similar species** • *Quercus x turneri* (below) *Quercus x hispanica* (p296) and several other obscure, exotic evergreen oaks.

Quercus x turneri Willd.

Turner's oak

Natural range
This hybrid can occur naturally where the parent species' natural ranges overlap (p298 and above).

Cultivated distribution
A potential urban tree which looks like a small common oak but keeps most of its leaves on through the winter.

Description • A variable, medium-sized hybrid tree (*Quercus ilex* x *Quercus robur*) up to 15 m tall. The dark, 5–10 cm, semi-evergreen leaves are tapered at the base and have three to five rather indistinct lobes. On some individuals early growth is rapid **7**. It then slows and the tree usually takes on the general appearance of its Common oak parent **8** except for the dark green, leathery foliage. Flowers are similar to those of both parents and some individuals produce acorns **9**. These however cannot be relied upon to produce authentic progeny and tend to throw back to either parent. **Habitat and Ecology** • An artificial hybrid but sometimes spontaneous individuals occur. **Similar species** • The original form, at first called *Quercus pseudoturneri* (Schneid) Henry, if propagated vegetatively is less variable than seedlings. It was produced before 1785 at Turner's nurseries in Essex.

1
2
3
4
5
6
7
8
9

FAMILY Fagaceae

Quercus suber L.

Cork oak

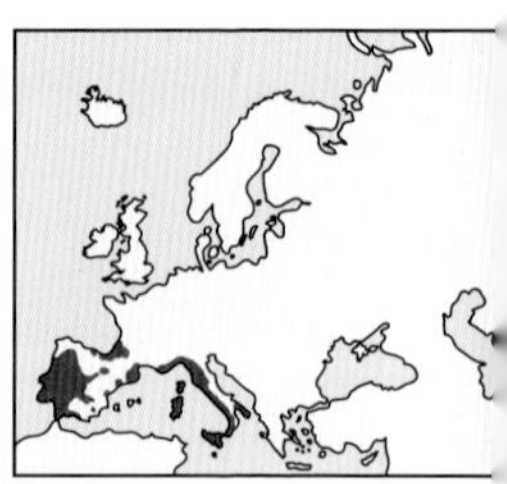

Natural range

Cultivated distribution
Only grown in Northern Europe as an ornamental curiosity. Introduced in 1699 but probably confused from the start with var. *occidentalis* which is more hardy. Also confused with some cultivars of *Quercus x hispanica* and the plethora of seedlings which have arisen from them. With climate change in Northern Europe this tree now has greater potential for amenity planting in city open spaces.

Description • A tree that is occasionally found in mild districts in northern Europe. Northern trees are generally short stemmed often with several large, low limbs probably reflecting early frost damage. The oldest surviving trees in Britain are mostly in semi-woodland situations protected from radiation frost [1]. From a distance, Cork oak looks like a pale leaved Holm oak (p292), a billowing, rounded evergreen tree up to 20 m tall and eventually almost as wide. Stems become massive and around 1 m in diameter [2]. The bark is distinctive. In the natural state (i.e. not harvested every eight to ten years to make bottle corks, etc.) it is deeply furrowed with broad, smooth-edged, vertical ridges. On an old tree it will be 4–8 cm thick, soft to the touch and pale brown. Freshly harvested trees are startling orange-brown until the exposed underbark weathers. Shoots are grey-brown with short, velvety, grey hairs at first. Buds are chestnut coloured, 2–4 mm long in clusters. A new flush of growth occurs each spring but previous year's leaves remain until they become dysfunctional [3]. The foliage becomes very dense, dark green and pendulous towards the branch tips [4]. Leaves are ovate to oblong, 3–6 cm long. Some have forward-pointing teeth with or without shallow lobes. Some are undulating with a zigzag midrib. Occasional leaves do not conform to any fixed pattern and may even be three lobed [3]. The upper surface is deep lustrous green, the underside is obscured by short, pale, ashy-grey tomentum. The flowers appear with the new leaves in spring. They are insignificant, greenish, pendulous male catkins and tiny females resembling enlarged buds on short spur shoots. Acorns ripen in one season to golden brown and enlarge to 2–3 cm long. They remain half obscured by the cup which has extended tangled scales like Turkey oak (p303 [4]) but shorter. **Habitat and Ecology** • Cultivated in Europe for centuries for cork and as summer fodder so the precise Natural range and habitat has become obscured. **Similar species** • The variety *occidentalis* (Gay) Arcang. is more deciduous and the acorns sometimes take two seasons to ripen. Another 'cork barked' tree is *Phellodendron amurense* (p406) but the foliage and shape of the tree are quite different. Some evergreen forms of *Quercus x hispanica* (p296) closely resemble Cork oak but the bark is always much harder and dense.

Cork oak acorn

1
2
3
4

FAMILY Fagaceae

Quercus x hispanica Lam.

Spanish oak

Description • A hybrid of this kind is inevitably variable. The parents, *Quercus cerris* Turkey oak (p302) and *Quercus suber* Cork oak (p294), are completely different in appearance. Furthermore, fertile acorns are produced so that subsequent generations become even more diverse until positive identification can only be described as speculative. The bark is also variable, pale or dark grey-brown, corky or fairly hard **1**, and on a stem up to 1 m diameter. Huge trees, 30 m tall are frequent. Leaves are elliptic, oval or ovate with a wedge shaped, sometimes oblique, base and around seven pairs of triangular or rounded lobes **2**. They are semi-evergreen or completely evergreen, often depending on the severity of the winter. Male catkins are pendulous strings of tiny flowers with reddish anthers until the yellow pollen is shed. Females are in small clusters developing into 3 cm acorns in scaly cups after two years. This hybrid is usually represented in cultivation by one of its named cultivars. 'Lucombeana', The Exeter oak, was produced around 1763 by Mr Lucombe a nurseryman from St Thomas, Exeter. It is a massive tree, intermediate between the parents, with semi-evergreen foliage **3**. The stem looks corky from some distance away but is actually rough and hard to the touch **4**. Open-grown specimens become huge with billowing, dense, rich green foliage **5**. Mr Lucombe only produced trees vegetatively so that his strain remained pure. Subsequent nurserymen have unfortunately grown seed from them and wrongly retained the original name 'Lucombeana' so most modern trees are of dubious antecedence. Another distinct cultivar 'Ambrozyana' was raised in 1909 by Count Ambrozy at Mlynany in Czechoslovakia. It is more evergreen than 'Lucombeana' but has similar hard, dark grey bark **6**. More often seen amongst evergreen variants in Britain is 'Fulhamensis' raised near London around 1760. It too has been subsequently grown from dubious seed and to some extent has lost its original identity. The bark is much closer to Cork oak, deeply fissured and corky. 'Crispa' is one of the more successful seedlings of Exeter oak. It is a small tree with corky bark and stiff, evergreen, grey-backed leaves. These often have pointed lobes and many are narrowed (waisted) towards the centre.
Habitat and Ecology • The hybrid occurs naturally in southern Europe where the ranges of the parents overlap, in open woods and deciduous forests. **Similar species** • A confused set of cultivated forms and their progeny. Some are reminiscent of Turkey oak in summer.

Natural range
The cross is possible in the wild but most trees are of cultivated origin.

Cultivated distribution
Extensively planted in large parks and country estates especially on lime rich ground. Many specimens now may be the result of spontaneous hybridization and backcrossing within collections where original trees were planted. It is important to raise new material vegetatively from known authentic trees or the old named cultivars will be lost for ever.

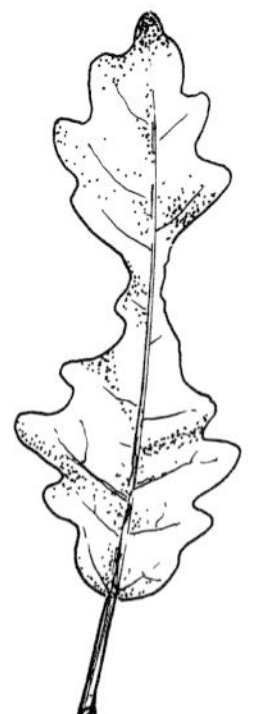

'Crispa'

FAMILY Fagaceae

Quercus robur L.

Common oak

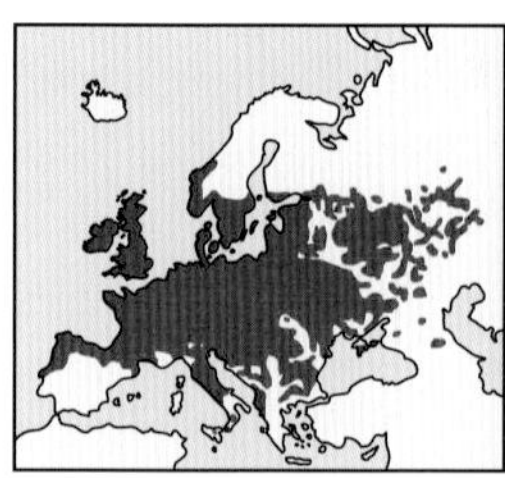

Natural range

Cultivated distribution
Planted and managed for timber and 'tan-bark', for tanning leather, for hundreds of years. Notably used for ship and house building until the start of the twentieth century. There are ornamental forms in cultivation including upright and weeping trees. One of the strangest leaf types is 'Filicifolia' **8**.

Description • An oak tree is a familiar sight to most people. Which Oak is of little consequence to many of them, but the one most frequently seen in Europe will probably be the Common oak. It is found in the countryside, high up on hills and mountain slopes and also in urban situations. Potentially a big tree, 20–25 m tall with a rounded, billowing, bright green top in summer **1**. It is equally impressive in winter when the leaves are off and the strength of the stem and structure of the crooked branches can be appreciated **2**. Stems may exceed 2 m in diameter but half that size is more common **3**. The bark is smooth, grey-green or pale brown at first becoming vertically fissured and increasingly grey and rough with age **3** and **4**. At around 200 years old branches start to die back and fall when hit by severe storms. This 'dead wood' is a vital habitat for invertebrates and should always be left under the tree if this is practicable **4**. New, shorter top growth will replace any losses if the tree is left alone. Young shoots are olive-brown and slightly bloomed. The buds are light brown and pentagonal in cross-section. Leaves are roundly-lobed but variable, some have narrow, forward-pointing lobes, others have a more even outline **5**. The petiole is short, although it too is variable in length. Most leaves have an auricled (lobed) base on one or both sides. Autumn foliage colour is yellow ochre then rich golden-brown late in the year. New growth is also yellowish and summer 'Lammas' growth is often tinged with red. Flowers appear in spring amongst the new leaves. Males are thin, yellow, 4–6 cm catkins **6**. Females are small and hidden at the base of new shoots. They resemble tiny, closed acorn cups. These rapidly expand into familiar acorns in long stalked cups by the autumn **7**. They ripen to glossy or slightly bloomed purplish-brown before falling. Many are predated by Knopper gall wasps which transform them into grotesque, woody green and brown, sticky galls. **Habitat and Ecology** • A climax woodland species but found in many different situations. Very tolerant of salinity in the soil and salt spray but old trees are intolerant of sudden changes in ground water levels (due to water abstraction or building development). **Similar species** • Sessile oak (p300) and other obscure deciduous oaks including the Balkan pedunculate oak, *Quercus pedunculiflora* K. Koch, from South East Europe.

Knopper gall (Andricus quercuscalicis)

1
2
3
4
5
6
7
8

FAMILY Fagaceae

Quercus petraea (Matt.) Liebl.

Sessile oak

Description • A large tree usually growing in rocky uplands as an isolated specimen with a domed top **1**, or in a forest of long, straight stems **2**. In either location branches are sinuous, often (but not always) upswept to heights of 20–30 m. The bark is smooth, purplish glossy brown at first soon becoming grey-brown, often in lateral, translucent, silvery bands reminiscent of birch (p162) **3**, then in time craggy, fissured and silver grey. Buds are 3–5 mm long in clusters and vaguely pentagonal in cross-section. Leaves are large and distinctive (when compared to Common oak, p298), 8–14 cm long and 4–7 cm wide with even, rounded, forward-pointing lobes and sinuses **4**. The leaf base is usually wedge shaped on a 2–3 cm petiole. In the autumn the foliage turns to rich yellow ochre and brown **5**. Flowers consist of male catkins emerging in spring from the tip of the previous season's growth. They are 5–8 cm long, pendulous and greenish-yellow. Female flowers are tightly held on adjacent new shoots in clusters or singly. From the start they are recognizable as tiny, closed acorn cups from which during the summer acorns ripen and fall. The stalkless acorn cup **6** is a good feature distinguishing this species from Common oak. **Habitat and Ecology** • Sessile oak is a tree of upland areas often forming pure forests on steep mountain slopes **7**. In cultivation it is happy growing in lowland hedgerows and plantations. Ancient trees 1000 years or more old with stems over 3 m in diameter occur. **Similar species** • Most often confused with Common oak. There are intermediate forms of both species and considerable foliage variation, even within a single tree. Hybrids do occur but they are infrequent. The semi-evergreen *Quercus canariensis* (p306) has similar looking leaves in summer and tree size.

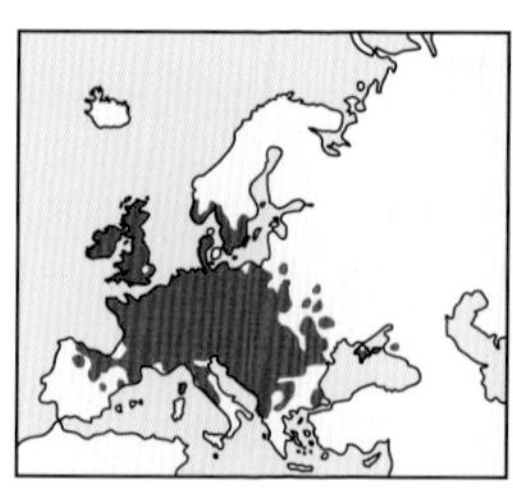

Natural range

Cultivated distribution
Probably a better quality timber tree than Common oak and highly prized for that throughout Europe, especially in the barrel and cask manufacturing districts of France where durability and straight grain are important. Traditionally the tree provided excellent tanning bark and charcoal for smelting and gunpowder. Widely planted on neutral to acid ground in exposed uplands.

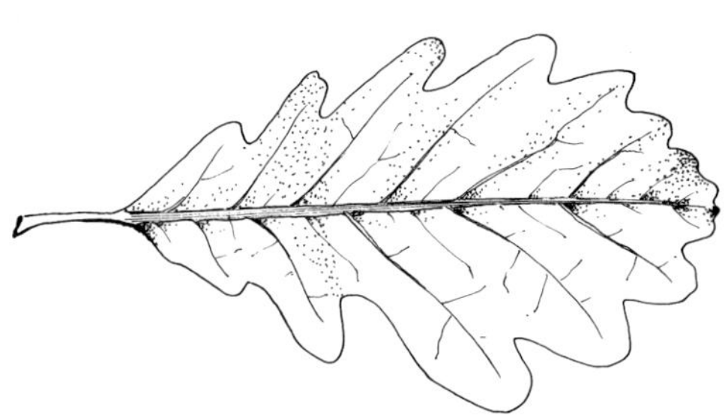

FAMILY Fagaceae

Quercus cerris L.

Turkey oak

Description • A very large deciduous tree, 20–40 m tall with a single stem **1**, or sometimes a spreading crown and large branches reaching 20 m in all directions **2**. Stems often exceed 1 m diameter **3**. The bark is exceptionally rough and hard although from a distance it looks corky and soft **3**. Vertical ridges and fissures are evenly arranged from an early age giving an orderly appearance. It is brown when young, dark brown in deep shade, but bleaches to silver-grey in the sun and rain. Shoots are pale grey-brown and distinctly pubescent with light coloured hairs. In the first winter they are darker **4**. Buds are distinctive (for this whole group of oaks) having thin, projecting stipules, two or three times the length of the bud giving a whiskery appearance. They are pale pinkish-brown. Some shrivelled stipules remain on the shoot all season and may be a good aid to its identity even in winter. The rough leathery and lustrous dark green leaves have an evergreen appearance in summer. They have seven to ten lobes, sometimes more or less in pairs **5**. The overall narrow oblong shape and depth of lobe is variable. Leaf length also varies considerably between 6–12 cm. There is however a uniformity in all this variation and once seen Turkey oak leaves are easily recognized again. Male pendulous catkins are crimson, appearing in early summer at the base of new shoots. Dead straw-coloured catkins sometimes persist on the tree adding to the whiskery appearance of the shoots. Female flowers on short shoots are usually in clusters of around five. They develop in the first year into 1–2 cm, 'mossy', closed acorn cups **4**. These expand to reveal ripe fruits the following year, 2–3 cm acorns in a distinctive cup covered in a tangle of recurved, bristly scales. **Habitat and Ecology** • In nature a forest tree but it also grows perfectly well in the open. **Similar species** • Superficially like most other oaks but close examination places this species in the *Cerris* group of oaks (botanically a section within the genus *Quercus*) which includes Cork oak (p294) and *Quercus x hispanica* (p296).

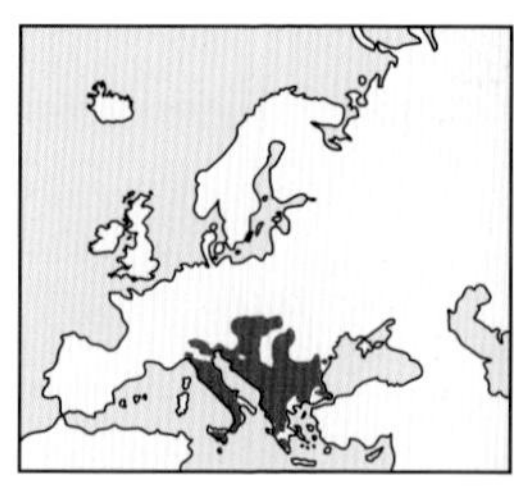

Natural range

Cultivated distribution
In cultivation in Britain since 1735 but now only found as a naturalized relic of old plantations. The timber is not particularly durable and the heartwood resists impregnation with preservatives. Although standing trees give the illusion of containing excellent timber with vigorous, straight growth, the wood inside is often split and shaken and of inferior quality.

Quercus cerris

1

2

3

4

5

FAMILY Fagaceae

Quercus frainetto Ten.
Hungarian oak

Natural range

Description • Probably the most vigorous of all oaks growing in Northern Europe. Specimens 35 m tall are known with stems over 1.5 m in diameter. Most trees encountered will be considerably less, but still very impressive. This is one of the few oaks that will be 'large' within the lifetime of the person who planted it. In 30 years it may exceed 10 m in height **1**. The stem often divides into huge, main, upswept limbs at the base of the domed crown 4–6 m above the ground. The bark is pale grey evenly divided into shallow fissures and small ridges. It becomes more craggy with age **2**. Shoots are finely pubescent, pale grey-green with light brown prominent buds. The deep green leaves are distinctive: no other oak is quite like this species. They are ovate, pubescent at first, up to 22 cm long and 10 cm wide, the widest part being above the centre **3**. There are up to ten regularly spaced pairs of rounded lobes many of which are further sub-divided evenly into three smaller round lobes and sinuses. The stiff texture ensures that fallen leaves remain intact on the ground well into the winter. A useful diagnostic feature at a time when the tree gives very little else away. Female flowers appear in the leaf axils on new side shoots. Globose, 2 cm long acorns soon follow with scaly sessile cups that half enclose them. They ripen to glossy purplish-brown and fall in one season. **Habitat and Ecology** • Able to thrive in pure and mixed deciduous woodland and also in open situations. Hardy as far north as Scotland. **Similar species** • Like Sessile oak (p300) in winter and closely related to *Quercus macranthera* (p310) and *Quercus pyrenaica* (p308).

Cultivated distribution
Brought into cultivation as an ornamental tree in 1838 and immediately became very popular with landowners as an amenity status symbol. For a time it was thought to be a potential timber producer too, but some cut trees have been rendered useless because of radial and ring shakes in the wood reminiscent of Turkey oak (p302). Most modern plantings are of the grafted cultivar 'Hungarian Crown' a superb tree with upswept branches and a rounded top. Sometimes however graft incompatibility will cause stems to break off in a storm causing the loss of half-grown specimens before they achieve their full amenity potential.

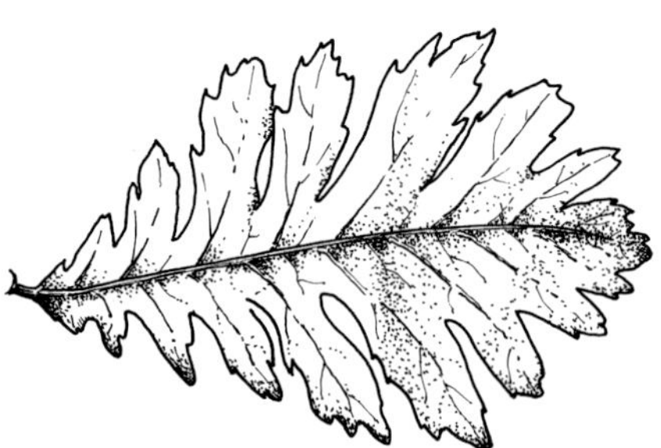

Quercus frainetto 'Hungarian Crown'

FAMILY Fagaceae

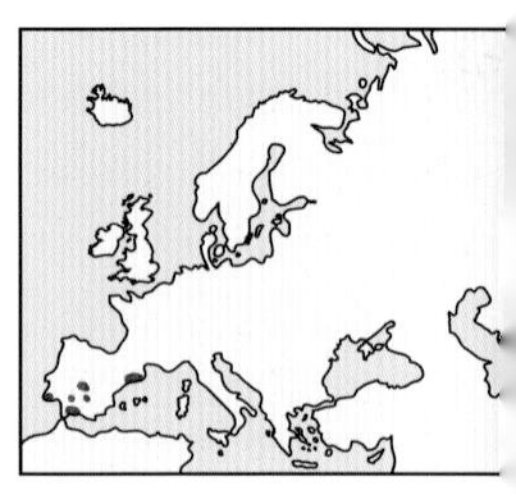

Natural range

Quercus canariensis Willd.
Algerian oak or Mirbeck oak

Description • A stately tree up to 30 m tall with a straight, vertical, persistent stem ultimately around 90 cm in diameter **1**. The outline is domed with ascending limbs and horizontal or slightly pendulous smaller branches. The foliage is usually luxuriant and thick so the canopy appears solid and casts dense shade. Except in very severe winters this tree is evergreen, so it is also good shelter from cold winds and snow. The leaves usually remain in place until thickening shoots and a new flush of foliage finally pushes them off in the spring. The bark is grey-brown and smooth at first then very rough, fissured and craggy. Generally more ridged and scaly than Common oak (p298), which it otherwise resembles **2**. Buds are pale brown with light coloured pubescence but they are well-hidden amongst the tenacious foliage. Leaves are large, 15–20cm long, obovate or oblong with a wedge shaped tapering base and 3 cm petiole. The margins are divided into 8–12 pairs of rounded lobes with triangular sinuses. The largest pair is about one-third of the way along, and the smallest at the tip. In dry weather particularly leaves become hooded as the midrib arches upwards. They are rich green in summer **3** and stay fairly bright in winter with just a few yellowish or brown individuals. There is no hint of sombre deep green usually associated with evergreens. If a 'normal' looking oak tree is encountered in full leaf in winter it is likely to be this species. Flowers appear on new emerging growth. Male catkins are pendulous and yellow coloured. Females are globular resembling small, closed acorn cups. Acorns are roundish, 2–3 cm long, held in almost stalkless scaly cups. They ripen and fall in one season. **Habitat and Ecology** • Deciduous woodland in hot, often dry situations. This tree does not have to endure much severe weather in its native range. **Similar species** • *Quercus x turneri* (p292) and *Quercus x hispanica* cvs. (p296) have similar semi-evergreen foliage but the leaves are less evenly shaped and smaller. Vigorous Sessile oak (p300) also looks similar in the summer. There is a hybrid between this species and Common oak (p298) with intermediate characteristics. Most seedlings raised from cultivated trees will be forms of this hybrid.

Cultivated distribution
Very much under used in Northern Europe where it is fairly hardy. Introduced to Britain in 1845 and eagerly planted in specialist collections and on country estate pleasure grounds. Som[e] original trees and early plantings still survive. Seed produced in cultivation ofte[n] seems to have been contaminated by other compatible oaks.

3

FAMILY Fagaceae

Quercus pyrenaica Willd.
Pyrenean oak

Natural range

Description • A medium to large tree, 15–20 m tall with a stem ultimately 75 cm in diameter. It comes from a diverse natural range in Spain and North Africa so there appear to be various forms in cultivation. Often it is a low-spreading specimen with a short stem and irregular branches but elsewhere it may be a tall, domed forest tree. The bark is grey-brown and smooth at first becoming grey, rough and deeply fissured into squarish divisions **1**. In cultivation the pendulous form of Pyrenean oak is often grafted on to Common oak (p298) some 3 m or so up the stem so the bark you see may not be what it seems. Shoots are densely hairy with grey, stellate pubescence. Buds are light brown with a basal fringe of free-tipped scales, sometimes a useful winter diagnostic feature. The 10–16 cm leaves are obovate with a rounded tip and tapering base leading to a slender, downy, 2–3 cm petiole **2**. There are around five pairs of rounded, more or less forward-pointing lobes cut almost halfway to the midrib. The upper surface is grey-green with some deciduous early pubescence but the underside is persistently hairy, sometimes felted with pale grey tomentum. Male flowers are pendulous, yellow, thread-like catkins in early summer appearing after the foliage has fully emerged. Female flowers are globular in leaf axils which rapidly produce subsessile, 2 cm acorns often in small clusters almost half enclosed by a scaly, tomentose cup. **Habitat and Ecology** • Open mixed woodland, hillside thickets and isolated in warm countryside. **Similar species** • Hungarian oak (p304) and Caucasian oak (p310). This species has an affinity with Common oak in parts of its Natural range and hybrids may occur between the two.

Cultivated distribution
Rarely grown for amenity as a species but pendulous forms, originally called *Quercus pyrenaica* subsp. *pendula* (Dipp.) Schwarz, L., are common in old collections, arboreta and botanic gardens. This form has narrow, hooded leaves with fewer lobes. Modern examples are mostly the clonal cultivar 'Pendula' which has strongly weeping branches and is always top-grafted **3**. In some old specialist oak collections, after 1822, this species was often labelled *Quercus toza* DC.

2

FAMILY Fagaceae

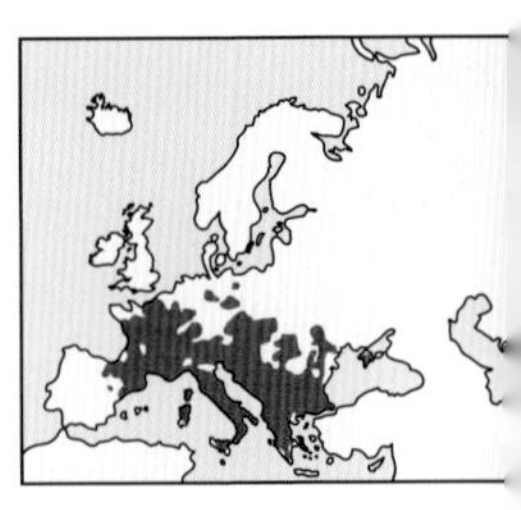

Quercus pubescens Willd.
Downy oak

Description • A deciduous tree reminiscent of Common oak (p298) ultimately 18 m tall with a stem up to 1 m diameter. The outline is rounded often on a short trunk when in an open situation **1**, but having a long, straight stem in forest conditions. The bark is grey becoming fissured and ridged into squarish plates **2**. Shoots are greenish-brown covered with dense, buff-coloured, felted pubescence. The 5–10 cm leaves are obovate with a rounded end and tapered towards a subcordate base. There are approximately six pairs of round, marginal lobes with undulating round sinuses **3**. The upper side is lustrous deep green with some stellate hairs, the underside is grey-green, more densely pubescent with prominent, forward-pointing veins. The petiole is short, seldom more than 1 cm long. Male flowers are slender, lax catkins, females are globular like tiny closed acorn cups **4**. The small, ovoid acorn, about 1.5 cm long, is half enclosed by the cup which has appressed scales. **Habitat and Ecology** • Woodland, thickets and in small clumps on exposed but mostly warm hillsides. **Similar species** • This is a variable tree which in some of its forms resembles several different oaks.

Natural range
Extends from Europe throug the Caucasus to Central Asia and possibly Northern India.

Cultivated distribution
Seldom grown in Northern Europe. Present but not recognized in some collections. Slow-growing provenances, possibly qualifying as subspecies, mal excellent large garden or parkland specimen trees.

Quercus macranthera Fisch. and Mey
Caucasian oak

Description • A 20 m tall columnar tree with luxuriant foliage and a persistent straight stem **5**, ultimately 1 m in diameter. Main limbs are mostly ascending with shortish horizontal branches. Bark is purplish-brown at first becoming grey and gradually developing an intricate pattern of vertical fissures and scaly ridges. Shoots are densely pubescent at first and buds are large with extending stipules. Some terminal buds are 1.5 cm long even before they begin to expand in the spring. Leaves are large, up to 20 cm long, with 7–11 pairs of ovate lobes **6**. Upper sides are rich green and the undersides are paler with thin, variable tomentum. Petioles are 1.5 cm long and also pubescent. Male catkins are pendulous, about 8 cm long and slender. Female flowers are globular and sessile. Acorns are 2 cm long, half enclosed by the cup, which has narrow, pointed scales, the lowest are usually free. **Habitat and Ecology** • Grows in mixed and pure woodlands. **Similar species** • The foliage resembles *Quercus canariensis* (p306).

Natural range
Northern Iran, the Caucasu and round the southern hal of the Caspian sea.

Cultivated distribution
In Northern Europe its kno timber is probably inferior t the closely related Sessile oa (p300). As an amenity tree where space permits it is ideal. In an open situation i spreads out until it may be almost as wide as it is tall, a reaches a mature state in a relatively short time.

1
2
3
4
5
6

FAMILY Ginkgoaceae

Ginkgo biloba L.
Maidenhair tree

Description • The peculiar, fan-shaped, thick, rubbery leaves **1** make this tree easy to recognize in summer. It is a historical curiosity, a relic of a primitive family of great trees that were prominent 160 million years ago. It is a gaunt, spiky, often semi-fastigiate tree seldom exceeding 20 m in height **2**. Huge stems over 1 m in diameter occur in Northern Europe but they are infrequent. The bark is grey-brown becoming dull grey in old age **3**. Vertical ridges form a lattice pattern and then become exaggerated like extended buttresses. Shoots are glabrous, pale green then buff before turning light grey in the second year. The 7 cm leaves are shaped like a duck's foot: the Chinese name Ya-chuo-tze means that. Even the venation of the leaf adheres to the analogy. The leaf has a central notch or occasionally three notches in it **1**. Autumn foliage colour is butter yellow. Flowers, on separate male and female trees, occur on side spur shoots. Male catkins are pale green, 2–3 cm long. Female flowers are held on a long, 4–5 cm stalk. They are fertilized in a unique and primitive way like ferns. The yellowish-brown, 3–4 cm ovoid, plum-like fruit contains an edible seed but the fleshy outer casing has a horrible smell. **Habitat and Ecology** • This is a living fossil tree completely removed from its original natural habitat. Its tolerance of hot, dry summers and cold winters, and even air pollution, give some clues to what early Jurassic conditions might have been like. **Similar species** • A monotypic genus but there are a few variable cultivated forms. 'Fastigiata' is a slender but unpredictable cultivar, usually male. 'Pendula' is a low-domed bush, like a mushroom, on a short, thick stem seldom over 2 m tall. Most spreading or pendulous branched individuals are female.

Maidenhair tree fruit

Natural range

Thought to have been Eastern and South West China but cultivated elsewhere in the Far East at least since the eighth century, according to a Chinese herbalist. This has confused any natural occurrence. Preglacial fossils show world-wide distribution.

Cultivated distribution

Recognized as a good urban tree (male plants) and used extensively in cities all over the temperate world. Grows easily from seed and transplants well but saplings are relished by mice. The fine grain, yellowish-brown wood resembles maple but is not load bearing or durable. The whole tree has valuable medicinal properties.

2

3

FAMILY Hamamelidaceae

Parrotia persica (DC.) C.A. Mey.

Persian ironwood

Description • Although specimens 15 m tall are known this tree is usually a smaller, rounded, bushy plant around 6 m high and at least as wide. Strangely, individuals planted close to the Atlantic coast tend to have no single trunk whereas further east short, distinct stems occur. Closely related to Witch hazel (*Hamamelis* L.), Persian ironwood produces it flowers in winter and also has good autumn foliage colour. The outline is domed but ragged round the edges usually with dense tangled branches reaching down to the ground **1**. The smooth, thin bark is reminiscent of a Plane tree (p288) flaking off in substantial, irregular shaped pieces. The ground colour is dark purplish-brown with orange-buff exfoliated patches that gradually mature over several years back to the original colour **2**. This attractive, multicoloured effect occurs all the way along main branches down to about 10 cm in diameter and is a good diagnostic feature. Young shoots are grey-green becoming light grey-brown after one year. Buds are dark blackish-brown with short, glandular, felted hairs like the brown budded forms of Ash (p410). On emergence the leaves are coppery-pink soon becoming fresh green **3**. Leaves always tend to droop downwards giving the impression (usually quite wrongly) that they are short of water. They are 6–12 cm long, irregularly round toothed, obovate to oval with a blunt, pointed tip and wedge-shaped base. The upper surface is deep glossy green in summer reminiscent of an evergreen. However, in the autumn, the foliage colour is spectacular orange and red just before it falls **4**. The flowers emerge from enlarged, dark, velvety scaled buds in midwinter. They have no petals but the red stamens are remarkable **5**. Female parts of the flower remain more or less out of sight. The fruit, an ovoid capsule like an enlarged bud, ripens through the summer then splits open to reveal a single, shiny seed. **Habitat and Ecology** • Usually an understorey to mixed woodland but also grows in isolated thickets often in harsh, dry summer and cold winter climatic conditions. **Similar species** • Nothing is quite like this plant as a whole but individual parts resemble several other trees (above).

Natural range
Asia Minor, Northern Iran and neighbouring states.

Cultivated distribution
Cultivated around 1840 in Northern Europe after being discovered and named after F.W. Parrot, a German surgeon who is credited with being the first person to climb Mount Ararat in Turkey. Widely grown and popular in gardens and parks particularly as an autumn and winter feature.

Parrotia seeds

FAMILY Aceraceae

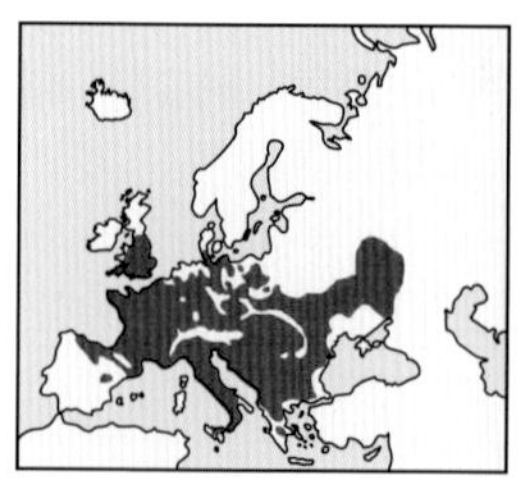

Acer campestre L.
Field maple

Description • The only Maple native in Britain, this tree usually plays a supporting role in deciduous woodlands, never a dominant species but nearly always present, particularly on woodland edges and along open ride sides. This is not a large tree even in prime open conditions, rarely exceeding 15 m. Field maple is a common native hedgerow species. Its round domed or layered top is distinctive in summer **1**. The twiggy short branches that usually develop close to the burry stem become clear in winter **2**. Young shoots are green, soon becoming deep red-brown when exposed to sunlight. Trimmed plants in hedgerows show up as sections of bright red, upright twigs in winter. The small palmate leaves have five wedge-shaped lobes and a long petiole **3**. They turn pink and gold in the autumn **4**. The flowers are usually bisexual but entirely male trees are known. In lax, drooping clusters, they are pale yellow with narrow petals dominated by prominent, deep yellow stamens. Some develop into paired winged seeds that are deep pink throughout the summer **3**. Very large stem diameters are unusual. Big old trees often consist of several stems, the result of past coppicing or hedge cutting. The bark is grey-brown or fawn-brown developing shallow, vertical fissures and ridges **5** usually with burrs. Some individuals produce numerous prominent burrs, once a source of 'birds-eye Maple' wood for veneers before superior American 'burry maples' were discovered and brought to Europe. Some young trees produce very corky, light brown bark: in extreme cases the branches develop exaggerated vertical 'wings' **6**. Trees can be long-lived, up to 500 years: often they were originally growing on wood boundaries and ancient hedge banks. Sometimes when the woods and hedges have been cut down the Maples remain marooned in the open **7** or amongst urban development. **Habitat and Ecology** • Fertile, moist lowland soils suit this tree, so it is an essential component of well-managed agricultural land. Its small size means trees seldom blow down or break. It is a good refuge, nest site and food plant for numerous organisms and provides nectar for bees. **Similar species** • Several small-leaved maples. There are several cultivated forms, 'Elsrijk' is a dense conical tree, suitable for street planting, developed in Holland in 1953.

Natural range
Extends down Europe to West Asia and North Africa.

Cultivated distribution
Managed since prehistoric times as a live hedge plant and for its wood. A few remnants of ancient pure maple woods can be found in some places. The ecological and wildlife benefits of planting the tree in Britain are now better understood, so it is enjoying wider use in modern planting schemes.

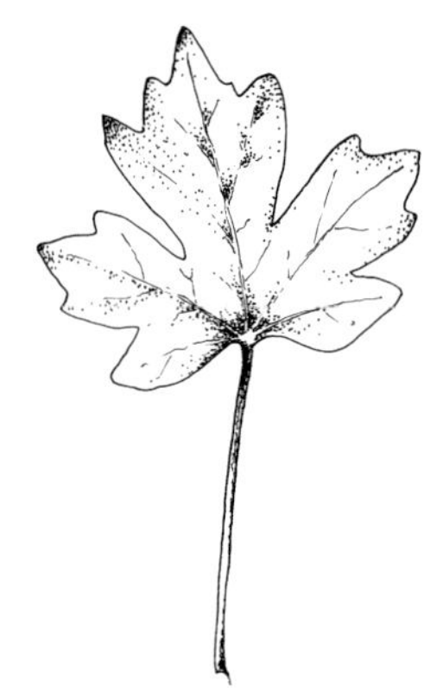

FAMILY Aceraceae

Acer opalus Mill.
Italian maple

Description • What seemed to be a simple tree to identify has now been split into several subspecies each of which appears to have a multitude of confusing and invalid synonyms. Italian maple, in the broad sense, is a rounded or domed tree up to 15 m tall with a stem diameter of 50–80 cm. The bark is smooth and brownish-grey for many years, eventually becoming flaky with shallow fissures revealing pale orange underbark **1**. Shoots are dark brown becoming brownish-grey. Leaves are variable, sometimes reminiscent of Sycamore (p362) but smaller, without most of the teeth and with slightly more rounded lobes **2**. Irregular three-lobed leaves are also common with completely untoothed margins **3**. The upper side becomes dark green at the end of the summer, but the underside remains pale with some tomentum and distinctly raised main veins **4**. Petioles are as long as the leaf blade, yellowish-green with a pink sunlit side. Flowers in short, pendulous corymbs are yellow and appear before the leaves. Clusters of paired seeds each have a 2–3 cm, dry, thin membraneous wing. **Habitat and Ecology** • Mixed deciduous woodland and thickets on warm lower mountain slopes. **Similar species** • The hybrid *Acer x coriaceum* Tausch, between this and *Acer monspessulanum* (p320), has smaller intermediate leaves **5**.

Natural range
Much of the Mediterranean edge from the Pyrenees to the Balkans, Caucasus and Iran. The population is divided into eastern and western subspecies.

Cultivated distribution
Rare in cultivation in Northern Europe. This tree has no particular ornamental merit; it is variable and its complicated taxonomy does not endear it to non-specialist nurserymen.

Acer hyrcanum Fisch. and Mey.
Balkan maple

Description • Originally this was thought to be a subspecies of Field maple (p316), but later a subspecies of Italian maple (above). Now it is accepted as a legitimate species but has been sub-divided into around seven subspecies. It is a 6–10 m tall tree with a 50 cm, brownish-grey, fairly smooth stem **6**. Some forms only make a shrubby bush. The 6–8 cm leaves resemble Sycamore in shape but may vary **7**. Flowers are yellowish-green in pendulous racemes appearing with the young leaves. The membraneous seed wings are held on the paired seeds at an acute angle. **Habitat and Ecology** • Hot, dry hillsides and scrubby woodland. **Similar species** • The whole *Monspessulana* series of Maples appears to consist of intermediate forms and indefinable subspecies.

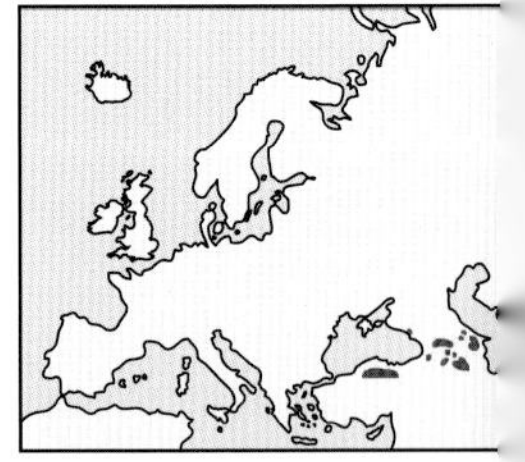

Natural range
The Caucasus, through the Balkan States into Turkey, the Lebanon and Iran.

Cultivated distribution
Rare in Northern Europe, slow-growing and of no commercial or ornamental merit. Some provenances are tender.

1

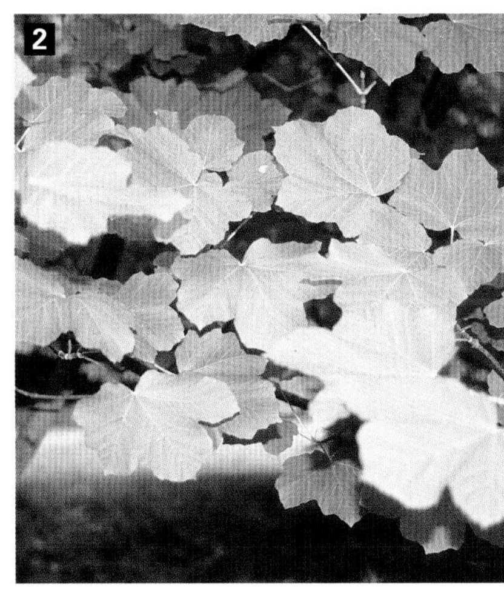
2

3

4

5

6

7

FAMILY Aceraceae

Acer monspessulanum L.
Montpelier maple

Description • A tree to 10 m, or a densely-branched shrub with a rounded top and often twisted short stem up to 60 cm diameter. The bark becomes fissured into shallow plates, yellowish-brown in the shade but bleached pale grey in the open **1**. Shoots are green turning pale reddish-brown after one or two years. The foliage is dense and deep shiny green. Each 5–7 cm leathery leaf is three-lobed with rounded tips and a wedge shaped base, with a distinct notch at the point of attachment to the 5 cm petiole **2**. In the autumn the foliage turns to butter yellow, but in mild districts some trees stay semi-evergreen. Flowers are in greenish-yellow, pendulous corymbs. Seeds in pairs have 2.5 cm wings that are tinged red in summer then ripen to pale brown **3**. **Habitat and Ecology** • Warm but often exposed places. In many natural habitats it is threatened by grazing goats. Also in unfavourable situations it fails to set fertile seed. **Similar species** • *Acer sempervirens* (below) and, superficially, *Acer campestre* (p316) but this species has sub-divided, five-lobed leaves.

Natural range
Southern and Central Europe to the Ukraine, Iran and the Caucasus.

Cultivated distribution
Seldom found in cultivation in Northern Europe. Not an obvious choice as an amenity tree but certainly of botanical and conservation interest. There are several recognized regional subspecies. Provenances from cool areas such as the Caucasus or the Ukraine are likely to thrive rather better in Northern Europe than from Algeria or Southern France.

Acer sempervirens L.
Cretan maple

Description • Rarely for a Maple this species is more or less evergreen, only shedding leaves in the coldest winters. It is a densely branched shrub or small tree seldom exceeding 8 m in height with a stem less than 50 cm diameter, often stunted and short. The bark is dark brownish-grey eventually fissuring to reveal pale orange underbark and developing small, fixed scales **4**. Shoots are green with dark brown buds, glabrous or minutely hairy. The leaves are small, mostly under 4 cm long and extremely variable **5**. Most are three lobed with three main veins. They are deep glossy green, giving the foliage a distinctive healthy appearance **6**. Flowers are in small, sparse, pendulous corymbs quickly developing into pairs of seeds with widely spreading wings. **Habitat and Ecology** • Hot, dry mountain sides where the form of the tree has probably been influenced by centuries of sheep and goat grazing, a selection pressure that has favoured the survival of small, twiggy, stunted plants. **Similar species** • Variable foliage has prompted some botanists to describe five or six different forms of this species. The only other evergreen maple is the very rare *Acer obtusifolium* Sibth. and Smith.

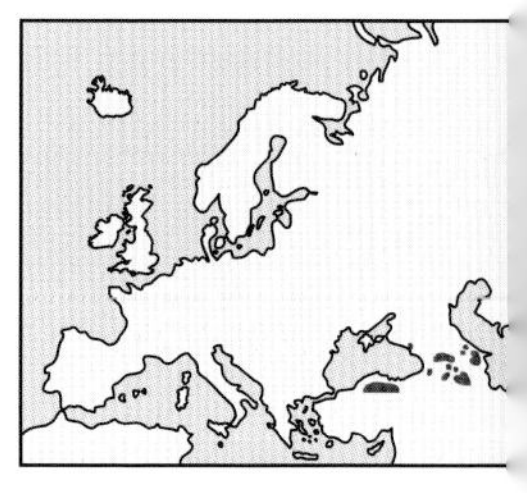

Natural range

Cultivated distribution
Infrequent in cultivation probably because it is tender. Old specimens often have multiple stems **4** usually due to regrowth after frost damage in the past. A venerable specimen in the Cambridge University Botanic Garden has survived many harsh winters but it is growing in thick cover.

1
2
3
4
5
6

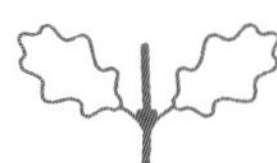

FAMILY Scrophulariaceae

Paulownia tomentosa (Thumb.) Steud.

Empress tree

Description • Usually a fast-growing tree, less than 15 m tall but a later batch of seed sent from China in 1907, probably variety *lanata*, produced huge trees around 25 m tall. The bark is greenish at first bristling with glandular hairs **1**: it turns brownish or purplish-grey but remains smooth until very old. The large leaves are ovate with a slender point, sometimes with two similarly pointed, intermediate lobes, and a cordate base. On the tree they are 25–35 cm long but on coppice regrowth they may exceed 60 cm **2**. The foliage is entirely covered with mucus rich, glandular hairs that trap aphids and other small insects. Flowers occur in spectacular, terminal, erect panicles. They are fragrant and heliotropic **3**. The fruit is a woody, pointed, 5 cm capsule **4** packed with tiny winged seeds. **Habitat and Ecology** • Cultivated for centuries in China on field margins as a kind of living 'fly-paper'. Said to have originally come from mixed deciduous forest, but full light, fertile moist soil and hot sunshine are required. **Similar species** • Superficially like *Catalpa* species (p124); also *Paulownia fargesii* (below).

Natural range
Central China to 1220 m elevation, also naturalized in Japan and Northern China.

Cultivated distribution
Introduced to France in 1834 and still widely grown there. In Northern Europe the early flowers are usually spoilt by frost in the spring and seed is hardly ever set. The wood is ultra-lightweight, stable and has a lustrous radial sheen. Used in Japan (Kiri) for superior cabinet work and musical instruments. Named after Princess Anna Paulownia of The Netherlands.

Paulownia fargesii Franch

Foxglove tree

Description • Originally thought to be a variety of the Empress tree (above) this species is difficult to distinguish from it with certainty. It is fast-growing, 15 m tall with smooth grey bark. Young shoots and foliage are less hairy and by the end of the summer may be completely glabrous. The leaves are smaller than the Empress tree. Tubular fragrant flowers appear in 20–30 cm upright panicles, cream in bud **5**, then white flushed with pale lavender and ultimately 6 cm long. Fruits are oval capsules ripening brown then splitting to release numerous tiny winged seeds **6**. **Habitat and Ecology** • Moist, fertile, open woodland away from direct exposure to strong wind. **Similar species** • Empress tree (above).

Natural range
Western China.

Cultivated distribution
Introduced to Europe in the early 1900s but identification was always confused. Very rare in cultivation although thought to be more hardy in Northern Europe than the Empress tree.

1
2
3
4
5
6

FAMILY Rosaceae

Sorbus torminalis (L.) Crantz

Wild service tree

Natural range

Description • Potentially a large tree over 20 m tall usually with a straight stem up to 1 m in diameter. Although infrequently utilized this contains valuable, strong, heavy white wood that has a decorative, occasionally wavy grain. Often this tree has a number, sometimes a large number, of separate stems originating as suckers covering a large area of ground, encouraged to spread in the past by coppicing. The sucker stems become interspersed with other tree species in mixed woodland so their vegetative origin is not at first obvious. The bark soon becomes fissured and ridged with squarish scales which peel off occasionally **1**. Shoots are green becoming olive-brown with thin, white tomentum at first. The leaves are reminiscent of Maple, around 8–12 cm in length with a long, almost white petiole **2**. There is a characteristic large pair of triangular toothed lobes at the base then three or more additional lobes decreasing in size towards the tip. Leaves are uniformly green on both surfaces **3** unlike most other broad-leaved *Sorbus* species, notably *Sorbus aria* (p190). In the autumn they turn bright orange-brown and red **4**. Flowers are in numerous terminal corymbs all over the crown of the tree appearing in late spring after the leaves are fully expanded. Each one is 12 mm across with five dull white petals. The stalks are pale green and sparsely woolly. Fruits in open branched clusters are obovoid, up to 18 mm long and green with a russet-brown sunlit side. Seeds are around 4 mm across. **Habitat and Ecology** • In woods and thickets, occasionally hedgerows on heavy clay soils. **Similar species** • Some exotic apple species with lobed leaves and *Sorbus intermedia* (p192) which has similar shaped leaves but rounded lobes. Some familiar aspects of Pear and other *Sorbus* species may be present especially the bark and fruit.

Cultivated distribution
Formerly grown as an orchard tree. The 'bletted' fruit is edible and was reckoned to be a cure for indigestion. The Latin *tormina* means 'the gripes'. There is speculation about whether eating the fruit was the cure or the cause. Increasingly this tree is planted as an ornamental and as an environmentally valuable species. The French in particular are researching it as a potential high-quality wood producer.

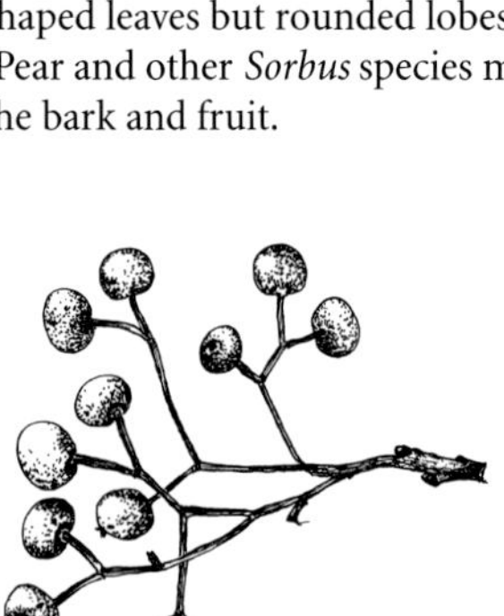

Wild service tree fruit

FAMILY Rosaceae

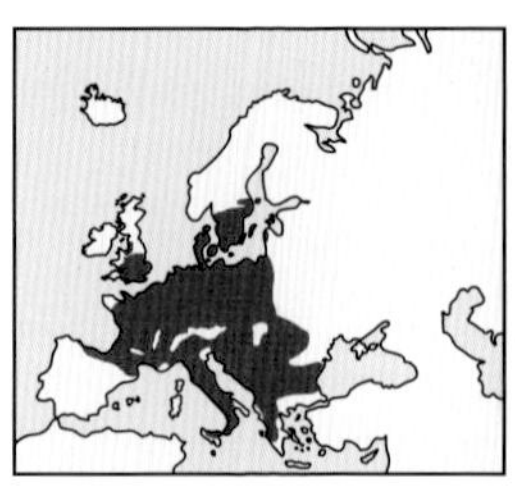

Crataegus laevigata (Poir.) DC.
Midland thorn

Description • Generally this is a rare tree. It can occasionally hybridize with Common hawthorn so its precise range is indistinct. It is likely that intermediate forms are variants of either species and not true hybrids. It may be 12 m tall but is usually considerably less with a rounded crown and one or more main stems. It is found in mixed woodland **1** or along old woodland boundaries, even after the woodland has been cleared and given way to agriculture. The bark is grey-brown becoming scaly and fissured in old age. Shoots are glossy green with a purplish-brown side in full light. Leaves have shallow, rounded toothed lobes with acute sinuses, cut less than half way to the midrib, and a wedge shaped base. They are distinctly glossy green on the upper side. Clearly different to Common hawthorn **2** (Common right, Midland left). The flowers, in tight clusters, are white with five petals, numerous stamens and two, sometimes three styles **3**. The fruit is a 1 cm red berry **4**, but it has two seeds compared to Common hawthorn's one, the most reliable distinguishing feature. When trimmed regularly as a hedge this species produces stipules at the base of each petiole which are lobed and roughly crescent shaped. **Habitat and Ecology** • An open woodland and hedgerow species characteristic of ancient woodland especially on moist clay soils. Valuable for bees in spring and a safe nesting site for small birds. The berries (haws) are food for thrushes and other birds. **Similar species** • When not in flower 'Paul's Scarlet' (below) and other cultivated forms.

Natural range

Cultivated distribution
Not in cultivation as a species except when lumped together with Common hawthorn for hedging. There are many forms and cultivars, some still listed under the former species name *oxyacantha.*

Crataegus laevigata 'Pauls Scarlet'

Description • An outstanding and robust garden tree that has been cultivated since 1858. It is exactly like the species (above) except for a profusion of double pink blossom in late spring **5** which are like miniature 1 cm roses in compact corymbs **6**. The cultivar was discovered on the white double form 'Plena' in Hertfordshire and propagated by the nurseryman William Paul. **Habitat and Ecology** • A garden plant but good nest site for small birds. **Similar species** • The species itself and other cultivars when not in flower.

Natural range
None.

Cultivated distribution
Since 1866 this has been a popular garden tree. It is completely hardy, tolerates very poor ground conditions and atmospheric pollution but still produces an outstanding display of pink flowers. It is used in parks and gardens all over Northern Europe.

1
2
3
4
5
6

FAMILY Rosaceae

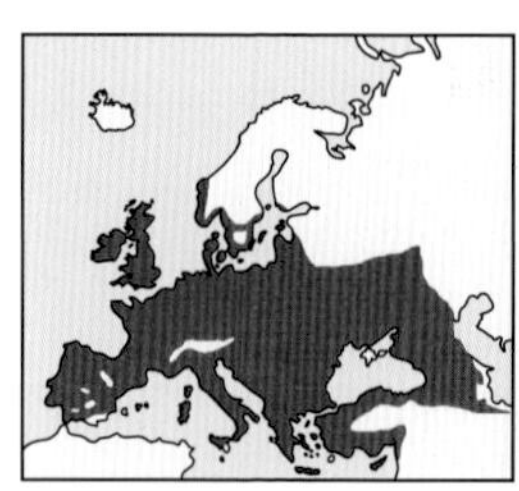

Crataegus monogyna Jacq.
Common hawthorn

Description • A familiar hedgerow plant which if not regularly cut back will make a tree 6–10 m tall. A spectacular sight in May when it is covered in white or palest pink blossom **1**. It is also called the 'May tree' because of this memorable display. Ancient trees exist **2**, some may be 500 years old. Survivors are largely because of folklore and superstition which obliged country people to respect the tree **3**. This ancient tree is growing on the boundary of a monastic site which seems to be a common practice. Even bringing the blossom into the house was, and still is, considered unlucky. In Ireland under the eighth century legal code, there were severe penalties for damaging Hawthorn trees. In former times they were managed as wood pasture pollards partly perhaps to encourage bees. Relics of pollarding can still be found now mostly half hidden in woodlands **4**. Their relatively small size belies their ancient origins. Given freedom to grow this is a round topped tree, often as broad as it is high, with one or more stems and a dense twiggy head of sharp, formidably spined foliage. The solitary 1–3 cm thorns are woody and persist on the branches indefinitely, which is why this is such a good hedgerow species. The bark is grey-brown, hard and scaly in old trees. Stems around 50 cm diameter occur sometimes in clusters of two or three adding up to a diameter in excess of 1 m. Leaves appear in spring before the flowers. They are deeply cut with two or three, occasionally five, pairs of lobes each ending with around five teeth **5**. Lobes vary in size and number, some individuals have an almost 'cut-leaved' appearance. On vigorous shoots lobed, 5–10 mm stipules accompany the young leaves. These often disguise a developing thorn at the base of each 1–3 cm petiole. Flowers occur in tightly packed corymbs on lateral branches. Each bloom is like a 1–1.5 cm single rose with numerous stamens but a single style **6**. The bright red, 10 mm berries contain a single, hard-shelled seed **7**. A distinguishing characteristic between this and Midland thorn (p326). **Habitat and Ecology** • Woodlands, hedgerows, open heaths and moors at low elevation on mineral soils. **Similar species** • Midland thorn and hybrids between this and Midland thorn or exotic species and cultivars.

Natural range
Extends from Europe to Central Asia.

Cultivated distribution
The hard wood was valued in ancient times for manufacturing and as fuel. The berries are edible although they consist mostly of the stone which is not. The flesh is bland raw but makes excellent 'hedgerow jam' or jelly. Since land enclosures in Britain this has been the favourite agricultural stock hedging species. A notable cultivar 'Biflora' is the Glastonbury thorn said to have miraculously grown from Joseph of Arimathea's staff. It flowers regularly on Old Christmas Day (7th January).

1
2
3
4
5
6
7

FAMILY Rosaceae

Crataegus laciniata Ucria (C. orientalis Pallas ex Bieb.)

Oriental thorn

Description • A round topped tree seldom more than 4 m tall with very few thorns **1**. Young shoots are covered with pale grey felt. Leaves, 3–5 cm long, are more or less oval with two to four pairs of narrow toothed lobes cut almost to the midrib. The base is square or wedge shaped **2**. The leaf blades are grey felted on the underside all season and downy on the upper side at first, giving the foliage a distinctive grey-green colour like sage. The petiole is 2 cm long with a pair of toothed stipules on rapidly growing young branches. The flowers on mealy stalks in compact corymbs of 6–14 are white with very long stamens **2**. Fruits are globose, green then orange or red and 2 cm long in clusters of three to ten **3**. **Habitat and Ecology** • Open scrub woodland in the wild. Planted in parks and gardens. **Similar species** • *Crataegus heldreichii* Boiss. is a western extension of the species into Greece. It has smaller leaves. *Crataegus schraderiana* Ledeb., formerly a variety, has dark purplish-red fruit.

Natural range
The Far East.

Cultivated distribution
Introduced to Europe in 1810 and widely planted especially in Southern England.

Crataegus crus-galli L.

Cockspur thorn

Description • A medium-sized tree with a strong, upright stem **4** and rounded crown at first becoming untidy and spreading. The dark green, glossy, 6–10 cm leaves are obovate, strongly tapered to a wedge-shaped base with ragged forward-pointing teeth confined to the upper half **5**. Formidable woody thorns up to 9 cm long are characteristic **6**. Flowers are white in tight corymbs around 8 cm across. The 2 cm globose fruits are deep red **7**. **Habitat and Ecology** • Open, exposed, scrubby woodland or as a park specimen. **Similar species** • *Crataegus x lavellei* (below) and many other cultivated entire leaved thorns.

Natural range
Southern Quebec, Ontario and south to Michigan, Iowa, Kansas and east Texas. Also Georgia and north Florida.

Cultivated distribution
Introduced to Europe in 1691, a favourite very hardy autumn colour feature and garden tree. Exact identification is difficult, in America 25 synonyms have been recorded.

Crataegus x lavallei Herincq ex Lav.

Hybrid cockspur thorn

Description • This is a common 5–7 m, round topped tree with glossy, deep green foliage and numerous corymbs of white flowers **8**. The leaves resemble *Crataegus crus-galli*, which is thought to be the pollen parent. Fruits are orange-red and russet, about 2 cm long and pear-shaped. Fiery autumn foliage colour is distinctive. **Habitat and Ecology** • An artificial French hybrid. **Similar species** • Many, including *Crataegus prunifolia* (Lamb.) Pers. **9**.

Natural range
None, but of American antecedence.

Cultivated distribution
Produced in France and first described in 1880, but confusingly described again in 1883 as something else. A popular, hardy ornamental thorn frequently planted in parks and gardens.

1
2
3
4
5
6
7
8
9

FAMILY Araliaceae

Kalopanax septemlobus (Thunb.) Koidz. (Kalopanax pictus (Thunb.) Naki)

Prickly castor-oil tree

Description • An infrequent, small to medium-sized tree with alternate leaves which otherwise superficially resemble Maple. The stem however is distinctive and very different, covered with viciously sharp, triangular, woody prickles **1**. The dark grey-brown, horizontally spreading branches are also very spiny **2**. Shoots are thick, bloomed olive-green and free of prickles only for the first year. Leaves are 8–18 cm long, palmately lobed like Sycamore (p362). Petioles are around 10 cm long, yellowish with a red side in full light and an enlarged base. Yellowish flowers occur in terminal umbels in midsummer **3**. They are followed by globose, 5 mm, black berries that resemble ivy and which, if not taken by birds, remain on the tree until midwinter. **Habitat and Ecology** • Formidable forests or mixed with other broadleaved species in the Far East. **Similar species** • Only the stems of *Aralia spinosa* L., Devils walking stick, resemble this species but its bi-pinnate leaves are quite different.

Natural range
Japan, Korea and the Pacific Islands and coast of Russia. Central and Northern China.

Cultivated distribution
Occurs over a wide area of Northern Europe but infrequent. Usually confined to specialist collections and botanic gardens. The thorns may be a safety risk in some public places. The variety *maximowiczii* (Van Houtte) Li, is often planted in place of the true species in gardens now.

FAMILY Hamamelidaceae

Liquidambar styraciflua L.

Sweet gum

Description • The alternate leaves resemble some species of Maple. Like many maples they provide conspicuous autumn colour – yellow, red, orange, crimson and finally purplish-brown. Stems are rough with small, corky, vertical ridges and plates. When dry the bark is pale brown **4**, but seems very dark when wet with rain. Trees 30 m tall are known but most reach maturity at half that height in cultivation **5**. The 8–14 cm leaves are palmate usually with five lobes and a long petiole **6**. Margins have irregular, shallow or almost non-existent, teeth **7**. The upper side is lustrous green, the underside paler and shiny with prominent, light coloured main veins. Flowers are in pendulous inflorescences which develop into 2–3 cm fruit clusters like the Plane tree (p288). Black winged, 4 mm seeds are shed when the seed clusters disintegrate. **Habitat and Ecology** • Deciduous, damp woodland including swampy bottomlands (in America), often as a pioneer species on cleared or storm devastated ground. **Similar species** • *Liquidambar orientalis* Mill. from Asia Minor is a smaller tree with more deeply cut leaves **8**.

Natural range
Southern states of North America from Texas to Florida and north to Connecticut and Illinois.

Cultivated distribution
Introduced to England in 1681 as an ornamental amenity tree. The timber was also imported on a vast scale in the early 1900s to build 'tar-block' city streets. Heartwood is called satin walnut, much valued for furniture making, joinery and veneers. Thrives best in cultivation on damp, lime-free soils in full light.

1
2
3
4
5
6
7
8

FAMILY Betulaceae

Alnus incana (L.) Moench.

Grey alder

Description • An aggressive pioneer tree, shrub or coppice of indeterminate size and shape because of the severe environmental conditions in which it frequently grows. In fertile sheltered conditions it makes a 10–20 m tall tree **1**. Stems 30–60 cm in diameter are known **3**. In extreme habitats such as sand dunes **2** or at high elevation stems crowd together, survive for a short time, die back or fall over and then re-grow from basal suckers or coppice. In this way sites are often improved sufficiently for other tree species to survive amongst the alders. The bark is greenish-grey and usually bleached by sun and wind **2**. Older stems become lightly fissured like ash (p408). Shoots are downy at first, soon turning scaly and pinkish-grey with tiny orange lenticels. The buds with only two outer scales are purplish-red with raised glandular pores. The 5–10 cm, variable leaves are oval, ovate or obovate with an acute tip and rounded or wedge shaped base. Each of 10–12 parallel veins ends in a small pointed lobe with intermediate teeth. The upper surface is dull green, the underside is felted grey, especially along the veins and down the petiole. Showy flowers appear in early spring before the leaves emerge. Males consist of pendulous catkins in clusters of three to six, red-brown all winter **4** then opening briefly with a flourish of yellow pollen. Clusters of exquisite, carmine-pink female catkins, 0.5 cm long **5**, develop into green strobiles 'cones' which turn brown the following year and eventually shed wind-blown winged seed. **Habitat and Ecology** • Mountains, sub-arctic tundra, stream sides, damp rocky scree sites and dune slacks. Often in harsh conditions where few other trees will grow. Its distribution extends round the world beyond Europe as subspecies rugosa (*Alnus rugosa* (Du Roi) Spreng.) Speckled alder in North America. **Similar species** • *Alnus hirsuta* (Spach) Rupr. has slightly larger leaves. It appears to replace Grey alder in Siberia and the far east. Grey woolly-backed leaves also occur on several *Sorbus* species, some of which resemble Grey alder, notably *Sorbus intermedia* (p192) and *Sorbus latifolia* (p194). A hybrid between Grey alder and Common alder (p336) is known.

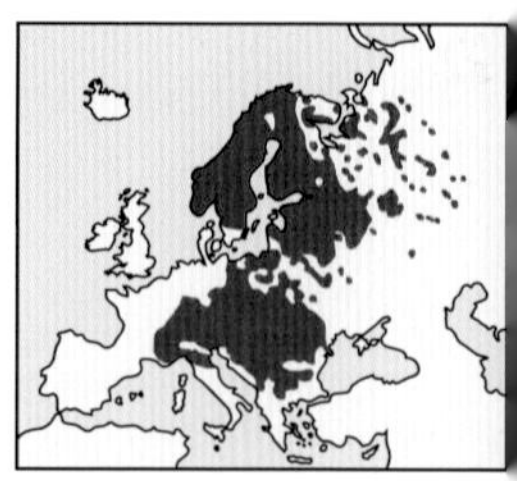

Natural range

Cultivated distribution
The species is planted for shelter to protect plantations of more valuable and less hardy species. It can fix atmospheric nitrogen in the soil (p336). Also used on derelict land and capped rubbish tips. There are several ornamental cultivars. 'Aurea' is a yellow-leaved form with red male catkins. 'Laciniata', in cultivation since 1861, has deeply cut leaves **6**.

1
2
3
4
5
6

FAMILY Betulaceae

Alnus glutinosa (L.) Gaertn.
Common alder

Description • A common, widely distributed and familiar wetland tree in Northern Europe. Stems up to 25 m tall are known but most are shorter. The outline is roundly pointed at first even when grown as multi-stemmed coppice **1**. This is a tree that thrives near or even in water **2**. Old stems around 1 m in diameter occur and coppice stumps often exceed this size. The bark is purplish brown at first and smooth, cracking and eventually bleaching to grey-brown **2**. Fissures in old stems reveal orange-brown under layers of younger bark. Shoots are bloomed purple-brown and glandular, clammy when touched. Buds are stalked with only two grey, outer scales. Leaves are variable, more or less round with a wedge shaped base and usually a distinctive nick in the apex. The leaf margins have various degrees of undulation and numbers of irregular, shallow teeth; some are almost entire **3** while others are lobed and have acute teeth. On newly cut coppice leaves are larger, 15–13 cm, often with rounded lobes and pronounced teeth. The upper side is dark green and quite sticky at first. The underside is light green and less glutinous, with six to eight pairs of pale parallel veins, each with a tuft of white axillary hairs and terminating at the point of a lobe. Flowers develop on the tree over winter as tightly-closed green or purplish-brown catkins. Drooping 7–10 cm male catkins extend in the first warm days of spring **4** in clusters of three to five. Females, also in clusters, are small, upright, deep red catkins about 6 mm long. These develop into green 'cones' in the first year **5** turning black and opening to shed the winged seed the following season. Seeds are able to fly in the wind or float in water to reach suitable germination sites, particularly gravel banks and mud flats. **Habitat and Ecology** • An environmentally valuable wetland tree providing food and shelter for numerous organisms. A critical component of 'alder carr', a transition stage between sedge fen and damp woodland. In association with the fungus *Frankia* alder root nodules are able to fix and utilize atmospheric nitrogen. Consequently the annual deposition of nitrogen-rich alder leaf litter benefits all nearby ground vegetation. Common alder survives on very poor soils up to 80 per cent of which may consist of stones and other non-rootable material. **Similar species** • Although variable this species is not difficult to identify. Only alders have woody, black, cone-like structures (strobiles) which are continually replaced on the tree so they are always present in one form or another.

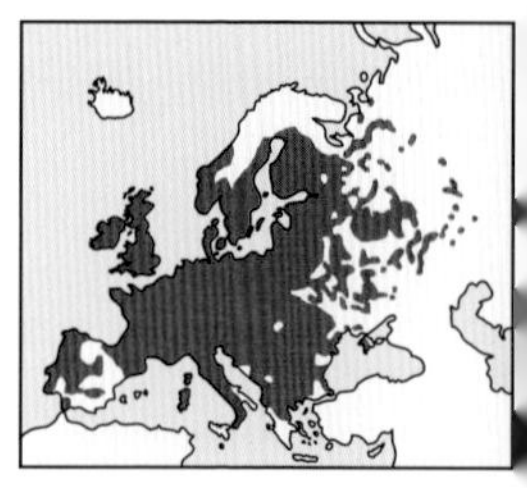

Natural range

Cultivated distribution
Alder wood has traditionally been used for engineering works in or near water (e.g. pumps, piles, sluices, troughs and bank reinforcements). Punts and small boats were made from it where good-quality elm timber was unavailable. Clogs were made from coppice poles and alder charcoal was favoured for manufacturing gunpowder. 'Scots mahogany' was freshly cut, green alder wood steeped for a long period in a peat bog. There are several cut-leaved variants and cultivars (e.g. forma *incisa* **6**, and 'Imperialis' **7** which has deeply cut leaves). Upright and golden variants also occur in cultivation.

1

2

3

5

6

7

FAMILY Betulaceae

Alnus subcordata Mey.
Caucasian alder

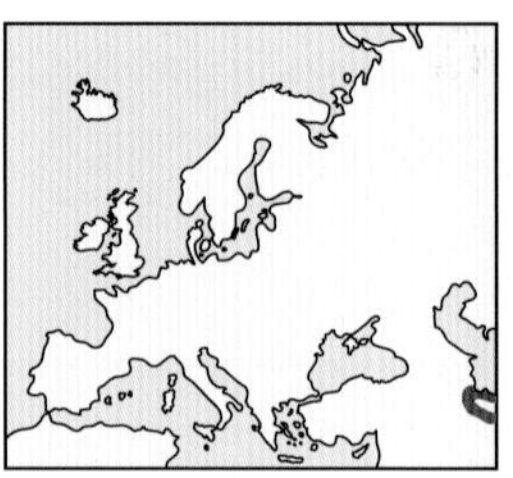

Description • A puzzling tree in the field because of its variability. It may be 15–20 m tall with a good, straight stem and vigorous growth **1**. Annual shoot extension of 2 m has been measured on young, established plants growing in sheltered conditions with moist, fertile soil but such rapid growth would not normally be expected in nature. The bark is reddish-brown and smooth at first, becoming pinkish-grey or brown and rough with age. Vertical fissures develop and although long they are never deep **2**. Young shoots are usually silky pubescent for two to three years, and olive-brown to light green near the growing points. The buds are not distinctly stalked. They have only two outer scales which turn yellow and cling on to the shoot like stipules after the leaves emerge. Petioles are pink, shading to pale green, 2–3 cm long and glandular pubescent. The midrib often picks up the pink or reddish colour of the petiole. Leaves vary from shallow lobed to ovate or oblong-ovate, 5–16 cm long. The tip may be short-acuminate or indistinct and blunt. Leaf bases are often cordate to some extent, but may be asymmetrical like elm. Teeth along the margins vary in size and shape and some trees have finely serrated leaves with hardly any lobes **3** while others are coarsely toothed with exaggerated points at the ends of eight to ten parallel veins. With a lens it is possible to see a minute white bristle or small number of bristles in between each tooth. The foliage is light green (compared to Italian alder p276) and turns yellow late in the autumn. Leaves are pubescent at first but becoming glabrous except along the veins on the underside. Catkins are similar to other alders. Mature strobiles 'cones' are large, up to 2.5cm long in clusters of one to four. **Habitat and Ecology** • Will thrive in a wide range of conditions but doubtfully hardy in the north. The close proximity of water is not essential for survival. **Similar species** • A difficult tree to identify without finding the blackish 'cones'. The bark and stem resemble Turkish hazel (p158). Some leaves are elm-like or reminiscent of Cherry (p142), Buckthorn (p278), Southern beech (p198) or Goat willow (p240). There are also other Asiatic alders which closely resemble this species but they are rare in Europe. So too is the hybrid with common alder (p336). The sub-Arctic *Alnus viridis* (Chaix) DC. Complex. *Alnus sinuata* (Reg.) Rydb. in North America has similar variable foliage but it is never more than a shrub.

Natural range
The Caucasus Mountains and Northern Iran. The north side of the Elburz Mountains by the Caspian Sea. Introgression with Common alder occurs on the western side of the range.

Cultivated distribution
The date of introduction to Britain is uncertain; 1838 is the earliest recorded plant. The tree was well-established in France by 1861. Occasionally planted in tree collections, small plantations, parks and gardens today, but generally infrequent in cultivation.

FAMILY Betulaceae

Alnus rubra Bong.
Red alder

Description • A vigorous, potentially large tree up to 25 m tall with a narrow crown at first, eventually becoming wide-spreading in an open situation **1**. Often seen in a plantation environment where stems are slender, erect and drawn up. The bark is pale grey and smooth **2** only fissuring on very old stems. Twigs are glandular and reddish-brown giving leafless plantations in winter a distinctive red 'haze' reminiscent of Japanese larch (p66). Fast-growing young shoots tend to be three-sided in a spiral. Buds are 8 mm long, acute to slightly rounded with only two visible outer scales, heavily resin-coated and glabrous. Leaves have distinctive rolled back margins **3**. They are up to 15 cm long, ovate to elliptic with an acute tip. The base is more or less rounded. Although revolute the margins retain obvious, doubly-serrate teeth forming small lobes at the end of each parallel vein. Some provenances (seed origins) are more distinctly lobed than others. Petioles are up to 22 mm long and sparsely pubescent and glandular. Deciduous stipules, which soon fall away, are light green or light brown. Female catkins in clusters of around eight are erect, 5–7 mm long, and produced during the previous growing season. They develop into green 'cones' which ripen to almost black, shed seed but then remain on the tree until eventually broken off by the wind. Fruit in various stages of development remains on the tree for up to three years. Pendulous male catkins appear in spring before the leaves; they are usually in clusters of three and extend to 15 cm in length **4**. Each one has numerous red scales each of which supports three flowers. Individual flowers have four yellow stamens. Seeds are flat with two lateral wings along the margins, 2–2.5 mm long and pale brown. They can fly a short distance in the air and float for days on water. **Habitat and Ecology** • A coastal and river-side species colonizing sand and shingle banks, rocky ground, flood-plains and even peaty sites. It is an aggressive pioneer, relentlessly invading newly disturbed ground particularly following floods. Trees grow at great density at first then selectively die out as weak individuals are suppressed. Sometimes whole populations will compete with one another until all the stems are so weak and crowns so sparse that they collapse. **Similar species** • Once the genus has been identified this species is easy to determine by its revolute leaves, even from fallen dead leaves in winter.

Natural range
Along the Pacific coast from south-west Alaska to central California. Also the Columbia River and its tributaries to east Washington and Idaho.

Cultivated distribution
In America an important furniture, pulp and board timber producer. Grown on a small scale in European plantations and for nitrogen enrichment of soil in mixed forests. Unlike most alders it will tolerate upland acid peaty soils. Growth is rapid but seldom sustained. Occasionally used for amenity planting.

1

2

3

4

FAMILY Fagaceae

Fagus Sylvatica L. 'Heterophylla group'

Cut-leaved beech

Description • Spontaneous forms of ornamental Cut-leaved beech occur, but less frequently in the wild than Copper beech (p86). They have variable amounts of leaf mutilation. In the past named trees such as 'Incisa', 'Quercifolia' and 'Laciniata' have been available in the nursery trade. The consensus now is that all cultivars (except 'Aspleniifolia', below) should be lumped together as the 'Heterophylla group'. The resulting group is rather variable and includes grafted and seedling trees. The leaves are variously lobed and some are vaguely oak-like [1]. Trees may eventually be very large with stems like Common beech (p86). **Habitat and Ecology** • Mostly found in cultivation. **Similar species** • A unique but variable group, difficult to identify except in a general sense.

Natural range
Found very occasionally throughout the range of Common beech (p86).

Cultivated distribution
See below. The advantage of planting 'Heterophylla' is that it is on its own roots and will not revert.

Fagus sylvatica L. 'Aspleniifolia'

Fern-leaved beech

Description • The extreme cut-leaved form of Beech, first cultivated in 1804, has leaves reduced almost to the midrib and main veins [2]. Many trees formerly named 'Laciniata' have been included under this cultivar name now. Identification is aided to some extent by the presence of a graft mark on the stem. This may be at the base or some way up [3]. At its best this is a big 15–20 m tall, rounded tree with tightly packed foliage which appears to have a clipped outline. Unfortunately the symmetry is often broken and spoiled by rogue branches that have reverted back to Common beech, presumably from the rootstock. They usually stick out, generally on the inaccessible extremities of the crown. **Habitat and Ecology** • A cultivated tree. **Similar species** • The leaves are vaguely like *Alnus glutinosa* 'Incisa' (p336) and *Alnus incana* 'Laciniata' (p334) but the size of tree, outline and type of stem are distinct.

Natural range
Originally as Common beech but now exclusively found in cultivation.

Cultivated distribution
Cut-leaved beeches of one sort or another are frequently used in urban and rural park landscaping. More obscure types are only found in specialist collections. There are various coloured forms including 'Tricolor' which has somewhat ragged purple pink and white leaves. 'Luteovariegata' is similar in yellow and green. 'Rohan Gold' is a small, compact tree [4] with faintly golden-brown indented leaves [5]. 'Rohanii', the Cut-leaved copper beech [6] has individual leaves which are interesting but overall the tree is uninspiring. An even more severely cut-leaved purple form is 'Ansorgei' which originated in 1891. It is often an ugly, deformed shape.

1
2
3
4
5
6

FAMILY Fagaceae

Quercus rubra L.

Red oak

Description • A large tree with an open, rounded outline and distinctive, large, spiky, deep green, 20 cm leaves, and a smooth grey stem. Young trees grow rapidly reaching 10 m in about 15 years on a good site **1**. Ultimately they may reach 25 m with a stem 80 cm in diameter. The name 'Red' implies red autumn foliage which is true in its native America but less often seen in Europe **2**. The bark is dark grey-brown on young wood becoming grey on older stems with shallow, paler, vertical fissures **3**. Very old trees become more furrowed often exposing some orange-brown inner bark when expansion is rapid. The leaves are broadly elliptical and divided into 7–11 shallow lobes with triangular bristle-tipped points. The upper surface is relatively dull green, less shiny than Scarlet oak (below). The underside is pale with prominent main veins each with a tuft of hairs in the axil. The acorns take two years to mature. In the first year they are almost enclosed by a light brown cup **4**. In the second year they expand to around 3 cm long. **Habitat and Ecology** • Almost any type of soil in moist woodlands. **Similar species** • Other American Red oaks (below and p346).

Natural range
East and Central North America from Cape Breton Island to Ontario then south to Texas, Minnesota, Oklahoma and Georgia.

Cultivated distribution
Introduced to Europe in 1800 and widely planted mainly as an ornamental but the timber is also good. In America this is an important lumber species used for furniture, structural and agricultural work especially fencing.

Quercus coccinea Muenchh.

Scarlet oak

Description • A fine, open crowned, 25 m tall tree with a persistent straight stem and spreading branches **5**. The bark is smooth for many years, purplish-grey with very shallow, grey-brown vertical fissures **6**. The leaves are very like Red oak (above) but more shiny on the upper surface and with soft, light-coloured hairs in the vein axils on the underside. The triangular points are often sub-divided into bristle-tipped lobes separated by rounded sinuses **7**. They tend to be more skeletal than Red oak but less so than Pin oak (p346). The broadly ovate 2 cm acorns take two years to mature. Then they are held in flat cups with large, tightly pressed scales **8**. **Habitat and Ecology** • Pure and mixed forests often on poor rocky or acid soils to 900 m elevation, also infertile sands and gravel banks. Soon colonizes disturbed ground. **Similar species** • Other Red oaks especially Pin oak and *Quercus shumardii* Buckl. that originates from nearly the same Natural range **9**.

Natural range
North East America from Maine to Georgia then west to Mississippi.

Cultivated distribution
Introduced in 1691 and planted frequently in Northern Europe ever since that time. A good shade tree and urban open space amenity specimen. The foliage colour can be spectacular but most years it is rather patchy.

1
2
3
4
5
6
7
8
9

FAMILY Fagaceae

Quercus palustris Muenchh.

Pin oak

Description • Potentially a large tree up to 27 m tall with a straight, persistent, 80 cm diameter stem and mainly horizontal branches with a slightly pendulous extremities. A diagnostic feature, particularly in winter when the leaves are off, is an accumulation of short, truncated, angular twigs along the lower branches that resemble pins. These spur shoots are not spiny in the strict sense but they are stiff and woody. When young this tree grows rapidly upwards with a vaguely conical outline and picturesque, tiered branches **1**. The bark is purplish-grey and brown on the young growth, becoming pale grey and smooth for many years, eventually developing randomly spaced, vertical fissures **2**. In old age these fissures divide the main stem into broad, smooth, grey sections. The leaves are 8–13 cm long and elliptical, although an outline is hard to see, with four to six pairs of deeply cut lobes each terminating in a triangular point with a bristle tip. Some lobes have two or three additional intermediate points. The sinuses are semicircular, in some instances reaching almost to the midrib **3**. Healthy foliage is yellow at first **1** then bright green, glossy on the upper surface of the leaves and paler below. Autumn colour is good but will vary from tree to tree. Some individuals are reliably orange-red, others are shiny chestnut-brown. Often bright autumn foliage colour is limited to a small part of the crown of the tree. Petioles are slender, 2–5 cm long. Male flowers are short, lax catkins, females are sessile and globular, expanding only slightly into embryonic acorns in the first year. These mature a year later into stout, little, 1 cm acorns in flat cups with appressed scales. **Habitat and Ecology** • A wetland tree thriving in pure forests on poorly drained sites such as upland clays and grass moorlands. Also floodplains and gravel banks but not rich alluvial soils. **Similar species** • Several American 'Red' oaks particularly those species with deeply incised leaves such as *Quercus shumardii* (p345 **9**), Black oak, *Quercus velutina* Lam. and Northern pin oak, *Quercus ellipsoidalis* E.J. Hill, a smaller tree introduced to Europe in 1902 but seldom planted and even less often recognized when it is.

Natural range
Eastern Central North America with scattered distribution out to the Atlantic coast between New York State to North Carolina. The main population is centred on Illinois and Indiana.

Cultivated distribution
Introduced to Northern Europe before 1770 and soon recognized as a valuable, tough, site tolerant amenity tree. It has a fibrous root system and no tap root so is easy to transplant even as a 'heavy standard' tree 4–5 m tall. Recently put to good use in numerous urban situations where the poor soils and wet, sour conditions under tarmac and concrete suit it very well **1**.

F367 HGY

FAMILY Aceraceae

Acer macrophyllum Pursh
Oregon maple

Description • A vigorous tree up to 25 m tall resembling Norway maple (p360) but with much larger leaves and smoother, grey bark. Open grown specimens develop a broad-domed top **1**. Stems may exceed 80 cm diameter. It is rarely seen in woodland in Europe but looks promising as a plantation tree **2**. Shoots are green with a purplish-brown sunlit side. Buds are obscured by the bases of the petioles which contain milky sap. At 4–5 mm these seem exceptionally small when the size of the leaves they produce is realized. The outline of each palmate leaf is more or less round, up to 35 cm across and deeply divided into five lobes which are further sub-divided by triangular prominent teeth **3**. The foliage all faces up to the light in stratified horizontal layers. Drooping, 10–15 cm clusters of pale yellow, fragrant flowers attract bees and other insects. Large-winged seeds in pairs have detachable, stiff bristles protecting them from predation. **Habitat and Ecology** • Deciduous forests and open woodland especially near water. **Similar species** • Some Norway maple trees and the leaves of Plane (p286).

Natural range
Western North America, British Columbia, Oregon and California including the Sierra Nevada.

Cultivated distribution
Uncommon as an ornamental park tree. Unsuitable as a street tree because of the excessively large leaves shed in autumn and high soil water requirements. Grown as an upland plantation species on a limited scale as far north as West Scotland **2**.

Acer saccharum Marsh.
Sugar maple

Description • This is a variable tree in Northern Europe because it has been collected and imported since 1735 from a wide range of climatic zones and habitats, from Canada to Georgia. It is a tree 12–20 m tall with an open outline and long, generally up-swept branches **4**. The stem, up to 1 m diameter, has light grey-brown bark which becomes finely fissured and ridged **5**. The leaves have five palmate lobes cut halfway to the centre with rounded sinuses. Margins are entire except for remote, triangular, whisker tipped teeth. The leaves have a cordate base and five palmate lobes cut halfway to the centre with round sinuses. The green and pink petioles have swollen bases enclosing next year's bud and the sap is watery (some similar looking maples have 'milky' sap). Yellow bell-shaped flowers in pendulous clusters are quickly followed by twinned seeds with membraneous wings held at an acute angle. **Habitat and Ecology** • Upland broadleaved moist forests. **Similar species** • Norway maple.

Natural range
Eastern North America, Manitoba to Nova Scotia, south to North Carolina and west to Kansas.

Cultivated distribution
The provider of Maple syrup which is hardly ever harvested in Northern Europe. The timber 'Rock maple' is extremely hard and decorative including spiral grain and 'bird's-eye' effects. As an ornamental this tree has outstanding yellow, red and purple autumn foliage colours, but these are less dramatic in Europe.

1
HIRE SHOP

2

3

4

5

FAMILY Aceraceae

Acer rubrum L.

Red maple

Description • The natural range of this species is so vast that provenances in cultivation vary considerably in appearance. An average tree will ultimately be 18–25 m tall with a stem diameter around 80 cm. Most specimens growing in Europe seem to have a compact, narrow outline **1**. The common name is appropriate because this tree is red in part through the year from winter twigs to spring flowers and then autumn foliage colour. The bark is thin and grey, smooth for many years then randomly cracked vertically, but remaining smooth between the widely-spaced fissures **2**. The 6–10 cm, long, dark green leaves are palmate or three-lobed with shallow, rounded points and variable numbers of irregular teeth. The underside is grey-green and the long petiole is often red on the upper side **3**. The foliage turns brilliant red in the autumn **4**, but most years this feature is less reliable in Europe than it is in America. The flowers are reddish in short, pendulous, slender-stalked clusters appearing before the leaves. Confusingly this tree can be all male **5**, all female, or bisexual **6**. Seed production and fertility cannot always be relied upon in cultivation. **Habitat and Ecology** • Wet sites in mixed woodland, river flood plains or along streams on mountain sides up to 1800 m elevation in America. **Similar species** • Other Maple species and cultivars particularly *Acer saccharinum* (below).

Natural range
North America from Newfoundland to Manitoba then south to Florida and west to Texas.

Cultivated distribution
The species is infrequent but there are several popular cultivars 'Scanlon' and 'Columnare' are upright forms. 'October Glory' has outstanding, autumn foliage colour.

Acer saccharinum L.

Silver maple

Description • A large, fast-growing tree up to 25 m tall often with a stem 90 cm in diameter. It has an open, spreading crown and very light foliage **7**. The bark is grey, vertically ridged and fissured **8**. The deeply-cut, five-lobed leaves are 8–15 cm long, light to mid-green on the upper side and silvery white on the underside. The long petioles encourage them to flutter and turn over in the slightest breeze. In the autumn the upper side of each leaf turns yellow while the lower side is silvery-cream. Fallen leaves give an interesting two-colour effect on the ground. Some trees produce copious, epicormic growth on the main stem. This causes a 'bird's-eye' effect in the timber. The same seed production problems described for Red maple (above) apply. **Habitat and Ecology** • Wet sites, flood plain forests and swampy ground. **Similar species** • The silver-backed leaves are unique.

Natural range
Central North America from Ontario to New Brunswick and Minnesota, then south to Oklahoma and Northern Florida.

Cultivated distribution
Widely planted as an urban, open space tree but subsequently found to be unstable, likely to drop branches and clog up drains with its roots. There are several decorative forms including some with finely cut leaves.

1
2
3
4
5
6
7
8

FAMILY Aceraceae

Acer palmatum Thumb. ex Murray

Smooth Japanese maple

Description • The wild form of this tree is rare in Europe and may not exist at all. Most of the trees imported from Japan since 1820 have come from cultivated sources. For centuries the Japanese perfected many hundreds of different ornamental cultivars. These and more recent selections from American and European nurseries have produced a bewildering array of very different-looking individuals. To add to the confusion most of these will hybridize freely and new generations of seedlings continue to appear. This is truly a species in an active and very rapid state of evolution. Stems are always dark grey-green, gnarled but smooth **1**. The outline is variable but a low dome is common until middle age **2**. Then, as branches die back and break off, with luck a picturesque 'Japanese' looking tree develops. Typical foliage (subspecies *palmatum*) has 10 cm, roundish leaves with five to seven long, tapered lobes divided about halfway to the base **3**. They all face upwards to the light forming a continuous layer or, in old age, a series of tiered layers. The long points droop downwards especially when wet with rain. Shoots are bright green with or without a reddish side. Another common form has leaves with lobes cut down almost to the base (subspecies matsumurae) **4**. Flowers are small and in corymbs, but they are attractive because the sepals are often purple or red and the petals are pale yellow. The small winged seeds in pairs may also be red during the summer ripening to dull yellowish-brown. **Habitat and Ecology** • A woodland species. Very large specimens still exist in what appears to be a natural habitat in South East Asia. Humus-rich soils are best and semi-shade ensures that the light-sensitive foliage remains healthy. **Similar species** • There are many obscure maples in cultivation with similar looking leaves. There are also several hundred *Acer palmatum* variants, but confusingly some have leaves quite unlike the species, for example, 'Ribesifolium' whose leaves resemble those of a flowering currant (*Ribes sanguineum*).

Natural range
China, Korea and Japan.

Cultivated distribution
Of the tree forms 'Osakazuki' **5** is one of the oldest and best-known cultivars. The foliage flushes pale orange in spring, turns bright green in summer then vivid red in the autumn. Quite different in summer is 'Atropurpureum' an important pre-1910 Dutch clone that has purple foliage **6**. In the autumn it too turns fiery red. There are numerous seedlings of it in cultivation but none is as good as the original clone. Many cultivars of *Acer palmatum* are stunted shrubs.

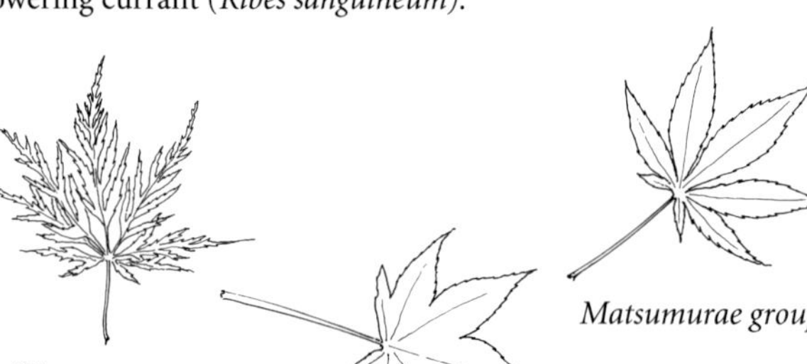

Dissectum group

Septemlobum group

Matsumurae group

Amoenum group

1
2
3
4
5
6

FAMILY Aceraceae

Acer japonicum Thunb.
Full moon maple

Description • Ultimately one of the largest ornamental Japanese maples, up to 15 m tall on a good, sheltered site. Stems are often forked from near to or at ground level, and multiple stem diameters around 70 cm are known **1**. Branches and main stems twist and turn in a picturesque fashion, supporting light foliage in a series of tiered domes. The bark is grey and although gnarled in old age remains fairly smooth. Shoots are green with a purplish-brown side facing the light. Buds are attractive, often with bright red, outer scales. The leaves are more or less round in outline, 8–12 cm across, with 9–11 short-pointed, triangular lobes **2**. The upper surface is dull green with prominent raised veins. Margins are double-toothed with soft, forward-pointing teeth. The autumn foliage colour progresses through yellows and reds, usually having all the colours and green represented at any one time. Flowers are a distinctive purplish red, unfolding just as the leaves begin to appear, in drooping corymbs. Seeds are in winged pairs in small, pendulous, reddish clusters. **Habitat and Ecology** • A mountain slope species in woods and thickets, often in semi-shade under larger broad-leaved trees. **Similar species** • Other round leaved, multiple lobed Maples including *Acer sieboldianum* Miquel, *Acer shirasawanum* Koidz. and *Acer circinatum* (p356).

Natural range
Japan, but mostly imported from cultivated sources.

Cultivated distribution
The true species (*Acer japonicum*)is seldom seen in Western gardens. The golden form 'Aureum', now called *Acer shirasawanum* 'Aureum', is popular. The cut-leaved type 'Aconitifolium' is also much sought after. It has exceptional autumn foliage colour. 'Vitifolium', named in 1876 in Britain, is highly prized but remains infrequent. Only grafted plants should be grown, as seedlings seldom come true to type and their autumn colour is generally disappointing.

Acer japonicum 'Vitifolium'
Vine-leaved Japanese maple

Description • Very like the species but larger in all its parts. Multiple, forked trees are around 15 m tall and equally wide. The leaves are larger and the autumn foliage colour is exceptional **3** lasting for about a month depending on the weather. Green leaves fade to cream then yellow, red and purple. All these colours occur on the tree at the same time and often all within a single leaf. **Habitat and Ecology** • Unknown in the wild. **Similar species** • None are as luxuriant or brightly-coloured as this cultivar.

Natural range
None.

Cultivated distribution
Rare in cultivation until recently.

1

2

3

FAMILY Aceraceae

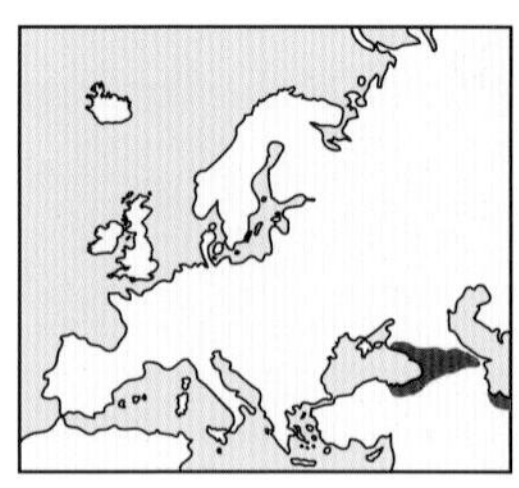

Acer cappadocicum Gledit.

Cappadocian maple

Description • Probably the best way to identify this tree is to search for suckers round the base of the stem: there are usually plenty of them, some even well beyond the limits of the canopy. This is a billowing, medium-sized tree usually less than 15 m tall **1**. The leaves are five to seven lobed with entire margins and long, pointed tips to each lobe **2**. Outstanding butter yellow, autumn foliage colour is another distinctive feature. The shoots are green with a red side in full light, glabrous and glossy, slightly bloomed at first. When cut they reveal milky latex-like sap. Stems are usually straight, up to 50 cm diameter, with grey, shallow fissures and indistinct ridges **3**. Flowers are in terminal corymbs on side shoots followed by bunches of winged seeds **2**. **Habitat and Ecology** • Mixed, moist woodland. Self-perpetuated dense thickets of suckers. **Similar species** • No tree with leaves of this sort suckers so freely.

Natural range

Cultivated distribution
Widely grown in the past on country estates and now difficult to get rid of because of excessive root spread.

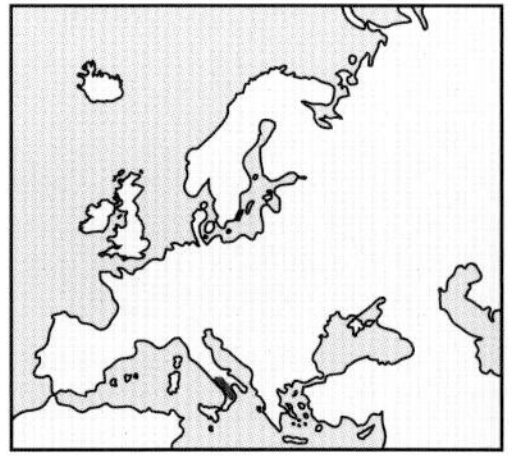

Acer lobelii Ten. (Acer cappadocicum subsp. lobelii (Ten.) Murray)

Lobel's maple

Description • A compact, narrow crowned tree around 15 m tall with upright branches **5**. The five-lobed entire leaves are 12–15 cm wide with wavy margins **4**. It is considered by some authorities to be only a subspecies of *cappadocicum*. The bark is grey with shallow ridges in old age. Shoots are distinctly bloomed at first, then glaucous and green, sometimes purplish on the exposed side. They exude milky sap if cut. Flowers occur in short, terminal corymbs on side shoots. They are bright yellowish-green and followed by pairs of flat fruits with almost horizontally spread wings. **Habitat and Ecology** • Mountain sides and rocky ground in a limited area of Calabria and the Bay of Naples. **Similar species** • Other *Acer cappadocicum* subspecies, but none are as fastigiate.

Natural range

Cultivated distribution
Not widely planted but present in many specialist tree collections.

Acer circinatum Pursh.

Vine maple

Description • A densely branched, twisted or reclining tree around 8 m tall with seven to nine lobed leaves, 6–11 cm across **6**. Shoots are green with a brown exposed side, white spots and some waxy bloom. Petioles are long with a swollen base. Flowers in small, terminal corymbs emerge with the new leaves. The petals are white over wine-red sepals. The paired, brilliant red fruits are around 3 cm across **7**. **Habitat and Ecology** • Moist stream sides and deep valley woodlands, layering freely and eventually forming dense thickets. **Similar species** • Vine-leaved Japanese maple (p352), *Acer japonicum* (p354) and other more obscure multi-lobed *Acer* species.

Natural range
North West America, from British Columbia along the Pacific coast to Northern California.

Cultivated distribution
In cultivation, but worthy of greater use. A hardy tree with summer interest followed by dramatic, orange and red, autumn foliage colours.

1
2
3
4
5
6
7

FAMILY Aceraceae

Acer velutinum var. vanvolxemii (Mast.) Rehd.

Vanvolxem's maple

Description • The species *Acer velutinum* Boiss., the Velvet maple, is a large, fast-growing, 25 m tree from the Caucasus and Iran. In cultivation in Northern Europe it is generally represented by the variety *vanvolxemii.* However seed-grown specimens may be variable, either close to the species or another variety *glabrescens* (Boiss. and Buhse) Murray, which has very glabrous leaves. This tree is basically like a vigorous Sycamore eventually with a rounded outline **1** and clean, thin-barked, grey-green stem **2**. Old grafted or budded trees (on to Sycamore rootstocks usually) only betray the 'graft line' by a slight change to smoother, *vanvolxemii* bark. The palmate leaves are huge **3**, up to 25 cm across, only exceeded by a vigorous *Acer macrophyllum* (p348). They are deep green with paler, slightly glaucous backs and pale brown, woolly hairs along the main veins. Petioles are 10–25 cm long. **Habitat and Ecology** • Originally a moist woodland species, without too much exposure to strong winds that would quickly shred the leaves. **Similar species** • Vigorous Sycamore.

Natural range
East of the species range in Georgia and the Eastern Caucasus Mountains.

Cultivated distribution
Introduced probably as the species around 1873 but described properly as the variety in 1938. Trees from that time survive in collections. New plants from seed are grown now but they may be dubious. Budding or grafting is to be preferred.

Acer heldreichii Orph. ex Boiss.

Balkan maple

Description • A medium-sized, 8–12 m tall tree vaguely similar to Sycamore (p362). A rounded, domed top usually forms in open situations **4**. The 8–12 cm leaves differ from Sycamore by being smaller and more deeply divided **5**. Petioles are as long as the leaf, yellow with a pink side where they face the sun. Young shoots are green, soon turning grey-brown. Larger branches and for many years the stem, have smooth, thin, grey-green bark **6**. Flowers are on male or female, upright, yellow racemes. Females develop into paired, 5 cm, obtusely winged seeds in bunches which droop under their own weight as they expand. **Habitat and Ecology** • Cool, sheltered valleys high up in the mountains of Greece and the Balkans. **Similar species** • Very close to *Acer heldreichii* subsp. *trautvetteri* (Medv.) Murray (formerly listed as a species).

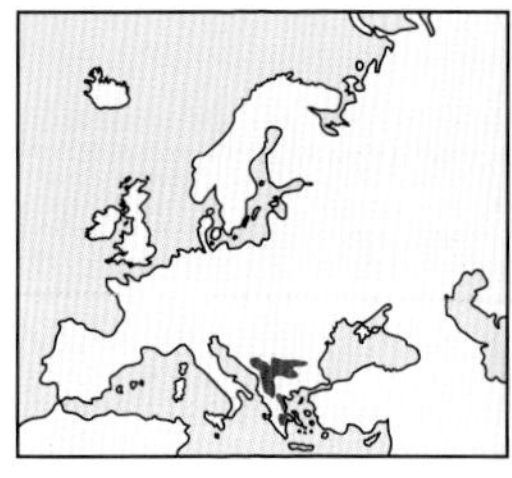

Natural range

Cultivated distribution
Seldom seen in cultivation because of its limited merit as an ornamental. Autumn foliage colour is dull yellow. Trees are less tolerant in towns or exposed places than Sycamore.

FAMILY Aceraceae

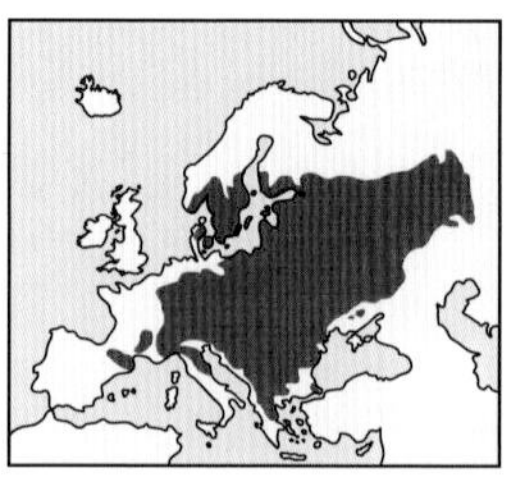

Acer platanoides L.

Norway maple

Description • This Maple, with leaves most like the stylized Canadian flag, has become one of the most widely-planted amenity trees in Northern Europe. It appears in urban open spaces, shopping centres and parks everywhere. Ultimately it reaches 25 m in height with a stem over 1 m in diameter. It will certainly outgrow the space allotted to it in many urban planting schemes. The outline is rounded like a huge, green cloud **1**. The bark is very pale brownish-grey, smooth at first, but becoming finely ridged and fissured in quite an intricate pattern of vertical and diagonal shapes **2**. Shoots are green for one year and then brown, often with a reddish tinge on the upper side. Buds are prominent in opposite pairs and terminal clusters. They are roundish, 5–10 mm long with green scales tinted with crimson. The 15–20 cm leaves are subcordate and five-lobed but the three main lobes are larger than the others **3**. Margins are more or less straight between a small number of slender points. Petioles are as long as the leaf they support, round, pale green with a red, sunny side and swollen at the base. If cut they exude milky sap. The foliage turns yellow in the autumn. Flowers appear before the leaves **4**, briefly turning the whole tree yellow in early spring. Fruits are paired winged, flat seeds in pendulous clusters, with the wings spread out at a wide angle. **Habitat and Ecology** • A woodland species able to withstand severe climatic conditions. Also grows perfectly well in full light. **Similar species** • There are several other maples of this sort with entire leaf margins but none is as frequently seen in cultivation as this familiar species and its many ornamental forms.

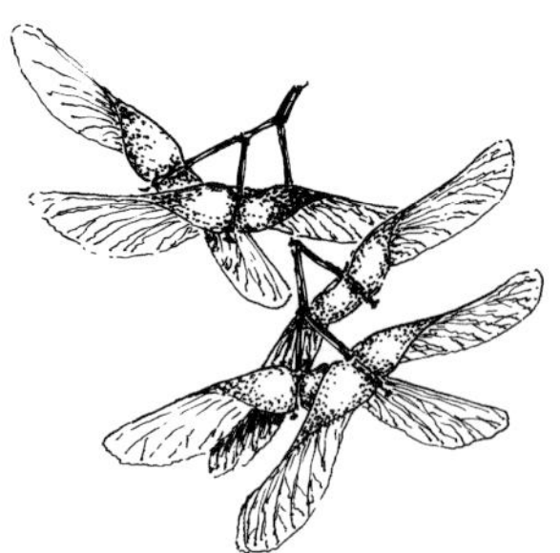

Natural range

Cultivated distribution
The species has been in cultivation for a very long time and has provided nurserymen with many cultivated forms, for example, Eagle's claw maple 'Laciniatum' back in 1683, and the popular yellow variegated cultivar 'Drummondii' produced in 1903 **5**. There are several coppery or red types – 'Schwedleri' is a big, crimson-purple-leaved, 1864 tree but its place has mostly been taken now by the more fashionable 'Crimson King' **6** produced in 1946.

FAMILY Aceraceae

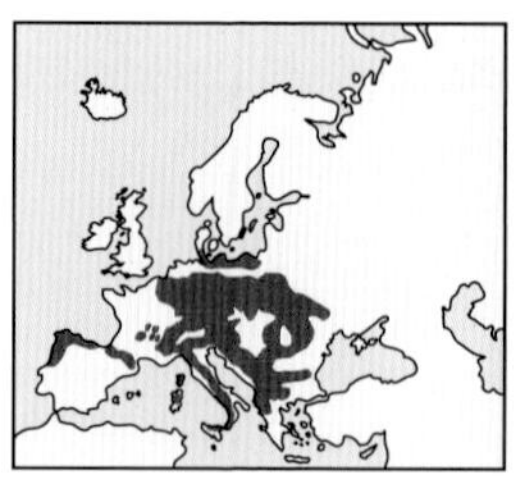

Acer pseudoplatanus L.
Sycamore

Description • Europe's largest maple, this tree grows to more than 40 m tall with massive stems up to 2 m in diameter **1**. The branches are heavy and spreading, and trees often develop a hard, rounded outline because the stout twigs in winter and the foliage in summer look as if they have been clipped **2**. In exposed places, where this tree originated and thrives, any rogue shoot that extended beyond the line of the canopy was soon cut back by the wind. Stems are straight, in sheltered places, with flaking, pale orange and grey-green bark **1**. The long-stalked leaves are palmate and up to 18 cm across. They are five-lobed with rounded teeth and a cordate base (see p365 **3**). In late summer they are often infested with flying aphids, that rain down if any branch is touched, and also the familiar, 'tar-spot', black dots on the leaves caused by the harmless fungus *Rhytisma acerinum.* This infection provides quite a useful diagnostic feature for identifying Sycamore. Flowers are numerous and hang down in compact racemes providing a feast for bees and nectar-feeding insects. Female flowers occupy the base of the inflorescence, males the centre and sterile florets the end **3**. Seeds in pairs rapidly develop in bunches, even before the male and sterile components have dropped off **4**. They become flushed with red then ripen to light brown. The dry membranous wings are aerodynamic. They cause the liberated seeds to spin, but the seed itself is so heavy they do not travel very far. Forests of seedlings appear right up to the base of the parent tree. **Habitat and Ecology** • Adapted to harsh climatic conditions and poor quality soils. Equally able to thrive on exposed moorland, near the sea or in polluted city centres. A good soil moisture regime is essential even if it happens to be under tarmac. This is an opportunistic pioneer where there is sufficient light, for example, in woodland clearings and forest road lines where it will become naturalized over a wide area. **Similar species** • There are numerous cultivated forms (p364) and closely related named species from the fringes of the Natural range (e.g. *Acer heldreichii* and *Acer velutinum* (p358)).

Natural range

Cultivated distribution
Moved beyond the boundaries of its native range into Northern Europe at an early date. In Britain, possibly the earliest evidence for it is a stone carving in Oxford dated 1282. The Welsh name *Masarnwydd mwyaf* (Great maple), in use when the tree was infrequent in England, suggests introduction to the British Isles by Celtic people. This is a superb timber tree but its future is seriously threatened now by the introduced American grey squirrel that often girdles the stem and kills the top of the tree.

FAMILY Aceraceae

Acer pseudoplatanus L. cvs.
Ornamental Sycamore cultivars

Description • Cultivars are divided by specialists into six groups. Firstly, green leaved trees of various shapes (e.g. 'Erectum', an upright Dutch cultivar); then trees with five-lobed leaves that are variegated or red at first; leaves with five lobes that are purple on the underside; three-lobed leaves; more or less triangular leaves; and finally various aberrant forms such as 'Crispum' a German form with asymmetric screwed-up leaves. In complete contrast to this a fine cultivar, particularly for town parks and urban open spaces, is 'Corstorphinense', the Golden sycamore discovered in Edinburgh in the seventeenth century. It is a fast-growing tree **1** that has clear, yellow leaves in the spring **2**. These turn green in summer. 'Purpureum', or forma *purpureum* Loud., has dark green leaves with purple on the underside **3**. Old, specially selected trees have the most dramatic colour; they are usually grafted. The purple characteristic is quite common and seedlings with various shades of this colour appear frequently. In a strong wind this tree excels in summer when the leaves show their backs. The original selection was introduced in 1883 as 'Atropurpureum', also called 'Spaethii' after the Nurserymen in Berlin who selected it. A similar Belgium cultivar 'Purpurascens' also has purple seed wings. 'Variegatum' is another medium to large tree that is found in many forms. Basically they all have five-lobed leaves that are splashed and speckled with yellow **4**. 'Variegatum' itself is now usually listed as forma *variegatum* (Weston) Rehd. and includes a range of plants occurring in the wild or in cultivation from wild collected seed. A superior variegated type is 'Leopoldii', an 1864 tree produced in Belgium and named in honour of King Leopold I. Its young leaves are pink. The German cultivar 'Tricolor' is another fast-growing form with interesting pink, white and green variegation. **Habitat and Ecology** • All of these trees are ecologically the same as Sycamore but they have been taken into cultivation because of their curious attributes. **Similar species** • A variable group but all have affinities with the species. There have been over 60 named forms of Sycamore in cultivation. Many have failed to retain their cultivar names and been reduced to group status.

Natural range
None, but may occur anywhere within the species range (p362).

Cultivated distribution
In the mid- to late nineteenth century there was a mania for new forms, especially in Germany and Holland. Some are stunted individuals such as 'Prinz Handjery' which combines purple backed leaves with variegation and pink flushing but is prone to aphid attack and sunburn. 'Brilliantissimum', bred from it in 1905, is a better garden plant, brightly coloured in spring and remaining small.

1
2
3
4

FAMILY Oleaceae

Fraxinus excelsior f. diversifolia (Ait.) Lingelsh

One-leaved ash

Description • A rare but perfectly natural form of Common ash (p408) which is easily overlooked in winter and even in summer but for close inspection. In every respect, except for the leaves, it is like Common ash. Potentially a large tree around 20 m tall with a stem approaching 1 m in diameter **1**. The bark is silver grey becoming finely latticed with diagonal ridges at maturity **2**. Wild trees have flawless stems but cultivated specimens often show bulging signs of grafting, sometimes at the base or 2–3 m up the stem if they are top-worked like Weeping ash (p410). The tree illustrated **1** was probably a top-worked example of a weeping form. In old age it has started to break up and is certainly no longer weeping. However a weeping form, 'Diversifolia Pendula', is said to still be in cultivation. The stout twigs are ash-grey with prominent black velvety opposite buds. The foliage separates this form from the species although the leaves are infinitely variable. On the tree leaves are sparse and allow light through to the ground below **3**. Individual leaves may be single or tri-foliate, sometimes with an additional rudimentary pair of leaflets so technically they are pinnate. Some ovate pointed leaflets are entire others have several irregular points. A variety of different leaf shapes can appear on the tree at the same time **4**. Some individuals however have mostly single leaves **5**, these have been selected and propagated by the nursery trade since 1804 as 'Monophylla'. **Habitat and Ecology** • A spontaneous but very rare occurrence in natural ash woodlands. Usually less able to compete with normal ash trees and confined to open boundaries where there is sufficient light. **Similar species** • Foliage is unique but the tree is exactly like Common ash.

Natural range
In ash woodlands from the British Isles to the Caucasus and Western Russia.

Cultivated distribution
Only cultivated and grown as a curiosity with no merit as an ornamental specimen or as an urban open space tree. It has arisen independently many times but appears to have been first noticed in cultivation in 1789. 'Monophylla' was grown in Paris by Rene Desfontaines in 1804. 'Heterophylla' appeared in Copenhagen the same year. Some surviving trees are probably these actual clones, others are more recent selections.

1

2

3

4

5

FAMILY Hippocastanaceae

Aesculus hippocastanum L.

Common horse chestnut

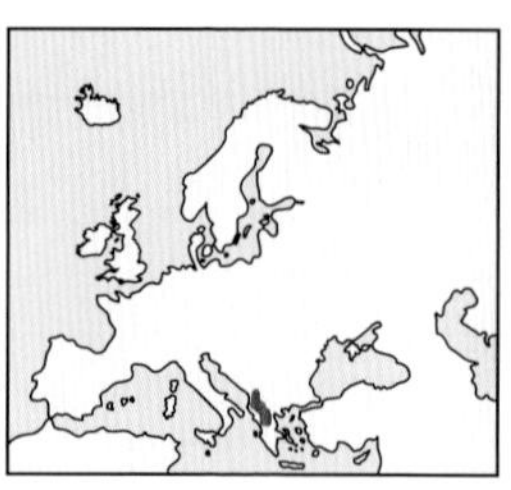

Natural range

Cultivated distribution
This tree is believed to have reached Northern Europe through Vienna in 1576. In the nineteenth century it was extensively planted on country estates for shade and as avenues. In many areas it is naturalized. It grows easily from seed and quickly becomes established but it is short-lived and rapidly declines after 100 years. There are named, weeping, upright, cut-leaved and double-flowered cultivars.

Description • The most obvious diagnostic characteristic of any Horse chestnut in summer is the distinctive leaf shape. This species is a large, fast-growing tree reaching 30 m in height. The trunk can expand to around 1.5 m diameter in 150 years: anything larger is likely to have suffered stem and top damage which will in some way have lightened the heavily branched crown. Green Horse chestnut wood is extremely heavy and brittle. The outline of the mature tree is squarish with irregular, spiky, upper branches **1**. Young trees are conical at first then rounded, apparently ideal urban trees, but almost always they get too big for the situation they are in. Only the cultivar 'Pyramidalis' produced in 1895 retains its narrow form. The bark is pinkish-brown to grey with rough, peeling scales. Eventually pronounced buttresses extend up the stem until it is distinctly fluted **2**. Shoots are light brown with characteristic 'horse-shoe' leaf scars **3** and prominent, opposite pointed, 2–3cm, glossy brown 'sticky buds'. The leaves are digitate, having a more or less round outline divided into five to seven obovate leaflets all joined in one place to the top of the petiole. Each leaflet has a short point, double-toothed margin and long, tapered base. The petiole is equal in length to the leaf. The flowers make an unmistakable statement in spring. They are in numerous 20–30 cm, upright, terminal panicles, often covering the whole tree just after the new leaves have emerged **4**. Each individual flower has five white petals arranged in a loose cup shape with a blotch of carmine-pink and yellow inside. The stamens and stigma extend beyond the petals giving a whiskery look to the whole tightly packed inflorescence. Small spiky green fruits develop almost immediately as the flowers finish but most of them soon fall off. Fully developed fruits, in small clusters, are greenish-brown, 5 cm husks each containing one or two seeds **5**. These are bright, glossy, 'chestnut' brown with a pinkish-grey, non-shiny point of attachment (hilum). **Habitat and Ecology** • In nature, a mixed deciduous woodland tree in mountain valleys in South East Europe. Widely grown as a parkland species, avenue and urban, open space tree. **Similar species** • Other *Aesculus* species especially Japanese horse chestnut, *Aesculus turbinata* Blume, which appears to be identical except for the much enlarged hilum on the seeds (conkers).

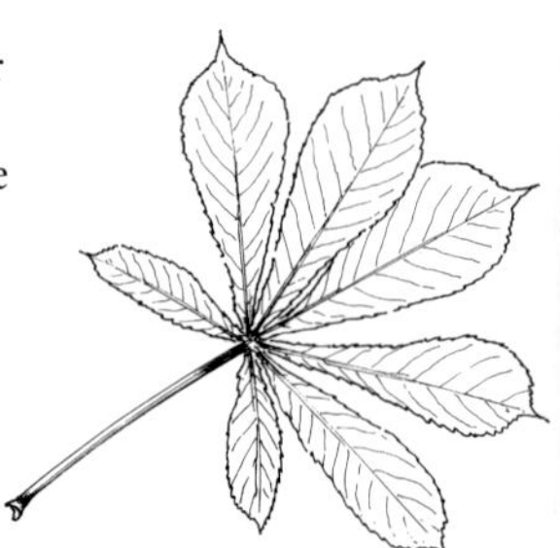

1
2
3
4
5

FAMILY
Hippocastanaceae

Aesculus x carnea Hayne

Pink horse chestnut

Description • A deciduous, heavily-branched, untidy tree ultimately 15–20 m tall with a stem diameter generally less than 80 cm. Young trees make shapely, urban, open-space specimens **1**, but they do not age very well. A frequent and unsightly problem is a genetic disorder known as bud proliferation. This causes canker-like swellings on branches which in extreme cases kills the wood above the damaged area. In winter these abnormalities are a good indication of the identity of the tree. It is a hybrid between Common horse chestnut and *Aesculus pavia* L., the Red buckeye, a medium-sized, crimson-flowered tree from the Southern United States, introduced to Europe in 1711 but rarely grown here. The hybrid was cultivated around 1820. Much of the development work was done in France and a French cultivar 'Briotii' (formerly Madame Briot) probably represents the best of *Aesculus x carnea.* It has the brightest, deep pink flowers and is often justifiably called Red horse chestnut **2**. Authentic plants are all grafted but unfortunately graft incompatibility is another common problem with this tree. Pink horse chestnut is a variable hybrid: some individuals are more or less sterile while others set fertile seed and produce new variants. The foliage is fairly uninspiring: leaves have twisted lobes and are prone to deformities. There is no autumn colour. The short-lived flowers are various shades of pink with yellow markings. The flower and leaf illustrated **3** are from a seedling when it was only five years old, a definite advantage where quick colour is needed in a planting scheme. The fruits have few or no prickles. **Habitat and Ecology** • An entirely artificial plant but naturalized in some places. **Similar species** • None, although individual clones are difficult to sort out. Many seedlings have been distributed as 'Pink' or 'Red' horse chestnut. Most of them are poor quality imitations of the original named cultivars. The flowers are often washed out pink, unlike the plant **3** produced in 1990 at Bristol, which was a lucky accident.

Natural range
An artificial hybrid produced several times in the nineteenth century.

Cultivated distribution
In its long history of cultivation several distinct forms have been produced. A weeping tree 'Pendula' was once fashionable but it is seldom seen now. Its high-level graft becomes unsafe with age. An early backcross with Common horse chestnut named 'Plantierensis', with pale blush-pink flowers, was produced vegetatively in the nursery trade for a time, but so many crosses of the same sort occur spontaneously that it was hardly worth while.

3

FAMILY
Hippocastanaceae

Aesculus indica (Colebr. ex Cambess.) Hook.

Indian horse chestnut

Description • A superior ornamental horse chestnut, this tree is seldom over 18 m tall with a full, rounded top and a clean, straight stem. It is one of the best, hardy, deciduous trees in cultivation. The foliage is healthy and bright green and the flowers appear in midsummer when few other trees are flowering **1**. This is later than any other *Aesculus* species. The stem is smooth for many years, then becomes scaly, eventually developing shallow fissures working up from the base **2**. The leaves are usually seven-lobed although five to nine lobes are possible **3**. They flush pink in spring, turn green in summer then shrivel up in the autumn without a further display of colour. Leaflets are obovate to lanceolate and the longest may exceed 25 cm in length. Margins are finely toothed towards an abrupt, pointed tip. The petiole is 12–18 cm long, often inclined downwards under the weight of the luxuriant leaflets. Flowers are in terminal panicles, 20–30 cm long, held vertically or almost so **4**. Each individual cup-shaped flower has four white petals with a pink and yellow spot inside. The stamens project beyond the petals **5**. In this species flowers are less tightly packed on the inflorescence giving an open, Orchid-like appearance. The fruits develop through the summer but do not ripen until after the leaves have fallen. The husks are green then brown without spines. The seeds are very dark, glossy brown, characteristically with a very small hilum **6**. **Habitat and Ecology** • A mountain side and valley species in mixed woodland or in isolated clumps. **Similar species** • Some obscure, exotic Horse chestnut and Buckeye species.

Natural range
Northern India, Afghanistan and parts of Nepal in the foothills of the Himalayas.

Cultivated distribution
Introduced to Northern Europe in 1851. An immediate success with estate owners looking for a really exotic tree, and nurserymen because it is so easy to grow from seed. In town planting it had the advantage of fruiting so late that small boys did not bother with the conkers.
A magnificent, free-flowering form 'Sydney Pearce' **7** was raised at Kew in London in 1928. It remains a firm favourite, urban, open-space tree, possibly as frequently seen in cultivation as the species.

1
2
3
4
5
6
7

FAMILY Leguminosae

Laburnum alpinum (Mill.) Bercht. and Presl

Alpine laburnum

Description • In the wild state a rounded, often wind-pruned, small tree **1**, in cultivation more like common laburnum. The fragrant, yellow flowers appear in early summer, in shorter but more dense, 10–15 cm, pendulous racemens. Each pea-like bloom is 2 cm long on a virtually hairless stalk **2**. The distinctive, 6 cm, flanged seed-pods are flat but waisted between each seed. They turn from green in summer to pale brown. The trifoliate leaves are indistinguishable from other laburnums. Bark remains smooth for many years ageing from golden brown to purplish-grey. **Habitat and Ecology** • A mountain species on moist rocky ground. In cultivation it is an ideal choice for damp places. The seeds in particular are poisonous to humans. **Similar species** • Other laburnums.

Natural range
Mainly in alpine situations across Europe from the French Alps to the Czech Republic.

Cultivated distribution
Occasionally found in parks and gardens but more likely to be replaced by *Laburnum x watereri* in modern planting schemes.

Laburnum anagyroides Medikus

Common laburnum

Description • A familiar garden tree best known for its golden yellow chains of spring flowers **3**. Specimens reach 12 m in favourable circumstances and ancient stems, usually in a rotten or hollow state, become very large **4** up to 1.4 m diameter. The arching branches develop into an untidy, ascending crown with drooping extremities. Shoots and buds are grey and hairy, a useful identification feature in winter. Thin trifoliate leaves **5** are entire with glaucous undersides. Individual pointed leaflets are 3–8 cm long on a 5–6 cm petiole. The brown seed-pods lack the flange of *Laburnum alpinum*, seeds are glossy black **6** and poisonous. **Habitat and Ecology** • A tree of open woodlands but now represented mostly by naturalized escapes from cultivation. **Similar species** • Other laburnums.

Natural range
Southern and Central Europe

Cultivated distribution
An extremely common garden tree and naturalized escape throughout Northern Europe.

Laburnum x watereri (Kirchner) Dipp.

Hybrid laburnum

Description • A hybrid between alpine and common laburnum made in Holland in the late nineteenth century usually represented by 'Vossii' **7**, a good cultivar with long racemes of bright yellow flowers in spring. 'Alford's Weeping' is a pendulous cultivar selected in England in 1965. **Habitat and Ecology** • Seldom recorded in the wild state. **Similar species** • Other *laburnums.*

Laburnocytissus adamii Schneid. Adam`s laburnum is a curious graft hybrid between *Laburnum anagyroides* and the broom *Cytissus purpureus* Scop. A small tree bearing both golden and purple spring flowers in separate clusters. Created in Paris in 1825 but remains rare.

Natural range
None, although the cross may be possible naturally where the ranges (above) overlap.

Cultivated distribution
Hybrid laburnums are extremely common in parks and gardens throughout Europe but because of their poisonous seeds they are less popular today **8**.

1
2
3
4
5
6
7
8

FAMILY Aceraceae

Acer griseum (Franch.) Pax

Paper-bark maple

Description • The peeling, cinnamon-brown paper bark is characteristic **1**. This is usually a small tree, seldom over 10 m tall with a neat, rounded outline. The peeling bark feature continues along the main branches well into the crown and provides a valuable amenity feature, particularly in winter. Stems do not usually exceed 60 cm in diameter. Shoots are greenish-grey for one year, then dark brown. They begin to peel on healthy trees after five or six years. The foliage is always short and dense **2**. The trifoliate leaves are characteristic **3**. Very few Maples have leaves of this sort split into three distinct sections. The pubescent petiole is red-brown on the sunlit side and green on the underside, with a central lobe about 10 cm long. In the autumn the foliage colours are yellow then red. The greyish underside of the leaf provides a more subdued range of contrasting colours, particularly noticeable when the leaves fall onto the ground. The yellow flowers on the tips of side shoots are in clusters of only three and appear after most of the leaves have emerged. Paired fruits in clusters of three are plump, green and pubescent, wings held at an acute angle **4**. They ripen to pale brown in one season but for some reason many trees in Northern Europe fail to set fertile seed. This group of Maples is andro-dioecious, having either bisexual or all male flowers on separate trees. Seeds only appear on bisexual plants. **Habitat and Ecology** • In mixed deciduous woodland comparable to Field maple (p316) in Northern Europe. **Similar species** • The bark resembles River birch *Betula nigra* (p166) but the colour is different and the form of the tree is completely different. The leaves are like Nikko maple *Acer maximowicziana* Miquel, and *Acer triflorum* Komarov.

Natural range
Central China.

Cultivated distribution
Frequent in parks and gardens as a bark feature and because of its relatively small ultimate size. It will grow on lime-rich soils but is less luxuriant than when planted on a rich, moist, neutral site with some side shade. Introduced to the west in 1901, some original specimens are still in existence.

1

2

3

4

FAMILY Rosaceae

Sorbus domestica L.

Service tree

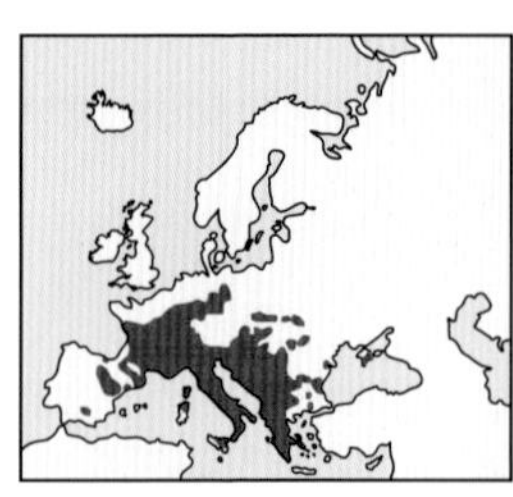

Natural range

Cultivated distribution
Formerly cultivated for food especially in France where several superior types were developed. Said to have been eaten, or pressed and fermented into a drink, mostly by poorer people in rural areas. It was gathered when ripe and stored for some time in order to make it sweet like the Medlar (p90).

Description • A puzzle of a tree, clearly not far removed from a pear in general appearance. The leaves are superficially like Mountain ash (p382) although this species is not that closely related to Mountain ash. The bark is also distinctive, similar to *Sorbus torminalis* (p324). Usually this is a medium-sized tree, around 15 m tall and like a fruit tree in general appearance **1**. The bark is yellowish at first, purplish-brown after two to three years then becoming progressively pinkish-grey with tightly packed, vertical ridges and furrows on the stem **2**. Shoots are silky pubescent at first with waxy, green buds. The 20–25 cm leaves are pinnate with seven to ten pairs of sessile 3–8 cm leaflets. These are sometimes unequal at the base and sharply toothed, but only in the upper half. Dull green above and paler below with some silky hairs **3**. Flowers in spring are in short domed or pyramidal, pubescent corymbs up to 15 cm across. Individual flowers are around 16 mm in diameter with five white petals. Fruits are of two distinct kinds, formerly listed as 'maliformis' forma *pomifera* (Hayne) Rehd. apple-shaped and 'pyriformis' forma *pyriformis* (Hayne) Rehd. pear-shaped. They contain stone cells which are a feature of edible pears. The fruit varies in size and quality suggesting past selection and cultivation. The largest, around 4 cm long, can be found mostly in Southern Europe. They are green with a dark red flush on the sunlit side. Until they are almost rotten (bletted) they are inedible. **Habitat and Ecology** • The natural environment of this species has been blurred by past cultivation and subsequent neglect. It is virtually impossible to distinguish between escapes and wild plants. **Similar species** • Mountain ash and other pinnate *Sorbus* species and cultivars.

forma pyriformis

forma pomifera

1

2

3

FAMILY Rosaceae

Sorbus x hybrida L.
Swedish service tree

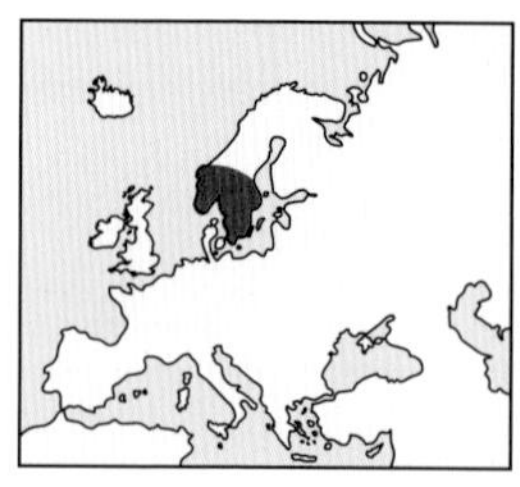

Natural range

Cultivated distribution
Occasionally grown in parks, gardens and urban open spaces as the 1924 cultivar 'Gibbsii' where climatic conditions are severe. Naturalized in some places but does not always come true from seed.

Description • A deciduous tree up to 12 m tall with a stem diameter around 40 cm. The outline is compact and rounded. The bark is greyish-brown, smooth at first becoming shallowly fissured. Shoots are light green and pubescent when emerging then dark brown in the second and subsequent years. The 8–12 cm leaves are typical of this hybrid group, probably a cross between Mountain ash (p382) and *Sorbus rupicola* (p190), broadly ovoid with eight to ten pairs of lateral veins and two or three pairs of free leaflets at the base **1**. Margins are toothed and lobed. This is a fully fertile hybrid producing terminal corymbs of creamy white, 2 cm flowers **2** followed by globose, 15 mm, scarlet berries, but subsequently in cultivation some variable progeny. **Habitat and Ecology** • A very hardy tree or shrub growing on mountain sides, some close to the Arctic circle. **Similar species** • Hybrid *Sorbus* (below).

Sorbus x thuringiaca (Ilse) Fritsch
Thuringian service tree

Natural range
Central Europe (*x thuringiaca*).

Cultivated distribution
Widely grown in parks and gardens usually as 'Decurrens' which has additional free leaflets and 'Fastigiata' a slender, upright form ideal for town planting.

Description • A small to medium-sized tree up to 15 m tall with a rounded, fairly compact outline **3**. It is a hybrid between Whitebeam (p190) and Mountain ash (p382) with foliage intermediate between the two. The leaves are oblong with a broad point made up of shallow lobes decreasing in size towards the tip. The basal two or three pairs of lobes are completely separated **4**. Flowers in early summer are in large 10–15 cm corymbs on the tips of side shoots. Individual flowers are creamy-white, around 15 mm across with five petals and numerous stamens. The fruit resembles that of Mountain ash but it ripens brownish-red. **Habitat and Ecology** • Spontaneous trees sometimes occur where the parents grow together. **Similar species** • Other Mountain ash hybrids. There is a similar looking hybrid in Central Ireland between Mountain ash and *Sorbus hibernica* (p190). Also *Sorbus pseudofennica* E. Warb., the Arran service tree, a 7 m rounded tree with white felted foliage **5** and partially pinnate leaves **6**. It is endemic only to Glen Catacol in Arran on granite.

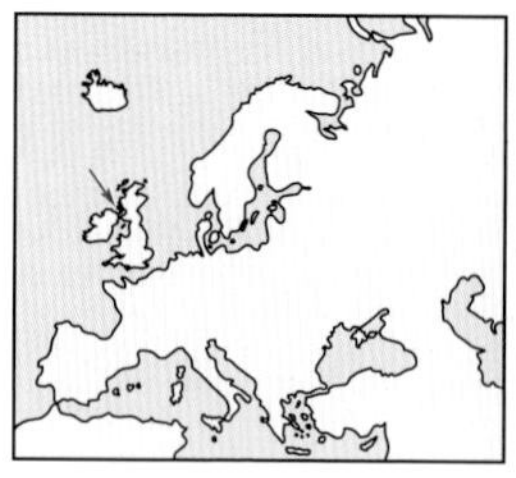

Natural range
S. pseudofennica

1
2 
3 
4 
5 
6

FAMILY Rosaceae

Sorbus aucuparia L.

Mountain ash

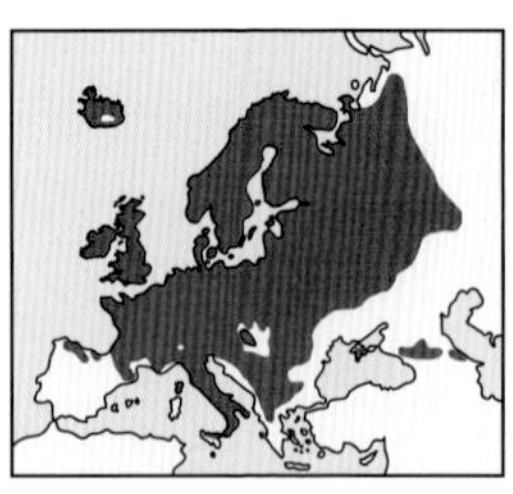

Description • A tough upland or sub-tundra tree that can also be found on neutral or acid soils in mild lowland situations. In an exposed situation it may struggle to reach 5 m in height **1**, but as a component of woodland or in the lowland agricultural landscape it may reach 10 m **2**. It is also a well-known ornamental garden and park species. On a favourable site stems are straight at first, with smooth, silvery-buff bark that gradually fissures very slightly and may peel a little **3**. Ultimately 60–80 cm diameter could be attained but this may consist of several stems that have fused together **4**. Shoots are green for the first season with pale, silky indumentum, then purplish-brown and glabrous. Buds are dark brown with distinctive, forward-pointing, fine, white hairs on the fringes of the scales. Leaves are 15–20 cm long, pinnate with five to nine pairs of 3–6 cm leaflets. Each of these is sessile except for a short stalk between the end pair and the terminal leaflet. Margins have distinct teeth almost to the base which is often oblique. Tapered on the lower side and rounded on the other. The upper surface is matt green and the underside is pale green with prominent veins and some pale pubescence. The top of the grooved rachis may be dark red when exposed to full light. Flowers are small, creamy white, numerous in flat topped dense corymbs up to 14 cm across **5** appearing with the leaves in late spring. These are followed by familiar clusters of 1 cm, orange-scarlet berries in the autumn **6** often covering the whole tree and persisting until the deciduous foliage changes to yellow and brown. **Habitat and Ecology** • Originally an upland tree often growing to the tree line on mountains but also thriving lower down on acid heaths and in open woodland. **Similar species** • There are many cultivated forms and exotic *Sorbus* species with pinnate leaves: these are seldom encountered in the wild but are common in gardens and parks. 'Aspleniifolia' has lacy, deeply toothed foliage. 'Edulis' is similar to the species but larger, stronger and very hardy. It produces substantial bunches of large berries that are said to be edible. There is also an upright form 'Fastigiata' but it tends to be lax and weak, however backcrosses with the species are better.

Natural range
Extends from Europe to Turkey, the Caucasus and the coastal fringe of North Africa.

Cultivated distribution
Not cultivated as a species, but survives very well often where few other woody plants will exist. There are cultivated forms and selections, several of which have particularly upright branches. Some have leaf margins with exaggerated teeth and others have been selected for their bright red or prolific berries.

1
2
3
4
5
6

FAMILY Leguminosae

Robinia pseudoacacia L.

Black locust or False Acacia

Description • A fast-growing, gaunt, untidy deciduous tree standing 15–20 m tall **1** with frequent suckers. Stems often over 60 cm diameter **2** with rough, deeply furrowed bark: burrs are common **3**. Shoots are red-brown, glabrous with pairs of viciously sharp spines (modified stipules) on either side of the bud. Spines are exaggerated on young sucker growth. The buds are completely obscured by the base of the petiole in summer. Leaflets are four to nine in pairs, oval, 3–4 cm long, untoothed and thin, each with a small bristle tip. Deep pea-pod green and glabrous, after emerging with silky hairs. The light foliage flushes late and falls early. White, drooping racemes of 1–2 cm pea flowers **4** occur in early summer on shoot tips followed by 5–10 cm brown seed pods containing nought to ten flat seeds. **Habitat and Ecology** • In America, this tree prefers dry, stony ground between 150–1500 m elevation, often in open woodland created by the tree's own suckers. In Europe, it grows well on poor ground including landfill, reclaimed sites and rubbish tips. The durable timber is of exceptional quality **5**. **Similar species** • Several green cultivated forms occur. Also *Gleditsia* (p386) and *Sophora* (below). *Robinia pseudoacacia* 'Frisia' **6** is a superb, golden leaved, ornamental form raised in Holland in 1935 and widely grown in parks and gardens. The golden-yellow foliage keeps its colour throughout the summer months.

Natural range
Southern Canada, Pennsylvania, Ohio, to Alabama also from Missouri to Oklahoma. Naturalized across the United States from Maine to California.

Cultivated distribution
Introduced to Europe soon after 1607 as an ornamental landscape and amenity tree, and also for its durable timber. Widely planted in urban situations but liable to shed brittle branches in strong wind.

Sophora japonica L.

Pagoda tree

Description • Usually a medium-sized tree **7**, but occasionally exceeding 20 m in height. Stems are generally straight with vertically ridged, brownish-grey bark **8**. Young shoots are downy, soon becoming distinctly deep bottle green and glabrous. The bud is obscured by the petiole base. Leaves 15–20 cm long consist of 9–15 ovate to oblong pointed, 3–4 cm leaflets **9**. These often fold in half along the midrib in hot weather. The tip of each has a short, glandular projection. Some leaves are more or less opposite. Very large, showy panicles of creamy-white pea flowers occur in late summer **7**. The flat, green seed-pods, 5–8 cm long, contain up to five seeds. **Habitat and Ecology** • Inhabits mixed woodland in China. **Similar species** • The distinct green shoot colour makes this tree unique even in winter.

Natural range
Probably only northern provinces of China, but obscured by cultivation from ancient times.

Cultivated distribution
In China this tree was traditionally planted on the graves of scholars and priests. It is sometimes called the Scholars' tree. It was also grown throughout Japan from an early date and introduced to Europe from there in 1753.

1
2
3
4
5
6
7
8
9

FAMILY Leguminosae

Gleditsia triacanthos L.

Honey locust

Description • The foliage is light **1** so it does not obscure street lights or block gutters or drains in an urban situation, and it has viciously sharp thorns that may discourage casual vandalism **2**. It is a fairly large tree, around 20 m tall at maturity, with a stem 50–70 cm in diameter. The crown is uneven or becomes tiered and flat topped on some old specimens. The bark is soon vertically fissured and rough with rigid branched thorns here and there **2**. The shoot is green becoming brown in the second year and increasingly grey with age. Leaves, up to 20 cm long, are pinnate or sometimes bi-pinnate, with 6–16 pairs of oval to ovate-lanceolate, 3–4 cm long leaflets, and bi-pinnate leaves have considerably more. Leaflets have small, forward-pointing, soft teeth along the margins. They are thin, almost translucent, and pale to mid-green **1**. Young growth is yellowish and the autumn colour is gold. Short clusters of yellowish-green separate male or female flowers appear in early summer. Some trees are all single sex. Female or monecious specimens produce flat, green seed-pods from the centre of each flower that expand dramatically to 30–40 cm in length, often twisting as they ripen to dark brown. The seeds are also flat and dark brown. The pulp around them is said to be edible. **Habitat and Ecology** • Moist woodland. **Similar species** • In winter, *Robinia* (p384). The foliage and bark are superficially like Kentucky coffee-tree (p392), also *Gleditsia aquatica* Marsh. a wetland segregate species.

Natural range
Eastern and Central North America from New England to South Dakota including Southern Ontario then extending to the borders of Texas and Florida.

Cultivated distribution
Few trees are as useful as this in tough, urban conditions. It is tolerant of air pollution, smoke and dust. Frequently planted as an urban, open space tree until more ornamental cultivars became popular. The original introduction to Europe was around 1700. In America it is used for hedging.

Gleditsia triancanthos L. 'Sunburst'

Description • A yellow leaved cultivar of forma *intermis*, the thornless Honey locust. It makes an attractive small to medium-sized tree, well-suited to urban conditions **3**. Stems are usually straight with fissured, grey-brown bark. The leaves are like the species but in full light remain yellow all summer **4**. **Habitat and Ecology** • The thornless form occurs in the wild with the species but the yellow leaved cultivar is a horticultural selection. **Similar species** • Other cultivated forms and superficially *Robinia pseudoacacia* 'Frisia' (p384).

Natural range
None.

Cultivated distribution
First cultivated in 1953 and extensively grown as a city tree.

FAMILY Juglandaceae

Pterocarya fraxinifolia (Lam.) Spach

Caucasian wingnut

Description • A very distinctive tree which at first glance resembles a whole forest. It is an extremely large suckering plant often covering in excess of 400m^2. Heights of 35 m are also on record and a stem 2 m in diameter is known. More often though up to 50 smaller, 40–60 cm diameter stems come into being with further new shoots appearing beyond the existing canopy. Young trees are columnar with ascending branches and a rounded, compact canopy **1**. The tree illustrated is 27 years old. The invasive root suckers are encouraged to proliferate whenever they are damaged by vehicles or machinery or, sadistically, when any attempt is made to cut them back. The bark is grey-brown soon becoming deeply fissured and scaly **2**. Young shoots are green and scurfy at first then light brown by the end of the first year, by which time they may have extended up to 1.5 m. The pith is chambered like Walnut (p394 and 395 **4**). Buds are leafy without protective scales. The leaves are pinnate, up to 45 cm long on established trees but over 60 cm long on new, fast-growing suckers. There are 11–25 leaflets arranged in pairs and increasing in size from 8 cm at the base to 12 cm towards the tip. They are thin and glabrous except for scattered stellate hairs in the vein axils and along the midrib on the underside. The long leaves tend to droop downwards under their own weight until the leaflets resemble the steps of a ladder. A feature shared with Black walnut (p396). Flowers are in drooping catkins at the base of new growth in spring. The females rapidly develop into 20–40 cm long strings of two-winged, 1 cm nutlets **3**. **Habitat and Ecology** • Requires moist soil and a good water supply to thrive. Often in clonal thickets like small woods. **Similar species** • Other suckering Wingnut species and the hybrid *Pterocarya x rehderiana* (p390). The foliage superficially resembles Black walnut (p396). If a tree is found that has all the features of a wingnut but is not suckering it is likely to be *Pterocarya stenoptera* C. DC. A better choice for planting where space is limited.

Natural range
Iran and the Caucasus to the Caspian Sea coast.

Cultivated distribution
Seldom grown in cultivation because of its invasive tendencies. Introduced to Britain in 1782 and usually planted by a lake or river where it could find adequate moisture but would be unable to spread in one direction at least.The variety *dumosa* Schneid. is a dwarf form. Both have good, yellow, autumn foliage colour.

Seeds

1

2

3

FAMILY Juglandaceae

Pterocarya x rehderana Schneid.
Hybrid wingnut

Description • A suckering tree able to create a forest of stems in a remarkably short time. The Hybrid wingnut was raised by the Arnold Arboretum in the USA in 1879. It is the most vigorous of all. Trees over 25 m tall with a main stem over 1 m diameter are known **1**. The bark on numerous stems **2** is grey, developing deep, vertical ridges and fissures in old age. Shoots are stout and the stalked winter buds do not have protective scales. The leaves are pinnate, up to 50 cm long with around nine pairs of oblong-elliptic pointed and irregularly toothed leaflets. The rachis is distinctly grooved. Spring flowers occur in catkins up to 15 cm long. Males are yellowish, females are pale green quickly developing into the unique fruit. Long 30–40 cm chains of oval winged seeds. This wholly artificial hybrid is between the massive *Pterocarya stenoptera* C. DC **3**, which has 8–11 pairs of leaflets but does not have multiple stems, and *Pterocarya fraxinifolia* (Lam.) Spach, the multi-stemmed Caucasian wingnut (p388). **Habitat and Ecology** • Damp woodlands. **Similar species** • The fruits are unique and few other trees sucker so successfully. Tree of Heaven (p404) is superficially similar.

Natural range
The hybrid has no Natural range. *Pterocarya stenoptera* is Chinese with a variety in Vietnam. *Pterocarya fraxinifolia* is a native species from Northern Iran to the Caucasus Mountains.

Cultivated distribution
Used sparingly in cultivation because it can be invasive. Found in older tree collections from time to time as a curiosity. Some research into the possibility of using this plant as a short rotation, coppice biomass crop has been carried out.

FAMILY LEGUMINOSAE

Cladrastis lutea K Koch
Yellow wood

Description • A small to medium-sized tree rare in cultivation and in the wild. The largest stems are around 50 cm with pale grey, lacy ridges and orange-brown fissures forming an intricate pattern **4**. The outline is rounded and the foliage vigorous **5**. Leaves are pinnately compound, up to 30 cm long with five or six pairs of 5–8 cm, elliptical leaflets. The rachis completely encloses the following year's bud. The autumn foliage colour is brilliant yellow **6**, but this is nothing compared to the yellow colour of the freshly cut heart wood. Flowers, seldom seen in Europe, are white in pendulous clusters followed by 5–8 cm, flat pods each containing up to six small beans. **Habitat and Ecology** • Limestone regions especially. Moist soils in woodland on mountain slopes and along stream sides. **Similar species** • None.

Natural range
A limited area in the East and Central USA. Parts of Virginia, North Carolina, Georgia and Eastern Oklahoma.

Cultivated distribution
Introduced to Europe in 1812 but not widely planted. The branches are said to be brittle.

1
2
3
4
5
6

FAMILY Leguminosae

Gymnocladus dioicus (L.) K. Koch

Kentucky coffee tree

Description • The best distinguishing feature is the huge, bi-pinnate, pea-green leaf. In excess of 60 cm long with up to 100 entire, ovate, pointed, 5–8 cm leaflets **1**. Trees reach 17 m with a stem diameter of over 50 cm. Old bark is grey with vertical ridges **2**. Thornless shoots are pubescent at first then pale and glabrous sometimes bloomed. On cut stems the light coloured pith is conspicuous. Buds occur above the leaf axils. Male and female nectar rich flowers occur on separate trees and attract bees. Male flowers are 1.2 cm long, greenish white, stalked and pubescent in short dense panicles. Females, in larger 25 cm inflorescences, have four or five greenish-white, spreading petals. These develop into red-brown, 15–25 cm leathery pods containing 2 cm seeds. **Habitat and Ecology** • Alluvial flood plains and riversides in full light. The tree flushes late in the spring and so avoids early frosts. It is fairly tender in Northern Europe but thrives in towns. **Similar species** • The only tree grown in Europe with similar leaves is *Aralia spinosa* L. but its stem is viciously spiny.

Natural range
Eastern North America west to Ontario and Oklahoma.

Cultivated distribution
Widely planted as an urban open space tree in Europe and America. Introduced prior to 1748. Roasted seeds were formerly used as a coffee substitute.

FAMILY SAPINDACEAE

Koelreuteria paniculata Laxm.

Pride of India

Description • A rounded tree usually around 10 m tall **3** on a rough barked stem **4**. Leaves are pinnate or occasionally bi-pinnate around 30 cm long. Leaflets are irregularly crenate to lobed, a distinctive feature **5**. The spectacular summer flowers **6** are golden-yellow, each one about 1 cm across with four narrow petals and a cluster of red stamens, in a terminal 30–40 cm panicle of about 100. They are quickly followed by the papery, bladder-like fruits each divided into three with a single, dark brown seed at the base. The ripe fruits give the whole tree a distinctive, pinkish-brown autumn appearance **7**. **Habitat and Ecology** • Mixed open woodland. In cultivation it thrives best in full light in mild districts. **Similar species** • The leaves and flowers are unique. Seed pods resemble Bladder senna (*Colutea* L.). The variety *apiculata* (Redh. and Wils.) Rehd., formerly a species in its own right, has all bi-pinnate leaves. It flowers more freely than the species.

Natural range
East Asia, China, Korea and Japan.

Cultivated distribution
In China the flowers have medicinal use and the seeds are made into decorative necklaces. Introduced to England by the Earl of Coventry in 1763. Widely grown as a garden ornament.

1
2
3
4
5
6
7

FAMILY Juglandaceae

Juglans regia L.

Common walnut

Description • Best recognized from a distance by its open branch arrangement and light grey bark although confusingly in some trees this is smooth and in others it may become fissured or very scaly. This is a thick twigged tree, 15–25 m tall with a rounded or irregular outline **1**. The shape and branch arrangement is especially distinctive in winter when the leaves are off **2**. The bark is smooth and pale grey at first developing furrows and scaly plates at maturity **3**. Young shoots are stout and if cut lengthways through the centre reveal a distinctive chambered pith **4**, a feature unique to this genus and *Pterocarya* (pp388–391). They emerge green and glabrous but gradually change to dark brown after about two years, then grey as they mature and become branches. Buds have only two outer, visible scales which are very dark grey. Pinnate leaves 20–40 cm long have five to seven leaflets, occasionally more. Each leaflet is oval, slightly (or not) toothed, and pointed at each end. They range in size from 8–20 cm long, the smallest pair towards the base of the leaf and the largest at the end **5**. When crushed they are aromatic but less so than Black Walnut (p396). Stout petioles are flanged and swollen towards the base. In the spring, flowers appear with the leaves, males in 8–10 cm, pendulous, yellowish-grey catkins and small, green females in clusters towards the shoot tip. These develop into familiar edible walnuts encased in a smooth, hard, green husk **6**. **Habitat and Ecology** • Prefers open, frost-free conditions and full light from above but also benefits from side shelter provided by mixed woodland. Grows best on warm, fertile, well-drained soils, but fruits best under some physical stress such as storm damage or a good beating with a stick. **Similar species** • Various obscure Walnut and Hickory (p398) species.

Natural range
A vast area from South-east Europe to the foothills of the Himalays and into China. Much obscured by centuries of cultivation.

Cultivated distribution
Introduced from the Greek to the Roman Empire and distributed to Northern Europe at that time over 2000 years ago. Selected fruiting forms were cultivated by the great monastic houses some of which are still grown as orchard trees today **7**. The decorative and very stable wood, traditionally harvested by digging up the root with the stem, is still produced for high-quality furniture and veneers. There are also ornamental garden forms such as the cut-leaved 'Laciniata' **8**.

FAMILY Juglandaceae

Juglans nigra L.

Black walnut

Description • A large tree up to 36 m tall with distinctive, dark brown, rough bark like Oak (p298) and long, pinnate leaves with many leaflets. Trees grow well as woodland on a good site **1** and produce timber in around 60–80 years **2**. The bark colour in this photograph is obscured by a healthy growth of lichen resulting from the clean air in the trees' Welsh location. The wood is extremely valuable being very dark brown like Laburnum **3** (p374). The bark is hard and roughly ridged, and furrowed vertically in a diagonal lattice eventually cracking horizontally across the ridges. It is dark brown, especially when wet with rain, becoming grey-brown as it weathers **4**. Bright green, flexible, slightly drooping leaves are 30–60 cm long with 9–21 stalkless, lanceolate to oval, 6–12 cm, glabrous leaflets, each with a finely toothed margin and a long drawn out point **5**. In early summer they are aromatic without even being crushed. In the autumn they turn clear yellow before falling. The brown twigs are stout with chambered pith (p395 **4**). Male flowers are small but occur tightly packed together in pendulous catkins. Females in clusters of two to five appear near the tips of side shoots. These develop into aromatic, green, 4–6 cm, oval husks each containing a thick-shelled, edible seed **6**. In many parts of Europe fertile (and edible) seed is not produced, although warmer climatic conditions do seem to favour seed production now in places where formerly it did not occur. Opening the aromatic husks will stain the fingers dark brown. **Habitat and Ecology** • Well drained but moist, warm soils; not cold, wet clays. Will grow equally well as a forest or open woodland tree. **Similar species** • Rare American Walnuts and some species of Hickory (page 398), but the latter do not have compartmentalized pith (p395 **4**).

Natural range
A large part of the Eastern and Central United States, from New England to the Florida state line then west to Texas and north to South Dakota and Southern Ontario. Growing in many places to over 1200 m elevation.

Cultivated distribution
Imported to Europe before 1656 but difficult to propagate, transplant and tend, so remains rare in cultivation. The wood is ideal for quality furniture, veneers and gun stocks. It makes a good, large amenity, structure tree with outstanding autumn foliage colour.

Black walnut flowers

1
2
3
4
5
6

FAMILY Juglandaceae

Carya cordiformis (Wang.) K. Koch
Bitternut

Description • A potentially valuable but seldom seen timber tree in Europe. The wood has very high strength and elasticity particularly when cut from coppice re-growth. Specimens over 28 m tall are known with a spreading irregular outline **1**. In its native America stems over 1 m diameter occur. The bark is grey and although finely fissured and scaly it looks relatively smooth **2**. The distinctive buds are bright yellow on olive-brown shoots. The leaves are around 30 cm long, pinnate usually with about nine leaflets, the largest towards the tip. The top pair and terminal leaflets may be 15 cm long by 6 cm wide: their large size is a diagnostic feature. Each leaflet is ovate to elliptic with an acute point and tapering base. The margins are evenly toothed. In the autumn the foliage is strikingly golden yellow. Male catkins are in threes and pendulous, appearing just before the leaves. Females are smaller on the shoot tips. The inedible nuts are not usually produced at all in Northern Europe. **Habitat and Ecology** • A wetland species which is very hardy in its native North America but seems rather tender in parts of Europe. **Similar species** • Hybridizes with *Carya glabra* Sweet, *Carya illinoinensis* (Wang.) K. Koch and *Carya ovata* (below). Similar to some Walnuts but lacks the characteristic compartmentalized pith.

Natural range
Eastern North America from South East Canada to Florida and west as far as Eastern Texas.

Cultivated distribution
Introduced to Britain in 1766 but never widely planted. All *Carya* species resent root disturbance and are difficult to transplant.

Carya ovata (Mill.) K. Koch
Shagbark hickory

Description • Identifiable immediately by its curled, flaky bark which becomes exaggerated as the tree expands but never seems to fall off **3**. The individual flakes of bark are actually very strong and can only be broken with difficulty. The pinnate leaves only have five leaflets but may be up to 65 cm long **4**. Male catkins are prominent, 13 cm long in clusters. Female flowers are smaller. The edible fruit is enclosed in a thick, green, grooved husk but is seldom produced in Europe. **Habitat and Ecology** • Northern provenances extend into fairly severe climatic conditions in Eastern Canada but the species also occurs in very different conditions encountered in Northern Mexico. **Similar species** • Other Hickory species and hybrids until the characteristic bark develops.

Natural range
A huge and diverse range across North America, from Quebec and Maine south to Georgia and west to Minnesota, South East Texas and North East Mexico.

Cultivated distribution
Grown as a curiosity in specialist collections for its bark and autumn foliage colour. Hickory generally has not been cultivated to its full potential in Europe. High-quality timber producers such as Mockernut, *Carya tomentosa* (Poir.) Nutt. **5**, would grow well on sandy sites and areas subject to seasonal flooding.

1
2
3
4
5

FAMILY Caprifoliaceae

Sambucus nigra L.

Common elder

Description • An aggressive, pioneer species growing freely from seeds in hedgerows on reformed or abandoned ground or in gardens. Usually distributed by birds who relish the fruits in late summer. Although usually seen as a multi-stemmed bush this species can occasionally produce a single trunk up to 30 cm diameter **1**, or a gnarled bole 70 cm thick **2**. Height seldom exceeds 6 m in the open or 10 m in woodland where competition for light draws it up. The warm feeling, soft bark is yellowish-grey, blistered and peeling at first then vertically ridged and fissured. In old age these fissures become greatly exaggerated and where the air is clean lichens and moss colour the stem white, yellow and vivid green **2**. Shoots are thick but soft with exaggerated pith for several years, bright green initially **3** becoming grey-brown and corky at the end of the first year. Buds are opposite, dark greenish-brown and leafy. As soon as one year's leaves have fallen the following season's buds show signs of opening. In cold winters the emerging leaves are often bronze-green or dark brown. Each leaf is 10–25 cm long **3** with five to seven short-stalked leaflets. Margins have soft, forward-pointing, rounded, irregular teeth. The underside is distinctly whitish-green with a deeper green prominent midrib and main veins. The rachis and petiole are grooved on the upper side. A reliable display of creamy white flowers can be expected in early summer. They have a strong distinctive scent and attract numerous flying insects **4**. Each inflorescence is a flat corymb, 10–20 cm across, often supporting over 100 flowers **5**. Berries rapidly develop in abundance often bending down the fruiting terminal shoots **6**. Each round, juicy berry, containing three to five seeds, is about 5 mm across, ripening in early autumn to blackish-purple. The copious juice is wine red but stains purple. Even bird droppings are purple at this time of year and each dropping is well supplied with viable seeds. Starlings in particular are attracted to Elder fruit. **Habitat and Ecology** • An aggressive pioneer able to colonize derelict ground, woodland edges, hedgerows, marshes and sand dunes. It will grow as an underwood species with a light deciduous canopy (e.g. poplar). **Similar species** • None.

Natural range
Extends from Europe into West Asia and North Africa.

Cultivated distribution
Elder as a species is not cultivated although a very good cordial and wine can be made from the flowers and berries. Cultivars however are widely grown. There are various cut-leaf forms and foliage colours. 'Guincho Purple' has black leaves and attractive pink flowers **7**. Golden elder 'Aurea' has bright yellow foliage which matures to deep yellow by the end of the summer **8**.

1
2
3
4
5
6
7
8

FAMILY Aceraceae

Acer negundo L.

Box elder or Ashleaf maple

Description • Rarely seen as a natural green-leaved tree because in cultivation most specimens are variegated **1**. However, these do frequently revert and the variegation can be totally destroyed by vigorous, green-leaved, rogue branches. In nature this is a medium-sized, fast-growing tree usually with a short stem and long, spreading branches forming an open, rounded outline. Heights seldom exceed 15 m and the bole is unlikely to exceed 80 cm in diameter. The leaves are unlike those of most other maples: they are pinnate or trifoliate with three to seven leaflets. Each leaflet is elliptical or oval with a drawn-out point and occasional long, exaggerated, forward-pointing teeth, sometimes distinctly like small lobes. Trifoliate leaves are around 12 cm long **2** with an even longer petiole. Pinnate leaves are 15–18 cm long also with a substantial petiole **3**. They are fresh green and lustrous on the upper side and paler below. The bark is fawn or pale brown, becoming grey in old age with shallow, vertical fissures developing upwards from the base **4**. Twigs are glabrous, more or less green, often with some white bloom. As they age they become pale brown with greyish-purple bloom. Provenances from segregate populations in California have particularly attractive coloured shoots and strong foliage. Flowers occur in drooping clusters, male and female on separate trees, before the leaves appear in spring. Seeds in pairs each have a membraneous wing held almost parallel to its twin. They tend to hang on the tree all winter in tattered, drooping, wind-blown bunches **5**. **Habitat and Ecology** • Mixed woodlands, field margins and stream sides. Thrives in wet, fertile ground even at high elevation, up to 2400 m in the Southern USA. **Similar species** • Uniquely for a Maple the leaves resemble Elder (p400) and the wood is like Box (p122), hence the common name.

Natural range
A large part of Eastern and Central North America with isolated populations in Southern Texas, New Mexico and California. In Canada it occurs from Southern Ontario to Southern Alberta.

Cultivated distribution
Extensively used as a hardy shade tree in America. In Europe it is also a common tree in parks and gardens usually represented by the variegated forms. The most exotic of these is 'Flamingo' which has bright pink, white, green and light brown markings on the foliage **6**.

1

2

3

4

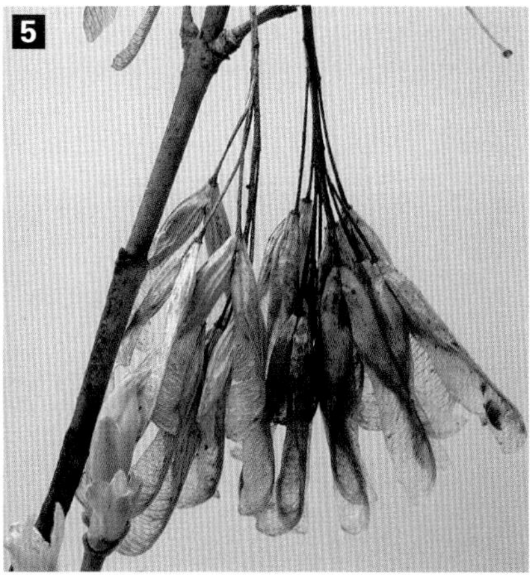

5

6

FAMILY Simaroubaceae

Ailanthus altissima (Mill.) Swingle

Tree of Heaven

Description • Tree of Heaven is an apt name for this vigorous, suckering plant. Once established it streaks upwards at a furious rate. If prevented from doing so by being cut back it will send up new trees from the root system, sometimes a surprisingly long way from the original stump. Tarmac, concrete and brick walls will not stop it. This is a large, 20–30 m, straight tree with a stem diameter approaching 1 m. The crown is rounded or consists of a series of rounded domes **1**. The bark is dark grey-brown on young stems, becoming paler grey and fissured at maturity with smooth, soft, vertical ridges **2**. Shoots are stout with very fine felted hairs, green at first, maturing to pale golden-brown with distinctive pale buff, spaced-out lenticels and large leaf scars. The leaves are a good diagnostic feature. Most of them are around 60 cm long, pinnate with 15–41 pointed, 7–12 cm leaflets **3**. By the end of the growing season the rachis along the centre of the leaf is deep yellow with an upper, red side **4**. The bottom pairs of leaflets develop an exaggerated heart-shaped base in which there are enlarged glands giving off a strong, spicy smell which on hot, still, summer days can cause some people to feel unwell. The base of the leaf stalk is enlarged but does not enclose the bud. The flowers in summer are spectacular because of the numbers produced, greenish-white terminal panicles extending beyond the limits of the foliage **3**. Male and female flowers may be in separate inflorescences or occur together; male flowers have an unpleasant smell. Another diagnostic and spectacular feature of this tree is its fruit. Quite suddenly in early autumn the whole top of the tree turns red as the winged seeds mature **1** and **4**. **Habitat and Ecology** • A deciduous forest species. If left alone it will eventually form clonal forests. **Similar species** • The only other species likely to be encountered in Northern Europe is *Ailanthus vilmoriniana* Dode. but it is rarely grown. The shoots and foliage are more pubescent. It is less hardy and a smaller tree from Western China.

Natural range
Northern China, but naturalized in many adjacent areas and also in North America.

Cultivated distribution
Cultivated as an ornamental following its introduction from China in 1751 and extensively planted as a shade tree at first. When it became obvious that it had antisocial habits including excessive size, rather odd smells and invasiveness, its popularity waned. However, existing planted trees proved harder to get rid of than could have been imagined. Roots have been known to spring back into life ten years after the stump had been grubbed out. A sapling persistently and mysteriously re-appears in a hostile place beside the railway track just outside London Liverpool Street station despite the best efforts of the line maintenance staff to physically or chemically remove it.

FAMILY Rutaceae

Phellodendron amurense Rupr.

Amur cork tree

Description • A shapely, 12 m tall tree with a persistent, straight stem and spreading branches **1**. The outline is columnar with a broad base. The best all year round diagnostic feature is the bark. It is soft and corky with light grey-brown fissures and indistinct, darker grey ridges forming a diagonal and vertical lattice pattern **2**. Branches are orange-grey or yellowish with smooth bark. Shoots are stout and reddish-brown with distinct leaf scars round the buds when the leaves have fallen in the autumn. Buds are in opposite pairs totally encased all summer in the swollen base of the petiole. Leaves are 25–35 cm long, alternate pinnate with 5–11 pairs of leaflets. They are aromatic when crushed. Individual leaflets are mostly between 5–9 cm long but occasionally on vigorous growth they are up to 14 cm long. The smallest is always towards the base of the leaf. They are ovate or narrowly oval with an abrupt point often inclined slightly to one side. The base may be rounded or wedge shaped with a short stalk attached to the rachis **3**. Margins appear to be entire but minute teeth can sometimes be detected. In hot weather or periods of drought each leaflet folds upwards along the midrib to reduce transpiration. Flowers are 6 mm across with five to eight yellowish-green petals in terminal panicles 8–10 cm high on separate male and female trees in early summer. The fruit is a 1 cm black berry in clusters of 60–80 until the wind and birds reduce them to just a handful as they ripen in the autumn when the leaves change colour and begin to fall. If crushed the berries smell of turpentine. They each contain five hard-shelled seeds. **Habitat and Ecology** • In deciduous forests on the lower slopes of high mountain ranges. At lower elevations the natural habitat has become indistinct because of centuries of cultivation for cork. **Similar species** • The soft, light bark is distinct. There are eight or nine species of *Phellodendron*, the nearest to the Amur cork tree is *Phellodendron piriforme* E. Wolf, which has oblique-based leaflets. It is very rare in cultivation. There is also a variable hybrid with *Phellodendron japonicum* Maxim., which was formerly regarded as a variety of this species.

Natural range
Japan, Korea, Manchuria and parts of China growing along side different *Phellodendron* species in each place.

Cultivated distribution
Introduced to Europe around 1856 and many times subsequently. A hardy and decorative ornamental tree especially because of the distinctive bark and autumn colour feature of contrasting pale yellow leaves and black berries.

1

2

3

FAMILY Oleaceae

Fraxinus excelsior L.

Common ash

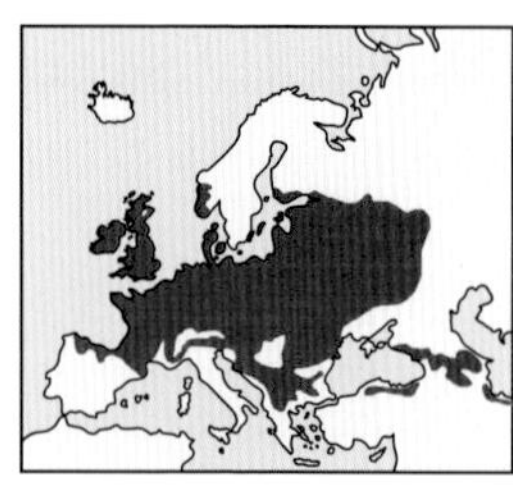

Natural range

Cultivated distribution
Cultivated since ancient times for its valuable, flexible, straight grained wood used for agricultural and military equipment and as a living fence or hedge species. The timber withstands pressure, shock and bending but is not durable in contact with wet ground. Ideal for fence rails but not the posts. Growing Ash in plantations requires particular skill: frequent thinning out is essential so that final crop trees do not become suppressed. Any that do are unlikely to recover their former vigour.

Description • A tall, open crowned, deciduous, 20–30 m tree with a stem diameter around 1 m at maturity. A tree that demands light, growing at its best in an open situation **1**. The massive, upswept limbs support curving then ultimately down-curved branches and a tangle of stout, angular shoots. The bark is light grey or fawn, smooth at first becoming ridged and fissured with an intricate lattice pattern, eventually becoming rough, more or less like oak (p298) **2**. Shoots are relatively thick, usually ash-grey, greenish-grey or sometimes purplish-brown, with opposite, velvety black buds **3**. In late winter lateral flower buds swell and become conspicuous, gradually exposing dark maroon, tightly packed male anthers **4**, or female styles and stigmas. None of the flowers have petals. Male and female may be on the same tree or on separate trees, a situation that can change from year to year. Male flowers eventually erupt and shed pollen **5** then female flowers expand into familiar bunches of 3–5 cm Ash 'keys' **6**. At this stage in late summer seed can be picked and planted before it goes into 18 months of dormancy. Ripe, single-winged, flat seeds are brown and often hang on the bare branches until the following spring **7**. The leaves are 16–30 cm long, pinnate with 5–11 narrowly oval, pointed leaflets. Margins are slightly toothed, mostly towards the tip of the leaflet. Leaves occur in clusters and fan out at the shoot tips giving the foliage an open, bunchy appearance. **Habitat and Ecology** • A light-demanding, open woodland or hedgerow tree which prefers damp, alkaline soils but is able to survive almost anywhere. **Similar species** • Several obscure Ash species have similar looking foliage but not the black buds.

1

2

4

5

6

7

FAMILY Oleaceae

Fraxinus excelsior L. 'Pendula'

Weeping ash

Description • In nature, pendulous forms of Common ash (p408) occasionally occur. It does not appear to be a response to environmental conditions. In 1990 a strongly weeping, spontaneous tree was found in a remote and open part of Salisbury Plain creeping about close to the ground amongst ordinary trees many miles from any habitation or other cultivated specimens. Weeping ash is potentially a large-spreading tree, its height is governed in cultivation by the height of the graft stock. Nineteenth century trees were generally grafted 4–6 m above the ground producing a well-proportioned tree about 8 m tall in 100 years **1**. Old grafts often swell up into grotesque lumps of woody growth. The foliage is exactly like Common ash with grey shoots, black buds and pinnate leaves. **Habitat and Ecology** • Spontaneous examples occasionally occur in ash woodlands and hedgerows. **Similar species** • None.

Natural range
Occurs with normal populations of Common ash as a rare aberrant form.

Cultivated distribution
The original recorded plant occurred near Cambridge around 1760. It was grafted on to Common ash and distributed widely. This very pendulous clone is probably still in cultivation.

Fraxinus excelsior L. 'Jaspidea'

Golden ash

Description • Golden describes the current shoots which are dusty-yellow at first **3** becoming brighter when leafless the following winter. However trees do also produce a brief period of golden-yellow autumn foliage colour **2** and the fruits are bunches of butter-yellow keys **3**. Except for the shoot colour this tree is like Common ash although because it is grafted it is unlikely to reach such a large ultimate size. The tallest in the British Isles (1996) were 21 m. The buds are velvety-black and contrast dramatically with the shoots. **Habitat and Ecology** • A variant of common ash originally found in the wild. Ash frequently produces variable shoot colours but these generally range from grey to green and purple. **Similar species** • The shoots and black buds are distinctive.

Natural range
Unknown but must have occurred originally with Common ash.

Cultivated distribution
There is confusion about the origin of this tree in cultivation because another cultivar 'Aurea' was thought to be synonymous. 1873 is suggested for 'Aurea' but 'Jaspidea' is clearly a different much larger plant. It is widely used as an urban, open space tree **2**, but may outgrow its space in some built up locations.

1

2

3

FAMILY Oleaceae

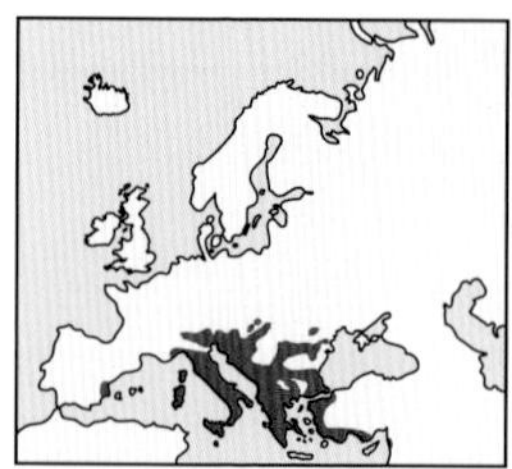

Fraxinus ornus L

Manna ash

Description • In Northern Europe this species is usually represented by planted ornamental trees, many of which have been grafted. Often the bulging, incompatible graft union is the first indication of what the tree might be **1**. Modern plants are produced using more sophisticated propagation techniques so young trees do not have graft incompatibility **2**. They develop into a perfect urban tree shape **3**. Old specimens may exceed 15 m in height with a round top almost as wide as it is high. Stems over 70 cm diameter are rare. Defects become evident before then which make them unsafe. The bark is exactly like Common ash (p408), smooth and grey at first becoming lightly furrowed and ridged in old age. Often the much rougher lower stem you see on an old specimen is actually the Common ash rootstock **1**. Branches are spreading and sinuous with angular, grey-green shoots. The buds are in opposite pairs and clustered at the tip. They are velvety grey-brown. In winter the buds clearly distinguish this species from Common ash which has black buds. The foliage is lush and relatively dense for an Ash. Leaves are 20–25 cm long with five to nine leaflets. They are 4–7 cm long and more or less oval with a broad point at each end. Some leaflets have an unequal base so the stalk may only be 5 mm long on the lower side and 8–10 mm long on the other side. Margins are more or less entire or with only a vague suggestion of shallow, rounded teeth. The flowers are dramatic **4**, massed in axillary panicles 30 cm across, occupying whole shoot tips and appearing with and projecting beyond the new leaves in late spring. Individual flowers are only 10 mm across with four narrow, 6 mm, cream petals, they are scented like new mown hay. Single winged, 2 cm seeds develop in huge, pendulous bunches **5**. **Habitat and Ecology** • A woodland tree in its native region. **Similar species** • The regional variant *Fraxinus ornus* subsp. *rotundifolia* (Lam.) Ten. has rounded leaflets. There are many other obscure flowering Ash species such as *Fraxinus mariesii* Hook. but they are rare in cultivation.

Natural range

Cultivated distribution
This tree has been in general cultivation in Northern Europe since before 1700. It does not appear to have been used extensively but is represented in many old tree collections. The cultivar 'Pendula', which is not usually very pendulous, may be recognized by its graft union high up on the stem. Various new, upright forms have been cultivated especially for urban use including 'Obelisk' and 'Fastigiata Pyramidalis'. The round-leaved 'Arie Peters' is also a 'designed city tree' probably selected from subspecies *rotundifolia*.

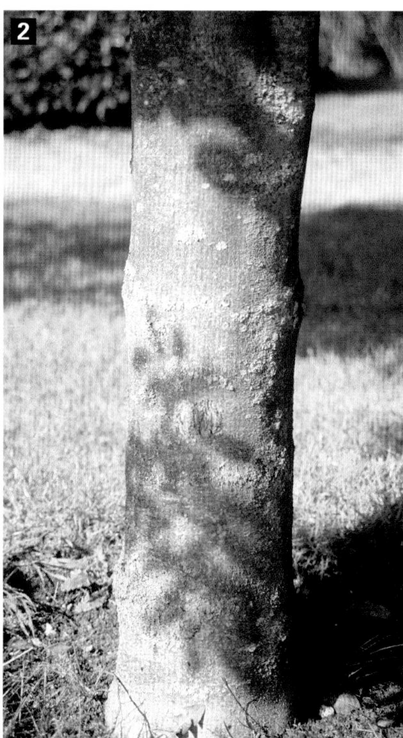

FAMILY Oleaceae

Fraxinus angustifolia Vahl

Narrow-leaved ash

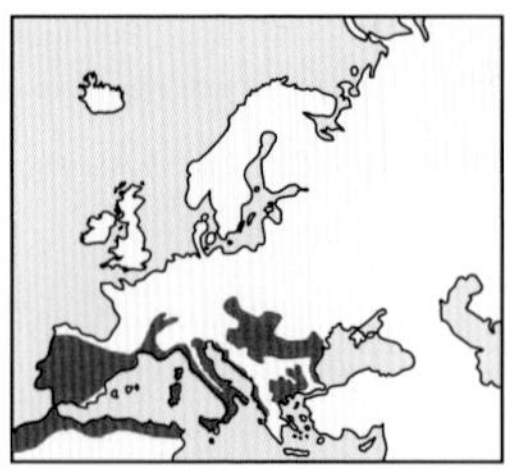

Natural range

Cultivated distribution
Narrow-leaved ash is infrequent but subspecies *oxycarpa* is used fairly widely in town parks and urban open spaces. Its shape and light foliage are ideal but ultimate size may be limiting **5**. 'Raywood' is becoming extremely popular. Since its introduction in 1928 it has been planted in most European cities and towns. The lacy foliage turns ruby-purple in the autumn if the preceding summer weather conditions have been right.

Description • This species, seldom seen in its pure form in Northern Europe, is generally replaced with the subspecies *oxycarpa* (Caucasian ash) in cultivation. Narrow-leaved ash is a big tree around 25 m tall with a domed top and light, airy foliage **1**. The stem may reach 1 m in diameter **2**. The shoots are olive-green, glabrous and stout. The buds in opposite pairs and terminal clusters are dark coffee brown and velvety. Leaves are pinnate, about 20 cm long, with 7–11 pairs of ovate to elliptic 3–6 cm leaflets in stalkless pairs. Each deep green leaflet has soft, forward-pointing teeth in the upper two thirds of the blade, a tapered base and an acute point. The rachis, leaf stalk, is pale yellow and slightly winged towards the bottom end. Flowers have no petals and seeds are like Common ash (p408). The form usually cultivated is *Fraxinus angustifolia* subsp. *oxycarpa* (M. Bieb. ex Willd.) Franco and Rocha Alfonso, formerly called *Fraxinus oxycarpa* M. Bieb. ex Willd. It is similar to the species but has smaller leaves with three to seven narrow, oval leaflets, rounded pointed or notched at the tip and tapered towards the base. Margins have small, forward-pointing, soft teeth often turned outwards. The rachis is pale yellow and winged towards the base. In the autumn a good display of golden yellow foliage colour makes this a sought after amenity tree **3**. Closely allied is *Fraxinus angustifolia* 'Raywood', a decorative tree which has very narrow, willow like leaflets, 6–9 cm long but only 1–1.5 cm wide, broadest near the base then tapering to a long, thin point. Each leaflet has widely spaced, forward-pointing, curved, glandular teeth. The general colour is pale to mid-green, slightly lighter on the underside. **Habitat and Ecology** • In Northern Europe these trees are only found in cultivated situations. **Similar species** • There are many 'look-alike' Ash species from Asia and America but none have such narrow leaflets as these. Although not common, exotic species do appear in large tree collections and old gardens. For example, a potential forest species in Europe is Green ash *Fraxinus pennsylvanica* Marsh. **4**. An American timber tree it produces a straight, high-quality stem and its seed grows easily without going into a period of dormancy.

1

2

3

4

5

Bibliography and further reading

*Bailey, L.H. and E.Z. (1976) *Hortus Third*, revised by Liberty Hyde Bailey Hortorium, Cornell University, Macmillan Publishing Co. New York.

Bean, W.J. (1976) *Trees and Shrubs hardy in the British Isles*, eighth edition Revised, John Murray, London.

Brooker, M.I.H. and Evans, J. (1983) *A Key to Eucalyptus in Britain and Ireland*, Forestry Commission Booklet 50, HMSO, London.

Elwes, H.J. and Henry, A.H. (1909) *The Trees of Great Britain and Ireland*, S.R. Publishers, Wakefield, Yorks.

Forrest, M. (1988) *Trees and Shrubs cultivated in Ireland*, Boethius Press, Co. Kilkenny, Ireland.

Hillier, H. (1972) (first published) *The Hillier Manual of Trees and Shrubs*, David and Charles, Newton Abbot, Devon.

Jalas, J., Suominen, J. *et al.* (1972–1991) *Atlas Florae Europapeae*, The Committee for Mapping the Flora of Europe & Societas Biologica Fennica Vanamo, Helsinki.

Jobling, J. (1990) *Poplars for Wood Production and Amenity*, Bulletin 92, Forestry Commission, London.

Johnson, O. (2003) *Champion Trees of Britain and Ireland*, The Trustees of the Tree Register of the British Isles (www.tree-register.org), Whittet Books Ltd., Suffolk, England.

*Krussmann, G. (1984) *Manual of Cultivated Broad-leaved Trees and Shrubs*, B.T. Batsford Ltd., London.

Krussmann, G. (1985) *Manual of Cultivated Conifers*, B.T. Batsford Ltd., London.

Little, E.L. (1988) *The Audubon Society Field Guide to North American Trees*, Western Region, seventh edition, A.A. Knopf, Inc., New York.

Little, E.L. (1993) *The Audubon Society Field Guide to North American Trees*, Eastern Region, thirteenth edition, A.A. Knopf, Inc., New York.

Meikle, R.D. (1984) *Willows and Poplars of Great Britain and Ireland*, Botanical Society of the British Isles, London.

Meusel, H., Jager, E., Rauschert, S., Weinert, E. (1975 and 1978) *Vergleichende Chorologie der Zentraleuropaischen Flora*, VEB Gustav Fischer Verlag, Jena.

Mitchell, A.F. (1972) *Conifers in the British Isles*, Forestry Commission Booklet 33, HMSO, London.

More, D. and White, J.E.J. (2003) *Cassell's Trees of Britain and Northern Europe*, Cassell and Co., London.

*Rehder, A. (1940) *Manual of Cultivated Trees and Shrubs Hardy in North America*, Dioscorides Press, Portland, Oregon.

Rushforth, K. (1999) *Trees of Britain and Europe*, Harper Collins, London.

Stace, C. (1991) *New Flora of the British Isles*, Cambridge University Press.

Strouts, R.G. and Winter, T.G. (1994) *Diagnosis of Ill Health in Trees*, Research for Amenity Trees No.2, Department of the Environment and Forestry Commission, London.

Tutin, T.G. *et al.* (1980) *Flora Europaea*, Cambridge University Press.

van Gelderen, D.M., de Jong, P.C. and Oterdoom, H.J. (1991) *Maples of the World*, Timber Press, Portland, Oregon.

Walter, K.S. (ed.) *et al.* (1995) *Catalogue of Plants Growing at the Royal Botanic Garden*, Edinburgh.

White, J.E.J. (1995) *Forest and Woodland Trees in Britain*, Oxford University Press.

* Titles marked thus contain lists of authors of scientific names cited in this work.

Glossary of technical and botanical terms

Aberrant – Unusual form of growth, deformity or colour.
Acuminate – Having a long tapering point.
Acute – Sharply angled or pointed.
Adpressed – (Hairs) pressed against the stem or foliage.
Alkalinity (Alkaline) – A measure of lime-rich soil above pH 7.
Alluvial – Sand, silt or gravel deposited by running water.
Amenity planting – Planting trees to enhance a landscape.
Andro-dioecious – Having male and bisexual flowers on separate trees.
Androgynous – Mixed female and male flowers on the same plant.
Andro-monoecious – Having separate, single-sex male flowers and bisexual flowers, but no purely female flowers, on the same plant.
Anthers – Male, pollen-bearing capsules borne on the tips of the stamens.
Apomict (Apomictic) – A plant that can produce fruit without the need for sexual fusion.
Appressed – See adpressed.
Arboreal – Connected with trees or formed like a tree.
Arboriculture – The science of tree care.
Axil (Axillary) – Emanating from between the upper side of a leaf or flower stalk and the stem.
Backcross – The result of hybrid progeny subsequently breeding with either one of the original parent species.
Binomial – A system of nomenclature giving two names to an organism (genus and species).
Bi-pinnate – See Pinnate.
Bisexual – A flower containing male and female sexual organs.
Bletted – Fruit that has started to rot but is still edible.
Bloom – A white powdery or waxy deposit on some stems or fruit.
Bract (Stipule) – A scaly or leafy appendage situated where a flower stalk (pedicel) leaves the stem.
Broadleaved – A tree with flat leaf blades (deciduous or evergreen) that is not a conifer.
Calyx – An outer whorl of leafy organs (sepals) at the base of a flower. A persistent calyx will remain on the top of a fruit permanently, a deciduous calyx will fall away as the fruit swells.
Callous (Callus) – An abnormal woody swelling of new growth surrounding an injury or diseased section of stem or branch.
Canker – Enlargement and fissuring associated with a discharge of moisture or slime, on the stem or branches of a tree, caused by fungal or bacterial disease infection.
Chimera – Two or more genetically different plants fused together by a mutation or deliberate grafting.
Ciliate – Fine hairs forming a fringe.
Climax woodland – Consisting of trees environmentally suited to a particular site that have evolved naturally at the expense of pioneer and less well-suited intermediate species.
Clone – A plant reproduced vegetatively, by cuttings or grafting, etc.
Conifer (Coniferous) – A cone bearing tree with needle or scale like foliage.
Coppice (Coppicing) – An ancient system of woodland management requiring periodic cutting back to a stump at ground level, usually at 7–25 year intervals depending on the species or required product.
Cordate – Heart shaped.
Corymb – A flat or domed inflorescence.
Crenate (Leaf margin) – Having rounded, shallow teeth.

Crown (of a tree) – All of the branches, twigs and foliage. The whole top of the tree.
Cultivar – A variety or strain produced artificially by using horticultural or agricultural techniques.
Cuspidate – Terminating abruptly in a sharp point.
Deciduous – Shedding, usually leaves in the autumn or bark in spring, but also hairs or cone scales.
Decussate – Alternating pairs (of leaves or buds) at right angles on a shoot.
Digitate – A palmate leaf with finger-like lobes.
Dioecious – Separate male and female plants.
Drupe – A fleshy fruit with one or more seeds protected by a hard shell.
Dysfunctional – Part of a tree stem or a branch which is no longer alive.
Elliptic (Elliptical) – Ellipse-shaped.
Endemic – Found wild exclusively in one region.
Epicormic – New shoots and foliage emanating from a mature stem or large branch (water shoots).
Exfoliating – Shedding (usually bark).
Exserted – Projecting (e.g. stamens from a flower bud or bracts from between cone scales).
Fascicled – Densely clustered (e.g. Pine needles in bundles of two, three or five).
Fastigiate – A very narrow tree with upswept branches, like Lombardy poplar.
Genus – See the Introduction.
Glabrous – Without hair (on leaves or shoots).
Glandular – Having glands (secreting organs) usually on twigs and leaves.
Globose – Vaguely spherical.
Globular – Spherical or consisting of globules.
Heartwood – Dead wood at the centre of a stem or branch providing strength and rigidity and a place for waste substances from the actively growing part of the tree.
Heliotropic – Movement of leaves and flowers following the sun.
Hilum – The scar left on a seed where it was attached.
Indumentum – Covering of short hair or felt.
Inflorescence – A cluster of flowers originating from a single point on the stem.
Intergeneric (hybrid) – A hybrid between plants from separate genera.
Interspecific (hybrid) – A hybrid between different species.
Involucre – A conspicuous bract (or bracts) within an inflorescence.
Lanceolate – Narrow, lance shaped (leaf) broadest at a point just below the middle.
Lenticels – Raised respiratory pores on the young stems of plants.
Lopping – The removal of large branches by tree surgery.
Microspecies – A distinctive segregate of a true species, often originating as a hybrid which has resulted in a population of apomictic progeny.
Monoecious – Separate male and female flowers on the same plant.
Monoculture – Plantations of a single species.
Monopodial – Having a single stem (trunk).
Naturalized – A plant that has become established in an area beyond its native or natural distribution.
Nodal (Node) – The place where side branches leave the stem.
Nothomorph (Nothovar) – Minor taxonomic rank below, but similar to, variety. See the Introduction.
Obovate (leaf) – Egg shaped, towards the tip.
Obovoid – Egg shaped, broadest below the centre.
Ovate (leaf) – Egg shaped but flat, broadest towards the base.
Ovoid – Egg shaped in three dimensions.
Palmate (leaf) – Shaped like a hand.
Panicle – An inflorescence, similar to a raceme but having branched stalks.
Pedunculate – Having flowers or a single flower on a stalk.
Pedicel – Flower (fruit) stalk.
Petiole – The leaf stalk.
Pinnate – A compound leaf with more than three leaflets arranged in two ranks along a common axis (rachis). Bi-pinnate is a pinnate leaf which also has pinnate leaflets.
Pollarding – An ancient form of tree management involving the periodic removal of all the branches as an alternative to felling.
Polymorphic – Having more than one morphological feature.
Provenance – A separate region within the natural distribution of a species.
Pruinose – Bloomed white (not grey, etc.).
Pubescent – Hairy (foliage).
Pulvini – Pegs to which spruce needles are attached.

Raceme – An inflorescence with many individually stalked flowers along a central stem.
Rachis – The central rib of a pinnate leaf.
Recurved – Curved downwards (like many fir cones) or backwards (petals).
Reticulate – Net veined.
Revolute – Rolled back leaf margin.
Riparian – River side.
Rootstock – The root on to which another plant is grafted.
Scion – The shoot or bud of a plant that is grafted onto the root or stem of another.
Segregate (botanical meaning) – A population of plants within a species which has become geographically isolated.
Semi-evergreen – Foliage mostly retained over winter and shed the following spring.
Sepals – The outer protective part of a flower.
Serrate – Saw toothed (leaf margin).
Sessile – Without a stalk.
Sinuate – Wavy edged (leaf margin).
Sinus – The inward curving space between lobes.
Socketing – An inverted cone-shaped void in soft soil round the base of a newly planted tree caused by the wind blowing the plant round and round. A cause of instability, death or leaning.
Stamens – The male parts of a flower supporting the anthers.
Stellate – Having star shaped hairs (on foliage).
Stigma – The receptive female part of a flower.
Stipule – A leafy bract at the base of a leaf stalk.
Stomata – Breathing pores, usually concentrated on the underside of a leaf.
Stone cells – Gritty cells found in the fruit of pears and similar species.
Striae – Longitudinal ridges.
Style – The female part of a flower between the ovary and the stigma.
Subspecies – A segregate taxonomic rank less than a species usually originating as a regionally isolated natural population. See the Introduction.
Suckers (suckering) – Shoots produced from surface roots.
Taxonomy – The craft, based on scientific observation and methods, of classification, from the Greek taxis (arrangement) and nomia (a suffix related to nomos meaning law).
Tomentose (tomentum) – Densely hairy or woolly.
Tree line – The upward limit of tree growth on a mountain side.
Trifoliate – Having three leaflets.
Truncate – As if cut cleanly across.
Umbel – Flat-topped inflorescence with pedicels all emanating from a single point. In a compound umbel pedicels further sub-divide.
Undulate – Wavy edge or surface.
Variety – A taxonomic rank subordinate to species that originates as a spontaneous morphological variant.
Vegetative propagation – Any method of reproducing plants not using seeds.
Venation – The arrangement of veins on a leaf.

Index of scientific plant names

General index